SO-CON-888

The ANSWER BOOK

A self-help guide with hundreds of practical answers to common questions on home maintenance, improvements and repairs

compiled by the
Editors of The FAMILY HANDYMAN® Magazine

Copyright© 1981 by The Webb Company

All rights reserved. No part of this book may be reproduced without permission in writing from the publisher, except by a reviewer who may quote brief passages or reproduce illustrations in a review with appropriate credit; nor may any part of this book be reproduced, stored in a retrieval system, or transmitted in any form or by any means—electronic, photocopying, recording, or other—without permission in writing from the publisher. Printed in the United States of America.

Library of Congress Cataloging in Publication Data
Main entry under title:
Answer Book No. 1
Includes index.
1. Dwellings—Maintenance and repair—
Amateurs' manuals. I. Family Handyman
Cloth Edition R1838—3
ISBN 08359—1838—6
Paper Edition R1837—5
ISBN 08359—1837—8   81-21139

Acknowledgments

Special thanks are due to Phil Scheller, the original "Ask Handyman" columnist and to Lura LaBarge who has so ably answered countless readers' questions in more recent years; to Gene Schnaser, Rudy Schnasse, Jim Stanley, Gary Branson and Ed Jackson who all contributed to the editing and organization of this book; to Ron Chamberlain, Tim Himsel, John Baskerville and Robert Scharff and Associates, Ltd. for their efforts in illustrations, design and typography; and to Dianne Talmage for copy checking and proof coordination.

Howard Jones, Publisher
The FAMILY HANDYMAN® Magazine

Safety First—This book has been written and edited in good faith by the Editors of The FAMILY HANDYMAN® Magazine, and is based on information believed to be accurate. The publisher and authors cannot, however, assume responsibility for any personal injuries, damage to property or other accidents which might result from anyone carrying out the projects and procedures described on these pages, or from the usuage of manufactured products described in this book. In most areas, building permits and inspection are required for construction and modification of buildings and the systems within a structure—particularly electrical, heating and plumbing. In any home improvement project, always comply with local laws to be sure that repairs and improvements are done safely and in accordance with applicable codes and safety regulations.

The ANSWER BOOK - NO. 1   Contents

The ANSWER BOOK NO. 1

INTRODUCTION

The Answer Book is a reference you can count on to help you become self-sufficient at home improvement, maintenance and repair. It is written and edited with the philosophy that the time and money you put into improving your home are among the best investments you can make.

Take a quick look at the table of contents. You will see an enormous range of subject matter, from overall plans from homes to extremely detailed repair instructions: thousands of individual items representing *real* problems and their solutions. Not theory, but practical stuff you can put to work right away in your own home.

This book was a long time in the making. It has been drawn from 30 years of producing America's foremost do-it-yourself publication, The FAMILY HANDYMAN® Magazine.

In fact, the term "do-it-yourself" originated about the same time the magazine did—in the days after World War II when hundreds of thousands of young couples searched desperately for homes where they could raise

families. They faced the worst housing shortage of this century. Prices soared and labor costs were without precedent. When they finally found a home it was often too small, run down, and old; or if new, a mass-produced house of inferior quality.

With labor costs higher than anyone could remember, these families could not afford to pay for outside help for repairing, maintaining or improving their new homes. They learned to "do it themselves," falling back on the pioneer tradition of self-reliance and self-sufficiency. These ideals would come to the fore once again in the "back to the earth" movements of more recent decades.

The do-it-yourselfers of the late '40s and early '50s created an enormous demand for tools and building materials suited to their needs. Manufacturers adapted industrial power tools for home use as light-duty hand drills and power saws, as well as combination bench tools which could turn a basement or a garage into a flexible and effective workshop. Makers of build-

ing materials came out with such convenient items as prefinished wallboard, ready-to-install wallpaper, easy-to-cut floor tiles, vastly improved adhesives and standard-sized lumber.

One of the big needs of the do-it-yourselfers was a source of information on how to tackle jobs ranging from building bedrooms in attics to waterproofing leaky basements. More than 30 years ago, in 1951, The FAMILY HANDYMAN Magazine was launched in New York to give these non-expert homeowners just what they wanted: directions for jobs they could do around the house, clearly written in non-technical language, and illustrated with carefully planned photographs, diagrams, and line drawings. The emphasis was on a step-by-step approach.

The reaction from homeowners was enthusiastic, and soon The FAMILY HANDYMAN Magazine became indispensable to hundreds of thousands of subscribers. From the start, readers took the trouble to write in with special problems. The editors not only answered their letters but devoted a long column in each issue to specific solutions. The "Ask Handyman" column quickly became the best-read department of the magazine.

In 1977 The FAMILY HANDYMAN Magazine was purchased by the Webb Company, one of the Midwest's leading magazine publishers, and moved from New York to a new home on the banks of the Mississippi in St. Paul, Minnesota. Within three years, paid circulation doubled to more than a million subscribers. Why the big jump? Partly because of improved production and editorial standards . . . the magazine looked better and offered more . . . and partly because in the 1980s we are once again facing a housing crisis.

In fact, economists agree that three-quarters of the families looking for a home today will be unable to buy a new house. Just as in the late '40s, if they buy at all, they are buying houses that need plenty of improvements and repairs. Very few are willing to pay $25 or more per hour to get this work done for them. So The FAMILY HANDYMAN is more indispensable than ever. It continues as the nation's foremost do-it-yourself publication.

Today, the "Ask Handyman" column, in which the editors apply their expertise to solve reader problems on a raft of different how-to projects, is still the most popular. More than 300 questions are answered by mail each month; a select few, the most useful and interesting, go into the column.

Most homeowners write in before embarking on a project. Sometimes they are looking for basic plans and ideas; more often they want to check on correct procedures, tools and materials. Besides "how-to" information, many answers include the names of government agencies, trade associations, books and publishers, technical experts, special products and their sources, and specialty stores or mail order houses. Leading categories of questions are: furniture repair, restoration, refinishing, upholstery and hardware; arts and crafts, which range from picture framing to wood carving; workshop and tools, including both hand and power tools; and painting and finishing. Plumbing and electricity pose perennial puzzles to homeowners, but the fact is that some simple explanations go a long way toward letting them do many important repairs themselves.

Much of the material in this book has been selected from the past 30 years of the "Ask Handyman" column. The best and most interesting problems and solutions have been chosen; all information has been checked and updated.

Supplementary material includes handy hints, tricks and time-savers, tips from old timers, basic skills and techniques in using tools, and useful advice on emergency repairs that can save you a lot of money and headaches when something breaks down.

You will find this to be the most diverse and readable volume available on many aspects of home maintenance, repair and improvement, offering invaluable, often hard-to-find information on thousands of nagging problems about building or fixing things around the house.

This book is meant as much for browsing as for specific troubleshooting. Flipping through it gives a relaxed education in an amazing number of technical areas. You will want to keep it on your desk, the kitchen counter, your workbench—even next to your bed—so that you can grab it and look up something fast, or just sit back and read for hours, picking up ideas and techniques. However you use it, you will be the company of a vast number of people who find both savings and satisfaction in doing it themselves.

Structural Problems

Construction, plans, models...Foundations, footings...Porches, basements, stoops, breezeways, sunroof decks...Railings... Stairways...Steps.

Do-it-yourself home

Q. **Where can I find a book written for the do-it-yourself homebuilder which will guide me in building my own home?**
R.L., Dayton, Ohio

A. Two books we can think of provide quite a bit of information on house carpentry. One is a paperback that costs $4.25 and is entitled *"Wood Frame House Construction,"* U.S. Dept. of Agriculture, Forest Service, Agriculture Handbook No. 73 (Order Stock No. 001-000-03528-2) available from the U.S. Government Printing Office, Washington, D.C. 20402. The closest to a how-to book is *"Practical House Carpentry—Simplified Methods of Building,"* by J. Douglas Wilson, a McGraw-Hill paperback that costs $4.95.

Two books which treat the subject in more detail are *"De Cristoforo's Housebuilding Illustrated"* (Popular Science/Harper & Row) and *"Carpentry and Building Construction,"* by John Feirer and Gilbert Hutchings (Scribners). The last is truly encyclopedic in its treatment of the subject, with over 2000 excellent diagrams and illustrations. Check bookstores and libraries for these.

Construction schedule

Q. **This coming spring, on a wooded, hillside lot, I am having a site cleared, excavation dug, foundation walls and cellar floor poured (measurements 35' x 24') and a two-story house erected. The materials are being left for me inside the house, so that I can do all of the interior finishing myself. The pipes, sewage, septic tank and tile bed will be installed and outlets for the all-electric baseboard heating will exist. I will be employing local teenagers to help with the interior trim work under my direction. I am a handyman myself, but would like your advice on what jobs I should do first. I don't want to have to undo some of the work already done because I didn't think of doing things in the proper order. Can you help me out?**
K.R., San Francisco, Calif.

A. You are obviously acting as your own general contractor and will be directly subcontracting the heating, plumbing and electrical work. Go over your plans in detail with these subcontractors and make clear to them just how far they are to carry out their work before you come in and do yours. For instance, the plumber can rough in the fixtures, let you do the tilework and then complete his installation—if you stick to his schedule. The same can be the case with the electrician: he can wire to the boxes, let you finish the ceiling, and then return to install the fixtures.

In general, try to do the jobs that need doing first; finish the bathroom and the kitchen and the installing of the appliances and fixtures, then install the cabinets in the wall surfaces, paint or wallpaper the wall, then do the floors and finally finish the trimming out. If you paint or finish the trim before installing it, there is a much smaller chance of spilling paint on the flooring. Work from the ceiling downwards whenever possible, and install the messiest finishes first, leaving the prefinished items until later. Details will vary from house to house; so there is no fast rule. Think each detail through as carefully as possible and try to figure out what will cause the least damage to what is already installed as you determine your work order.

One last thought: if you plan to live in the house as you get it finished up, take steps to prevent unnecessary clean-up work. Give raw wood a sealer coat, for example, even if you plan to delay painting for months.

Scale model home

Q. My husband and I have made our own house plans. We'd like to build a scale model, 1":1', before we build the real thing. Do you know where we can obtain scale pieces of wood to make walls, order doors and windows, etc.? The house model will be 65" on a side.

P.G., Pekin, Ill.

A. You've chosen the scale most miniature furniture and dollhouse builders use so you should have no problem finding materials. Northeastern Scale Models, Box 425, Methuen, Mass. 01844 has moldings and operating windows. Catalog and sample molding packet is $2. Other sources carry the Northeastern products plus those of additional manufacturers. Two such places are Craft Products Miniatures, 2200 Dean St., St. Charles, Ill. 60174 (their "Doll Houses and Furnishings" catalog is $1.50) and Shaker Miniatures, 2913 Huntington Rd., Cleveland, Ohio 44120 ($1.50 for literature). These include such items as shingles, parquet flooring, and hardware for those 6-1/2" high doors—all to scale. Carry the model far enough to check out the floor plan in action by providing some representation of furniture to scale.

Building log houses

Q. We are interested in building a log house. Could you tell us where we might get information on how to go about it?

G.C., Lethbridge, Alberta

A. There are two books on the subject: *"Shelters, Shacks and Shanties"* by D.C. Beard, published by Charles Scribner's Sons, 597 Fifth Ave., New York, N.Y. 10017, and *"How to Build Your Home in the Woods"* by Bradford Angier, published by Hart Publishing Co., 15 W. 4th St., New York, N.Y. 10011.

Log cabins

Q. Do you know of a company processing logs for complete homes? There is a good demand for such structures in my area.

L.T., Sullivan, Mo.

A. Following is a partial listing of major log home kit manufacturers. Some will do the total construction job, some sell and erect home packages, some sell just logs.

The companies listed without an asterisk are members of the Log Homes Council, which is part of the National Association of Home Manufacturers, 6521 Arlington Blvd., Falls Church, Va. 22042. The Log Homes Council roster includes 21 companies, and they sell 70% of all pre-cut log homes, according to E.T. Fillion, chairman of the council. Fillion says that 80% of log home owners do some of the construction work themselves.

Air-Lock Log Co., Dept. FH, P.O. Box 2506, Las Vegas, N.M. 87701; **Alta Industries Ltd.,** Dept. FH, P.O. Box 88, Halcottsville, N.Y. 12438; **Authentic Homes Corp.,** Dept. FH, P.O. Box 1288, Laramie, Wyo. 82070; **Beaver Log Homes,** Dept. FH, P.O. Box 1966, Grand Island, Neb. 68801; **Boyne Falls Log Homes,** Dept. FH, Highway 131, Boyne Falls, Mich. 49713; **Cabin Log Co. of America,** Dept. FH, 2809 Highway 167N, Lafayette, La. 70507; **Green Mountain Cabins,** Dept. FH, Box 190, Chester, Vt. 05143; **Justus Co.,** Dept. FH, P.O. Box 98300, Tacoma, Wash. 98499; **Lincoln Logs Ltd.*,** Dept. FH, 11 County Line Rd., Chestertown, N.Y. 12817; **Lodge Log,** Dept. FH, 3200 Gowen Rd., Boise, Ida. 83705; **Logcrafters*,** Dept. FH, P.O. Box 286, Lookout Mountain, Tenn. 37350; **Lok-N-Logs,** Dept FH, Rt. #2, Box 212, Sherburne, N.Y. 13460; **Lumber Enterprises,** Dept. FH, Gallatin Rd., Bozeman, Mont. 59715; **National Log Construction Co.*,** Dept. FH, P.O. Box 69, Thompson Falls, Mont. 59873; **New England Log Homes,** P.O. Box 5056, Hamden, Conn. 06518; **Northeastern Log Homes,** Dept. FH, P.O.

Box 126, Groton, Vt. 05046; **Northern Products Log Homes,** Dept. FH, Bomarc Rd., Bangor, Maine 04401; **Real Log Homes,** National Information Center, Dept. FH, Box 202, Hartland, Vt. 05048; **Rocky Mountain Log Homes,** Dept. FH, 3353 Highway 93 S., Hamilton, Mont. 59840; **Rustic Log Homes,** Dept. FH, 204 W. Ridge St., Kings Mountain, N.C. 28086; **Rustics of Lindbergh Lake,** Dept. FH, Condon, Mont. 59826; **Timber Log Homes*,** Austin Drive, Marlborough, Conn. 06447; **Ward Cabin Co.*,** Dept. FH, P.O. Box 72, Houlton, Maine 04730; **Western Valley Log Homes,** Dept. FH, P.O. Box D, Hamilton, Mont. 59840; **Wilderness Log Homes*,** Dept. FH, R.R. 2, Plymouth, Wis. 53073.

Dome kits

Q. I would like to build a geodesic dome for a home. How can I find out more about this?

B.M., Astoria, Ore.

A. Keeping up with the dome home situation is complicated. Many firms are local or regional and do not come to our attention. The best single organization to get in touch with is the National Dome Association, 2506 Gross Point Rd., Evanston, Ill. 60201. One source of kits and/or plans you might want to investigate is Geodesic Domes, 10290 Davison Rd., Davison, Mich. 48423. Send a self-addressed, stamped envelope. And, for $6.00, Monterey Domes, P. O. Box 5621, Riverside, Calif. 92517 will send a copy of their 80-page color catalog of shell dome kits in sizes from 300 to 3,500 sq. ft. priced from $3,995.

Try a tipi or yurt

Q. Before we got around to building our truly different A-frame home, everyone had one. Before we got around to building our geodesic dome, everyone had one. Now this summer we want to build a shelter for living close to nature that is truly different and we want to build it before everyone else does. What do you suggest?

D.T., Iron Mtn., Mich.

A. We suggest that you go to your nearest bookseller (or your library) for a copy of *"The Indian Tipi—Its History, Construction and Use"* by Reginald and Gladys Laubin (published by Univ. of Oklahoma Press and also available now in paperback in the Walden Series by Ballentine Books). Also check up on *"The Yurt Book,"* an oversize paperback by Len Charney, the correct title of which is *"Build a Yurt—The Low Cost Mongolian Round House."* It's published by Collier Books, Div. of MacMillan.

You can order various sizes and choice of materials—made to order tipi with option liner—hand-crafted by people who care from Nomadics Tipi Makers, 17671 Snow Creek Rd., Bend, Ore. 97701. $1 will get you their catalog.

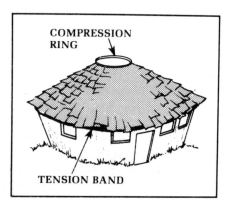

COMPRESSION RING

TENSION BAND

The yurt idea is one that is open for your own individual interpretation. The basis is adapting the Mongolian model to this country and our available materials. Canvas, wood slats, tarpaper and polyester resin-coated parachutes are reasonable roofing and siding substitutes for yak hides. For a dollar plus postage, you can obtain a delightful booklet outlining the basics of yurt construction entitled "Home's Where the Yurt Is" from Jim Steinman at Box 53, West Danby, N.Y. 14896. Although they can be made very cheaply from

scrap materials, a reasonable figure for a more conventionally built yurt would be around $600.

Another source of yurt information is William S. Copperthwaite, Director, The Yurt Foundation, Bucks Harbor, Maine 04618. They offer a poster guide, beautifully drawn and lettered, containing a brief history of yurts, for $10. They also offer workshops in yurt building for interested groups. There are also several posters available for the same price of $10. One is a plan diagram of a 32' diameter concentric yurt with a central raised section. Both this and the guide show wood plank siding and incorporate the tension band, compression ring roofing method that's essential to the yurt design.

Underground homes

Q. Do you know where I can get information on underground homes?

C.M., Kennewick, Wash.

A. You might want to start with the feature article by Ray Lorenz in The FAMILY HANDYMAN, No. 206 Edition, February 1980, page 12. (You can obtain a copy of that issue by sending $2 to the Back Issue Dept., The FAMILY HANDYMAN, 1999 Shepard Road, St. Paul, Minn. 55116.) *"Earth Sheltered Housing Design"* by the Underground Space Center, University of Minnesota is $10.95 in paperback, published by Van Nostrand Reinhold (VNR/Litton Educational Publishing, 135 West 50th St., New York, N.Y. 10020). Mother's Bookshelf, P.O. Box 70, Hendersonville, N.C. 28791 also carries this title and a number of others listed under "Energy Efficient Building" in its mail order catalog, which is available free upon written request. There are underground and in-ground homes as well as earth-covered ones, and various types in between. What's best for you depends a lot on where you are and how you live.

Vacation homes

Q. In the 64th Edition of The FAMILY HANDYMAN, Sept./Oct. 1961, you showed a vacation cottage. Are these plans available and what is the current price?

T.S., Pittsburgh, Pa.

A. You're too late to get plans for the 1961 vacation home, but we've got good news for you. A co-operative effort between The FAMILY HANDYMAN Magazine and Home Building Plan Service of Portland, Oregon, has resulted in a new special publication. This book contains over 100 plans varying from A-frames to contemporary designs. Although it's titled "Recreation & Holiday Homes," it also contains some unique designs for year-round homes, and complete blueprints are available for any design you choose. Price is $2 plus 50¢ postage. Send your check to Handyman Home Plans Service, 1999 Shepard Rd., St. Paul, Minn. 55116.

House plans

Q. Do you have a book of house plans? We would like to build a ranch-style home.

R.M., Sacramento, Calif.

A. The Handyman Library includes five books with house plans; two of the most popular are *Recreation & Holiday Homes* and *Homes for the 80's.* Send $2 plus 50¢ postage for each to The Family Handyman Library, 1999 Shepard Road, St. Paul, Minn. 55116.

Home Planners, 2371 Research Drive, Farmington Hills, Mich. 48024, offers collections of plans in five categories for $10.95 (over 1,000 designs). Other plans sources include Home Building Plan Service, Inc., Studio 14 N. 2235 N.E. Sandy Blvd., Portland, Ore. 97232; National Home Planning Service, 37 Mountain Ave., Springfield, N.J. 07081; Spectrum-3 Design Associates, Suite 277, 5331 S.W. Macadam Ave., Portland, Ore. 97201, and W.L. Corley Plan Service, P.O. Box

90430, Atlanta, Ga. 30364. All have catalogs showing at least one perspective view of each house, the floor plan and information for study and comparison. Once you select the plan you'd like, you can order as many sets of working drawings and details as you need.

Concrete block house

Q. I would like to build a house of cement blocks, but there are several questions I have not been able to get answered locally; so I hope you can give me some help.

1. Where can I get a detailed book, giving step-by-step instructions so that I can do the work?

2. How large a footing would be needed to support a wall 20' high. It will be built on pumice soil.

3. How does the insulating quality of blocks compare to 4" of insulation in a frame house?

4. Is the dead air in blocks sufficient or should the blocks be filled with something?

5. Which is better—a cement block or triple-wall metal chimney? I will be putting two in the basement and one in the living room so that I can use either oil or wood for heat.

N.W., Prospect, Ore.

A. One book that will come close to answering your questions is "Simplified Masonry Planning and Building" by J. Ralph Dalzell, published by McGraw Hill. Check with your bookseller and library or write to the McGraw Hill bookstore at 330 W. 42nd St., New York, N.Y. 10036.

Also the Portland Cement Association, 5420 Old Orchard Rd., Skokie, Illinois 60077 should be able to help you—either with one of their publications or by suggesting other titles.

Foundation caulking

Q. I have a ranch house with a slab foundation. The seal between the foundation and the walls is not tight. I would like to caulk around the house under the first row of shingles but there isn't room enough to use a regular caulking gun and I can't find one with a right angled nozzle. Any suggestions?

R.M., East Hartford, Conn.

A. You can substitue oakum caulking, the type used to caulk boat seams. Tap it up into the joint with a cold chisel and mallet.

Foundation walls

Q. I'm adding an enclosed sun room on one end of my ranch house which is built on a crawl space. When I butt the new wall to the old one at the foundation level, do I make the joint with cement or mortar or what? These will be block walls.

W.N., Herkimer, N.Y.

A. Give the old wall a coat of asphalt cement and mortar the new one against it. This way you will have a bit of give should settling be a shade different.

Walls on slab

Q. I am going to build a home in an area with a dampness problem. Could I build a concrete slab, allow 3' crawl space and put the foundation at the edge of this slab?

W.P., Bergenfield, N.J.

A. A solid slab of equal thickness throughout would crack from weight concentrated at the outer edges. You'd need a "floating" slab with the outer edges about 16" thick, tapering on the underside to about 5" thick at the center of the slab. The entire slab should be reinforced with steel rods.

Cement over brick

Q. We've about decided it is worthwhile to cover the crumbly brick foundation walls of our house with cement, both to improve appearance and prevent further destruction. What should we use and how is it applied?

H.F., Torrington, Mass.

A. You'll have to excavate downward as far as any damage extends to make it worthwhile. Clean the wall with a wire brush to remove all loose material, then wet the brick well. Mix 1 part cement, 2-1/2 parts sand and enough water to make a stiff mix that will not fall apart when rolled into a ball in your hand. Trowel this on at once to a thickness of 1/2", wait two weeks, then apply a silicone or other water repellent paint above grade.

Footing size

Q. I have heard there is a "rule of thumb" for determining the size of footings required for a given project. Could you tell me what this is?

F.R., New York, N.Y.

A. The rule which is pretty safe to follow for almost any building around a single family home is simple: Twice the wall thickness for the footing width, the wall thickness and the footing thickness the same. For an 8"-thick wall the footing would be 16" wide and 8" thick from top to bottom.

Shallow cellar

Q. I am considering the possibility of putting in a cement floor in my cellar. The cinderblock walls are all right but the dirt floor is leveled off at the bottom of the 8" footer, giving me only about 5-1/2' of standing room and I am 6'2". How am I going to dig the dirt down about 18" without undermining the footer?

T.K., Elmira, N.Y.

A. There is a standard way of going about deepening a cellar. Come inside the footing line 18", then dig down to the new depth plus the depth of the new footing and erect a new footing at that point. Then the new foundation wall is carried up to the top of the present footing and the resulting shelf covered with at least 2" of concrete. The excavating must be confined to an 8' length along any one wall only at any one time.

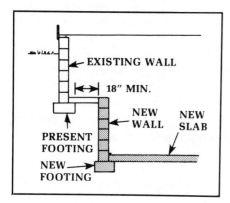

Enlarging basement

Q. I have a concrete block house with a half-basement and I would like to dig out the rest of the basement. I plan to pour short sections at a time and connect these sections with reinforcing rod. Will I have any trouble doing this?

R.J., Colorado Springs, Colo.

A. If you feel you MUST have the foundation for the full basement directly under the present foundation, hire a rigging contractor to jack up the whole house on heavy timbers, build your new foundation and then set the house back down on it. Your way is a hazard to the house as well as to the men doing the work.

Addition to house

Q. I want to add more rooms to the first floor of my house. I don't figure to build a basement, just a crawl space but there is a basement under the rest of the house. What do I need for a new foundation?

E.S., Whitestone, N.Y.

A. For a new foundation where there is to be no basement, an excavation must be made to at least 36" depth, and here a concrete footing

is made 16" wide and 8" deep. The 8" foundation wall is erected on its center. You may want to increase the 36" dimension to bring the top of the new foundation in line with the top of the old one to keep the floor levels identical—unless you plan a split level addition.

Pipe column support

Q. When I built my home I used 4" double strength pipe for support in the basement. I am told I put these in wrong and they will rust out. What can I do now?

K.C., New Philadelphia, Ohio

A. If the part of the pipe under the floor was not properly protected, it could rust away. Brace the girder and remove the pipe. Replace with a new one set on a cement base a bit above the present floor level.

Moving posts

Q. I would like to move a post in my cellar. There is a distance of 8' between the wall and this post and 8' to the next post. I wish to increase the space to 12' between wall and first post. The posts support the main beam. Can I do this?

F.S., Merrick, N.Y.

A. To simply move the post and do nothing more could be extremely dangerous. Assuming you have a standard triple 2x8 built-up beam, you would have to strengthen it with two addtional 2x8s, one on each side, bolted right through at 2' staggered intervals. Extend the two new 2x8s 2' beyond the new post location. Then set up temporary supports to hold the beam while you remove the old post. The new post will need a larger footing under it to carry the greater load and a larger bearing plate on top.

Removing column

Q. Part of my basement is a recreation room and right smack in

the center is a lally column. I've been told I can remove the column only by strengthening the beam over it which is now three 2x8s. Suggestions include using a 3x8 on each side of the beam, a steel channel bolted to each side or a 1/4" steel plate bolted to each side. Columns are 8' apart and 4" in diameter on concrete pads.

R.G., Upton, N.Y.

A. None of the suggested methods take into consideration the additional load on the end columns after removal of the center one. They would have to be strengthened first to avoid cracking the footings. Then we would favor the steel plate system as it requires shorter bolts and takes up less room.

Flagstone stoop

Q. I am making a poured concrete top on my new stoop which I want to cover with flagstones. Do I have to lay the stone immediately after the 48-hour waiting period or can I delay this operation several weeks?

G.C., Plainfield, N.J.

A. You can lay flagstone 24 hours after the slab is poured or any time thereafter so long as the concrete surface is soaked with water before the cement for the flagstone is spread on it. A waterproofing chemical in the mortar is not amiss.

Concrete porch

Q. I would like to build a concrete porch, open underneath with a concrete block wall along the front to support it. Can I build this front wall on a concrete sidewalk 4" thick?

R.B., Long Island City, N.Y.

A. Your foundation would crack the walk. Foundation wall should rest on a footing below frost depth.

Concrete porch floor

Q. To make a concrete floored porch without bringing the fill up to the underside of the floor slab I imagine reinforcing would be necessary. Could you tell me what size, spacing, etc?

B.A., Longview, Wash.

A. The average porch would need 1/2″ reinforcing bars spaced at 9″ intervals with lateral bars wired to these at similar spacing. Assuming the front edge rests on a block wall the house side would have to be built up from the footing ledge to the same height. You would need a form construction for pouring the in-place slab.

Brick over concrete

Q. At present I have a cement stoop in front of my house and have considered covering it over with brick. Must I chip or roughen the cement before applying the brick?

J.W., Rockville Center, N.Y.

A. Soak the old cement thoroughly, and make sure it is free of dirt or oil. Then cement bricks to it using a mix of 1 part mortar cement to 2 parts sand. When the job is finished, a coat of clear masonry silicone water repellent would be a good idea.

Stoop replacement

Q. We want to remove the small wooden platform that serves as a back stoop and add on a larger open porch. The house foundation is concrete block and we figured to align the foundation walls for the new porch to that. How is the joint made watertight between porch foundation and the house foundation?

G.H., Petoskey, Mich.

A. You can use expansion strips or asphalt coating on the old surface and join against this to avoid cracks but it will leave a visible seam. Or you can wet the old surface thoroughly and mortar the new wall up to it.

Screened porch

Q. I'm building a concrete porch or patio which we'd like to screen in. Do I put up the framework after the concrete is finished and if so, how is it anchored to the concrete? Or should I imbed the framework in the concrete when it is poured?

A.E., Great Bend, Kan.

A. Set anchor bolts of 12″ x 1/2″ size in wet concrete to serve as anchors for porch sills and corner posts. All woodwork is put up after concrete has set.

Foundation for stoop

Q. I want to replace my porch with a brick stoop but the ground slopes. I do not know if I make an excavation starting at the lowest point or at the highest point for the footings.

L.T., Cochituate, Mass.

A. It is best to excavate to frost depth, starting at the lowest corner and leveling off from that point. A largish stoop on a steep slope might make a stepped foundation more practical but this would seldom be the case. The average depth should always remain at frost level.

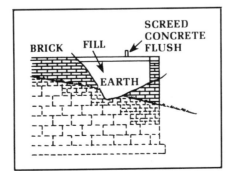

Pitch or slope

Q. Is there any easy way to get the right pitch or slope to drain the cement floor part of my brick stoop? It is 4′ square.

E.W., Dowagiac, Mich.

A. You need about 1/4″ per foot drop to ensure good drainage; in 4′ this would be 1″. Lay your brick wall so the front is 1″ lower than porch height at the house side and taper the end walls to this slope. Then use these walls as a guide to sloping the concrete floor.

Storage under porch

Q. I plan to enclose the lower portion of my porches. I'd like to use cement to weatherproof the areas so they can be used as storage, keeping them as inconspicuous as possible. I'll appreciate any suggestions.

L.S., Corona, N.Y.

A. Since the wall will not have to bear any weight, you can use 4″-thick 8″ x 16″ blocks on an 8″ wide footing 4″ thick, started about 16″ to 20″ below grade. Leave room on top of these walls for a tapered sill to fit snugly under the porch edge support timbers. By striking the mortar joints flush, your wall will be smooth surfaced and can be painted if desired. You will have to provide some sort of door of course. If the enclosed area is dirt floored, excavate to grade and level off, then put down a layer of polyethylene film sealed to the wall with plastic adhesive which will keep the storage area quite dry and lessen moisture migration upwards to the porch timbers.

Add a porch

Q. What is the easiest way to make a concrete porch? This will be outside my kitchen and I'd like it to be about 7′ x 9′. As it need be only two steps up from the ground,

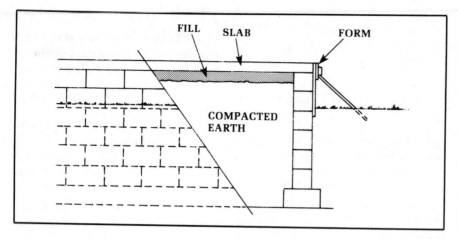

FILL   SLAB   FORM

COMPACTED EARTH

I thought concrete would be best to use and just paint it.

C.F., Moline, Ill.

A. Make a foundation for the porch of 8"x8"x16" concrete blocks on a footing at frost depth 16" wide and 8" thick. Fill inside with dirt, compacting it to within 4" of the top, then crushed rock fill as a base for a 4" slab. You'll need forms around the outside to contain this slab and either use cap blocks on the foundation wall's top course or stuff them well with crumpled paper or you'll be pouring your slab down inside the wall. Cracks are likely where the slab crosses the wall this way if the center fill is not well compacted.

Extended stoop

Q. I wish to extend my front stoop by 5' on each side. It is poured concrete 18" high. I plan to use cinder block on a footing faced with white brick with poured concrete for the slab top. How do I prepare the ground for the footing and what do I use for fill before pouring the slab?

H.G., Plainview, N.Y.

A. Make a trench 20" wide at the bottom and fill with rubble or poured concrete to form a footing 8" thick. Lay the block on this and face with 4" blocks to the ground level, then continue this portion with the face brick. You can fill between these new foundation walls and the existing stoop with compacted earth but leave room for 3" to 4" of crushed stone fill under the slab.

Support porch floor

Q. I have a question where a wood floored porch meets the 8" x 8" x 16" concrete blocks of my house. Can I cut into these blocks for porch floor supports or do I have to make a foundation wall on all four sides of the porch for the floor?

P.F., Frostburg, Md.

A. You can cement 4" blocks to the house foundation for the full length of the porch to provide a bearing surface for the floor joists. Or you could bolt on a steel angle, attaching it with lag screws in lead anchors for which holes are drilled in the house foundation. The angle should be predrilled for these holes and for screws to attach the joists or a nailing plate.

Pre-cast concrete

Q. I am getting tired trying to keep a wooden porch in shape. Is there an easy way to make a concrete one about 8' wide and maybe 10' or 12' long at the end of my house? I do not want to make a stoop out of it.

P.S., Uniontown, Pa.

A. You can use pre-cast beams, already reinforced for this job.

They could be rested on a steel angle bolted to the house foundation and on a foundation wall carried down to frost depth on the side away from the house, leaving the ends open. Seal the joints with expansion strips and apply a surface of cement.

Enclosing porch

Q. We have a 12' x 13' porch with a concrete floor and a pitched roof supported on corner posts of wood. We cannot decide whether to enclose the porch so it may be screened-in in summer or enclose it permanently as an added room. We would like to know if we can do both and what the difficulties would be.

J.S., Clifton, N.J.

A. There are one or two difficulties to be considered in this halfway approach. The corner and other posts should be removed and replaced with studs at 16" intervals for a finished room. But 16" intervals is difficult to fit with standard screens and storm sash. As a compromise use double 2x4 studs on 32" centers. When framed this will accomodate 30" stock sash. You will probably have to add short studs between the doubled ones to brace the sheathing if and when you enclose. Set in rough headers and sills for your sash and make your door opening to fit a stock combination door.

Small porch enclosure

Q. I have a 4' x 4' cement stoop in the rear of my house and want to enclose it. If you could tell me how to frame it, including a shed roof, I could probably figure out the rest. We'll use storm sash on the two window sides, a door on the wall parallel to the house.

A.C., Cranston, R.I.

A. Use double 2x3 corner posts as roof supports. Anchor to a square plate at the base. Bolt a 2x3 to the house and a double 2x4 from this to

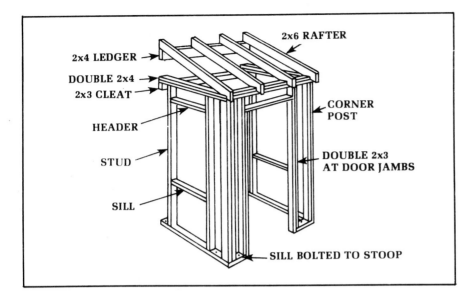

2x6 RAFTER

2x4 LEDGER

DOUBLE 2x4

2x3 CLEAT

HEADER

STUD

SILL

CORNER POST

DOUBLE 2x3 AT DOOR JAMBS

SILL BOLTED TO STOOP

the corner post and to join the posts. This is all level and a frame for the porch ceiling. The shed roof requires a 2x4 bolted to the house. Run 2x6 rafters from this ledger to the front edge of the frame. Make framework of 2x3 stock to enclose the storm sash. Use full height studs for the jambs, 2x3 sill and header as required. You'll need a doubled 2x3 stud at each side of the doorway too.

rot) set the panels on it and nail them to it and to each other and to the header or beam under the roof. It is almost as simple as it sounds. For a solid wall, a 2x4 stud frame most probably can be covered easily to match the rest of the house. You'll have to insulate, give the end walls and solid wall areas an interior finish and supply heat to have a room that is useable year around.

Corner post

Q. We have a 6′ x 8′ entrance porch. It is concrete but has a solid rail and corner post shingled like the house is. I would like to take all this off and substitute wrought or cast iron. We want to paint the house white and I think black iron would be much more attractive. I figure to have enough shingles from the railing to fill the space on the wall where the railing fits against it now. Do you think this is a practical project and how should I go at it?

R.T., Cleveland, Ohio

A. This could be quite effective, the way you have described it. It would be best to tear out the railing portions first, repair the house wall, then tackle the post substitution. Be certain you support the roof securely enough to do your work. Telescoping jack posts or 2x8s can be used, but plant them on something solid. You'll need a corner unit capable of carrying the weight. One manufacturer offers one with devices that fit into the bottom ends of the tubular sections for easy leveling on concrete. A jacket slips down to conceal the ends.

Enclose a breezeway

Q. We have a good sized roofed breezeway between house and garage that I would like to turn into a useable room. It has large framed screen panels at present that hook to a board on the bottom and a board on the top and the bottom is decaying so we have to do something. There are two 8″ square built-up wood posts on each side and the concrete floor is one step down from the house, one step up from the garage. Is there an easy, fairly quick way to enclose this?

W.S., Morristown, N.J.

A. There is if cost is no object. You can buy floor-to-ceiling triple slide window units in various widths that will fill in the walls for you. You provide the wood sill (use pressure treated lumber to avoid

Iron railing

Q. I am building a concrete stoop at my front entrance, using concrete blocks faced with brick. I plan using an iron railing around the sides and would appreciate any information you can give me on how to anchor it.

E.B., Troy, N.Y.

A. Part of the answer is going to depend on what anchorage is provided with the railing you buy. Some types are fitted with flanges through which screws can be set into lead anchors in the concrete. These may be inserted while the concrete is wet or set in drilled holes after the concrete has hardened. Some types of railing supports are simply an extension of the rail with a cross bar welded on for added strength. Make a hole for these in wet concrete, then

insert when the concrete is dry and pour melted lead into the holes around the post supports.

Porch pillars

Q. I am planning a 14′-square porch with a flat roof with 8″ x 8″ x 16″ blocks as pillars to hold up the floor. Should these be cemented together or will the fact that they are entirely underground hold the blocks together?

M.J., Lansing, Ill.

A. Blocks even on the footing they must have, would tend to slip under pressure and your pillars could collapse or crack the blocks under uneven pressures. They should be cemented together.

Iron posts

Q. We would like to do something about improving the appearance of our front porch. Can those wrought iron posts be used on an existing porch?

L.D., Saginaw, Mich.

A. Of course they can. Make sure the support for the porch floor is in good shape first, then provide temporary support for the porch roof while you make the exchange. The 3-point supports are usually used at corners while the 2-post panel units go between corner supports as necessary. Railing to match the design you select is easily set between corner or panel units. Attachment methods vary but most manufacturers offer sockets or angle clips suitable for wood floors as well as some device for concrete attachment. Select the type to suit your situation.

Roof supports

Q. We have an extended stoop, 12′ wide by 7′ deep, that we want to roof over coming out from the eaves with an intersecting gable roof. Will it be necessary to add to the present footing of the stoop to support the added roof weight?

K.R., Columbia, S.C.

A. It would be best to cut away the present stoop where posts supporting the new porch roof are to be placed. Then build a separate footing and base for these. A concentration of the extra weight could crack the stoop slab and tend eventually to cause a sagging roof. Use a strip of expansion joint material between post base and stoop.

Posts on concrete

Q. I plan using 4x4 fir posts to support a small roof over our front entrance. How would you advise anchoring them to the concrete porch?

K.W., Greenport, N.Y.

A. Attach a squared section of 2x6 to the bottom of the post, after treating both the base of the post and the block with wood preservative. Paint the underside of the block with asphalt and rest it on the concrete. Through the protruding flange of the block drive at least two brass screws into lead anchors set in holes drilled 1-1/4″ deep into the concrete.

New deck roof

Q. I am going to remodel my kitchen and remove the present shed roof and make it over into a sun deck. I am using light weight concrete blocks for the walls and intend using 2x10 rafters, if these will be strong enough to carry the load. The span is 12′. What pitch does it need to drain and what material to cover?

F.L., Newfield, N.J.

A. The 2x10s are more than adequate for the deck roof. Slope should be 1/4″ per foot for proper drainage. On a subfloor of 1x6 tongue and grooved stock plus tarpaper sealed at the joints you can use hardboard sealed at the joints, marine-type deck lumber with caulking and a varnish finish or, since you have support, quarry tile.

Front door overhang

Q. We have a brick house and would like to add a more finished look to the area over the front door. Do you have any suggestions about where I could get some ideas? I would prefer wood to aluminum, something not too difficult to make, and of course not too expensive.

M.S., Pittsburgh, Pa.

A. House plan catalogs in your library could be an idea source. Look through back issue files of "New Homes Guide" and "Home Remodeling Guide." House and Garden, House Beautiful, and Better Homes and Gardens will also be useful.

If what you are thinking of is simply for decoration and not for protection from the elements, a small, light lattice frame for any kind of vine would suit your purposes easily.

Concrete porch

Q. I want to build a concrete porch 10′ x 7′ with brick on the sides. Does it need a footing? It will only be two steps up from the ground. How far down into the ground must I carry the brick?

R.M., Columbus, Ohio

A. You go down to below frost, usually about 3′ for the footing. You can use 8″ concrete block for your foundation wall, going to the 8″ brick wall only at grade and save some of the cost of the brick.

New stairway

Q. I am remodeling my home and would like to install a stairway to my attic. I have only a limited space: A 7′ x 7′ room and a ceiling height of 9′2″. I would like to know what type of construction would be best.

W. S., Elgin, Ill.

A. There's a good deal more involved than a few dimensions in completely designing a stairway. Assuming you can use all of the 7′ dimension without walking through a wall you will need 14 risers of 8″ each and 13 treads of 7″ each. This makes a very steep, uncomfortable stairway. If you can use all of the 7' square area and still have a door you could construct a platform with portions of the stairs at right angles to each other. This could be managed with four or five steps in the turn. If headroom is available a landing can be made at the turning point.

Stairway headers

Q. I have just finished building new cellar stairs and notice that the header at the side of the stair-wall has a slight bow. There are five joists nailed into this header and there seems to be a gap of about 1/4" to 1/2" between joist ends and header. Your recommendations as to how to solve this problem would be welcome.

W. D., Toronto, Ontario

A. If nails are holding securely the slight gap will cause no trouble. In standard construction, sub-flooring would tie joists and header together and distribute floor load equally over all. If your header is not covered by flooring, it might be a good idea to set lag screws through header into joist ends to make sure the joists will not pull loose.

Basement stairway

Q. I plan to replace basement stairs in a space 7-1/2' long with a ceiling height of 6'. Headroom is ample and does not figure into the picture. I am wondering which is the best construction: To cut the stringers for each tread or to fasten cleats to the stringers to support the treads? The stairs rest against stone or cement at each end.

T. I., Westboro, Ontario

A. You will need 10 risers of 7-3/16" and 9 treads of 10" for a fairly comfortable stairway. For stronger construction use cleats rather than cutting into the string-ers. We would suggest you attach a 2"-thick header to the masonry at

the top of the flight and anchor the stringers to this rather than to attempt anchoring directly to the masonry.

Cellar hatch steps

Q. The doors to our cellar hatch-way were evidently replaced not too long before we bought this house but the steps are another matter. There are seven now and six are loose. Is there a quick and easy way to replace them?

E.J., Salem, Ohio

A. The quickest way is to use the metal stringers you set in place, then push in 2x10 treads. If you remove the existing steps and prepare the bulkhead according to manufacturer's directions, you'll find the job simple and quickly done.

Chairlift

Q. We recently purchased a tri-level home, despite the fact that I am physically handicapped. Carrying items up and down stairs is proving to be a chore. What ideas are available to ease problems handicapped people have in using stairways?

Z. K., Palm Desert, Calif.

A. A chairlift that parallels the stairway is a reasonable alterna-tive to an elevator. If you can't find a local source, write to American Stair-Glide, Dept. FH, 4001 E. 138th St., Grandview, Mo. 64030. But you might want to consider the advantages of a vertically travel-ling residential elevator. One of them is that you don't have to trans-fer between floors. Inclinator's "Elevette" is of a size to accom-modate a person in a wheelchair. If you can't find a listing in the yellow pages, write Inclinator Co. of America, Dept. FH, Box 1557, Harrisburg, Pa. 17105.

Rule of thumb

Q. There seems to be a rule of

thumb for just about everything. Is there one for stairs?

I.I., Glen Cove, N.Y.

A. Yes, there is. Usually it is stated thusly: "Twice the riser plus the tread equals about 25". You'll find this holds pretty true on the low, broad terrace steps with a 5" riser and 15" tread as well as the ladder-like attic steps with 9-1/2" riser height to 6" tread.

Strength of stringers

Q. In building wood steps for my porch, I am in a quandary as to how many carriages are needed. Would two 2x12s do? The finished carriages will be 7'2" long, with a step span of 40".

J.V., Silver Spring, Md.

A. These carriages—also called stringers or horses—carry all the weight. In your stairs, the two 2x12s will be adequate. For the 40" span, it would be best to use 2" stock for treads, unless you are putting in wood risers fastened to treads, which would serve as a brace. In that case, 1" stock could be used.

Cutting stringers

Q. Just how do you start to draw the pattern on a piece of lumber to make a stringer for porch steps? There are four steps to be cut. If I can get the lumber laid out correctly, I'll have the job beat.

C.L., Toronto, Ontario

A. For an on-the-job way to tackle this problem without a framing square, take a 2x10 at least 3' long for each side support. Square one end of the board and then measure off 7" along one edge to form a pattern "P". Set tip of pat-tern at point X and draw lines X-A and A-B. Now shift pattern and draw lines B-C and C-D. Repeat this for lines D-E and E-F. Extend the line E-F to point G and cut off the excess. Take pattern and set it along line X-Y as shown by dotted

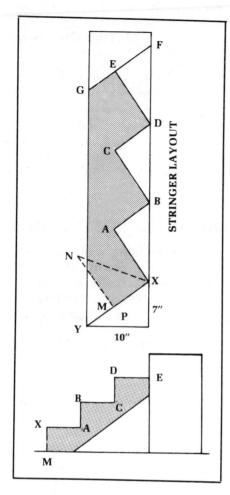

STRINGER LAYOUT

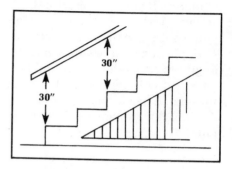

outline. Draw line M-N and cut off the excess. Sketch #2 shows the stringer in place. Point E is placed so that it is 8" below top of the porch.

Folding stairs

Q. I want to install a folding stairway to our attic. Would you please give me the necessary details for cutting through the ceiling and how do I construct the proper frame for a ready-built stairway which I am going to get from a local lumberyard?

G.S., Springfield, Pa.

A. You have to pick a spot where you will have headroom. Information that comes with the ready-built stair unit will specify the clearance needed and show size of opening required. You should try to run the long dimension of the stair opening the long

way of the joists, so that only one or at the most two need to be cut. First locate the joists; then, assuming the attic is floored, mark off the opening between the joists, cut through and lift the flooring. Mark through the ceiling below and cut out this side, leaving joists bare on both sides. Framing the opening consists of cutting through the joists vertically at each end and placing a piece of the cut out joist sawed off to a snug fit, across the ends. It is spiked into the cut joist ends and toenailed into the uncut ones at each side. Use 1" stock to frame the inside and you are ready for installation.

Open stair railing

Q. I have opened my stairway between living room and den on both sides. I had to retain a pillar from the foot of the stairs to the ceiling. Now I have to select some kind of railing for both sides. Could you solve this problem?

H.C., East Taunton, Mass.

A. The final solution will have to be up to you as this is pretty much a decorating problem. You can select the rail to blend with the room decor—aluminum, brass, wrought iron or stock wood. The "do-it-yourself-type" aluminum can be worked into quite a modern handrail but lacks the strength of wrought iron. For the most "open" effect a slender wood handrail with equally slender balusters, serves the purpose best in the wood line. Your lumber dealer has many stock patterns to select from.

Handrail placement

Q. I would like to know how high above the steps I should install a handrail. It will be placed on a plastered wall alongside the stairway. Please indicate if the measurement given is to be made from the front or back edge of the steps.

J.O., Rome, N.Y.

A. Measure straight up from the front edge of the tread 30" and set the rail at this point. If the railing continues beyond the stairs at the top, run the railing 6" higher before leveling off so it is 36" above the upper floor.

Loose stair dowels

Q. How can we tighten the dowels on our stairway banister?

C.R., Schenectady, N.Y.

A. The wood is obviously dry. Drill a small hole at an angle through the base of each dowel into the stair tread. Then drive in a 3" finishing nail. Use a drill bit 2/3 the nail diameter. An alternative method is to fill the crack around each baluster with a quick-drying liquid glue or one of the urea resin glues which are applied with a putty knife, then wiped clean before drying.

Reinforcing stringers

Q. I have a rather long stairway to my rear porch with 2x10 stringers and 7" risers with 9" treads. The stringers are spaced 39" apart and there is a good deal of "give" to them. I would like to know how to strengthen the stairway.

J.C., Flushing, N.Y.

A. You probably have sufficient room to work from below on this job, so you can do it the easy way by adding a 2x4 to each stringer. Cut these full length and bolt them to the inner side of each

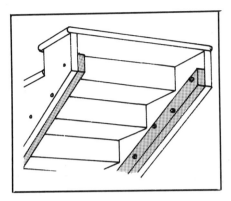

stringer, flush with the bottom edge. Use 1/4" bolts all the way through with washers on each side, staggering bolts along the 2x4 at 10" intervals.

Sagging stairway

Q. Can you tell me what is causing the treads and risers of my stairway to pull away from the baseboard and plaster along the wall? The gaps are from 3/8" to 1/2", and I'm worried.

C.K., Canton, Ohio

A. The explanation is generally a roomside stringer that has bowed, shrunk or rotted at the base permitting that side to drop slightly, pulling treads and risers with it. In all probability the pulled-away portions are also attached to a stringer on the wall side that would prevent collapse of the stairs. But if not, then there does exist a future hazard.

Separated stairway

Q. It seems like our whole stairway is coming away from the wall. The steps did fit up under a kind of baseboard on the wall side, the room side being open above the steps with just a railing along there. Is there any way we can get these risers and treads back where they belong without removing the baseboard and disturbing the plaster?

C.C., Omaha, Neb.

A. There is not much if any chance of getting things back into place without complete reconstruction. Nails must be removed the rest of the way before anything can be done. That means dismantling and the manner in which stairs are put together would require almost total removal down to rough framework. It would be advisable to check the foot of the stringer at the railing side to determine whether it has rotted. Also see if that stringer has pulled loose from the stairwell header. Major repairs are undoubtedly necessary in this case.

Spiral stairway

Q. Can you tell me where I can get or order a metal circular stairway? This is the type that has triangle-shaped treads that fasten to a 3" steel pipe and are adjustable. If these are not available, can you tell me if back issues of The FAMILY HANDYMAN have instructions on how to construct one of wood?

J.H., Marietta, Ga.

A. You will find it easier to order a metal circular stairway than to figure out how to build one of wood. You can order units which have triangle-shaped treads that fasten to a steel pipe and are adjustable from The Iron Shop, 400 Reed Rd., P.O. Box 128, Broomall, Pa. 19008; Mylen Industries, 650 Washington St., Box 350, Peekskill, N.Y. 10566; Duvinage Corp., Box 828, Hagerstown, Md. 21740; and American General Products, 1735 Holmes Rd., Ypsilanti, Mich. 48197.

Duvinage has only built-to-order units but they can be owner-installed. The others have more or less standard units, adjustable or "selectable" enough to suit almost any normal residential need. Write each company for the name of their local dealer, their residential catalog or brochure and their price list. Some do offer wood treads and the designs range from institutional to cleanly functional in the metal

units. You should be able to find a stairway that will suit your purposes and which the average home handyman can install.

Trap door

Q. We are adding a kitchen to our cabin with a spiral stair down to the basement. We realize this will let cold air from the basement upstairs. Can a trap door be used on the spiral staircase?

K.M., Hayward, Wis.

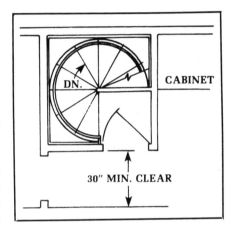

A. A trap door for a spiral stair isn't that simple. If you use a kit stair where the railing is within the diameter of the steps, you don't have just a round hole in the floor to put a trap door into. You have a square hole with a railing spiraling out of it. It might be possible to build a cover 4' to 6-1/2'-square, high enough to cover the stair railing. The sides of the cover could even do double duty as the stairwell rail. Even with a few folding panels, such a cover is not a trapdoor. Or you might simply close the stairway and weatherstrip the door.

Squeaking stairs

Q. I have trouble with squeaking stairs. They squeak so loudly that our house sounds haunted. Can you tell me the easiest way that I can get rid of these annoying noises?

H.Y., St. Louis, Mo.

A. Wood shrinkage and expansion probably lies behind the squeaks that bother you. In the process, nails become loose and allow the pieces to rub together, causing the noise. Two things—glue and screws—will work as curatives if you can get them into the right places. Pick out a tread that squeaks badly and have someone step up and down on it as you observe closely any motion in the three possible joints that make noise: 1) where the tread overlaps the riser below it; 2) where the tread joins the riser just above it; and 3) where the tread joins the wall or side stringer. Two screws put through the tread into the riser below are usually enough to stop trouble at this point. Space the screws equally across the tread. Countersink them and fill the holes with wood putty. Where an ornamental molding has been placed under the tread overhang, it should be secured with additional brads or very thin screws.

Pre-drill all screw holes to prevent any splitting. The back edges of some treads are cut into a tongue to fit into a groove in the riser above it. In this case, glue might be introduced into the joint from the stairway side. Use glue in an applicator bottle with a small opening. At the two ends, construction determines whether glue or screws will work best. If the tread ends are butted against the side stringers glue is your only hope. If the tread ends are inserted into grooves in the sides, toe-nailing with spirally grooved nails will serve to tie the pieces together. If the treads simply rest on stringer cut-outs, then screws are the best answer to tie them down.

Slippery steps

Q. Recently I built a new set of stairs for the back porch and finished them with porch and deck paint. During the summer rains they were very slippery when wet. I'll have to do something before winter sleet arrives. What can you suggest?

D.S., Oak Park, Ill.

A. If you still have some of the deck paint, thin it about 50% and apply a fast coat to the treads when the steps are clean and dry. Sprinkle this wet paint lightly but thoroughly with clean, fine, sharp sand. One treatment should last all winter.

Tread removal

Q. The stairway in my hall was covered with rubber treads that were pasted down with a black paste. Can you tell me how to remove this?

A.W., New York, N.Y.

A. It's likely that the paste was a form of linoleum paste which can be dissolved or softened with turpentine. Various lacquer, shellac and rubber cement solvents will also work as might some of the liquid paint brush cleaners. Once it has been softened it can be scraped up with a broad putty knife, a messy job. If you have an electric drill with a sander attachment you can use coarse sandpaper to take the paste off in the dry state. With this method you'll get to bare wood quickly. Hand sanding is too difficult and slow here.

Carpet on stairs

Q. I want to lay carpet on the stairs. What is the best way and can it be done so the carpet is attached to the stairs but removable?

M.R., Cedar Grove, N.J.

A. There is a type of fixture which consists of a metal bar or rod about 1/4″ in diameter which lays across the carpet at the rear of the tread. It is held by two fasteners at the ends just beyond the carpet edge, one of which permits removal of the rod. Only the top and bottom ends of the carpet have to be tacked down. Your hardware dealer can probably provide this sort of device.

Opening a stairway

Q. My enclosed stairway is placed against an outside wall. The partition that encloses it is part of my dining room wall. I would like to remove this wall and open the stairway. I am in some doubt as to how to go about it.

J.P., Allentown, Pa.

A. The upper portion of this type of partition can be removed completely but do provide a protective handrail. If the stairway stringer on the dining room side is not supported by studs, the lower part can be open too. If it is enclosing headroom for a basement stairway you will not want to open the understair area. Start the work by exposing the studs above the steps by removing plaster and lath or plaster board. At this point, you can probably determine whether the stringers are self supporting or not. As a rule, in a stairway between floors the stringer would have to be extremely strong to carry the load. It would be better in remodeling to retain two or more of the studs below the stringer and build recessed furniture, built-ins and the like under the steps using these studs as part of the framework.

Chapter 2

Remodeling Problems

**Additions...Archways...Bars...Basements...Bathrooms...
Bedrooms...Breakfast nooks...Closets...Kitchens...Laundry chutes
...Living rooms...Old house restoration...Room dividers & screens.**

House addition

Q. **We want to add a bedroom, a half-bath and a utility room to our house. It is brick and has pier and beam. Where do you think this would be best situated so it would look best?**

F.D., Denison, Tex.

A. In planning an addition, consider not only the looks of the altered house but the plan and the economies of construction, the orientation of the house and lot, and last but not least, building code and deed restrictions. Yours is one of the kind of questions that can only be answered finally by properly qualified personnel right there on the spot.

From the standpoints of workable plan, ease and consequent economy of construction and reasonable appearance, we can suggest the changes noted on the plan shown. Putting the new lavatory and the utility room, plus the extended hall, where your second bedroom is now, seems to fit. Simply adding two bedrooms at the end makes sense from here.

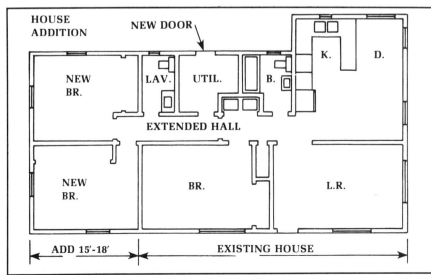

HOUSE ADDITION · NEW DOOR · NEW BR. · LAV. · UTIL. · B. · K. · D. · NEW BR. · EXTENDED HALL · BR. · L.R. · ADD 15'-18' · EXISTING HOUSE

Adding a new room

Q. **I am not sure of the best way to tie a new addition to my existing house, considering exposure of opened walls to weather and insects. Your suggestion would be appreciated.**

B.K., Ball, Md.

A. It is only necessary to cut into the present walls and roof to the sheathing and even this only at points where framing members are attached. Proceed with the new addition until it is entirely closed in, then break into the walls of the present structure to join the two.

Room addition

Q. **My husband and I want to make an opening along the wall between the kitchen and dining room to create a snack bar with a countertop. Do we need to set some type of I-beam or support along the top of this wall? There is a "brace" in the doorway entrance to the dining room, as if it used to be the**

main back door of the house. We need some sort of support when making the upper cut; what type is it and how would we put this in? The dining room walls are old lath with plaster hung and are covered with wallpaper. The side of the wall in the kitchen has drywall hung on it. The kitchen is also an addition.

E.S., Scottsdale, Pa.

A. Your letter and sketches imply it is probably not a partition wall and therefore, what you contemplate is not the safest thing in the world to do with it. At least, put in a post so the two spans could be slightly shorter than the doorway-plus-opening would be. Concerning the particular specification of your house, we advise proceeding as follows. In the partition wall you could do what you suggested if the corner is sufficiently well stabilized by counter built-ins. In a wall holding up the old house roof as well as the added kitchen roof, you will definitely need a beam to take these loads.

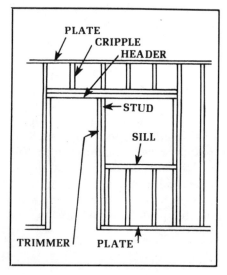

The size of the beam depends on the size of the load. In the gable end wall of an older home you might find uneven stud spacing (if this is the first floor of a two-story house and there is a window above this area) that would upset all your calculations. In a gable end wall of the existing house and the nonbearing "side" of an added kitchen area, you might double

the header and use the post shown. We suggest that you take off some of the wall surfacing on both sides and look for clues as to what you are apt to run into.

Dormer sky hooks

Q. I recently purchased a home with a story-and-a-half roof, intending to finish the second floor for additional space. I've been told it's possible to cut the roof and lift it forming a shed dormer and then merely frame it in. Is this possible and, if so, what must be done to maintain the roof strength?

R.M., Otis AFB, Mass.

A. It's possible, but not quite that simple. The house was not built with hinges at the roof ridge. It is not a job we would suggest for the lone do-it-yourself homeowner. You can get a good idea of what is involved from the story in *The Family Handyman*, August 1975.

You may find that you can't hope to complete the job alone and must hire the work done. Roof framing is not a job that can be done a little bit today and a little bit next weekend. However, you can panel and trim out on this kind of schedule.

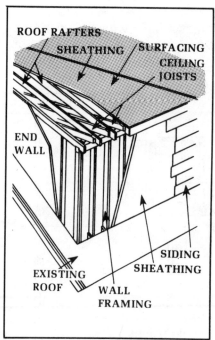

Covering for archway

Q. I have a messy kitchen which can be seen through an archway that is between the kitchen and the dining-living room. I would like to cover it up with something that could be there or not there according to what was needed at a given time. Do you have any ideas? My wife says it has to look pretty and she doesn't want a double-acting bar door effect which is the easy way to solve the problem. She wants something more modern and not bar-door looking.

N.G., Onondaga, N.Y.

A. You can cover the archway from view in the living room quite simply with a valance installation of a single-hung panel door sufficiently obscure to hide the kitchen clutter. Open, it will be a decorative panel alongside the archway, united in appearance by the valance. What you need is a few angle brackets to mount a strip from which the sliding door track can be mounted. Make sure you screw through the brackets into the studs. Mount the track according to the manufacturer's directions and cover the thing from view with a hardboard facing mounted on the valence. The hangers and track need only be those for a light door if you use a framed panel with fabric insets as indicated (hem top and bottom, secure with dowels run through door panel stiles) or other light-weight material. If you go to a plywood panel with a decorative mosaic or other heavy type of door, the track must be sized accordingly. The valence could also be extended a bit higher and include indirect lighting if that is desired.

Bar addition

Q. Enclosed is a sketch of our home that we have been in the process of remodeling for the last four years. The family room was recently added to the dining room area. The old wall was taken out as far down as the refrigerator and a cedar siding overhang was used to finish off the family room wall side. We would like to add a bar somewhere in between the kitchen and the dining area to serve functionally as well as in a decorative way and that would hide the kitchen from both areas. Is this project feasible and if so, how do we go about doing it? The dining room table, by the way, should not be moved.

E.A., Hartford, Wis.

A. A small bar at the end of the kitchen cabinets, as indicated, could serve as a pass-through section and a serving table for the dining room as well as a bar area. It could have storage underneath on both sides and would also screen the kitchen from the dining room, although not from the family room. You could also build a closet or put some nice decorative grillwork in front of the refrigerator to screen the kitchen from the family room if you so choose.

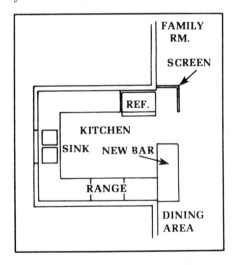

New basement look

Q. I want to make our unused basement into a sewing room, bar, etc. I am a housewife and would like to do the paneling and flooring myself, but would probably have the lighting and ceiling done by someone who really knows how. Before I begin I need to solve

a few problems. We have no water or seepage, but where the walls and floors meet they are dirty looking, which I presume is mildew. There is a musty smell even though we use a dehumidifier. Must I waterproof-paint our white painted concrete-block walls? Also, should I use a fiberglass sheeting of insulation before I apply a wood flooring over the cement floor before laying carpet?

C.L., Mansfield, Ohio

A. The dirty look you refer to may be dirt and it may be mildew. In either case you should waterproof before paneling. As to the floor, you should forget about laying a wood flooring and merely use an indoor-outdoor carpet layed directly over the concrete.

One-wall appearance

Q. What I would like to do is put up a wall in my basement to cover all the things seen to the right in the sketch, but still have access to these things. I thought of having multiple doors that will swing out, but when closed will look like a wall. Is this the best way? How should I stud, brace and hinge these doors? What size doors would be best and should they be paneled?

J.M., Cherry Tree, Pa.

A. You would have to frame the wall the full length of the basement and figure each opening as a single, hinged door or a pair of hinged doors. If they had to be over about 6′ in width, you'd have to increase the header size there, too. This is *not* the only way to achieve a one-wall effect, however. You can obtain an appearance that will please you and still have the openings your various-sized line-up of things requires. We suggest a pair of continuous sliding door tracks be installed along the whole run. (Is the CB radio room already walled in? The proportions your drawing indicate would give you a room about 3′ x 4′ with perhaps an

18″ door, not very comfortable.) Hang 2′ or 2-1/2′ wide doors, one in front and one in back and so on down the line. With an adequately supported, continuous track, you can stack the doors as shown to gain wider access where needed. The only drawback is the need to overlap the doors by eye to close the area most simply; any other method would be too costly.

We'd suggest you make a more detailed diagram of the items installed, dimension it carefully and work out on tracing paper laid over the original diagram the number of doors of different sizes that would be required to follow your hinged door framing method or the

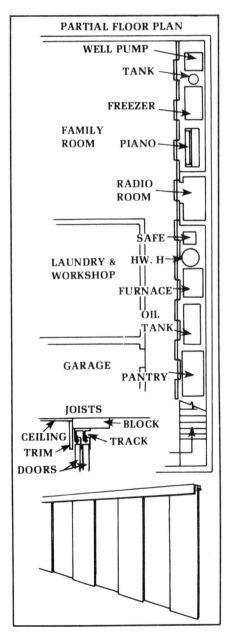

PARTIAL FLOOR PLAN

sliding one-front, one-back alternating doors suggestion. You won't be able to obtain one piece of track long enough (40') for your purposes, but you can butt end to end with good alignment if you are careful.

Basement finishing

Q. I would like to make a recreation room in my basement but am confused. At what stage is it most economical for the electrician to come in?

M.C., Akron, Ohio

A. Waterproof first. Then put up your wall and ceiling furring. With the strips in place, the outlet boxes and electrical fixtures can be positioned and the electrical work completed without difficulty. Wall paneling and ceiling tiles can be cut as necessary after the electrician is done.

Movie screen

Q. I would like to make a movie projection screen out of 1/4" plywood for one end of my cellar recreation room. Could you tell me how to treat the surface for best results?

L.M., Vineland, N.J.

A. If you insist on paint, spray it on if possible. Use a flat finish, interior grade, in pure white. But you'll get much better results gluing a screen fabric to the plywood. Check your local film supplier for the most up-to-date information on materials—used to be silk, more recently nylon or similar plastic type fabric materials. Make sure the adhesive you use is compatible with the screen fabric.

Permanent screen

Q. I went to a lot of trouble making a permanent projection screen to use in our basement playroom but now see one advantage of the portable types. Just how do I protect this wall mounted screen from the ravages of three kids?

S.K., Tottenville, N.Y.

A. You can go quite fancy if you like and give it double protection. We assume it is centered on a wall at least twice its width for this thought, though you could do it in half again the width. Get yourself a track for closet doors. Hang one set with black paint for a black board and the second set behind that with bulletin board covering and behind that let the screen stay. Run the track the full width and open both sets of sliding panels at show time.

Nautical rec room

Q. I will be building a rec room in my basement this summer, and I would like to finish it off with a seaman's touch. Do you know where I can get plans for a bar that is shaped like the stern of a ship? What I have in mind is making the rudder movable, and using this as the door into the bar area.

S.C., Harrisburg, Pa.

A. Most rudders have a tiller which would knock the glass out of the hand of anyone standing in the wrong place (unless you pivoted only the rudder part). On bigger boats the rudder is all wrong in proportion to serve as a door. You could get something of the effect you seek by just faking up the prow of a ship as a place to put one of the figurehead reproductions, letting the bar take over the rest of the ship. The dimensions shown here serve well for most home bar building. For some more ideas, get the catalogs from nautical places such as Preston's at 93 Main Street Wharf, Greenport, N.Y. 11944. They feature things like real ships' wheels, lanterns, prints, etc., to decorate a place as you wish.

Bathroom vanity

Q. I am interested in getting plans for a bathroom vanity. I want to build an approximately 8' long vanity top, which would incorporate the already existing lavatory into this space. Can you help me?

B.A., Charleston, S.C.

A. An 8' long bathroom vanity countertop seems a bit longer than most would measure so you'd probably have trouble finding complete details for exactly what you had in mind. You might think about combining the construction of a lavatory countertop with a cabinet section below and medicine cabinets above (diagram).

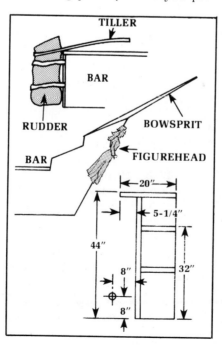

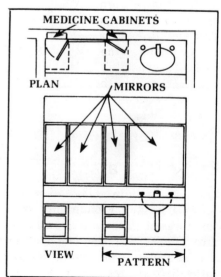

Bathroom storage

Q. Please help me get more storage space in my bathroom (see enclosed floor plan). The sink is built into a vanity 16″ wide by 20″ deep while the free-standing storage cabinet in the corner is 17″ wide by 19″ deep. There's a window sash in the window opening but it's closed by the paneling in the den/playroom on the other side of the wall. How do we get the most space for the least money?

H.M., Wingate, N.C.

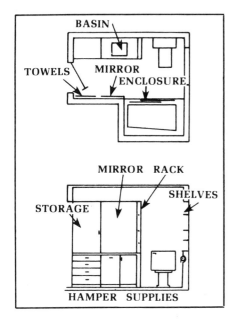

A. If you can move the door, building in storage will be greatly simplified, as shown. What you include depends on what you need to store. If there is no operating window in the bath, include some form of mechanical ventilation. You can use a reasonably large mirror opposite the storage area's mirror. You needn't let the unused window sit idle either. Remove the sash and parting strip and set in small shelves.

Enclosing a sink

Q. The sink in my bathroom is enclosed with a Formica top and has a 4″ skirt which is nailed securely to the wall tiles. The removal of the tiles would therefore be quite difficult. It is supported in the front by two metal legs attached to a tile floor. I would like to put in a plywood cabinet under this top, preferably one with two doors and drawers or shelves. The countertop will be 51-3/4″ long and 21″ wide. The skirt will be 4″ wide and will have a 10″ drawer within it. Can you help me with this remodeling project?

E.P., Port Jefferson Station, N.Y.

A. From your description it seems that you will need only one front panel and one end panel (with sliding or folding doors). You may wish these panels to fit flush with the floor of the room (Sketch A) or you may want to improve the plan by building a floor or platform to the cabinet attached to a base (Sketch B) which would allow toe room under the cabinet. Details of the latter type of construction are shown in the Section part of the diagram. The panels and base can be secured to the tiled floor and walls with angle braces after drilling holes in which fiber plugs are inserted to hold the screws. Or you may wish to use 1-1/2″ x 1-1/2″ cleats (blocks of wood) just inside the panels, attach them to the tiled floor and walls with a mastic cement, and then nail or screw the panels to the cleats. A third possibility is simply to attach the panels and base to the floor directly with a mastic cement.

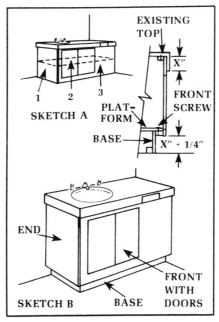

Bathroom planning

Q. We are trying to figure out whether or not we have the space for a powder room. Is there a minimum floor area necessary?

A.W., Milton, Mass.

A. You can tuck a powder room in a minimum space 4′0″ x 4′6″ or in a space 2′9″ wide by 6′0″ long. With the new corner lavatories you might shrink the 4′ dimension slightly if you don't mind the lavatory in your lap. Figure 15″ on either side of center for a water closet, 18″ clear in front of it. You stand in this same 30″ x 18″ area to use the lavatory whose size will govern the exact dimensions in the additional area needed.

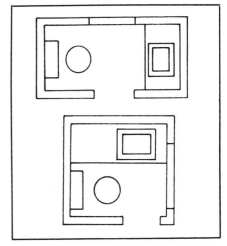

Locating accessories

Q. We want to finish a bathroom and have a number of questions: how high above the floor is a recessed toilet paper holder installed? How high above the bathtub and approximately in what area is a recessed soap holder installed? Where in relation to the lavatory is a recessed tumbler holder installed?

L.A., Chicago, Ill.

A. The bottom edge of the paper holder should be about level with the toilet seat though it can be higher if desired. It is most convenient if located 6″ ahead of the front edge of the seat. Soap dish generally goes one tile (4″) above the tub top in the center of the tub's length. A recessed tumbler holder is at the right of the sink from 12″ to 14″ above the rim, depending how tile works out in this area, if you are governed by that. Obviously one avoids cutting tiles to adhere exactly to any measurement in locating these accessories.

Medicine chest

Q. **At what height should a medicine cabinet 39-1/2″ x 22″ be placed over a bathroom sink? It has a 2″ chrome trim.**

H.Y., Bellwood, Ill.

A. Standard placement for a medicine chest is from 4′1″ to 4′6″ above the floor to the underside of the chest. This may be adjusted to suit average height of individuals using it, to match half tiles, wall limits, etc.

Bathroom rehab

Q. **We just bought an old home and are trying to fix it up on a limited budget. The bathroom is a horror. The walls are some kind of plastic paneling (if the walls were dishes, I'd say they were made of "melmac"). The sink is in a metal cabinet with a grey Formica top that we would like to disguise. The tub needs to be enclosed on the end and we do not know how to do it as it has rounded corners. The shower curtain bar is wired to the ceiling and is unattractive and inefficient. Also, do you think it would be possible to wallpaper over the plastic walls? I would like to panel half-way up and then wallpaper the rest of the way. Could you give us some advice on this matter?**

K.T., Pinedale, Wyo.

A. Our own theory is that color works wonders and paint is less expensive than plastering. If you insist on using the enclosure idea, get waterproof plywood (1/2″ to 3/4″) with the top surface snug and sound. Run a cleat across the fau-

cet end and a frame across the back. The front and end can be closed in with a simple framework covered with panel material. Use a good grade of caulk. The shower curtain bar would certainly be improved with proper attachment to the ceiling, or you might consider a makeshift building-in, somewhat as sketched, if you have access to a sheet of plastic. As for the walls, your unwanted plastic paneling should be removed. Wallpapering over it would be a waste of time and paneling half the way over the plastic is not too feasible either. Concerning the sink, a sheet of adhesive-backed vinyl surfacing over the gray, laminated plastic top and the metal cabinet in a really blinding color print will do

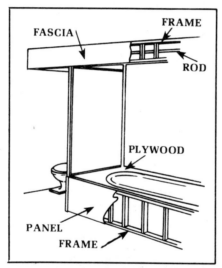

wonders. Generally, think through to the ideal final version. Do what you can towards it first. Don't do anything expensive that will have to be removed when you are able to head for the final version.

Arranging a bedroom

Q. **My 16-year-old daughter has a terribly arranged bedroom. In it is a 21″ television, a stereo table and two speakers. Also, there is a double bed and a double dresser. There is no place to sit. It needs a desk that has built-in units around it. The room is about 12′ x 11′. How can this room be rearranged?**

H.S., Elmira, N.Y.

A. With no sizes given on the pieces, we'd suggest you use the window wall, in spite of the heat,

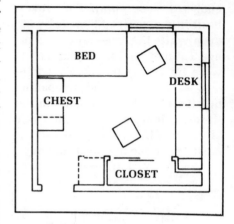

and build in the equivalent of the desk and the TV table with the stereo housed into or under the counter. What happens where the counter meets the closet depends on the closet doors. The two speakers will have to be hung from the walls or set on the desk and dresser. Move the bed out from the wall and flank it by two smaller storage units, such as night tables or chests. In this manner, you could use the double bed.

A girl's room

Q. **The only way we figure we can make more room in our daughter's bedroom is to remove the closet and to build drawers and a closet into the wall adjoining the foyer. However, since this would overhang the foyer, we would be limited to using just the top half of the wall in order to allow for head room in the foyer area. Does this project sound feasible? Also, do you have any ideas for a bed for a little girl?**

J.M., Billerica, Mass.

A. You could build into the wall as you indicate, but it would be a rather funny-looking thing from the entry side, and not very convenient for storage use, either.

Consider some of the following alterations that might make the tiny room more usable for a girl.

First, close up the hall wall to the existing hall closet. Remove the walls and door to the present bedroom closet. Close up the old bedroom door and relocate it as shown. Open the wall to get into the ex-hall closet from the end, making the opening as large as possible. You could build up over the stairs with a slanted floor, giving the same clearance as the bottom edge now provides, but do it the whole width of the downstairs. With a pullout rack you should not have to do this. (Broken line indicates this rack. Check local store fixture companies if you have trouble finding this hardware.)

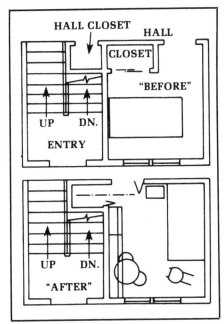

With the traffic pattern confined to this one corner of the room, there is a lot more play space available, especially if you use a built-in bunk-type bed. It needn't look spartan, but the box bottom with the three drawers does provide a lot of storage space. You can track curtains 18" long outlining the shape of the bed on the ceiling, with long drapes at the head of the bed tied back prettily to the wall. An older child might prefer built-in shelves with desk space and a sit-in-and-read chair. The clue to more space is in the tight fit of room and closet doors. Bifolds are suggested as the least space-taking style to use.

Breakfast nook

Q. I would like to build a breakfast nook in a small room between kitchen and dining room measuring 52" across by 58" long. Could you advise me as to measurements? My idea was to hang a table top from the wall 24" wide and 55" long with side benches 14" wide attached to the walls. We would of course slide in.

L.F., Scarsdale, N.Y.

A. A quick check of accepted minimum standard measurements will show you do not have enough room for table top and two benches. You need a 24" top and 20" from top to back of seat which adds up to 64" minimum. You could run a 24" wide counter along one wall and comfortably seat three on stools or small chairs in the 58" length, even squeeze in a fourth at the end for a light breakfast or lunch, though when full size plates are used 22" to each place is good, 20" acceptable.

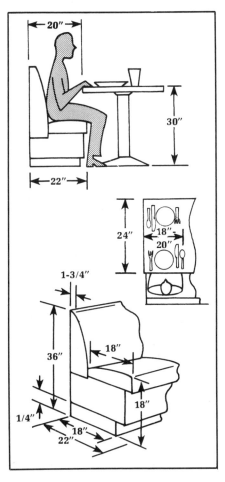

Storage benches

Q. I have been trying to locate plans for a breakfast nook that has storage space in the seats. Craft Patterns has discontinued this item. Do you have any suggestions for an L-shaped bench about 3' x 5'?

R.H., Roselle, Ill.

A. The basic dimensions of breakfast nooks will not change. We include here the diagram for this project in hopes that you can determine how to finalize it yourself. If you use 4" thick seats, the framing goes lower than for a bare-wood seat but a comfortable sitting

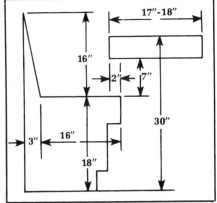

height is somewhere about 18" above the floor for the finished top surfaces. The table height that goes with that is still 30". An L-shaped bench, 3' x 5', is going to be very crowded for three people. Take the dimensions shown on the section and you will see it is almost 36" from back to opposite table edge, with one place setting taking at least 12" in depth. In 5', you would get a table about 40" long with one seat at the end, too. There would be just enough room for three people to sit at the table.

Closet window

Q. We have a large master bedroom, and I want to make a bathroom out of the existing closet. That means building a closet at the other end of the room, but there's a window on this wall. Can you advise me how to plan such a closet? Enclosing the window sounds like an expensive operation because of our home's brick exterior.

V.C., Williamsburg, Va.

A. Don't think about building a closet in front of the window. Instead, build a storage wall around it. A floor-to-ceiling storage unit will provide hanging space with some out-of-season storage above. Use shelves or closed storage beside and over the window, with a desk or vanity in front of it.

Underused closet

Q. We have a walk-in closet which is not used to its full capacity. My husband and I share it. What might help us make this closet more efficient?

C.M., Sharon, Pa.

A. Often a large walk-in closet has a rod down either side with a narrow shelf above. You may need more rod length for shorter things which suggests one rod above another. Other possibilities include more drawer space or a wider shelf for off-season storage of blankets or bathing suits.

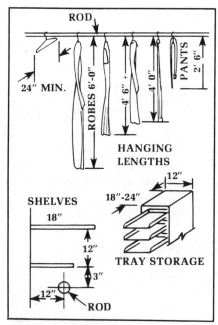

Cedar closet

Q. I have a poured cement foundation in my basement. I'm interested in building a cedar closet down there but am concerned about dampness and mildew. What is the proper procedure for construction?

P.K., North Ware, Vt.

A. In theory what you want to do is "wrap" the contents of the closet surrounded by the cedar material in a vapor barrier. You can start by building a wood frame floor unit and surface it with 5/8" plywood. Erect stud frame walls on the back and both ends, and surface them with 5/8" plywood on the outside. Top this with a ceiling unit similar to the floor. Line the interior with a plastic vapor barrier and cover with cedar. Hollow core doors, also lined with a vapor barrier and cedar, would finish the closet. You can get plans for a do-it-yourself cedar closet (using Cedarflake Panels) for 25¢ from Giles and Kendall, Box 188, Huntsville, Ala. 35804.

Closet renovation

Q. I want to use our daughter's closet which is in the same wall as ours. I read how to build a closet in a corner in **FAMILY HANDYMAN** and plan on building her one. I would like to know how to go about taking out our wall which is the back of her closet and making a wall for her where her doors were. I want to make a cork-like area for her that would serve as a giant bulletin board on her wall. Should I leave a partition between the two closets? Can I use her framework? Any help you can give me will be appreciated. We have plaster walls and ceilings.

C.S., Webster, N.Y.

A. Before you start taking out and moving around those walls, be sure you know what holds up the ceiling. The chances are that you are alright since you will be leaving the framing pretty much alone, but make certain before you remove what was the back and end of your

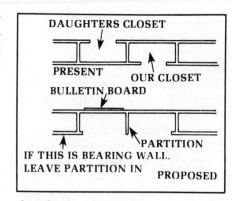

daughter's closet that you do not take away the support of the ceiling overhead. You will be replacing it with a doubled 2x6, at least for a header over the large-sized closet. But if it is a bearing wall now, it should be supported while you do the substituting. Otherwise your suggestion of leaving a partition is a good safety measure and saves some plaster patching, but it does depend on just how you want to finish off the doorway of your new large closet.

It's possible that the joists above run parallel to the closets in which case nailing is what you'd have to worry about, not bearing wall problems.

Built-in wardrobe

Q. I want to construct a built-in wardrobe along a 12" masonry wall in my master bedroom. On the right side, I can remove the existing closet and compensate for floor which is over the stairway. But on the left side, I have a double-hung window only 6" from the back wall and a radiator 21" from the same wall. I want my wardrobe 24" deep. How can I end the left side of my built-in wardrobe?

S.E., Bayside, N.Y.

A. You may be inviting a number of problems with the relocation of the closet. We don't know just what you intend to do with the 27" high stairway clearance shown on your sketch where it lies in front of the desired wardrobe. Put a seat on it? At the other end, a valance straight across the end of the room would unify the looks of whatever you do, but you'll still have to set back for the radiator and at an undetermined height up, for the window. The closet cannot run floor to ceiling at that end without some very difficult and peculiar situations. We suggest a narrow chest of drawers up to windowsill height, not over 21″ deep, perhaps with a long, narrow mirror above them, as the best solution.

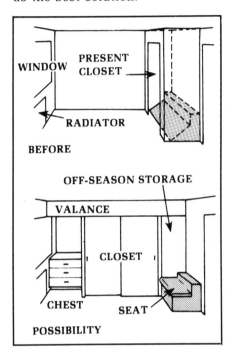

Closet improvement

Q. Although the closet in our master bedroom is 9′ wide and extends from floor to ceiling, much of the space is wasted because the present door opening is 5′ wide. We would like to make better use of this space and are considering bifold doors as the first step. What do you think?

P.D., Tipp City, Ohio

A. Bi-fold doors would be a good way to open up your closet space. To gain access to the entire area, it will be necessary to reframe the door opening from floor to ceiling for the entire 9′ width of your closet, as in drawing A. Or you could use the present 5′ door frame and install "partitions" at either end. This would create a 5′ long center closet which you could subdivide into a double-pole section and a single-pole section for full-length items. Then you could use the flanking 2′ areas for either drawer or shelf storage. Since the depth of this area (28″) may be too much for drawers, you might consider using regular hinged doors on both end spaces, as in drawing B. This way you could have shoe or other storage on the inside of the door and use the back of your closet space for drawers or shelves. If you decide to have shelves that run

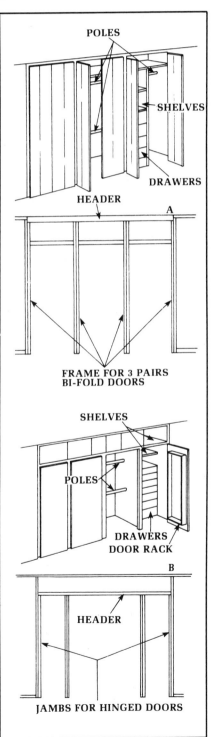

the full width of your closet, you may wish to have separate 12″ to 15″-high doors for access to this area rather than having doors that run from floor to ceiling. If you have a lighting fixture that is in an inconvenient spot, you will want to consider moving it as part of your project.

Kitchen planning

Q. I would like to remodel our kitchen but I really don't know how to rearrange it for greatest efficiency. I enclose a plan of its present arrangement. Can you tell me how to proceed?

A.S., Sheboygen, Wis.

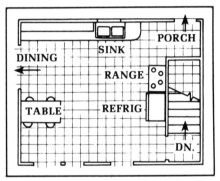

A. The first thing we notice in your floor plan is that you have an 8′ wall devoted to a range and refrigerator and a 14′ wall with only a sink and cabinets on it. Studies made at the University of Illinois confirm the value in steps saved of "centerizing" related storage and work space around each major appliance.

Thus you have a refrigerator for cold food storage which should be

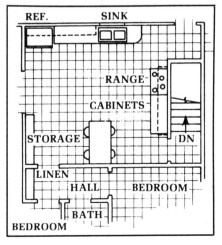

located at one side of the sink where such foods are most likely to be prepared. The sink is considered the center of things as it gets traffic coming and going, before, during and after meals. The first suggestion would be to locate the refrigerator to the left of the sink. How far to the left is both a matter of convenience and appearance. From the point of view of appearance, a big refrigerator usually looks best at the end of a line of cabinets. Also it is best if your refrigerator is hinged on the left side in this case, otherwise you always have to walk around the open door.

You would also be much better off to install wall and base cabinets next to the range in place of the refrigerator. Here you can store cooking and baking utensils as well as the dry foods, canned foods and condiments used in baking and cooking.

Obviously, the table should be moved so that it doesn't obstruct any doorway as shown in drawing at bottom.

Kitchen remodeling

Q. **We would like to remodel our kitchen but don't know how to place the various cabinets, appliances, etc. for best use. Enclosed plan shows how kitchen looks now.**

W.F., Maple Shade, N.J.

A. Please see our sketch of the plan for your kitchen. The biggest trouble people seem to encounter

in remodeling is drawing to scale. It is really quite simple if you get some graph paper and let each square equal one square foot. Measure your cabinets and appliances and cut out pieces of graph paper scaled to the same size as the various pieces in the kitchen and move them around on your drawn-to-scale floor plan. A quick check of your diagram will easily show which arrangement is best for you.

Kitchen refinishing

Q. **I am planning to remodel my kitchen and would like to know if there is any wood wall paneling which will resist grease and is easy to clean. Also, can you suggest any material that can be applied to countertops and to the wall behind the range which my wife can clean without difficulty?**

A.L., Syracuse, N.Y.

A. Most lumberyards now carry vinyl or acrylic-surfaced plywoods in a variety of woodgrain patterns. Such stores also carry hardboard panels with a printed woodgrain surface and very durable plastic finishes. Either of these types of panels are suitable for easy-to-maintain kitchen walls. As for the countertops, we suggest that you extend the backsplash up the wall behind the range until it meets the cabinets above. Then apply one of the new seamless floor coatings (a combination of decorative vinyl chips and liquid urethane) to the backsplash and countertop. These

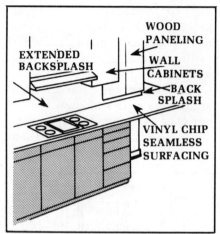

coatings are available at many hardware and paint stores and, like the paneling mentioned above, are easy to clean with a damp cloth or mild soap and water.

Pass-thru window

Q. **I wish to make a pass-through between my kitchen and dining room. The wall is plaster, 12' wide and 9' high. What height and size is the best and most attractive?**

E.E., Newburgh, N.Y.

A. A pass-through window should be about 40" to 42" above the floor for convenience. Go at least 36" in width. To prevent smoke, etc., from the kitchen making an exit this way, the top of the opening should be at least 12" below the kitchen ceiling. With your 9' ceiling, the opening might be 4' high. An opening the top of which is less than 5' from the floor is a bit inconvenient for the cook to look through. The counter should be at least 10" wide, or more if you customarily will use trays on it.

Making a pass-through is just about like installing a window. Rough frame the opening with 2x4s, a double 2x4 laid across the cut off studs below, a double 2x4 across the cut off ends above and a short stud between these preferably placed against full length studs at each side. Set in the counter or sill and face the inside of the opening with 1" stock wide enough to reach from wall surface on one side to that on

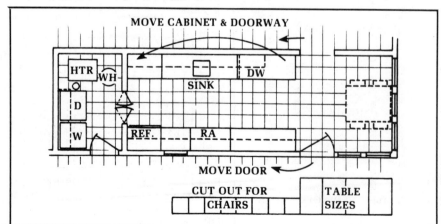

the other. Fit casing around the opening just as you have on the windows, nailing through into the edge of the trim and into the studs. Fancying it up from these bare essentials is a matter of personal taste.

Kitchen-bath

Q. I have a small, old house (built without plans or blueprints), situated on a city lot that measures 50′ x 100′. I am interested in remodeling the kitchen and the bathroom, but I cannot figure out a way to rearrange them for the greatest efficiency in the available space. My funds are limited, so the changes must be economical as well. Can you help me?

B.W., Tuskegee, Ala.

A. Rearranging plumbing is about the most expensive thing you can do to remodel. Wherever you can avoid moving plumbing fixtures, do so. If your bathroom fixtures are in reasonably good shape you should certainly leave them be. Do your remodeling there with color and texture in different paint and surfacing materials if you want a change.

Your kitchen situation is another matter. Is it possible for you to enlarge the kitchen either by enclosing the back porch and removing wall A or by removing wall B and combining dining and kitchen areas? Either way you would gain a long solid wall on which you could put your kitchen necessaries, leaving the rest of the room for dining. (See sketches.)

Incidentally, it would help you and many readers with planning problems if you worked things out to scale on graph paper. Just let each square equal either a 6″ x 6″ or a 1′ x 1′ square in your house. Then when you measure something you can draw it on the graph paper to scale, and show windows and doors at their proper positions, right where they really are.

Pie safe

Q. I want to make metal inserts for my kitchen cabinets like the old pie safe used. Is there an easy way to do this, quicker than using a nail and a hammer? I don't want to use tin because it will eventually change color. What other metal could I use?

B.N., Buffalo, N.Y.

A. Your best bet would be to check the decorative expanded aluminum panels available at lumber yards. These are produced by Reynolds in a wide range of patterns and styles. If you decide to make your own, don't try putting the pinholes in the metal inserts with a hammer and nail—you'll cause kinks in the metal. Copper or aluminum sheets should be used, and make the holes with a 1/8″ drill bit chucked into a drill press or electric drill.

Closet crisper

Q. In a recent issue a reader asked about building a closet crisper and using an electric light bulb to keep it dry. During World War II days in Mississippi, I found that the shelf or cupboard over the refrigerator provided ideal storage for crackers, cereals, etc. The hotter (and more humid) the day, the more the heat that came from the refrigerator, and this kept the upper shelf dehumidified.

L.S., Rockville, Md.

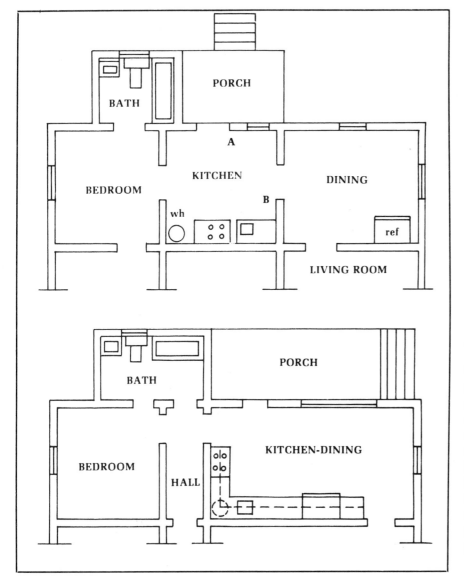

A. Thank you for your letter. You have a good point worth mentioning although today's refrigerators give off less heat. However, it's important not to locate cracker storage over a range where boiling water will add to the humidity, or over the sink with its hot water providing additional water vapor.

Cabinet problem

Q. I've been trying to redo the kitchen cabinets in my recently purchased older home. I had thought I could just remove the paint and use a varnish, but after a month of trying everything, I can't get the paint off. I have gone through several cans of paint remover. I believe that the cabinets were originally finished with an epoxy paint as the finish is as solid as steel. Giving up, I cleaned the cabinets and applied antiquing. But now the antiquing is chipping. What can I do?

M.B., Franklin Square, N.Y.

A. From your description, we're not positive about the original finish. Assuming the cabinets are wood, it seems your guess about epoxy may be correct. It's definitely a factory-applied, hard finish which is baked on. It's possible the chipping may result because the antiquing coating has no "tooth" to cling to. Suggest you try again. But first give the unyielding surface a rub with steel wool if on wood, and fine emery paper if it is on metal. This way the surface will be more receptive to a new coating.

Refinishing cabinets

Q. My wooden kitchen cabinets need refinishing. I plan to remove the old wax and varnish with Spic and Span and mineral spirits and then apply a fresh coat of stain, varnish and rewax. Is this a sound way of doing the job?

G.B., Piscataway, N.J.

A. You may not get all the varnish off with Spic and Span and mineral spirits and this may result in an uneven stain job. These materials would clean it sufficiently to get a decent varnish job. However, to completely remove the varnish, a good-quality paint remover would be a better substitute for the mineral spirits. In either case, sand it smooth again before you refinish.

Hiding holes

Q. I drilled the mounting holes for kitchen cabinet pulls on 3-3/4" centers. Now I can't find hardware I like to fit—it's all 3" centers. Any suggestions? I've already stained and lacquered the fronts so can't fill the holes and drill new ones without the "old" holes showing.

C.L., Mishawaka, Ind.

A. It's a shame you didn't get the hardware first. At least one mail order supplier has a contemporary pull with 3-3/4" centers (The Woodworkers' Store, 21801 Industrial Blvd., Rogers, Minn. 55374; catalog, $1). Or you can try to find a pull that has a large enough escutcheon or large enough pad ends to cover your too-far-apart holes (see sketch). You can plug the holes on the inside. From the outside you won't know the difference.

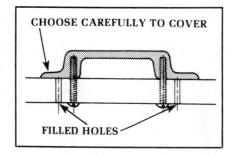

CHOOSE CAREFULLY TO COVER

FILLED HOLES

Damp doors

Q. Our kitchen cabinets are 3/4" birch plywood. The doors on several are so badly warped they will not stay closed. We have tried various types of catches but nothing helps. Have you any suggestions to offer, other than having new doors made?

N.N., Cliffside Park, N.J.

A. Birch plywood or anything else made of wood will warp if one side is absorbing more moisture than the other. This is what often happens in kitchen cabinets where the face of the door is finished and refinished and finished again, while the inside goes bare. Sometimes warped plywood doors can be corrected by removing them, taking off all finish, weighting to correct the warp while the door panel is in a horizontal position, and then refinishing both sides and all edges to thoroughly seal out all moisture. Unfortunately, there is no guarantee that you will be able to get the doors straight but it is worth a try before you buy new doors. In that case, cut the new doors and fit them first, then seal thoroughly, including all edges, before you install and finish them.

Painting cabinets

Q. I have metal kitchen cupboards made by American Kitchens. They are 22 years old and the finish has become dull and it's hard to keep clean. Is there a paint that would brighten them, or is there some other method of refurnishing them?

M.D., Fort Benton, Mont.

A. Yes, it's possible to paint metal cabinets and, depending on how neat a job you do, their appearance will be greatly improved. It takes quality materials, good preparation and patience. A spray paint job gives you better results on metal, but it also gives you an awful problem of masking the entire place to protect it from overspray. It is an almost impossible job in an installed kitchen. Often, if you start to spray you have to give up and use a brush. Further, there are other pitfalls.

You have a lot of vertical surfaces that are hard to paint with enamel. Metal is hard and smooth, so brushmarks show up more than on wood. You can partially get around this by using a pad applicator. There are also brushes that do not have bristles but instead have a piece of urethane foam which is discarded after use and that are remarkably smooth. If you have any rust problems, take care of them first. Careful preparation usually involves the slight roughing up of the present surface with fine sandpaper. However, if your cabinets are hard to clean now, they may be rough enough to hold paint well.

Refinishing cabinets

Q. I would like to refinish my white steel cabinets to go with the rest of my new kitchen. Can you offer any advice as to how to proceed?

J.M., Modesto, Calif.

A. You can give a new look to your cabinets by painting them or even giving them a wood-grain or antique finish. The secret lies in thoroughly cleaning the surface (any grease will prevent the paint from adhering) and then roughing it enough to provide a good tooth for the base coat. Depending on the design of your cabinets, you could also use adhesive-backed vinyl wall covering on the doors.

Hutch top cabinet

Q. Could you suggest a design for a hutch-type top on this base kitchen cabinet with doors on the top that are not see-through? I am planning to leave room for a canister set on the top, of which the tallest piece is 12".

A.D., Trenton, N.Y.

A. It appears that the hutch top you describe is a bookcase with two solid doors and without a bottom shelf. Most plans sources will show a piece of similar design that you could take the details from and

size to fit your base cabinet. Usually the top section would be set in a bit less than 1" from the edges of the base's top. The rudiments of its construction are shown on the attached sketch. The back of the hutch extends below the top of the cabinet and is screwed with either bolts or screws to the back of the base cabinet. The bottom edges of the hutch which rest on the cabinet top are glued.

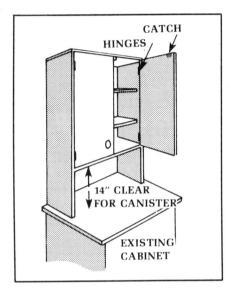

Counter sealer

Q. I am building counters on either side of the kitchen sink and I have encountered a problem in fitting the plywood counter tops against the sides of the sink. What can I use for a waterproof sealer between the sink and plywood edges?

M.J., Detroit Mich.

A. If yours is the type of sink that wasn't made for the built-in age, you have to devise a solution that's bound to be less than ideal. You can design the counters so the plywood edge rests on top of the rounded sink with a strip of aluminum angle (after painting the plywood to seal the edge), and caulk the joint with the type of sealing compound that's sold for filling cracks around a built-in bathtub. Caulk the concealed side of the joint under the counter top as well as the exposed edge.

Counter covering

Q. Please tell me an easy way I can recover kitchen counters, which now have linoleum tops, without removing the linoleum.

M.R., Columbus, Ohio

A. The easiest way to recover kitchen countertops with a solidly adhering linoleum top, is with one of the vinyl-flake urethane matrix pour-and-toss flooring methods. It works equally well on *countertops*. Two manufacturers of this material are Dap, Dayton, Ohio and Dur-A-Flex Inc., 100 Meadow St., Hartford, Conn. 06114.

Top to match

Q. I've seen some of the yard goods that coordinate countertops with floor covering and the colors are very nice but isn't the job of covering the counter too much for the home handyman?

J.R., Chicago, Ill.

A. Not at all, the sheet vinyl surfacings are flexible and easily worked. Cutting the wood fillet strip to length is simple and it just nails in place. Spread mastic, cut the vinyl a bit oversize and press in place rolling it up over the fillet against the backsplash. Incidentally, that is one advantage—no problems of leaking at this joint. Trim off the excess surfacing around the sink cutout and along the edges with a sharp linoleum knife. You can use metal edge molding along the front edge for the easiest job.

Tile on plastic

Q. We are having some work done in our kitchen. I understand you can't get laminated plastic off a plywood countertop once it is on. Is it possible to resurface the present counters with ceramic tile to match the new ones? I want to

33

have ceramic tile throughout kitchen and laundry areas.

L.L., Berwyn, Ill.

A. You are correct in your understanding. Getting laminated plastic off a plywood surface once it is on properly, is next to impossible. Up until recently you'd have had to discard the whole top and replace it with new plywood on which you could bond ceramic tile. However there is now on the market a new epoxy based ceramic tile grout. When mixed with 1/2 to 2/3 parts clean dry sand, this grout makes a good non-shrinking adhesive the use of which makes possible bonding ceramic tile over plastic laminates.

Laundry chute

Q. Where can I get plans for a laundry chute to go from the bathroom to the basement directly underneath?

J.Y, Shiremanstown, Pa.

A. Basically the laundry chute is fairly simple, but we'd advise against trying to incorporate it on an outside house wall. The size might be 12″ x 14″ or thereabouts, and the upper end can be incorporated in a bathroom built-in very easily. You could consider it

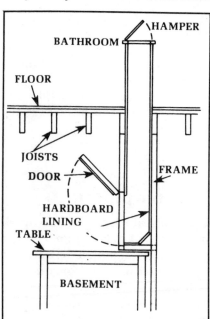

as a bottomless hamper extending down to the basement. With a door at the bottom that latches shut, you can drop the dirty clothes out on a sorting shelf or into a basket. One way you might do it is shown in the sketch. The important thing is to keep the inside surface as straight as possible and free of projecting nails or anything clothes could get caught on. Be aware of the sound transmission problems you can create when you cut the necessary hole in the floor. A tightly closing, gasketed door can help. Double walls with insulation surrounding the chute might be needed too.

Open living room

Q. We have a typical older home — L-shaped with three rooms downstairs, three up, and an open stairway in a closed-in hall. We'd like to remove the wall parallel to the stairway, between the hall and the living room, making a larger living room. Would this make the house colder, or would the heat from downstairs make the upstairs too hot?

E.L., Kandiyohi, Minn.

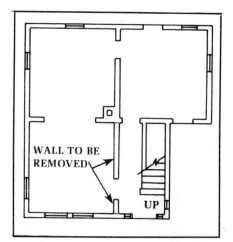

A. The state of your present heating system must be considered. It may require some alteration to meet the new conditions. If you make do with a system designed for separate rooms, you will probably have an overheated upstairs hall and a drafty downstairs. You

will have a more comfortable breezy home in summer, and one more easily fan-cooled. A seasonal "stairway encloser" would be a possibility. You'll need to investigate the structural problems involved, too.

Sunken living room

Q. Where can I get literature on remodeling an existing living room into a sunken living room? We have a basement under this room and I realize dropping the floor is going to lower the head space.

A.C., Ronkonkoma, N.Y.

A. To be effective the floor level should be at least two steps down, a minimum of about 15″ below the surrounding floor. That would most likely kill the use of any basement area underneath. If you have 9′ ceilings, it may be possible to build a platform "up" to get a sunken pit effect. You'll likely need local professional help to do such a job safely.

Old house restoration

Q. I am restoring an old house, and I need to find a wood filler to fill many holes and nicks in the old woodwork and doors, which I plan to paint. What I am hoping to find is some type of nonshrinking plastic filler that can be applied once and which, when done very smoothly, will require little or no sanding.

Also, the house has grayish-green slate fireplace hearths, which, under many coats of old paint, prove to be dry and ashy looking. Is there a preparation or shiny hard clear finish that can be applied that would not be affected by heat?

M.R., Richmond, Va.

A. Any of the readily available wood patching fillers will do well on reasonably sized nicks and holes without undue shrinking, and as you note, if you're neat, little sanding is needed. For really small blemishes, the finer texture of the vinyl spackling pastes may be preferred. If you've really got a lot to do, you might want to get painter's spackling putty, which is available at any place that serves the local painting trade.

On the fireplace hearth, please contact the Building Stone Institute, 420 Lexington Ave., New York, N.Y. 10017. They are the experts in the field and will be able to give you an authoritative answer.

You may be interested in The Old-House Journal, 69A Seventh Ave., Brooklyn, N.Y. 11217. Although this publication cannot undertake to answer specific questions, it carries many items of interest to anyone involved in the restoration of vintage houses.

Old home fix-up

Q. I recently bought a 50-year-old home in need of painting, repairs, cupboards, bath, electrical outlets, etc. Could you suggest any books or manuals that are geared to older houses and jobs of this nature?

K.W., Riverside, Calif.

A. It's likely that no one reference will solve your problems. Those geared to older homes are more apt to accent preservation, while those of a more practical nature separate carpentry jobs from plumbing, heating and wiring. Start at the beginning with something like "How to Buy and Fix up An Old House," prepared and edited by the staff of Home Tech Publications, Bethesda, Md. 20014. This one will also help you organize the jobs that have to be done and figure out how to handle payments. "Remodeling Old Houses Without Destroying Their Character," by George Stephen, is a Borzoi book published by Alfred A. Knopf that also would help. This book emphasizes design and planning. Check your town's build-

ing code on what you can and can't do, before you go too far.

Transom removal

Q. I have recently purchased an old house with high ceilings and transoms over the doors. I will use modern flush doors but would like to get rid of the transoms completely. Would you please tell me the best way to do this?

D.T., Rock Island, Ill.

A. Once the transoms are gone, you may miss the air circulation they afforded. Remove the header casing first, then the casings along the sides so they can be cut short to new door height or discarded. Remove the transom sash and set in a short central stud. You can use a piece of gypsum wallboard cut to size on each side of the wall, furring out just enough to bring it flush with the adjoining plaster. The crack between old plaster and new material is then filled in, sized and covered with wallpaper or painted.

Bedroom divider

Q. I have a daughter 3-1/2 years old and a son of 1-1/2 years. They both share the same room. I would like to divide the room into two smaller rooms with an inexpensive temporary partition. Can you tell me how to do this?

J.B., Deckerville, Mich.

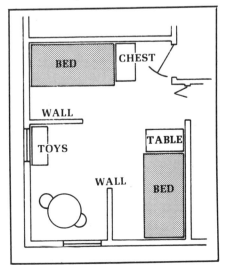

A. The room layout you've shown does not really lend itself to total subdivision. Considering the ages of your children, we advise that you settle for separating the sleeping areas into suggested "rooms" with a lightly constructed low partition, leaving the larger part of the room for joint occupancy. The use of color to separate "his" from "hers" areas would be a reasonable compromise as the children get older.

Entrance screen

Q. When you walk in our front door, you come right into the living room. While I'd like to use a closet right there to give a guest some chance to take off outer wraps, there is not enough room. Is there some material that could be used to build a screen of sorts to make entering the house, walking over to the closet (about 6' away) less of a performance? In other words I want a front entrance but have no room for it. Any suggestions would be most welcome.

S.T., South Orange, N.J.

A. Your difficulty is going to be selecting the material you like best. Any solid panel material such as plywood, hardboard, gypsum wallboard, etc. can very easily be framed between floor and ceiling to provide a solid partition at that point. You can even treat the floor differently in the entrance area to make the transition more deliberate. The easiest thing to do is build a 4' wide partition wall—set 2x3 plate at the ceiling directly over a 2x3 plate at the floor. Set four studs between the two and mount one 4' x 8' panel material on either side. Trim out as your living room is trimmed, capping the ends with a 1x4 board.

Chapter 3

Roofing Problems

**Roof gutters...Roof ice dams...Roof leaks...Roof replacement...
Roofing safety...Reroofing...Roof reinforcement...Roof joints...
Roof dormers...Skylights.**

Rain troughs

Q.   Is it necessary to have rain troughs on the eaves of a house? How important are they?

L.M., Midland, Mich.

A.   It isn't exactly necessary to have rain troughs on the eaves although it is usually a very good solution. Rain water hits the roof and runs straight down the slope. Without eaves, it drops off the entire edge, perhaps right in front

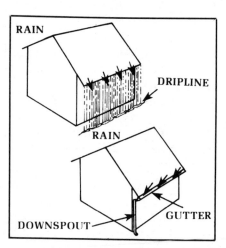

of your front door. It also tends to puddle up in a drip line equal to the overhang away from your house which may or may not run away from your house. Gutters collect the roof-water and convey it to downspouts which in turn direct the water to a place less inconvenient for its return to the earth. The choice is yours.

Vinyl gutters

Q.   Please tell me where I can find out who in this area carries the vinyl rain gutters you featured in your story in the April 1980 issue.

J.C., Johnstown, N.Y.

A.   Address any inquires you might have on the Raingo Gutter System to Mr. Tom Gallagher, Raingo Division, Genova, Inc., 7034 East Court St., Davison, Mich. 48423.

Rusted gutter liner

Q.   I have an old house with built-in or boxed in gutters at the edges of a Dutch gambrel roof. The metal lining has rusted. What is the proper way to repair them? Is it possible to reline them? We plan to reroof soon, too.

T.S., Steubenville, Ohio

A.   If the lining of your boxed gutter has rusted, the wood beneath may well be decayed. Repairing the liner is not the answer until you make sure the wood is still sound. Then, you can reline with metal, repair the liner (if it is not too far gone) with a repair kit available at your local hardware store, or replace the entire assembly with new gutters. Whatever you decide to do, do it before you reroof.

Asphalt for gutters

Q.   Is asphalt roof coating harmful to sheet metal gutters?

J.P., South Bend, Ind.

A.   You may use asphalt in any form on the inside of gutters and seal pin hole leaks or narrow cracks. If cracks are wide or holes are large, you can still use it, but with reinforcing. Apply a coating of asphalt to the metal all around the area to be repaired. Then stretch fiberglass cloth, clean burlap or loose weave canvas over the area and press down into the asphalt. Then apply more asphalt over this to conceal it.

Wood gutter drip

Q. How can I stop water from clinging to the bottoms of the wooden gutters around my house? This happens after every rain, gutter bottoms become streaked and frequent painting is necessary.
J.H., Saddle River, N.J.

A. Apply plenty of liquid floor wax to the bottom of the gutter with a brush.

Run-away rain

Q. Rain accumulating on two sides of my roof during moderate or heavy rainfall and making its way down a central valley, overshoots the eaves troughs completely. I can't raise the troughs due to necessity of maintaining present pitch to the downspouts. If there is a solution, I'd like to hear it.

J.P., Newburgh, N.Y.

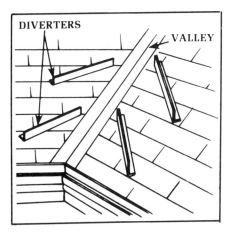

A. A sort of baffleboard series to divert the flow away from the valley and spread it out over the adjacent roof sections is the usual treatment. These can be made of aluminum bent at right angles or constructed of wood. They are usually about 2" or 3" high, can be set on top of the roofing as shown, but use a good dab of roofing ce-

ment around the nails that hold them on.

No fascia

Q. I would like to know if my house should have a fascia board under the wooden gutters which are apparently nailed to the plate of the roof. Will it be necessary to replace the first board with a wider one to meet the fascia and gutter and how do you keep this board from decaying?

N.I., Lyndhurst, N.J.

A. Nailing gutters to the top plate builds them in completely which is OK provided they are kept completely paint-sealed inside and out and not allowed to overflow. To remove them now would call for complete reconstruction. A fascia must be treated lumber, should be back painted before placing. You wouldn't have to widen the lower board; a metal strip slid up under the shingles and down over the fascia and gutter top edge so as to divert water into the gutter would do it. Use aluminum flashing if you do this.

Icy steps

Q. Our porch runs across the front of the house. The steps leading onto it run the full width of the porch. The gutter that should drain the water from the porch roof runs the full width of the house. Snow gets piled up on the roof and ice freezes in the gutter which causes dripping all across the steps which freezes and causes a very dangerous condition. Will heating tape help?
N.C., Saxonville, Mass.

A. It is possible, considering the severity of your climate, that the cable would not completely solve the problem if merely strung along the eaves above the gutters. Since the trouble presumably originates in frozen gutters, a cable placed within the gutters would keep the ice from forming there. No matter what snow and ice accumu-

late on the roof, as long as the melted part can flow down and out via the gutters, there would be no overflow.

Drywell directions

Q. My husband and I are interested in digging a drywell. Can you furnish us with general information and instructions for this project?

J.S., Ozone Park, N.Y.

A. Essentially a drywell is a big hole in the ground that allows water to seep away more slowly than it would from a puddle at the end of your downspout. The object is to direct water from where you don't want it to the drywell. This should be located in an area where the drainage is better or where you don't mind a bit of lingering damp ground. The easiest way to build your own drywell is by using a 55-gallon drum. Puncture it with many fairly large holes (not pin holes). Dig a hole deep enough so that the tip of the drum can be buried 12" to 14" below ground with a 3" or 4" pipe, pitching 1" for each foot of run, coming in at the top of the drum. Set the drum in the

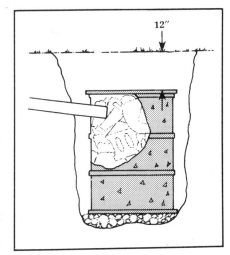

hole. If the hole is bumpy, put stones or gravel under the drum to keep it level. Fill the drum with bricks, rocks, etc. Place planks across the top of the drum and fill the hole with dirt.

Flooded dry well

Q. The home I just bought has a basement entrance from the rear lawn and a dry well at the bottom of the entrance. After each heavy rain, water enters the basement under the door as the dry well cannot carry off the excess water. Can you suggest what might be done for this?

D.S., Franklin Square, N.Y.

A. Possible solutions are: Deepen the dry well; run a pipe line from this dry well to another further removed from the house; construct a covered entrance to prevent water from falling into the entrance area; divert surface water from flowing into this entrance area from the surrounding territory.

Ice dams

Q. We've been told leaks in our attic are due to ice dams. What causes the ice to dam up?

D.E., Madison, Wis.

A. The overhang has no heat below or above and snow and ice stay frozen until the weather moderates. The top part of the roof has sufficient heat escaping from below to partly melt snow and ice.

MELTING SNOW MAKES A PUDDLE—THAT DRIPS. EAVES' FLASHINGS MUST RUN UP ROOF FAR ENOUGH TO DIVERT THIS DAMMED-UP WATER.

This water runs down to join the ice and snow lower down on the roof and freezes there, building up

the dam. The real solution is to insulate the ceiling heavily to reduce heat loss to the attic, and to increase attic ventilation so the underside of roof stays cold. This will reduce premature snow melt, which causes the ice dams.

Ice dam prevention

Q. What's the best way to prevent or at least cope with the formation of ice dams along the edge of the roof? The floor of the attic space is insulated and we use electric radiant heat in the flooring. The roof is low pitched and has a 2' overhang.

N.D., Andover, Mass.

A. You have two ways of offsetting the problem. You can use insulation so good that the snow will stay on the roof everywhere until the sun melts it in which case everything will go at the same time, or you can melt the ice dams along the edges with an electric heating cable. With the dams melting away as fast as formed, water from above will flow down and away in spite of adverse weather. If you are losing enough heat through the roof to melt snow and ice, it will be more economical in the long run to stop the heat loss and save the fuel money.

Heating cables

Q. I would like to install heating cables on my roof to prevent ice build-up. The cable package cautions one to be sure the cables do not touch or overlap. What is the reason for this?

W.M., Short Hills, N.J.

A. Allowing the cables to touch or overlap could cause them to overheat, melt the insulation and short out.

However, with electricity costs being what they are, you may want to consider other ways to prevent ice dams. See "Attic Ventilation" in Chapter 14 in this book.

Porch roof problem

Q. My house has a gable roof and the front entrance is in the center under the eaves. I wish to put a porch there using a gable roof for the porch also. The present stoop which I will retain is 10' wide, 7' deep and the ceiling of the roof will be 9' above the porch. Is there a rule of thumb to determine the angle of the gable I must use? What angle would you suggest so it will not be out of proportion to the width and length of the porch itself?

R.K., Cincinnati, Ohio

A. The angle of the new porch gable can be used to give the house a greater width or to accentuate the height as you wish. For convenience in construction a 45° angle is often suggested. That would be a 5' height which added to the 9' height would bring the roof peak 14' above the porch floor. Check to determine where this intersects the present roof. The higher the point of intersection the more roofing work you will have to do. Very likely a 3 on 12 pitch would be nearer an appropriate angle in your situation.

Changing roof angles

Q. I now have a raised porch outside my kitchen. It is about 9' x 9'. I would like to put a roof over it and screen it in. My problem is that my roof on my ranch house is pitched at such an angle that I can't continue the roof line over the porch.

H.I., Sysosset, N.Y.

A. You can open the covering at the end of the present roof rafters and expose the rafter ends back to the top plate. Place roof rafters in position against these spiking or bolting through for support and extend the new rafters out over the porch at a lesser angle, if you can provide headroom at the new porch ceiling. Or you can run the new rafters up and attach them to the present roof, tapering the ends of the new rafters on the underside to set down at the proper angle

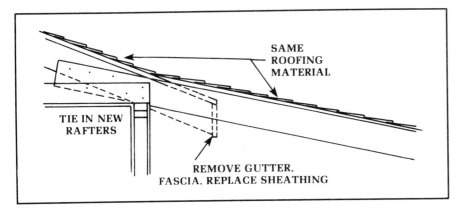

TIE IN NEW RAFTERS

SAME ROOFING MATERIAL

REMOVE GUTTER, FASCIA, REPLACE SHEATHING

over each existing roof rafter. They are spiked down through the present roof. Use 1x4 spacer-spreaders between these, nailing to roof.

Screened porch roof

Q. I want to roof my patio and screen it in, building the roof securely enough so that the room may possibly be enclosed at a long distant date. Can you tell me how to connect the rafters to the end wall of my frame house? They would have to come in just below the second floor level, the patio being two steps down from the floor.

S.G., Glencoe, Ill.

A. In making a roof of this nature you had best open the wall and attach the new rafters along side each stud, resting them on a ledger supported at each end, if your patio is very large, and nailed to each stud. We do not know what type of siding you have but insert flashing and bend it up out of the way while you build on the roof,

bringing it down on top of the new roof's shingles properly when you are done.

Leaking concrete deck

Q. I have a 4″ concrete deck roof covering the side porch attached to my house. The roof has steel beam supports. At each beam the concrete has cracked. Every time it rains the water leaks through these cracks. I have tried caulking compounds, plastic roofing cement, then paint, but the cracks seem to open up again. Can you suggest something to seal these cracks?

J.W., Toledo, Ohio

A. Asphalt seems the most likely material to use, heated to above 70° and worked into the cracks deeply with a trowel. If heated enough it will run like tar and still harden eventually so it can be painted over. Another way would be to force oakum caulking into the cracks to within 1/4″ of the surface. The last 1/4″ can be filled

with caulking compound as a base for paint.

Roofing paper "rug"

Q. The floors on our upstairs porches are covered with roofing paper and when people walk on them, they track the loose particles or flakes into their living rooms. Please inform me as to whether or not there is a paint or coating I can apply to this roofing paper to prevent this tracking.

T.L., Cleveland, Ohio

A. Roofing paper is not meant for traffic. There is an aluminum base paint that can be applied to roofing paper which might help, but you might find it more practical to make some other arrangement for protection of the roof and to stop the problem. A sort of duck-walk of wood slats on sleepers is an often used device over this type of roof and does very well. Use 1x3 slats spaced 1/4″ to 1/2″ apart on 2x2 sleepers made up in easy-to-handle sections.

Roof joint leaks

Q. My problem concerns the leaks along the joint between a wood shingle roof and a deck roof. My idea was to rip off the lowest row of shingles and lay a strip of flashing out over the deck and cover the other end with new shingles. I do not see any way to remove these shingles without laying a whole new roof.

W.P., Fairfield, Conn.

A. You have the right idea but there is no need to remove the lower course of shingles. You can bend a wide strip of flashing and slide it between this lower course and the one below it. If extended up 1″ to 2″ beyond the exposure point, you would prevent any moisture from getting under the shingles. Run the flashing over the flat roof a minimum of 6″ and nail down rust-resistant nails spaced no more than 4″ apart. Seal edge with asphalt and sprinkle with sand.

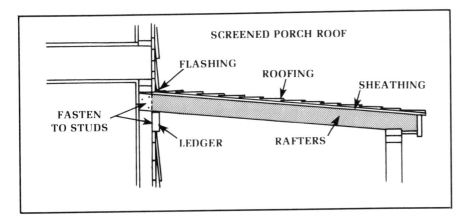

SCREENED PORCH ROOF

FLASHING

ROOFING

SHEATHING

FASTEN TO STUDS

LEDGER

RAFTERS

Metal deck leaks

Q. I have a tin covered deck roof which leaks in two places. Instead of patching it again I thought of putting on tar and roofing paper and then a platform to keep furniture legs from punching holes in the paper. I hope you can help me with this problem.

G.S., Milwaukee, Wis.

A. Your idea of a platform is a good one and will protect the metal roof. Coat the whole roof with asphalt, no paper. Make sectional duck walks of two 2x3 sleepers about 30" apart and across them, spaced 1/8" apart, place 1x3 strips of clear pine to form square platforms roughly 3' x 3'. Make enough of these to cover the roof. Asphalt will protect the sleepers from rot and the 1/8" cracks will provide adequate drainage yet be solid enough not to interfere with walking or furniture placement.

Deck joint leaks

Q. We have a concrete patio deck which is also the garage roof. We also have a leak where it meets the house. Have been told I need flashing. Would this be effective?

G.W., Mount Vernon, N.J.

A. Use metal flashing attached to the house wall about 6" above the patio floor, slipped under whatever kind of siding you have. Run it out onto the patio about 10" sealing it down with asphalt. Depending on what surfacing was used on the deck, you may need to add one now. If so, bring it over the flashing. You could also seal the house-patio joint with asphalt and pour 1/2" of waterproof cement over the entire patio to seal that. This would cost less, need no further maintenance and could be painted. If the slab is not reinforced the added weight might be too much, in which case a lighter weight waterproofing surface would be better.

Roof leak

Q. After a heavy rainstorm, my roof leaks in the vicinity of the valleys. I coated the valleys with roofing compound but it hasn't remedied the situation. What is my next move?

I.W., Hartford, Conn.

A. Your next move is to locate the leak and fix it. This is tricky because a roof leak doesn't always announce itself in the location of the actual leak. If you can get up into the attic under the bare rafters that's the easiest place to start. Use a good light. Find the point you first discover evidence of leakage and follow the water flow lines uphill to their source. If you can't inspect the underside, it can be done from outside but you have to hunt. Look over flashing around chimneys, roof vents, etc., and pay particular attention to the ridge cap as leaks at these points are common, too.

Leaks at eaves

Q. During rainy weather, there is a dripping of rain between the fascia board and rafter ends in my roof. My idea to correct this is to insert a strip of flashing under the bottom course of roof shingles and conduct it over the back edge of wood gutters. At the same time, I note that some of the wood gutters have pulled away from the fascia as much as 1/4" at the top. Is this flashing idea a good solution?

A.P., Braintree, Mass.

A. Since the fascia should have been brought up tight under the shingle ends there seems to be no other solution than the one you have in mind. Unless the gap behind the gutter indicates it is pulling loose, you need do no more than insert the flashing under the shingles, bend it over into the gutter and anchor it there with a rust-resistant nail every 4" or so.

Shingle spacings

Q. Our new home has cedar shingles, some of which are separated by as much as 1/4". Is this a natural occurence due to the hot dry summer past or are there steps I should take now? The only insulation we have in the house is building board and it would seem that the winter wind will get through these openings. If the solution is caulking, is there a type which is tinted or will we have to paint over it?

I.M., Suffern, N.Y.

A. Properly laid up cedar shingles are supposed to be 1/4" apart. The joints between the shingles in any one course should not be closer than 1-1/2" from aligning with the joints between shingles in the course below. As one course overlaps that below, it covers the joint underneath. There is little chance for wind or water to get

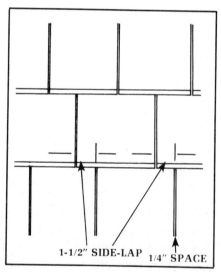

1-1/2" SIDE-LAP   1/4" SPACE

past the shingles. Don't fill the joints up. They are meant to allow a certain amount of movement of the wood shingles with changes in temperature and humidity.

Slate roof

Q. I am looking for information that might help me repair a slate roof. Can you help?

T.B., Bedford, Va.

A. Broken slates are best removed and replaced. Nails that no longer have a shingle to hold can be cut off with a hacksaw blade under the slate from the next row up, leaving the space clear for a new shingle to be inserted and nailed in place. Make the holes first by temporarily inserting the shingle, marking the existing holes and then makng them in the new slate by a sharp blow of your hammer on the end of a heavy nail or center punch. If you have to cut the slate to fit, score each side with cold chisel. (Make sure the scored lines are exactly back to back.) Tap along the scored line with the wanted edge well supported, until the unwanted portion breaks off. Coat the area that will be covered with roofing cement. Insert the trimmed, drilled slate and nail in place. If you need to remove a damaged slate still held by a nail or nails, you will need a slate puller which is a piece of strap iron bent and notched about as shown. You stick it up under the slate, hooking a nail in the slot. Hammer on the upright portion until the nail gives and you can remove the slate.

Incidentally, don't be upset with the daylight that can be seen through the lower parts of an old slate roof on a sunny day. Remember, you're sighting along the space between slates. That joint is sheltered by the whole slate in the next course up and for most of its length by slates in the course above that. It is like looking down a tunnel. What to look for in really old houses is rot and/or decay in the spaced roofers that support the slates. If you see daylight looking up at 90°

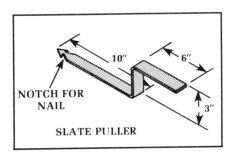

NOTCH FOR NAIL

10″   6″

3″

SLATE PULLER

to the slates, then stick a wire through the hole and find it on the outside roof surface. You'll find a cracked, broken or missing slate. Annual inspection of slate roofs is a good idea. Loose slates can often be salvaged. The most vulnerable spots seem to be around flues and vents made in the roof after it was initially built. Flashings here are apt to be poorly supported. Unless solid support can be supplied, continued repairs will have to be made.

Slate replacement

Q. A couple of slates are missing along the gable edge of my roof. I don't see any way to nail them back. Is there another way?

C.F., Elgin, Ill.

A. Where it is impossible to nail slates, you can cut a 1″ wide strip of 20-gage copper, nail that in the space where the slate belongs. Tap the slate into place on top of the strip, then bend the bottom end of the strip up over the lower edge of the slate to hold it in place.

Roof butts shingles

Q. Where our one-story breezeway joins our two-story house we

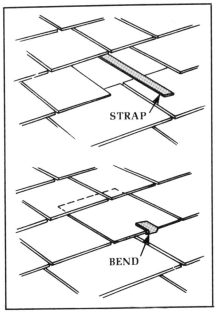

STRAP

BEND

have a leak. I've patched this joint repeatedly with asphalt cement but it always opens again. Now that we are reshingling the house seems like a good time to do something else. We intend to put cedar shingles on the wood siding. The abutting roof is already asphalt shingles. Have you any suggestions?

E.W., Bicknell, Ind.

A. This should be flashed as the roof is laid, extending shingle length flashing out onto the roof and up the wall as you go along, covering the wall leg later with the siding. With the roof already on, you are not going to be able to do

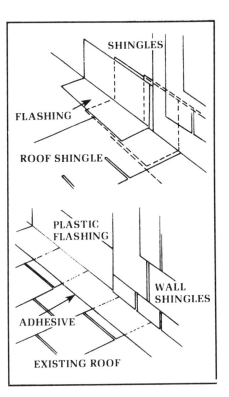

SHINGLES

FLASHING

ROOF SHINGLE

PLASTIC FLASHING

WALL SHINGLES

ADHESIVE

EXISTING ROOF

this. We'd suggest you try the tough, heavy gage plastic flashing now available, using the plastic adhesive with it. Let the material extend over the roof about 6″ and up the wall about 8″. Then apply and trim your wood shingles on the wall over the flashing. You'll be half right anyhow and it should be more satisfactory than patching with asphalt cement.

Flashing placement

Q. I'm installing a jack ventilator on our fairly steep shingled roof. Does the flange go under or over the shingles?

E.S., St. Catherines, Ontario

A. On any sloping roof set the flange on the sheathing. Then use metal flashing all around it. On the up slope and at both sides the flashing is placed under the shingles and run up the high sides of the ventilator at least 8″ so that water from above flows over the shingles onto the flashing and around the obstruction. On the down slope, flashing extends over the shingles so that water flowing around the obstacle flows over the flashing and back to the shingles. Coat all cuts and joints liberally with asphalt.

Low-pitch roof leaks

Q. A year ago we added a room to the rear of our house with a low shed roof. We applied asphalt shingles over this just as we had done about eight years ago on the house roof. There the roof is fine. We thought by using the same shingles we'd have a better looking house and a dry roof, but not so. What's wrong? We used the same felt underneath and both roofs are plywood.

L.R., Joplin, Mo.

A. Just how low is that shed roof pitched? If it is between 2″ and 4″ on 12″ you'd have been all right with asphalt shingles applied with the low-slope specifications in mind. You should use a double underlayment and special cemented eaves flashing strip and fasten shingle tabs down with quick setting cement. If it is lower than 2″, shingles are not a good choice at all. Roll roofing in the same color would be about as close as you could come to matched roofs. If it is wind-blown rain that gives you the most trouble, repairing any torn shingles and sticking down all the tabs now may save the day. You made no mention of the joint between new roof and old house. Poor flashing here would also result in a leaky roof.

Patching shingles

Q. After a severe wind and rain storm, I found that several of my asphalt shingles were damaged. A few of these roof shingles were lifted out of position and I was able to press them back into place. I was told I should rip them out and replace them. Is this necessary?

S.K., Silver Springs, Md.

A. You cannot leave the shingles in their present state. Examine them again. If there is a small crack or tear in the shingle, it can be waterproofed by applying roofing compound or asphalt mastic with a towel or putty knife. To prevent the edges from lifting, use rustproof nails at each corner and cover the heads with compound. If part of the shingle is torn away or badly ripped, it is necessary to remove the entire shingle and replace it with a new one. A special nail puller is needed for the job. Slip the head of the puller under the shingle. Hit the end outward with a hammer to shear the nail heads off. With nails removed, slip the torn shingle out. Slide a new shingle into position. Since you cannot nail from under the upper shingle, nail directly through it to hold the new shingle in place. Use coated nails and cover the head and surrounding area with roofing compound or asphalt.

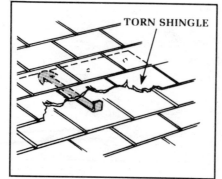

TORN SHINGLE

Roof too flat

Q. I built an addition to my dwelling and through error the roof is perfectly flat. In fact, it is slightly hollow in the center. Can you suggest a material with which I can build up that center to prevent water from lying there. The roof is spruce sheathing, rock-faced roofing paper cemented and nailed at all joints.

V.G., Halifax, Nova Scotia

A. You can build up layers of tar or asphalt covered with sand. After the first layer hardens, add others until proper thickness is obtained. If the depression is more than 1/2″ deep, you can use finely-crushed rock instead. For lighter weight, use vermiculite.

Bubbles and breaks

Q. The roof on our two-family house is made of roofing felt and hot asphalt. Some of the seams are opening and there are a few bubbles in one area where the very slight slope is in the opposite direction. Can these places be repaired long enough to postpone the need to re-surface the building?

B.M., Mount Vernon, Ind.

A. Well done patch work will last about six months, sometimes a good deal longer. At some convenient day, you will need to recover the roof, but to hold off that date coat the inside of gapping seams with roofing cement. Press down and tack tightly, dabbing the nail-heads with more cement. Bubbles are done about the same way but you have to slit them open first so as to reach the inside area to coat it with asphalt roofing cement. Then tack down with broad-head shingle nails as before. Do this work when the sun shines brightly on the roof so that the materials are as pliable as possible.

Melting snow

Q. Our roof has a low pitch and in winter when the snow melts, water leaks from the valley into our living room. I cemented over a hole that I thought was the cause of the problem, but the leak hasn't stopped. We'd like to solve the roof situation before we have the ceiling fixed.

F.C., Evansville, Wis.

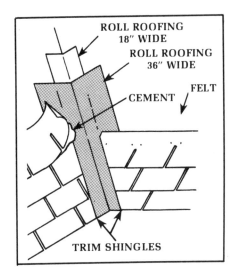

A. Good idea—fix the roof first and then the ceiling. Tracking down a roof leak is not always easy. The snow may be melting higher up on the roof than you think. This could easily result in a problem like yours if the valley flashing does not extend up far enough under the shingles.

Moss on the roof

Q. My lakefront retirement and vacation home has a leak in the roof on the north side only, off the dormers and near the toilet vent pipe. The roof is four years old. It is the third roof on the house in 25 years, and the firm that installed it is no longer in business. There is also green moss growing on the same side of the roof. There is insulation in the attic and no central heating system. Help!

E.L., Hamtramck, Mich.

A. If the leaks are localized, along the dormers and around the toilet vent pipe, it may be that the flashing at these points is not adequate. Green moss will not make the roof leak, but its presence indicates that surface moisture is not evaporating fast enough. We suggest that you prune back any overhanging trees so the moss cannot flourish. You can kill the present growth with a solution of zinc chloride (10%) or by running a strip of galvanized sheet metal along the ridge of the roof. Do *not* use any petroleum products on asphalt roofing.

Leaking roof

Q. I have a seven-year-old ranch-type home with a fireplace that leaks whenever it rains down the outside of the chimney. I have had several different roofers look at it and each one has stated that everything looks very well constructed. Each roofer has caulked and recaulked around the chimney as well as quite a distance from it. Although I have used at least 1-1/2 gallons of roofing cement and several tubes of caulking compound, nothing seems to stop the leaking. The rain still runs down into the attached garage below the attic. Do you have a solution?

C.K., Dubuque, Iowa

A. Have any of the roofers looked in the chimney? It is possible that water running down the inside of the flue has seeped through a crack in the terracotta. You might overcome this problem by inserting a cap above the chimney top or by coating the inside of the flue. We suggest that you have a good local mason check your chimney.

Reroofing

Q. The 20' x 20' roof area over my garage needs to be repaired. Originally I used plywood covered with cheap tarpaper. The paper has blown off in many places, The roof leaks and the plywood is disintegrating. Can I put Plyscore and roofing paper on what is left or must I tear it all off to the joists to repair it?

W.B., Transfer, Pa.

A. You don't have to tear your roof off to the bare joists, but it would certanly be advisable. Putting new plywood over what could turn out to be rotting material would be folly in the long haul. You cannot know for sure if the joists are affected unless you remove the old plywood. Apply new exterior decking plywood to carefully inspected joists. Staple 15-lb. roofing paper to the deck, then use heavy roll roofing, overlapped about 4", and coat the overlap seams with roofing cement.

Roofing safety

Q. My husband and son believe they can reroof our house and save money. My husband is 62 and sometimes unsteady. You have written about reroofing and safety rules. What do you suggest?

J.S., Monticello, Ga.

A. Reroofing a low-slope, one-story-high roof is one thing. Reroofing a steeply-pitched, many-gabled, two- or three-story Victorian home is another. Perhaps you might have a friend of your son's help him do the roof work. Necessary scaffolding can be rented rather than attempting to do the job with makeshift arrangements.

Wood shingles

Q. Where can I get information on buying and installing wood shingles?

A.B., Levittown, N.Y.

A. You should be able to buy cedar shingles at your local lumberyard or home center. Red Cedar Shingle and Handsplit Shake Bureau, Suite 275, 515 116th Ave. NE, Bellevue, Wash. 98004, is the best source for installation information.

Replacing old roof

Q. We have an old house with a composition roof that has been on for 20 years. This has developed cracks and leaks in the past year. We had thought of putting sheet aluminum on, but the lumberyard dealer tells us that it will cause the house to sweat and that would not be good. The pitch is very shallow, 1" to 4", so this does not provide much slope. The ceiling is drywall with 4" of glasswool insulation over it. There is a ventilator at each end, open at all times so the air can blow straight through. The roof is straight, running east and west. What would be your recommendation for this roof?

J.W., Moss Lake, Wash.

A. There is really no need to put aluminum sheet over your old roof. The simplest thing to do is what roofers would do in this situation. This is to staple on 15-lb. roofing felt, overlapping each strip about 4", then cover the paper with standard asphalt roofing shingles.

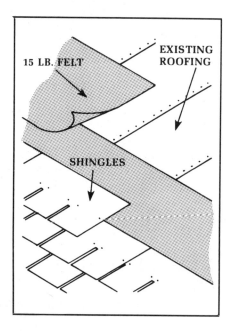

Roof replacement

Q. Our house has a studio addition with a roof slope of about 3/4 to 1" per running foot. It presently has composition shingles. The roof is about 15 years old and

needs replacement. We have about 15" of precipitation a year, and considerable freezing in winter. I am not sure that composition shingles are the best materials to use on the roof. Perhaps tarpaper with at least 50% overlap cemented with tar between three thicknesses would be better. What would you recommend for such a low sloping roof?

H.I., Billings, Mont.

A. We certainly would not recommend composition (asphalt) shingles. Your own suggestion would probably be much better. You could also use a built-up roof with gravel or marble chip surfacing. Contact your local roofing supplier and check out the specifications suggested by the manufacturer of the products he stocks. You will find a range of quality and price along with appropriate weight (thickness) of asphalt-saturated felt and appropriate adhesive suggestions. You may also find suggestions for concealed nailing practices. Wind considerations in your area should not be ignored.

Asphalt shingles

Q. Should we remove the old asphalt shingle roof before we put on a new one? The present roof never leaked in 10 years and the boards underneath seem to be in good condition. We are building an extension and want to do the whole roof area the same.

R.B., Bronx, N.Y.

A. You can put new asphalt shingles over old ones if you like. You will have to remove the old ridge, and in valleys the new shingles have to be carried out past the old ones to be sealed down to the flashing. The double course at the eaves may cause heavy rain on a steep slope to overshoot the gutter by the time you add two more layers. The old roof shingles may cause the new ones to lay in waves across the slope. With those reasons against over-roofing there

are two strong ones for: taking old shingles off is quite a job as you have to remove all nails too and the underlayment plus the fact that when the roof is bare, the house is defenseless against a sudden storm. If you have a passion for neatness and precision workmanship then it is best to take off the old ones and start over.

Shingle renovation

Q. I painted my exterior trim and windows with white exterior latex paint and unfortunately dripped a considerable amount on the old, dark-grey asphalt shingles of the roof. I attempted to remove some of the spots with remover and turpentine and removed more of the surface of the shingle than the white spots. Can you tell me how to remove the spots and renovate the shingles?

I.H., Boston, Mass.

A. Try black paint with a dry brush stipple of white or of a reasonably close grey touch-up for your dark grey asphalt roof. Blend out as much as possible and it won't look that bad.

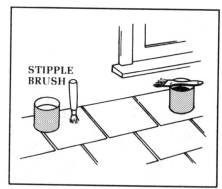

Reshingling

Q. The wood shingles on my cottage roof are badly curled, warped, chipped and sometimes gone entirely. The sheathing under the shingles is not solid but spaced 12" apart. What is the best and most economical way to re-roof with asphalt shingles?

C.N., Michigan City, Ind.

A. Remove the wood shingles. Asphalt shingles need solid sheathing. Remove enough of the roofers as you go to insert solid boards between the roofers or take all the roofers off and replace with plywood. Apply a layer of 15-lb. asphalt saturated felt over the roof deck, then lay the new shingles.

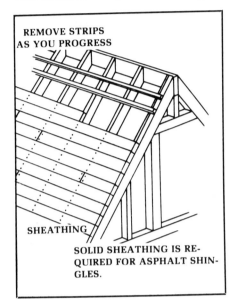

REMOVE STRIPS AS YOU PROGRESS

SHEATHING

SOLID SHEATHING IS REQUIRED FOR ASPHALT SHINGLES.

Horsefeathers

Q. Are horsefeathers necessary on a wood shingle roof before reroofing with asphalt shingles?
B.S., Freeport, N.Y.

A. Assuming the term "horsefeathers" is a local variant for

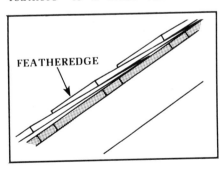

FEATHEREDGE

"featheredge" they are not necessary except for appearance. Installing them does take extra time and money. These triangular strips are tucked under the lower edge of each row of shingles to make the roof more level under the pliable asphalt shingles. Without them, the new roof might appear wavy.

Start shingling

Q. I've taken off old shingles and repaired the roof deck so am ready to start from scratch. Under asphalt butt shingles, what goes on first?
H.P., Somerville, Mass.

A. A 3″ metal drip edge should be installed along eaves and rakes bent downward over the edges of the roof deck to provide a drip. The whole deck is to be covered with 15-lb. asphalt saturated roofer's felt and eaves flashings. Flashing at all roof intersections is applied before you actually start with the shingles.

Applying cedar

Q. We are fixing up a bungalow and have removed the old roof surface, repaired the roof sheathing and built a garage linked to the house with a breezeway room. We would like to use cedar shingles on the roofs and will appreciate any information you have on proper application techniques.
W.S., Oak Park, Ill.

A. You should have no trouble doing a good job. Watch the pitch and exposure relationships on your various roofs to choose shingles the proper length. Do not use tarpaper over the roof deck, selecting a rosin sized building paper or an unsaturated felt. Begin laying the shingles with a double thickness at the bottom edge, letting

these shingles project over the edge so water runs into gutter properly. No matter how wide a shingle is, use only two nails, in no more than 3/4″ from the edges and set so the shingles in the next row up will cover the nails by 3/4″. You can easily align shingles by tacking a straight edge at the proper location. Flash valleys and against the house carefully, preferably with metal, and use the Boston or laced type hip and ridge cap methods. Use only rust resistant nails, and start from valleys so wider shingles occur at ends of courses, fitting widths in the centers. Leave 1/4″ spaces between shingles and jog joints at least 1-1/2″ in successive courses.

Cedar over asphalt

Q. We would like to improve the appearance of our bungalow and have made extensive repairs to it for this reason. Liking the looks of cedar shingles on a roof, we wonder if it is possible to put them over asphalt shingles in need of replacement or repair?
L.L., Newport, R.I.

A. Cedar shingles can be applied over asphalt shingles but the layer of asphalt may tend to act as a vapor barrier in the wrong place and permit condensation on the roof deck. It is better to remove the old shingles first. Also this way, you can easily make any necessary repairs to the roof sheathing, too.

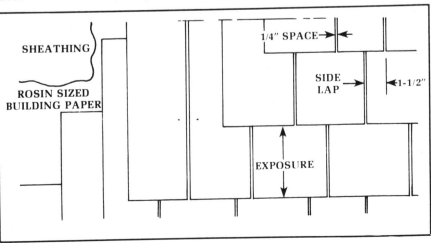

SHEATHING

ROSIN SIZED BUILDING PAPER

1/4″ SPACE

SIDE LAP

1-1/2″

EXPOSURE

Straight shingling

Q. How do you go about putting on asphalt butt shingles straight?
C.H., Reading, Pa.

A. Assuming you have prepared the roof deck properly and installed the felt underlay and flashings, install the starter course. The first course of shingles is aligned with it. Then make use of a chalk line to align the second course and each course therafter, measuring the spacing so as to expose an equal amount of each course to the weather. Vertical chalk lines are necessary also to make sure you'll come out even where upper courses run through above an intersecting roof or dormer.

The starter course is a row of shingles laid with the tabs facing up, over the eaves flashing strip and flush with its rake and eave edges. Cut about 3" off the first shingle to make sure all cut outs will be covered. The purpose is to back up and fill in the spaces between tabs.

Reinforcing roofs

Q. Do you have any information on the reinforcing of roofs?
C.B., Lake Zurich, Ill.

A. Simplest way to reinforce a roof is by setting up a new rafter alongside the old, spiking them together. There is no necessity of

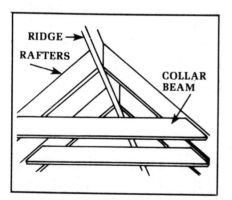

spiking the new ones to the top plate of the walls but they are toenailed into the ridge. Collar beams may be added for additional strength. These are cross members, 2x4s or 2x6s, set horizontally across each pair of rafters, 18" to 24" below the ridge. 2x6 vertical struts may be used between present rafters and floor joists though they will usually be in the way if any use is to be made of the attic space, and they may put strain on the joists that they weren't meant to handle.

Boxing eaves

Q. I have rafters that overhang the side of the house. As these are not boxed in, they take time to paint. The rafters slope and protrude about 17" from the side of the house. Will you give me some idea how to box these in?
P.G., Lorain, Ohio

A. The standard method when the rafter ends are cut off vertically is to apply one board across these ends, then run short lengths from

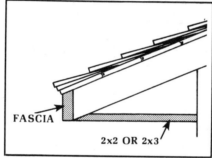

each end horizontally to contact the house wall. The underside is then covered. You may choose some type of ventilating panel arrangement. At the present time you probably have the area between rafters completely sealed so that no air circulates upward under the roof sheathing. The top board should be removed so that air entering the soffit can continue on up.

Extension

Q. My bungalow has a boxy silhouette, mostly because my roof stops nearly flush with the wall. How can I extend the roof to create a pleasant overhang without disturbing the existing roof?
G.H., Mandan, N.D.

A. The extensions are fairly simple. Remove the gutter and

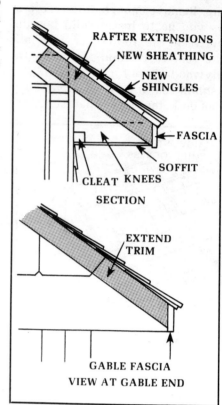

fascia board. Either remove the first sheathing board or pierce panel or diagonal sheathing for access to each roof rafter. Insert 2x4s beside each rafter flush with its upper edge and long enough to go at least 1' beyond the plate and out to provide the desired amount of overhang. The maximum is 18" to 24" determined by architectural considerations such as window height and visual proportion. Horizontal braces called "knees" are secured to the outer ends of the extensions and run back to a cleat on the house wall. A new fascia is applied to these projecting ends and the gutter replaced. The gable ends will also require attention. Easiest solution is to nail a fascia board of the correct width underneath the lower edge of the gable ends to bring them to the correct size.

Joining old and new

Q. I am building an addition with a gable roof at right angles to a gable roof on the old portion of

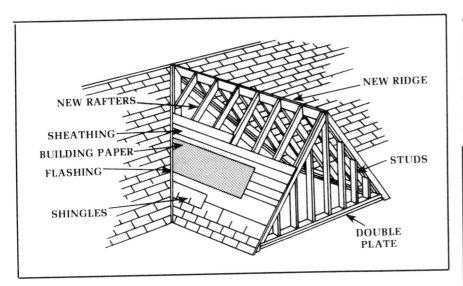

NEW RAFTERS
SHEATHING
BUILDING PAPER
FLASHING
SHINGLES
NEW RIDGE
STUDS
DOUBLE PLATE

the house. How do I join the new roof to the old one?

K.D., St. Louis, Mo.

A. Extend the ridge of the new roof to meet the old and set in rafters at standard spacing along this ridge extension, each rafter meeting the old roof to which angled ends are attached by nailing. Cover rafters with sheathing which also joins the old roof. Before shingling the new roof the valley formed on each side is covered with flashing and extended under the old shingles and across the new sheathing over which new shingles are applied.

Dormered attic

Q. We need to get better use out of our attic space and I want to put one or more dormers in the roof so we can make rooms there. Would installing four dormers on the roof be better than one large one in the rear of the house?

T.I., Providence, R.I.

A. The single dormer is preferable for a neater appearance and interior conveniece plus the fact that it is far simpler to build one than four. However your style of house will have something to do with this decision as will the possible room arrangements and the roof slope and size.

Room on top

Q. I have an addition to my home with a flat roof and now I wish to take that roof off and add a room on top. I can do carpentry work but can't work at this steadily, so I don't know quite how to get started at it. Do I have to take the present roofing paper off?

N.G., Pawtucket, R.I.

A. You might be able to build up the walls and put on the new roof for protection of this area before removal of the old roof. This way you wouldn't have to worry about the room below getting wet in bad weather. The paper will definitely have to come off eventually. Check the size of the present rafters to see if they are strong enough to support the floor of a new room.

Adding dormers

Q. My house measures 32' x 24' and has a hip roof. From top of ridge to ceiling is a distance of 8'. What can I do with the roof which will give me enough room to build two rooms?

L.W., Belleville, Ill.

A. You can add twin dormers, one on each long side of the house, using a partition to parallel the ridge in dividing the upper area or make a shed dormer by lifting

one side of the roof and divide the upstairs at right angles to ridge; whichever arrangement seems best, based on location of the stairwell. Two smaller dormers would probably be more attractive from the outside but would not provide enough room inside.

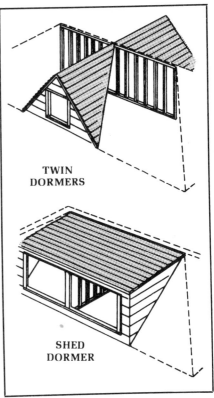

TWIN DORMERS

SHED DORMER

Roofing an addition

Q. I wish to place an addition to the side of my ranch house. The addition will have a gable-type roof to tie into the rancher roof. What is the best way to effect the roofing tie-in to preclude leakage? Both roofs are and will be asphalt shingles.

J.L., Green Lane, Pa.

A. Assuming you do not wish access between the two roofed areas as the "attic" level, the easiest thing to do is to strip down the rancher roof to bare sheathing in, and a bit beyond, the area where the roof of the addition will attach. Then figure your framing as indicated by the pitch of the two roofs. Your object is to attach the framing and then the sheathing for the new roof securely to the sheathing of the old roof and the framing under it *before* you apply the roof surfacing materials of your choice. Before you can prevent a leak at the joint you have to make the joint secure. Then apply your saturated felt and the shingles to align with those on the main roof, flashing the valleys as you go up. The one thing on your sketch which we'd suggest you consider carefully is that you show a lower eaves line on the addition. It will be a lot easier if you keep the same eaves line for the new roof (see illustration.)

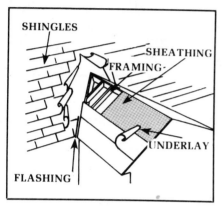

Knee walls

Q. **I started to reroof, using your step-by-step story as a guide, then halted suddenly when I was advised that the additional layer of shingles would put an undue weight strain on the house. I was told I should put up knee walls. I can't find reference to these nor do I know anything about them. Any descriptions or help you can give?**
C.K., Wickliffe, Ohio

A. An additional layer of asphalt or wood shingles does add

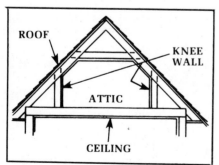

some weight, but rafter sizes and spacings should be designed with

a sufficient safety factor to accommodate this. Knee walls are most easily seen in the diagram. They are not generally used as braces for a failing roof since the load would simply be transferred to the ceiling joists below which could (and probably would) cause the plaster below to crack. Knee walls are the vertical walls, parallel to the eaves, designed to enclose usable space in your attic.

Roof rejuvenation

Q. **The gable roof on my garage is sagging in the middle and the roof covering is in poor repair. I figure on replacing the covering and fixing up the sheathing. Can I at the same time fix the sag?**
J.B., North Tonawanda, N.Y.

A. While the roof is stripped down, check to see whether the sag is caused by rafters cut too short or rotted at the ends, or by bulging sidewalls. Make the center rafters long enough to match the end ones, replace rotted timbers or correct the sprung sidewalls by installing collar beams joining all rafter pairs. Then re-roof from the rafters out.

Leaking skylight

Q. **I'm having trouble with leaks around the skylight and chimney of my flat roof. The rain seems to blow under the edge of the Plexiglass skylight (it extends about 2″ all around the opening). Every sealant I've tried has not lasted in this hot summer sun. Are there skylights which have integral aprons that could hang down around the skylight? If so, who makes them?**
P.S., Sierra Vista, Ariz.

A. Most skylights have some form of frame or at least a gasket under or around the edges. What you describe will probably always leak as there is no good way to tighten it down evenly along the entire perimeter. Ask the manu-

facturer of the unit you have for suggestions.

Installing skylight

Q. **When we recently bought our home, it was summertime, the sun was high, and the kitchen was bright. I am now finding it quite dark and would like to put a "bubble" in the roof. Do you have any suggestions?**
L.S., San Francisco, Calif.

A. You'll generally find residential-size skylights for sale at local building supply outlets. Distributors of plastic products also most likely stock these products. Tap Plastics, Dept. FH, 3011 Alvardo St., San Leandro, Calif. 94577 can give you the name and address of your nearest distributor. Also, Cadillac Plastic and Chemical Co., a Dayco Co., has 100 service centers throughout the world. Write them at 1221 Bowers St., Birmingham, Mich. 48012.

Installation is not that difficult. You mark the opening-to-be on the ceiling, then drill a hole in each corner to transfer the marks through the roof surface. Go on the roof, use the holes as guides. Remove the

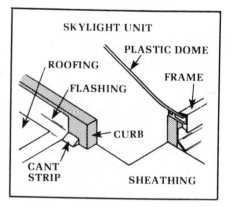

roofing and cut the opening through the sheathing.

You'll usually need to build a wooden curb to receive the skylight and may need a sleeve to bring the light from the roof to the room below. Make watertight joints as necessary where curb joins roof. Then set the unit over the curb and fasten in place.

Chapter 4

Siding Problems

Aluminum siding...Asbestos siding...Asphalt shingles...Brick & stone veneers...Cedar shingles & shakes...Clapboard siding... Stucco siding...Vinyl siding...Wood siding.

Aluminum siding

Q. I would like to cover my aging frame house with aluminum siding in a pastel shade, preferably the insulated type. So far I cannot find any reasonable instructions for the handyman to follow in this application. Can you advise me?
H.A., Bergenfield, N.J.

A. You need to secure a copy of the installation manual from the manufacturer of the siding you purchase for details. Generally a starter strip must be attached around the house exactly straight, meeting at all corners and starting at the lowest one. It is usually furred out and nailed on through slots provided. A system of acces- sory pieces are used around all openings and at corners and wall tops to receive the interlocking siding panels. The first panel inter- locks in the starter strip and is nailed along the top about every 16" in holes in the nailing bead on the panels. Subsequent panels in- terlock and are nailed in the same manner. Back up plates are used under every vertical joint. Any furring required is applied as you go along to keep the finished wall even. It is essential that you secure instructions from the manufac- turer on proper use of accessory pieces.

Siding situation

Q. An increasing number of homes are being resided with aluminum or vinyl siding. I've even seen new homes built with aluminum siding applied directly to the wall sheathing. I've con- sidered having aluminum siding put on my home, but the possi- bility of trapping too much mois- ture within the walls bothers me. Homes with wood exteriors some- times have this problem, yet alu- minum and vinyl are effective vapor barriers. Isn't there the pos- sibility of excessive trapping of moisture and rotting of wood construction with such sidings? Shouldn't more ventilation be pro- vided somehow?
L.S., Waltham, Mass.

A. Manufacturers of aluminum and vinyl siding are aware of its vapor barrier effectiveness and design ventilation methods ac- cordingly. Contact the manufac- turer of the siding you like and ask him for the particulars on this point. Your question is reasonable and you certainly cannot cure damp and rotting wood siding problems by covering them up with aluminum or vinyl as too many people seem to believe. How- ever, properly installed, these sidings should not cause nor con- tribute unduly to wood rot in ex- isting siding or wood construction.

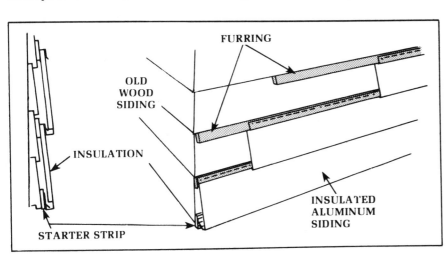

FURRING
OLD WOOD SIDING
INSULATION
STARTER STRIP
INSULATED ALUMINUM SIDING

Cleaning aluminum

Q. Is there any type of solution on the market to wash aluminum siding that's gotten dingy, or can it be painted over?

J.S., St. Paul, Minn.

A. Guess you missed the story on renovating siding that ran in our April 1980 issue. As suggested there, washing down the siding with Tackle and coating it with Guard may be your solution. Both are products of Aminco Industries, Dept. FH, 7533 Washington Ave. So., Minneapolis, Minn. 55435. If you want to try it first, they'll send you full instructions and samples of both products for $2.

Insulation or siding

Q. Our house has no insulation in the walls. We want to put on aluminum siding. Is it best to have insulation blown in between the walls or to put on insulated aluminum siding and rely on the air pockets between the inner and outer walls for insulation? Would we be wasting our money if we had both aluminum siding and blown-in insulation?

R.H., Jenkintown, Pa.

A. Aluminum siding is mainly a matter of appearance and freedom from painting for perhaps 15 to 20 years. Insulated aluminum siding usually has 1/2" of foamed plastic glued to the back of each panel. This, by itself, is not enough to compensate for the complete lack of insulation in your house. Blown insulation will completely fill the cavities between the walls and give you a full 3-1/2" as well as 6" under the attic floor.

Cleaning asbestos

Q. Please advise the best method of cleaning asbestos cement siding.

A.S., Houston, Tex.

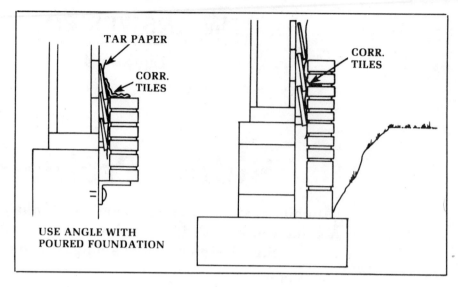

TAR PAPER

CORR. TILES

CORR. TILES

USE ANGLE WITH POURED FOUNDATION

A. Strong detergents and scrubbing are the best methods. The job is simplified with powered scrubbing equipment some of which is water-powered and fits on a hose in place of a nozzle. You'll need a good rinse anyway so the hose is necessary. Once cleaned and dry, you should use a coat of clear silicone water repellent on the older type asbestos cement to prevent further dirt penetration. The new types generally have a silicone finish.

Stone facing

Q. I saw a stone front on a house in our neighborhood that I swear is real stone and it was a frame house a week ago. The corners appear to be solid stone. How is this accomplished?

N.P., Weehawken, N.J.

A. You probably saw one of the facing jobs done with thin natural stone. Mitered corner stones or the factory fabricated corners are done so accurately it takes close examination to see they are really only 3/4" or 1" thick. Installed with care and good judgement such corners do appear to be solid stone.

Angle iron

Q. I am considering putting brick veneer on the front of my frame house to a height of about 4' but there is no lip on the foundation to start on. I wish to avoid the construction of a new foundation for the veneer. Would it be practical to attach an iron angle to the foundation to support the bricks?

W.B., Whitestone, N.Y.

A. Your method would be practical if you have a poured concrete foundation. The angle would need to be a minimum of 3/8" steel with a bearing leg 3-1/2" to 4". Anchors should be spaced at 2' intervals in 2" deep holes. If you have a block foundation, excavate to the footing, using blocks to grade, bricks above.

Adding brick veneer

Q. I plan adding brick veneer to the outside of my home. Do I put brick against the wall or leave an air space? Also if I leave a space, how do I keep the brick from toppling?

E.T., San Antonio, Tex.

A. Cover the present frame walls with asphalt saturated felt and erect the veneer wall 1" away from it. To hold the veneer in place use corrugated metal strip fasteners which are nailed to the house wall and extend into the mortar joints as the brick is laid.

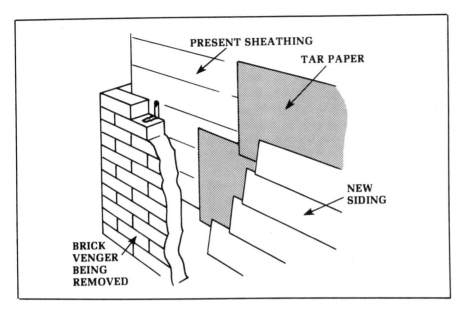

PRESENT SHEATHING

TAR PAPER

NEW SIDING

BRICK VENGER BEING REMOVED

mix, 1 part powdered sodium silicate, 1/2 part asbestos fiber or other binder, 4 parts sand, dry color if desired and water to make a fairly stiff mix. Marble dust, powdered quartz, pulverized mica and other materials are sometimes pressed into the damp surface to color and add sparkle to the material.

Thin stone

Q. I would like to face a portion of our remodeled house with real stone but have not got the footings to support 4″ veneer. Do I have to use the artificial stone or is there some way to attach a ledge to the wall for real stone?

E.F., Skokie, Ill.

A. There not only is "some way" to attach a ledge to the wall for a real stone facing but a whole system that will give you just what you want. A number of quarries are producing thin stone 3/4″ to 1″ thick, grooved top and bottom and controlled in thickness, height and finish. You need sound sheathing covered with asphalt paper to start with. A special starter strip supports the first course of stone, subsequent courses are attached by clips fitted into the grooves in the stone and held to the sheathing by screws. When stone is all attached, mortar is applied with a caulking gun, the joints struck for a finished appearance.

Replacing brick

Q. I have an old 11-room house of brick veneer. In several places the brick is loose from the frame. Would it be practical to remove all the brick and apply wood siding?

R.B., White Bear Lake, Minn.

A. If the brick is bulging outward this may indicate a wall in danger of collapse and removal of the brick is the best solution. You would expose sheathing of some sort which should be covered with tarpaper as the base for new siding to be nailed to. It is possible that the sheathing has rotted and may have to be replaced. You may have some trouble at doors and windows as reducing the total wall thickness could leave them protruding in which case they would have to be taken out and reset.

Making stone

Q. Is it possible for me to make an artificial stone and put this up on my frame house? I would like a list of ingredients and how to mix them if possible.

C.C., Brooklyn, N.Y.

A. There are two methods used for application of artificial stone. In one process, the stone is pre-cast and put up like ceramic tile with cement mortar to hold it to wire lath nailed over the frame wall. The other way, material is placed in a mold and immediately pressed —mold and all—against the lath and its thin cement coating where it adheres and dries in place. The general formula is 1 part portland cement with or without a 10% lime

Waterproofing stone

Q. I want to put a stone facing on the front of my house which is now asphalt siding and not very attractive. Do I have to cover the asphalt with anything, building paper, etc., first?

H.W., Burlington, Iowa

A. No, provided the asphalt siding is intact. It is ample waterproofing for the house wall.

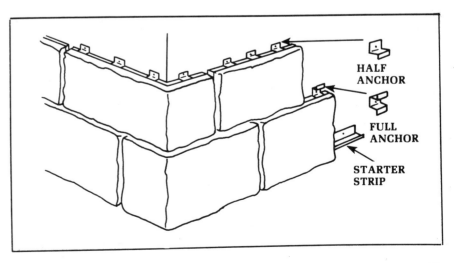

HALF ANCHOR

FULL ANCHOR

STARTER STRIP

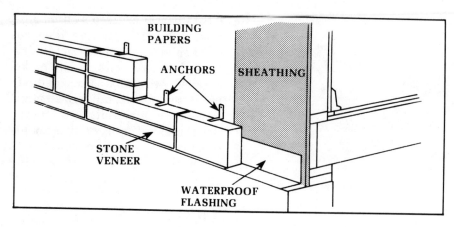

Stone veneer

Q. I have heard there is some genuine stone that can be applied like brick veneer. Could you tell me if this is so?

S.M., Bartow, Fla.

A. You have heard correctly. A number of producers offer various types of genuine stone materials in 3″ or 4″ thicknesses and controlled sizes and finishes for veneer applications similar to brick veneer. You need a footing to support the veneer and masonry anchors are used to tie it to sheathing or masonry backing.

Covering wood siding

Q. Our house sits on cement block foundation walls that rise about 2-1/2′ from the ground to where the wood siding starts. We would like to run bricks or "stone look" siding about 18″ up over the wood siding, starting at ground level. We are concerned about termites if we bring the bricks or siding up over the wood. Is there anything we can use between the original wood siding and cement blocks and the material we use to keep out termites? Also what is the best thing to use to waterproof and finish cement blocks?

H.H., Spearville, Kans.

A. Wood siding covered up in the way you describe will get damp and decay and will certainly attract termites if you have any near you. Try the method suggested by the drawing as one possible way.

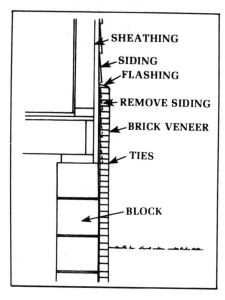

Parging or plastering with a good waterproof cement on both sides can make the walls resistant to moisture and provide a nice finished appearance.

Artificial stone

Q. I would like to install a stone facing on the front of my house using precast stones. In installing the stone over the wire mesh I am wondering if all the weight would be too much burden for the fasteners for the mesh.

W.H., Buffalo, N.Y.

A. Use rustproof nails and secure the mesh to every stud. Overlap mesh sections tightly and nail about 3″ apart. The nails used are usually long, driven about 2/3 of the way in, then bent over and hammered tight. As long as you have the mesh secured rigidly with nonrusting fasteners the weight won't tear it loose.

Corner treatment

Q. We are putting on one row of shingles at a time on the sidewalls of our house but are confused about what to do at the corners. Should the meeting shingles be mitered?

M.S., Cincinnati, Ohio

A. They can be mitered at exterior corners but laced corners are apt to be better and more easily made. Interior corners should be made by nailing a square strip in the corner and butting the side of each shingle against it. To make a laced corner, place the corner shingle in the course first, lining it up with first one wall face and in the next course, the other wall face.

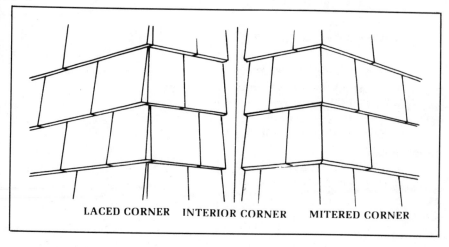

LACED CORNER INTERIOR CORNER MITERED CORNER

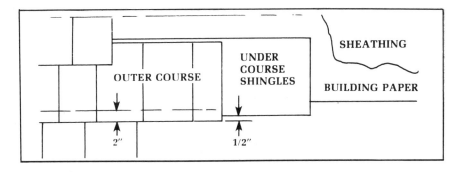

OUTER COURSE | UNDER COURSE SHINGLES | SHEATHING | BUILDING PAPER

2" | 1/2"

culties at door and window trim occur, and it is difficult to lay the shingles neatly. The big reason for leaving them on is avoiding hard work. Taking off clapboards and getting sheathing in shape for shingles takes time and effort. We think you should, as it may disclose the condition which causes the moisture to accumulate behind the clapboards and ruin your paintwork. This should be corrected.

Cedar over paper

Q. I'm building my own ranch house and have used wood sheathing over which I intend to put topgrade cedar shingles. I went to buy tarpaper for the walls under the shingles but the dealer is trying to sell me something else. What should be used?

R.C., McAlister, Okla.

A. If the something else the dealer is trying to sell you is rosinsized sheathing paper, he is correct. He'd be right suggesting unsaturated deadening felt or asbestos paper, too.

Shingle patterns

Q. We want to resurface our clapboard house with cedar shingles. How do we get the deep shadow line, wide shingle effect?

C.S., Oswego, N.Y.

A. That is double coursing, a method of applying the shingles in two layers for each course. More economical than it sounds, it uses a low cost shingle for the concealed layer and 16" or 18" shingles or processed shakes are most often used for the outer layer. Shingles are fastened by butt nailing, one nail about 3/4" in from each edge of a shingle. It is important to use galvanized or other rust resistant nails, 5d small headed type on the outer shingles, a single 3d nail for the undercourse shingle.

Cedar over asphalt

Q. I wish to cover the asphalt shingles of my house with cedar

shingles but I have been told I need felt. Is this so?

L.E., Wilmington, Del.

A. No, put your shingles on over the asphalt ones without felt. There is no more danger of moisture being trapped under them with the asphalt shingles than with felt.

Covering clapboards?

Q. Our home is 12 years old. We now have clapboards but the paint blisters and peels so we want to put on cedar shingles. Should we remove the clapboards before shingling or should we shingle over them? The house is insulated and we wonder if shingling over the present siding would trap moisture in the walls.

J.C., Stoughton, Mass.

A. It would be best in this case to remove the clapboards. It is possible to lay shingles over clapboards but the thickness piles up, diffi-

Time is money

Q. We are completely re-siding our small home this summer but our biggest trouble is lack of time, along with the chronic complaint of lack of money. I thought perhaps you could suggest an exterior surfacing material that would be easy and fairly fast to apply. We have removed old stucco and most of the sheathing will be replaced with the structural insulation board type. Large sheets of plywood would go up faster I know but we prefer a shingled effect.

G.U., Franklinburg, N.Y.

A. Wide lap siding might be your best bet. If you prefer a more rustic look—and more expensive—you might investigate insulated shake units. They are about 4' in length, easy to handle and it only takes 22 or so to cover 100 square feet. Matching nails eliminate time consuming touch-up work and the material comes predecorated.

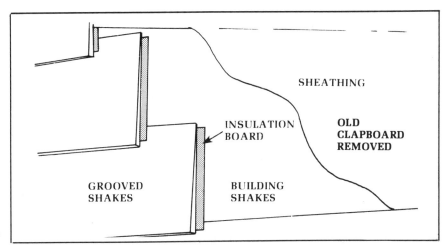

SHEATHING

INSULATION BOARD

OLD CLAPBOARD REMOVED

GROOVED SHAKES

BUILDING SHAKES

Shingles over siding

Q. We would like to put cedar shingles onto our house which is clapboard now, and uninsulated. It is quite old, about 100 years or so. How can this be done? Can insulating board be used under the shingles?

L.H., Amherst, Ohio

A. You can put cedar shingles directly over clapboard siding if

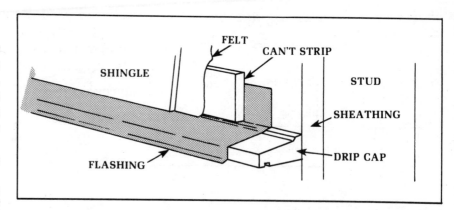

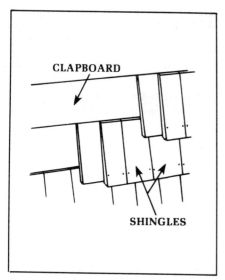

the siding is in reasonably good shape with no evidence of rotting. In so doing you will be adding considerable insulation from this extra material alone. You might also have insulation blown into the clapboard walls by a rock wool insulation contractor. They have the special equipment needed to do this with the minimum openings between studs which they repair when finished with the job. Then install the shingles yourself.

If you plan extensive interior work anyway, you can also break open the interior wall material in each stud space and pour in pellet or pouring insulation yourself. This requires a lot of break and patch work, but if you plan to panel or paper and have a lot of patch work to do anyway, now is the time to do the insulation, too. That, combined with the shingles on the exterior, would give you a well-insulated wall indeed. Of course you'll need storm sash, etc.

Drip cap

Q. I'm re-siding my house with shingles and have a bit of a question about the window heads. Mine have a drip cap now, attached to the wood sheathing. How does the row of shingles fit over it?

R.B., Phoenixville, Pa.

A. Use metal flashing first, over the drip cap, and up the sheathed wall. Then you need a wood cant strip, similar to the strip you started off with at the bottoms of the wall. Then the building felt comes down over that and finally you put that row of shingles in place.

Shingle gaps

Q. Spaces have developed between some of the exterior cedar shakes on the side of my house. How should I fill these in?

S.S., Berkley Heights, N.J.

A. There is no need to fill in spaces in between cedar shakes. The method of alignment and overlapping produces a shingle under the surface one so that the wall is still weathertight. These shingles contract when hot and dry but will swell when wet. Consequently any filler would be squeezed out or make the shingle bulge.

Mildewed shakes

Q. My newly purchased home has three sides covered with as-bestos shakes and one with wood. The wood shakes are on the east side and these have turned gray with mildew. Rather than having to paint one side of the house frequently, I would prefer to replace the wood shakes with asbestos shakes to match the rest of the house. The wood shakes are on the front. I have been told that asbestos shakes don't last. However, the ones on the house are like new but are ten years old.

Do you advise that I use asbestos shakes or would aluminum or vinyl be a better choice?

E.G., Patterson, N.Y.

A. Your problem seems to be an aesthetic one. Are you sure if the grayness of the wood is really mildew rather than the natural coloring of cedar shakes? Are they painted now? If the asbestos cement siding has been on 10 years, the chances of matching it with new siding applied now are not very good. However, this kind of siding lasts well. Your house was probably designed with the idea that the contrasting siding on the front made it look attractive. Give it some more thought before you go to the expense of making the change.

Clapboard repair

Q. I have recently purchased a 65-year-old house apparently not painted for 25 years. Some clapboards are faulty and decayed and there appear to be some leaks through them. How can they be replaced?

J.M., Manchester, N.H.

A. You can replace individual clapboards by first cutting the nails along the bottom edge with a hacksaw blade. Slip under the board, after raising it slightly with a pry bar. In some cases, this will loosen the nails enough to pull them out. Then raise the board above and repeat the nail removal. Slide the defective board out. Replace it with a new one and renail through the one above.

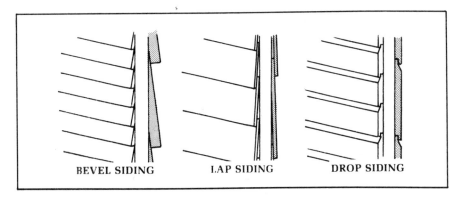

BEVEL SIDING   LAP SIDING   DROP SIDING

Preventing split wood

Q. **How can I prevent clapboards from cracking and splitting when I drive nails into the side of the house? I am sure I use the right size nails. Is it all right to drill holes first and then put the nail in?**

G.W., Bloomfield, N.J.

A. For one thing, you could use coated box nails which are thinner with the same length as common nails and the resin coating makes them hold better. An old trick is to tap the point of the nail first to blunt it a little. This results in less splitting. Drilling holes is all right but slow work. You'll find the going easier if the wood is damp rather than dry and brittle.

Discolored clapboards

Q. **The clapboards of my house have developed a lot of black marks that resemble water dripping on them. I believe this is due to poor insulation. Can you give me any idea of what I can do to correct this condition?**

S.O., Syracuse, N.Y.

A. Poor insulation is not apt to be the cause of this trouble. It may be water dripping from the roof or from a broken or sagging gutter; rain washing down over metal such as screens, exposed nail heads

or other metal attached to the house or water flowing down the sides of the window and door openings. The dirt originates as soot, usually oily. It sticks and stains. The other possibility is mildew on the paint. Either way, bleach and detergent scrubbing prior to repainting is about the only answer.

Sandblasting wood

Q. **We are considering having our wood clapboard house sandblasted to remove the old paint and wonder if you have any tips for us. We want the wood to be smooth, not with ridges resulting from the difference between the hard grain and the softer wood in between.**

A.C., Owings Mills, Md.

A. If you want the wood smooth without wearing away the softer wood while leaving the hard grain standing, don't have it sandblasted. Instead, use a belt sander—and a lot of care.

Sidings

Q. **In going over specifications for our house which we are having built from stock plans, our builder asked did we want bevel siding or lap siding, of wood or plywood or hardboard. Not knowing for sure what he was talking about I told him I'd have to think about it awhile. Could you please tell me what the difference is?**

S.H., Huntington, N.Y.

A. Bevel siding is thicker at the butt than at the top edge. It is made by sawing boards on the diagonal, now is also available with a plywood surface. Lap siding is the same thickness throughout, the overlap occurring in application to provide a closed joint. Both types are made in solid lumber as well as plywood and lap siding is also available in hardboard. Generally, the lap siding is less expensive, may have guide lines for right overlap in installation.

Overlay siding

Q. **Would you please tell me the advantage of overlay siding over lap or bevel siding?**

T.J., Bridgeport, Conn.

A. Bevel and lap siding both refer to shapes of siding boards while overlay refers to a surface treatment given to plywood. It is actually a phenolic resin and cellulose fiber overlay bonded to the plywood which gives a smooth, dense surface that takes less paint and holds it longer than untreated plywood. Overlay plywood siding is available in both lap or bevel styles.

V-grooved siding

Q. **I have seen a sheet or panel material that when painted looks like vertical boarding. Can you tell me what it is and how it is applied? Does it necessarily have to go over sheathing?**

F.B., Cairo, Ill.

A. You probably saw a V-grooved hardboard that very much resembles vertical boards from a little distance. It can be applied over sheathing or directly on 2x4 studs on 16" centers where it meets the requirements of FHA. All panel edges must be positioned on framing members. This is a shiplap joint and is fastened with galvanized box nails, 6d if no sheathing or wood sheathing is used, 8d for other sheathing materials. Space nails 6" apart on vertical joints, 12" apart at intermediate studs and at center between grooves at top and bottom edges. Caulk butted joints. Panels are factory primed and back painted. Be sure to paint all edges well.

Rusty siding

Q. The nails holding the siding to my house have rusted and are staining it. There was apparently no attempt made to countersink these nails. What is the most practical and economical way to correct this?

D.Y., Akron, Ohio

A. You can countersink the nails now and fill the resulting holes with putty or caulking compound before repainting. Or you can shellac the nail heads but this requires removal of paint from the nail heads first to make the shellac effective. Neither method costs much.

Dry rot

Q. Can you tell me what causes dry rot? I have heard it is caused by dampness.

R.N., Brooklyn, N.Y.

A. Dry rot is caused by a fungus that grows best in conditions of alternate drying and excess moisture. It spreads along the softer grain line of wood and eventually reduces it to an almost weightless, sponge-like consistency of little or no strength.

Expansion strips

Q. I was reading about expansion strips for hardboard siding. These go between the ends of adjacent siding pieces. The strips do not seem to be available locally. Can you tell me where I can get them?

D.L., Pueblo, Colo.

A. These strips are inserted as the siding is applied. An accessory item like this would not normally be found in hardware stores, but in a home center or building materials yard where the siding is purchased. They should be ordered to "come with" the siding you select, not purchased later. If you have a specific problem, write the manufacturer of the siding you are using.

Board and batten

Q. The exterior of my house is cedar board and batten. The 1x12 boards, planed one side, rough the other, were butted and nailed along the edges. A 1-5/8" wide batten was stapled over these vertical joints, hiding the nails. The boards have cracked and split loose at the nails, and the battens are working loose. What went wrong?

M.M., Plaquemine, La.

A. The 1x12 boards are going to move as they dry out. There is bound to be some shrinkage and cupping. Since you have nailed the edges down tightly, there is nothing else for the wood to do but split. There's enough movement so the battens work loose, too.

Proper installation makes allowances for this movement. One way this is done is to nail down the center of the wide boards, hold their edges protectively with batten strips that are nailed between the board edges.

Log cabin repairs

Q. My log cabin was built in 1945 by an amateur. The logs aren't perfectly straight, resulting in many big cracks between them. The logs were chinked with small sticks and oakum, then caulked. Because of shrinkage in both logs and caulk, I've been patching ever since. How can I reduce or stop this constant maintenance, yet retain the log appearance?

G.B., Lake, Mich.

A. It may be time to remove and replace mortar and chinking. If chinking is loosening, repack the oakum joints with new material, then apply new caulk to a clean surface. Repair one joint at a time; don't remove everything at once. Once repaired, it should need minimal attention in future years, but give it an annual checkup.

Peeling paint

Q. No matter what kind of paint I put on the outside of my house, it peels. What is the problem?

J.T., Geneva, Ohio

A. If your house is wood-sided and you are careful to scrape off any loose paint before repainting, the most probable cause of your

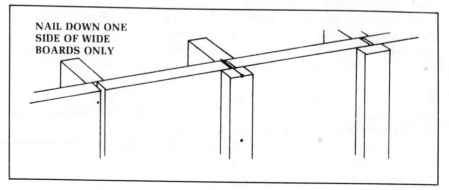

NAIL DOWN ONE
SIDE OF WIDE
BOARDS ONLY

problem is excessive moisture. You will have to track down and solve the cause of the wetness, then remove loose or peeling paint, prepare the surface and paint again.

A booklet called "The Menace of Moisture" may help you track down possible causes of excessive moisture. It was put out a few years ago by what is now the National Paint and Coatings Ass'n., 1500 Rhode Island Ave., N.W., Washington, D.C., 20005.

Flashing problem

Q. I have a problem in my 18-year-old house where a lower portion of the roof meets the siding. I removed all old paint and put on a good oil-base primer and finish coat last summer and the paint is peeling off again. I have enclosed a sketch to help explain the situation, and am wondering if the flashing was installed properly—it goes under the vertical siding and behind it. Moisture gets under the siding and into the wood. I caulked the area where the asbestos siding meets the wood last summer to no avail. Do you have a solution to my problem?

J.C., Lexington, Neb.

A. One thing that is noteworthy in your sketch is that the flashing is *under* the roof covering. The

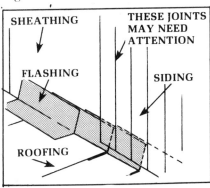

highest layer of flashing should always be on top of the abutting roof surfacing with the siding on top of that. Instead of trying to make a watertight joint between the surfacing and the siding backed by flashing, you should leave a

gap, allowing the flashing to work as shown.

Moisture problem

Q. Moisture escapes through the siding in my home. While recently drilled holes under the eaves have improved conditions, I am searching for a permanent solution. Would foam insulation inside the wall or outside board insulation covered with siding help me?

E.S., Canastola, N.Y.

A. Your real problem is reducing the relative humidity. For this, foam insulation doesn't help, and, in fact, by absorbing the moisture, it would rot the siding. Drill-

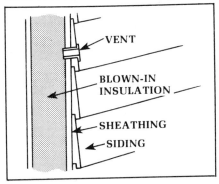

ing vent holes under the eaves was a good first step and to conserve heat, insulate, first in the attic and then in the sidewalls. The blown-in method, using mineral wool to insulate and installing the proper venting in each stud space can be done for you by most firms specializing in this work. While applying board insulation covered with shingles or sidings will also work, the blown-in method is better.

Moist siding

Q. We recently purchased an older two-story home. On the north side of the house we noticed that the paint was peeling and underneath the wood looks and feels moist. There are outside stairs above this area but there are no water pipes near it. We would like to paint the exterior

but wish to correct this problem before proceeding. Could you help us?

J.M., Delta, Ohio

A. You are right in correcting the dampness problem before painting the exterior. You don't need water pipes to have a leakage problem. You may have moisture at the bottom of your steps. It is difficult to track down a leak long distance, but we suggest that you look along the roof edge (you didn't say whether this is the gable end) under and around windows and of course along the house side of the stairway. You may get a clue from the pattern formed where the paint is peeling the worst. Be sure to scrape off excess material before painting and seal and prime the area after you stop the leakage.

Stuccoing concrete

Q. I am ready to stucco the foundation of my porch which is built of concrete block topped with a concrete slab floor. I would appreciate your advice on the procedure for applying the stucco.

M.S., Wilmington, Del.

A. Dig a small trench about 4" deep all around the foundation. This will give you room to apply the stucco without getting dirt mixed in it. Take a hose and wash down the exposed foundation thoroughly, leaving it wet. Mix 2-1/2 to 3 parts sand and 1 part portland cement with enough water to make a non-crumbling mass that doesn't run. When a trowel tip run over the surface causes water to ooze out, you know it's right. Trowel this mixture onto the wall about 3/8" thick. Work from the bottom up with a steel float and press the stucco into the block surface firmly at first, then smooth off. After a few hours, wet with a very fine spray. Keeping it wet in this manner for two or three days will allow the stucco to cure much harder. After curing, replace the earth in the trench.

Patching at corner

Q. I've been trying to get a good looking patch at the corner of our stucco-over-concrete block house without success. What is the secret?

L.S., Peoria, Ill.

A. Assuming you are using a proper mix and applying the stucco to clean, wet block, the trick is simple. Just press a length of 1x2 against the side not being worked and build up the stucco on the other side out to it. When you turn the corner, hold the stick against the freshly stuccoed side and run the stucco out to the stick again. This will give you a neat and sharply defined corner.

Resurfacing stucco

Q. I would like to improve the appearance of the stucco on my house. It is 10 years old and very dirty. Shall I spray a new coat of stucco over the old?

R.W., St. Paul, Minn.

A. You can't spray new stucco over a dirty, old coat as the dirt will prevent the new coat from adhering. Any treatment to make the old one a good base for new stucco might very well reveal it to be in good condition and clean again. The treatment used can be a mild sand-blasting, a steam cleaning or a rub-down with muriatic acid. This last method is one which you can handle yourself, if you are careful to protect your skin and eyes from the acid.

Stucco failure

Q. I have a home with a stucco exterior. Large chunks are coming off and the metal lath has rusted and pulled away from the wall. Can I fix it myself?

J.C., LaSalle, Ill.

A. You'll have to remove the old coating and the rusted wire lath and start over. Begin with new tarpaper covering over the wood supports and then new wire lath. Over this you may trowel plain cement, forcing it deeply into the wire lath. Stop about 1/4" to 1/8" from flush to leave room for the new stucco coat. As the cement coat dries, crosshatch to roughen the surface for keying on the stucco coating. Use at least 2-1/2 to 3 parts of sand to 1 part stucco cement which must include a waterproofing agent. Wet the base coat with a hose spray, then smooth on the stucco mix. Work it in and level off flush with the old surface.

Patching stucco

Q. The bottom edge of my stucco walls is crumbling and can be broken off with the fingers. Is there any way I can patch this?

C.B., Downey, Calif.

A. Don't patch loose stucco. The patch will merely pull off more of the old material. Circle the house with a mason's hammer, knocking off all the loose stucco. If it sounds hollow when tapped, chip it off. Soak the remaining sound stucco with a hose, after digging a small trench below grade all around the foundation. The new coat should extend that deep if the bottom edge is to be concealed. Apply the new mix to the wet wall and don't fill in the trench for a few days. Since you'll need to match the new stucco to the old anyway, apply a waterproof paint before backfilling.

Putting up vinyl

Q. After receiving incredibly high estimates from contractors, I have decided that the costs warrant a do-it-myself installation of vinyl siding on my home. Can you provide any information on this?

J.H., Rantoul, Ill.

A. Putting up vinyl siding would be basically similar to putting up wood clapboard siding. However, you need the specifications and the installation information that is provided from the manufacturer of the vinyl siding you will use. One should not buy building materials unless complete instructions from the manufacturer on the proper installation of the material accompany the purchase. Insist on complete information and if necessary, write to the company prior to making your purchase.

Vinyl-clad steel

Q. Some time ago I bought vinyl-covered steel siding from a magazine ad, but I have never received the application directions. Now that I need them, I can't find the information anywhere. Where can I write?

W.W., Raymond, Wash.

A. Allside, Inc., P.O. Box 2010, Akron, Ohio 44309 makes this type of siding. If you'll write to the V.P. Sales, at that address, requesting the information you need, it will be sent to you.

Aluminum covering

Q. Our church is considering re-siding the manse with aluminum siding. The existing wood lap siding does have some paint and mildew problems. Some members are concerned about continued deterioration. Is their concern justified?

D.J., Grundy Center, Iowa

A. The members are rightfully concerned. You do not cure a problem simply by covering it up. Mildew and many paint problems often indicate the presence of moisture where it shouldn't be. Check for leaks, eliminate the source of humid air (or allow it to escape without damage), kill the mildew, etc.—then consider re-siding.

Door Problems

Basement doors...Burglar proofing...Construction...Folding... Glass...Locks...Mirrors...Repair...Sliding...Stormdoors...Weatherstripping...Wrought iron.

Basement entrance

Q. We need direct access outdoors from our basement now that it is finished. You can get in through the attached garage at the front of the house but then have to go through the house to get to the back yard. There the basement floor is about 6′ below grade. Is it much of a job to install one of those metal cellar door units?

R.C., Pittsburgh, Pa.

A. It is not easy work to install a cellar entrance but it is a fairly simple job, and usually worth the effort in convenience. First you have to dig to expose part of the house foundation, then erect a retaining wall or bulkhead to hold back the earth. Breaking through the foundation for the entrance door can be made easier if you rent a pneumatic hammer with or without labor to use it. Carrying the bulkhead 6″ above grade and installing the basement entrance door should present no problems and the stairs necessary can be provided quickly with steel stringers attached to the bulkhead walls into which you tap 2x10 stock treads. Proper flashing and fastening of the metal unit is a matter of following the manufacturer's instructions carefully.

New cellar doors

Q. We have one of those old-fashioned houses with the wood cellar doors. The basement is not usable for much as the ceiling is low, but the doors form one side of our otherwise attractive terrace. Can those cellar door units be used to replace the wood ones? I think it would look better.

A.S., Kittaning, Pa.

A. Generally the answer is yes. You need a foundation wall sufficiently strong to support the unit and of a size to suit one of the standard units made. There is a variety of sizes and shapes available. You'd do well to measure carefully the masonry you have presently, discounting the wood superstructure which would be removed, and consult a local dealer. Meanwhile a light fence wall or simply a row of potted plants might camouflage your unattractive cellarway.

Leaking cellar door

Q. I am having a problem of leakage through joints around my outdoor cellarway. This is a metal unit and I didn't think they were supposed to leak.

C.F., Midland, Ontario

A. The possible leakage points of such a door unit would most likely be at the top along the house wall, a point that should have been given the usual flashing treatment at the time of installation. Depending on your exterior wall covering, you may be able to install this flashing properly now or use plastic flashing to cover the joint. The second possible point would be along the joint between sidewalls and the concrete base. This can be caulked on the outside and probably inside too. If the doors themselves leak, that is a matter for the manufacturer of the unit.

Shorter door

Q. I am building a partition wall in the basement beneath the floor beam. I would like to close off a sewing center behind the wall with bifold, louvered doors. The problem is that the beam and furnace plenums on either side of it measure only 75″ from the floor. I am unable to find doors in anything less than the standard 6'8" height. Can louvered doors be unglued, shortened, then reassembled?

W.M., Minneapolis, Minn.

A. You should be able to trim off the bottom and perhaps the top of a door to make it the right height. You will need to take off 5", perhaps 3-3/4" at the bottom and 1-1/4" at the top would do it. Your idea of taking the shutter door apart is also a possibility. We do not know of any source for non-standard doors, so you might have to get them made locally.

Burglarproof hinges

Q. How can one burglar-proof the pin in the hinge of a door that opens outwards?

G.C., Fayetteville, N.C.

A. Burglar-proofing the hinge pin on hinges installed as you've shown them would not be very effective. Any self-respecting burglar would just unscrew the hinge leaf and take it off along with the door.

If the hinges were butt hinges properly installed, you could drill and pin through the jamb leaf into the hinge pin blind if you did it with the door a bit open as in Sketch A, or through if you did it with the door shut as in Sketch B.

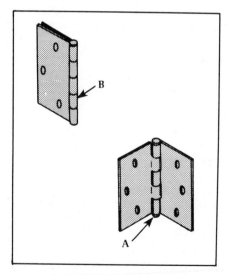

You can also pretty well guarantee a hinge pin will never come out if you peen over the end of it, but you have to be able to work on the hinge to do this.

If it is a pintle-type hinge, setting one up and one down does discourage people a bit. (It can keep a gate safe from Halloween kids for years), but it will not stop the determined thief.

Door in partition

Q. We plan a frame partition in our basement and will need to put a doorway in it. Is this done the same in the basement as in other parts of the house?

H.J., Pontiac, Mich.

MAKE SURE YOU HAVE THE SILL ON EITHER SIDE OF THE OPENING ATTACHED FIRMLY TO THE CONCRETE SLAB WITH SUITABLE FASTENERS

A. Essentially the same except you have no threshold. Build your frame partition as usual, leaving out the plate where the door is to go. At the doorway set a double stud on each side of the opening. Line the opening with 1" pine and hang the door in this framed opening. Run wall materials to the frame. Cover joint with casing as desired.

Making a door

Q. How would you recommend making a frame for a hollow core flush door with tempered hardboard faces so that the corner joints are invisible yet strong when the frame is covered?

D.C., Cleveland, Ohio

A. For a completely invisible joint, miter the corners and join with blind dowels glued in with brads set into the dowels on each side of the joint.

Window to door

Q. I want to remove a window and make a doorway to the yard. I think the window is about the same width as a door should be but the wall is solid brick. How do I go about this job?

R.D., Johnsonburg, Pa.

A. Start by removing the whole window and its rough frame, including the sill. Then enlarge the opening to door size, use a mason's hammer and a broad chisel. Start at the center of one side of the opening, removing one brick at a time and the mortar. In each alternate course, leave half of the brick sticking into the opening. Then go back and score these carefully all around before you snap them off with the mason's hammer. A little chisel work will finish any rough edges. Continue till the opening is a bit below the inside floor, as you have to allow for a cement cap over the wall to bring it to proper level. Set a metal threshold in the cement. The rough wood door frame of 1" stock is seated in mortar after pretreatment with preservative.

New door

Q. I'd like to hang a new exterior door using a wide window as my basic opening, but I'm not sure how to rough-frame it. Can you help?

A.K., East Lansing, Mich.

A. First you remove the window, its frame and all material inside and out to expose the house framing and rough window frame, as in the top sketch. This done, you can proceed to cut and add studs as necessary to end up with the rough door frame as shown in the lower sketch.

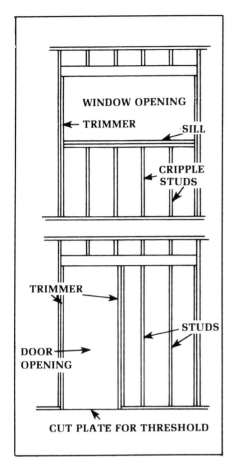

WINDOW OPENING

TRIMMER

SILL

CRIPPLE STUDS

TRIMMER

DOOR OPENING

STUDS

CUT PLATE FOR THRESHOLD

Opening aluminum

Q. We wish to put in a new door. There is aluminum siding on the house and we want to know how to cut it.

K.H., Lima, Ind.

A. You can cut the siding with an ordinary hack saw blade or with a utility saw that cuts metal or wood. This will do it if there is no wood sheathing under the metal. If there is wood sheathing it would be best to make a vertical cut in the scrap portion with tin snips, then bend both sections back and make a neat cut at the new edges of the opening. Remove the sheathing by cutting the sides of the new opening with a wood saw. Removal of the interior surface to the floor line will make this work easier.

Door to garage

Q. I wish to cut a door through my living room wall into my garage for easy access. Any information you can give me will be welcome.

A.L., Fair Lawn, N.J.

A. First of all check your local fire regulations in regard to such an opening. The door may have to be metal-clad or otherwise fireproofed or the project may be prohibited entirely. Some flush doors filled with asbestos fiber are considered fire safe. The procedure for installation, if permitted, is the same as for any other door.

Door framing

Q. I am starting to finish my "unfinished" second floor and have a question to which I can find no answer. It is: What should the width be between the 2x4s (studs) and the height from subfloor to header for a 32″ x 6′8″ door?

J.G., Cincinnati, Ohio

A. Door is framed as sketched. The space between double studs is 2″ wider than the door width; allow 1″ for top frame placed against header and 1″ for finish flooring. If you are putting a threshold in the doorway, add its thickness to the vertical measurement.

Interior doors

Q. Our problem is to make a door from the front hall into a bedroom. We are anxious to get details from beginning to end.

D.H., Stoneham, Mass.

A. Choose the door size first, then mark an opening large enough to allow for the door, a 1″ frame on each side, a double 2x4 on each side of that. Score the plaster with a sharp pointed tool on the mark, then break the plaster at the center of the opening with a hammer and start removing it in chunks to the marked line. It's best to make the opening alongside one wall stud against which the second short stud on that side can be nailed. Cut away plaster on both sides until studs are bared. Interior doors are usually 6′8″ high, and you will need 1″ framing above it plus 4″ for a double 2x4 lintel. Add 1″ more if you want a threshold. Cut the intervening studs at this point. Then frame the opening with the double 2x4 lintel and the double studs at each side. The lintel rests on the trimmer studs and the floor plate butts against them. Inside framing of the opening should be the thickness of the studs plus the thickness of the plaster on both sides. The header is first nailed up,

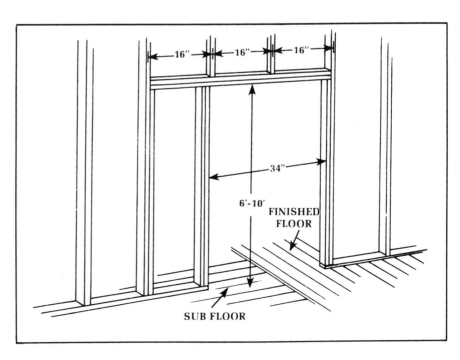

16″ 16″ 16″

34″

6′-10′

FINISHED FLOOR

SUB FLOOR

then the sides under it, all pieces attached with finishing nails to the studs and lintel. The casing is then put on, offset 1/8" and nailed to the frame on one edge and to the studs on the other. It should conceal plaster breaks. You can purchase a standard strip of door stop which is then cut and nailed to both sides and the header, after which the door is hung. Most interior doors can be hung with two butt hinges. You can use no-mortise hinges to save time. All bare wood should be given one and preferably two coats of shellac, then painted or varnished to match other wood trim.

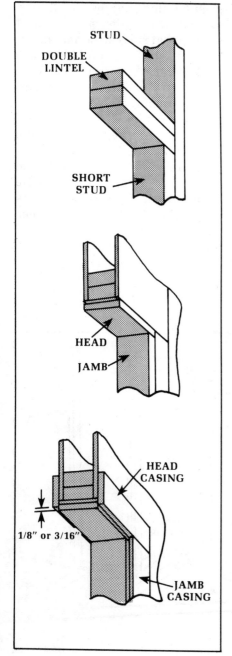

Make flush doors

Q. **Our house has all old fashioned four-panel doors. Is there some way to modernize them like building up the panel recesses?**

A.J., Greensboro, N.C.

A. You can convert the doors to flush doors by covering both sides with 1/4" plywood or with hardboard. First remove varnish. Then attach the new surfacing material with glue and brads spaced 3" apart along all edges and across the center rail. Since this makes the door thicker, you'll have to reset the stop strips.

Home-made door

Q. **We need a bathroom door but it is a very narrow, odd size. We can't afford to have it custom made. Can you tell us how to make one?**

F.D., Gary, Ind.

A. You can make a serviceable door, using a rectangular frame of 1x4 clear pine with a single cross brace at the center and 1x2 X-braces in the upper and lower halves. To reduce the chance of warping, join the framework with 1/4" hardwood dowels and glue. Attach 1/4" plywood to both sides of the framework with glue and brads spaced 3" apart and set in 3/4" from the outer edges.

Reversing a door

Q. **What is the easiest way to change the way a door opens?**

M.B., Williamsburgh, Iowa

A. First remove the door stop, then the hinge pins and the door. Remove the hinges from the door and the frame. If you want to swing the door out when it swung in before, simply reverse the hinges with the pin side opposite to its first position and remount the door. You'll have to reverse the latch too so the flat side still meets

the striker plate properly and usually you'll have to relocate the striker plate. If you want to set the lock and the hinges so the door swings open to the opposite hand, turn the door around and relocate hinges on the opposite frame, and, if you change the direction of swing, repeat as outlined above. Once the door is rehung, replace the stop strips, latch side strip first, then top, then hinge side.

Dog door

Q. **I would appreciate any ideas you might have on how to make a two-way door for my dogs. It would have to fit between 16" studs in the outside walls. I've seen some plastic ones but did not particularly like them.**

E.W., Richmondville, N.Y.

A. You should be able to build a simple, hinged-at-the-top style

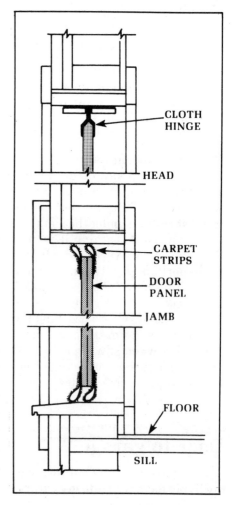

dog door yourself. The section drawings show how you might go at it. Size the opening to fit the dog and allow 6" or more above shoulder height so the door need not be fully opened each time. Make the panel proper somewhat smaller than the opening. You can make a top hinge of two strips of heavy fabric like canvas or duck. Weatherstrip the other three edges. Folded strips of carpet make a reasonably good seal that isn't too damaging to a slow-moving dog though they will require periodic replacement. If you want to get fancy, consider an insulated door panel.

Folding door

Q. Is it very difficult to install a folding door in a doorway now occupied by a swinging door?
S.F., Little Falls, Minn.

A. If the doorway is square, the job is quite simple. Remove present door, pry off door stops. Cut track to 1/8" less than inside measurement of doorway. Align overhead and mark for holes. Drill, and after sliding runners onto track, install track. Secure one edge of folding door to frame. Explicit details are usually given on installation diagrams accompanying these products.

Steel frame

Q. In redecorating my room, I wish to put in a folding door but my father says this cannot be done since the door frame is steel. How can I put a folding door in?
H.B., Flushing, N.Y.

A. With a high speed electric drill and a metal drill bit, make 1/4" diameter holes in the header for wood plugs or lead plugs to hold screws for attaching the folding door track. Three holes should be sufficient here but match them up if there are predrilled holes in the door track. You'll need at least one

hole on the side to anchor one side of the folding door and perhaps one or more on the opposite side if there is a latch. Some types of folding doors are complete with their own jamb and header pieces but you'd have to drill more holes to use this variety.

Shallow closet

Q. I have a closet under 24" deep and with only a regular door. We had considered putting in an accordian or a folding wood door till we found out they take up room from front to back when folded that would cut down the depth even more. I want to open the wall the full 36" and put in some kind of doors, not sliding, that will make it more accessible. Are two hinged doors the best I can do?
E.D., Teaneck, N.J.

A. Two hinged doors will do the job for you and at about 18" wide each would certainly not be unmanageable. However, you might consider bi-folding doors which would let you fold back two 9" panels on each side.

Folding shutter doors

Q. We have seen some of these shutter doors that just fold in half. How are they installed?
T.N., Sioux City, Iowa

A. The bi-fold hardware sets that make shutter doors fold in half vary some from one manufacturer to another and installation depends a bit on whether the doors come with the package or not. The first step would be to hinge the two panel pairs together properly. Fasten pivots at top and bottom jamb-side corners of each pair and the pivot assembly that will ride in the overhead track in the top meeting corner. There is probably an aligning device to install at the bottom, eliminating the need for any floor track. When you have the opening prepared, align the track on the

centerline and attach it to the head frame. Trim strips may be used to conceal the hardware if desired. Insert the doors in the track and make necessary adjustments in pivot mountings and aligner.

Glass door leaks

Q. The sliding glass patio door in my 10-year-old home has evidently sprung a leak. How can I eliminate the moisture that collects between the glass panels of this thermopane-type door?
E.M., Pittsburgh, Pa.

A. You can't. Thermopane™, Twindow™ and similar insulating glass panels are factory-sealed and there is no reasonable do-it-yourself method to repair them.

Log cabin lock

Q. Do you know how to make a "combination lock" with a latch string? I am building a log cabin and would like very much to use a latch string on my front door. Someone once told me about adjusting the latch string so that only the person knowing how could open the door. Please send instructions if you can.
T.W., Sedalia, Mo.

A. If you try to make a combination lock with a latch string, someone will yank hard enough to break

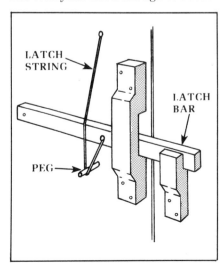

the string and then where will you be? You could, however, run the latch string under a peg or hook in such a way that you'd have to loosen the string to free it from the peg (or pull the peg out from outside) before pulling to lift the latch (see sketch). What is indexed as a "Combination Lock" is described in *"How to Build Your Home in the Woods"*—a very good little paperback by Bradford Angier,(Hart Publishing). This unique frontier lock involves a series of blocks that engage a groove in the door jamb. Unless all are turned just so, the door does not open. The latch string they mention is called a "secret lock." The "secret" is to find the latch string!

Mirror mounting

Q. **Can you please tell me how to hang a full length mirror on a plywood door? Some say it can't be done since the door is hollow.**

C.H., Hawthorne, N.Y.

A. The outer edge of the door is solid wood, about 3" wide. If your mirror reaches that, four clips can be used all around to hold it. If not, clips can be set into the core with special anchors at desired points.

Warped door

Q. **We have an old house and one of the solid oak doors has a bad warp. I have considered soaking it with water and then trying to flatten it out, but wonder if this is the best solution. The door is about 32" x 80" and I can't replace it. Can you give me any advice?**

J.R., Terre Haute, Ind.

A. Sometimes, if luck is with you, you can straighten a warped door. Take it off the hinges and lay it on sawhorses with the warped side up. Apply weight (concrete blocks are good) on the bellied-up area and check often to see if you are making any headway. You

must also try to stop the cause of warping. It may be that the finish on one side or the other of the door is not keeping moisture out. Perhaps the edges of the door are not very well sealed and allow moisture to penetrate there. Whatever you may find along these lines that can be remedied will help keep the door flat once you've managed to get it flat with the weights.

Stuck door

Q. **We have a door that sticks some at the bottom. Is there any way to fix it without using a plane and cutting into the finish?**

S.A., Chevy Chase, Md.

A. You bend the hinges. If the door is sticking at the bottom, take the top hinge off first. Put this hinge (with pin still in place) into a vise. Let the pin part of the hinge stick up out of the vise, with the two halves of the hinge in the vise. Then, with a hammer, bend the hinge so that when its re-installed it will raise up the door. If the sticking is other than at the bottom of the door, you bend the hinge or hinges as required.

Swollen door

Q. **I have a solid wood door with one glass pane next to my overhead garage door. In the winter a 3/8" gap appears at the top and the door sticks so tight on the sides it is almost impossible to open or close. The rest of the year it is fine. How can I fix this? I don't want to plane it as it works the rest of the year. Would weep holes in the edge be of any help? The edges are painted.**

E.V. Irvington, N.Y.

A. You blame the door only. How about the frame? You may discover the stop strip is loose and water gets under it, penetrates the raw wood and swells strip and frame. Remove the stop strips and paint the frame under them and the back of the strips. Replace the stop

strips. Check the door to be sure it is sealed and painted on the top and bottom edges. This will prevent moisture from entering through the end grain and swelling the door.

Sagging doors

Q. **One of my doors sags badly although I used three hinges in installation. There is a gap of almost 1/2" at the top and it rubs against the threshold at the bottom. I planed the threshold which helped for a while but it is again becoming difficult to close the door.**

D.M., Hunkers, Pa.

A. It seems likely that the frame around your door is changing shape due to shrinkage and settling of the house frame. Try setting the top hinge deeper by cutting out the mortise. Put one or more strips of cardboard under the jamb leaf of the bottom hinge. This should bring the door more nearly true in the frame. You can raise the threshold by removing it and setting the tapered end of a piece of siding under it, then replacing threshold. If you still find distortion you might correct it by trimming the door.

Clearance for doors

Q. **I understand that 5/8" is standard clearance between the bottom of inside doors and the floor. All our doors are about 1/2". Is it important to take off the other 1/8"?**

J.V., Gary, Ind.

A. That 1/8" can be totally ignored. There may be a rule for initial construction to take care of shrinkage and settling of the frame and to allow for a possible threshold or as clearance for deep-pile carpets. But if your doors are not scratching the floors, there is no reason to worry about the exact dimension. Occasionally doors are cut up 1" or so for reasons of ventilation or cold air return, but on the other hand they are often made close fitting to lessen sound transfer.

Door bottom clearance

Q. **We have to do something about trimming a bit off the bottom of our flush doors as they are marking our brand new carpet. I'm afraid I'll damage the door faces. Is there a technique that will avoid this?**

V.P., Hollywood, Calif.

A. Not really a trick, if you have a plane. Cut an 1/8" bevel along each edge, directing the plane at an angle of 45° away from the center of the door, across the grain of the plywood. Then plane away the resultant 1/8" of exposed core frame wood without damage to the plywood faces. If an 1/8" off won't be enough, increase the bevel.

Warped sliding doors

Q. **I thought plywood never warped. We have four sliding door panels across our closet wall and they are all out of whack. We had them off the hangers to apply that louver pattern wallpaper and I wonder if in replacing the hangers we might have done something wrong.**

E.T. Scarsdale, N.Y.

A. You may well have disturbed the adjustment in replacing the hangers. You probably have the type mounting with slotted holes for leveling the doors. You might check that point though it would have little to do with warping. Where you went astray there is in applying wallpaper to one side only. Plywood is a balanced construction and what you do to one side you should do to the other. You did not note the thickness used which would have some bearing and you may not have sealed and painted the exposed edges. Properly treated plywood

does not warp but if you permit moisture to be absorbed and there is any variation of temperature inside and outside the closet, warping may be assured.

Sliding door mirrors

Q. **I would like to close off my kitchen from the living room area by installing a sliding panel door. However, the area to the left of my opening (not an archway) is covered with decorative mirror squares. I want to cover the left side of the opening with these same mirror squares as well as the sliding panel door. This would give me a complete mirrored wall when the sliding panel door is covering the opening. Is this feasible? How would I install the mirrored sliding door?**

L.B., Denver, Colo.

A. Your idea is quite feasible. To compensate for the added thickness of the mirrors you should use 3/4" plywood for the panel instead of 1". You also will probably need a heavier tracking due to the added weight of the mirrors. Apply the mirrors with a strong mastic cement to the plywood very carefully. You might also want to run a plastic guide on the floor next to the panel to keep it on track. Having the door slip off its tracking could be disastrous for the mirrors.

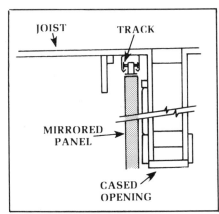

New sliding door

Q. **I would like to install a new sliding door in an exterior load-bearing wall that now has a win-**

dow and a warm air heating duct under it. What procedure should I follow?

J.L., Lee's Summit, Mo.

A. Measure the width and height of the new door and remove a corresponding area of plasterboard from the inside wall and the sheathing and siding of the outside wall. What you will then see will probably look like the first diagram.

Remove the existing studs and install a new header of two 2x6s or 2x8s standing on edge and resting

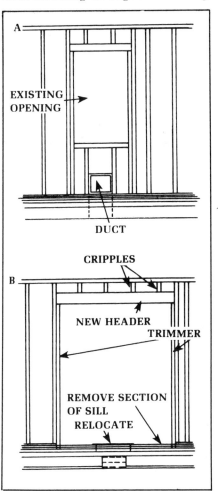

on the trimmer studs as shown in the second (lower) diagram. You will also have to remove part of the sill plate on the floor and move the warm-air duct to an opening in the floor in front of the door. Since you are working with a loadbearing wall don't forget to temporarily shore up the existing ceiling plate (horizontal 2x4) until you get the header in.

Storage doors

Q. I want to put some 4' x 4' sliding panels along the knee-wall of my attic for access to the storage space behind. Would 3/4" plywood be suitable for this?

E.V., Ridgewood, N.J.

A. You should think twice about using panels this wide. Even if you run your insulation between the storage area and the roof, you probably won't be supplying heat to the closet area directly. Those panels are not apt to remain true. Even 2' wide panels this high would be better as rolling doors hung with top mounted hardware to run on a track at the top. Plywood is suitable material, but it must be thoroughly sealed, including the edges.

Sliding closet door

Q. I would like to change and enlarge the door on a closet to a pair of sliding doors but am not familiar with the framework that is necessary to accomplish my purpose. It is a plywood paneled wall here and I don't know what pieces to take off or where to cut.

J.U., Mechanic Falls, Maine

A. First take the door off its hinges. Then remove the casings which will expose the door frame. Remove the frame pieces and if there is a saddle, that too. You'll see the rough framing and note that the lintel rests on a short stud at both ends and butts against a full height stud next to the short ones. Remove the lintel. Pry carefully from the inside so you don't disturb the wood paneling over the doorway. At the side you will increase, remove the short stud and cut the long one even with the remaining one over the opening. Saw STRAIGHT across the plywood to the new door opening width. If you don't stop on a full stud, insert one. Also insert a short stud inside the opening next to the full stud. Across the top run a new

lintel the proper length. Renail the paneling to the new lintel. You'll need new frame stock and new casings to finish off the opening for your new doors. Track, rollers and floor aligner are installed according to what type hardware you select.

Pocket door

Q. How can I make a swinging door into a sliding door that goes into a pocket?

J.S., Lynchburg, Pa.

A. To make a door that slides into a pocket, you have to take down the wall itself as high as the door and as deep as the door must slide in, so that the studs can be replaced with two matching 1x4 or 1x6 verticals between which the door can slide. The lintel over the door is removed and replaced with a longer one which reaches to the back of the pocket to support the sliding door hardware and the door. It's best to install small rollers or tiny wheels along the bottom of the door to guide it away from the sides of the pocket. You also need special hardware for a handle to pull the door out.

Sliding doors

Q. I want to install a sliding door in an interior wall. Can you give me some idea how this may be done?

L.D., Schwenksville, Pa.

A. You can get pre-framed pocket or sliding doors at your local lumber yard. The existing wall must be opened up to accommodate the width of the unit, and a double header installed above the door as mentioned directly above. It's best to buy or at least measure the unit you want to install before framing the rough opening, to be sure of a fit. Then install the door plumb in the opening.

If you're fairly handy it's not too tough a job. The major pitfall is in

noting that the nailers which run horizontally to the door frame are only 3/4" material. Don't use nails in the wallboard so long that you penetrate completely through both the wallboard and the nailers, or you'll ruin your door. The best bet for fastening wallboard to the nailers is to use stud adhesives and 7/8"-long wallboard screws.

Wood grille

Q. I am interested in making a sliding door from a decorative wood grille. I know that there is a company known as the Stanwood Corp. which makes these grilles. Can you give me their address?

R.F., Middletown, Conn.

A. The address is Stanwood Corp., 711 N. Broadway, Stanley, Wis. 54768.

Storm door

Q. Can you suggest a way to make a storm door out of a wooden crossbuck door? I can replace the screen in the opening with Plexiglas and trim, but I need to put a trim around the edges to make a flange like a storm door.

G.E., Chattanooga, Tenn.

A. The wooden storm doors we've seen have no flange, but fit into and against the door frame, as shown. If you can exchange the present screen for plastic and hold it in securely, there's no reason why your wood crossbuck door can't serve as a storm door too.

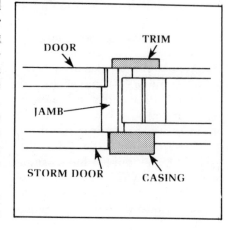

Your existing exterior door should be well weatherstripped to take advantage of the dead air space between the two doors.

Bowed door sill

Q. The door sill of my front door started to get a bow in it which caused the storm door to bind. I planed down the sill once but the bow continues to get worse. Can you advise me how this sill can be replaced and is it too much of a job to undertake?

B.K., Tinley Park, Ill.

A. The original door sill was probably cut too snug. Upon swelling from water absorption it took the only path open—up. The best way to replace a sill involves complete dismantling of the door frame. Remove the door first, then the casings from both sides and the threshold. This will reveal the door frame resting on the threshold and must come off to pry up the sill. Since the header jamb is attached to the sides, it is also removed. Get a new sill identical to the old one but cut ends so there is at least 1/2" clearance between sill and studs and then reassemble the door. If you withdrew all nails through the back of each part you will have no trouble using the parts again.

"Normal" door

Q. I got to talking with our lumber dealer when I bought a new wood frame storm door last week. He tells me that it is normal for a wooden door to bow out in the winter and bow in during the summer. Is this so?

N.M., St. Louis, Mo.

A. It's not necessarily "normal" for any wood door to bow out in winter and in during the summer. Just because they often do, that's not the way it has to be. If the door is sealed so no moisture can get to the wood, it won't bow in or out—ever. Moisture swells wood, and

heat (including sunshine) will dry it out on the side most rapidly warmed and a warped door is the result.

Bowed storm door

Q. Is there a practical way to take the "bow" out of a wooden storm door? It bows out about 3/4" at the top and bottom.

J.F., Johnstown, Pa.

A. You can counteract the bow by running a taut wire between screws set in the top and bottom rails inside the door with a turnbuckle in the center of the wire. As you tighten the turnbuckle, the door ends will be pulled inward straightening the door. You can speed up the process by using a small heater to dry out the inside surface of the door. When the bow is corrected, paint the door with a high quality paint to seal the wood thoroughly.

Door closers

Q. I have a problem common in our section of the country. The winds are heavy, and blow open or slam shut combination storm-and-screen doors. Standard door catches are torn out of the wood and the doors bang against the walls or rails and fall apart. Just what can we use to keep the doors from being wrecked?

R.E., Bellwood, Ill.

A. We'd suggest using door closers—a device with a fixed arm, compression chamber and spring which stops the door from opening too far thus saving the house wall and railing. At the same time, the closer forces the door to shut slowly enough not to slam but closing it regardless of wind. These devices are adjustable and can be set to serve your needs.

Weatherstripping

Q. Can you tell me if it is pos-

sible to purchase a one-yard piece of brass with felt weatherstripping for inside the bottom of a door? I need one in a wider width than the hardware stores carry. In the case of a door cut too short, is it possible to build up the sill?

D.C., Harrisburg, Pa.

A. Weatherstripping of brass comes in various widths. Check the builder's supply houses for a larger variety. They may be unhappy selling you just one piece, in which case a friendly builder might get it for you. If this question is connected with your last sentence, build up the too-short door and use a width of the weatherstripping that you can get. Building up the sill is more difficult than adding a strip to the door. If you really want to do a neat job, cut some more off the door to get it straight and smooth and add a good sized strip, securing it with glue and screws. Then apply the weatherstripping.

Wrought iron doors

Q. I am interested in replacing conventional exterior doors in my home with glass-paneled ones to give more light. Will you please advise me as to where I can obtain information on glass doors as well as on interior wrought iron doors.

J.L., Minneapolis, Minn.

A. The exterior doors you describe are pretty much a stock millwork item, assuming you have a standard size opening. We suggest your local building supplier as the easiest place to go for the information and the doors. Sears and Wards also carry such items in their catalogs. Sears also has interior iron doors.

Chapter 6

Window Problems

Aluminum...Basement...Burglar proofing...Cleaning...Condensation ...Construction...Conversion...Leaded glass...Leaks...Removing... Repairs...Replacement...Stained glass...Specialty glass...Stuck windows...Storms.

Aluminum windows

Q. I have been having trouble with my aluminum windows sticking and wonder if there is a special lubricant that will make them operate more easily. Can you help me?
D.M., Memphis, Tenn.

A. Aluminum sash can be lubricated. Use a silicone spray lubricant. This should prove a great help provided your sash runs are clean and true. You can also lubricate with paraffin or candle wax, or petroleum jelly; these won't injure the metal or drip oil. Some aluminum sash become pitted from weather action, and should be polished before lubricating with a fine wire brush along the sliding edges of both sash and frame.

Window parts

Q. Recently we purchased a home that is equipped with aluminum windows that slide on a plastic track. This track has become hard and cracked. Can you direct me to a source of replacement for these tracks?
J.S., Kent, Ohio

A. If you possibly can, try to find a manufacturer's name or trade name on the windows. One source we know of is Blaine Window Hardware, Dept. AB, 1919 Blaine Dr., Route 4, Hagerstown, Md. 21740. They stock replacement parts for windows, closet doors, and patio doors, and may possibly have what you need. Order a catalog ($1) or send a sample piece of the track, along with how much is required and ask for a quotation.

Sunken windows

Q. While filling in my yard for landscaping I discovered that my cellar windows are now about 2″ below grade. I do not like those curved galvanized shields. Is there another way? The foundation wall is poured concrete.
N.B., Saint Joseph, Mich.

A. You can make a waterproofed concrete window well if you find that more attractive. Come 3″ or so wider than the window opening and build a 4″ wall, 6″ above grade and about 18″ below. All else being equal, make the well at least the window height in the other direction.

Put in a concrete bottom with a drain into a tile line to your drywell.

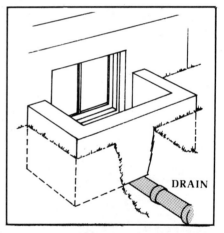

DRAIN

Leaky basement sash

Q. Is there some sort of weatherstrip or insulation for steel basement windows? The sash open in on a sliding rod, lock shut by turning a handle at the top. Even when locked, a great deal of cold air comes in.

H.W., Haddon Heights, N.J.

A. What you need here is a heavy, flexible weatherstrip which can be attached to the frame with plastic bonding cement or adhesive so that when the window is pressed shut it compresses the stripping, sealing the crack between sash and frame. If there are leaks around the frame where it fits against the masonry, seal them with caulking compound.

Burglar proofing

Q. I'm thinking of using plexiglass for windows instead of glass to make them burglar-proof. Do you think this will work?

G.L., Jersey City, N.J.

A. Acrylic sheets available to the home handyman have a high impact resistance, and are easy to drill and cut with common tools. However, no claims are made for it to be unbreakable. For burglar proofing, you may be better off using wired glass. Note: Plexiglas® is the registered trade name for acrylic sheet material made by Rohm & Haas Co.

Window seepage

Q. Condensation on and around my large picture window causes a problem with puddles of water on the window sill. I would like to arrange some drainage device so the water could flow into a collection point and thus save me from constantly drying the area. What suggestions would you have?

H.M., Malvern, Pa.

A. You should consider reducing the relative humidity of the room air. Keep the humid room air from hitting the cold window surface. Use an inside storm sash, tightly fitted, to keep the air from reaching the colder window surface or use an outside storm sash to help warm up its surface by providing trapped air insulation space.

You may also wish to investigate the idea of covering your window sills with a surface that can be wiped and will not be damaged by water. Getting rid of the cause of the water problem is still the best answer.

Sweating casements

Q. I have steel casement windows which sweat terribly even with storm sash. Is there any way to cure this or help reduce it?

E.D., Billerica, Mass.

A. The problem of curing sweating windows and storm sash is a universal headache. When warm, humid interior air hits a cold surface, condensation generally follows. With metal windows which remain cold there is apt to be some condensation on the metal with or without storm sash. If the window sash fit loose enough for warm interior air to reach the cold storm sash, condensation occurs there. If the storm sash fit loose enough for the cold to chill the interior window, warm air condenses there. If neither are loose the through metal is still cold and will sweat on the room side anyhow. Reducing excessive humidity within the house will help.

Frost on storm sash

Q. I had triple-track aluminum storm sash installed on my two-story home. Condensation forms on the inside of the storm sash and freezes. It's nearly impossible to open the sash for ventilation at night. When the temperature rises, the condensation melts, leaving water between the storm and inside sash. What can I do?

G.T., Summit, N.J.

A. Warm air with a relatively high water vapor content is reaching the inside surface of your storm sash. Most likely this is because your windows do not fit tightly. Weatherstripping can help, or you can remedy the loose fit mechanically. To do this, remove the stop strips and reset them tight against the sash. If there's a gap between the two sash at the check rail, felt weatherstripping is about the only answer. Two things to check: 1) If

you have no sidewall insulation below the windows, warm air from the basement can rise within the walls to the window area. Insulation applied from the basement can remedy this. 2) It's possible the putty or glazing compound holding the glass in the sash is loose, dried out or missing allowing warm "wet" air to reach the storm sash. Winter is not the right season to reglaze but you can prepare for spring repairs.

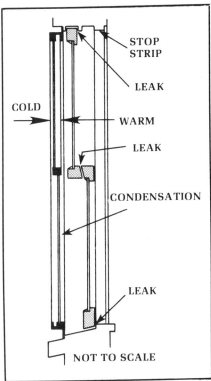

Wet thermopane

Q. I have a 4′ x 6′ Thermopane picture-type window that is about five years old. Recently moisture condensed on the inside of the outer pane. Can this be removed or remedied?

I.S., Philadelphia, Pa.

A. Thermopane is a registered trademark indicating a glass "sandwich" consisting of two sheets of glass sealed together at the perimeter and having the air between them removed in a vacuum process. Once the edge seal is broken, there is no real way to again create the vacuum, with the glass installed in the house. The condensation is not removable.

Water stains

Q. My home has been under construction for some time and the windows were installed last winter. They were undercoated on the exterior but unprotected inside. During cold weather they frosted up and as this melted, the pine sash became discolored by the water. Is there any wood bleaching material that will remove these water stains?
M.S., St. Paul, Minn.

A. Several household preparations will bleach out these stains. These include hydrogen peroxide and ammonia, as well as laundry bleach. Ammonia sometimes will darken or burn pine wood, however. Pat on with a cloth and allow to stand a few minutes, then rinse off with a damp sponge. When thoroughly dry, sand off the raised grain. For a commercial preparation try oxalic acid which is brushed on, allowed to stand 15 minutes, then neutralized with a solution of water and soda used as a rinse.

Rough windowframe

Q. Once I cut a hole through the frame wall of our house, what must be done to the opening before setting in a new window unit? Or do I just get one to fit between the studs left in the wall?
K.K., St. Louis, Mo.

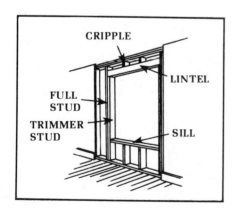

A. One would hope you knew the size of the window unit and allowed for rough framing before you cut the hole. You need a double

2x4 stud at each side, with the lintel (double 2x6 in a one-story house, double 2x8 in 1-1/2 story) resting on the inner pair of studs, butting against the outer ones. Set in a rough sill supported by short studs left after cutting the opening at the bottom. The short cut studs above the opening rest on and are toe-nailed to the new lintel.

Wider windows

Q. I wish to replace two small windows separated by a 24″ strip of wall with a single large picture window. The new opening will measure 88″ wide by 64″ high. These windows are on the first floor of a two-story house. When the studs between the windows are cut out, is a temporary support needed and what size header will be needed over the new opening?
C.D., Ocean Grove, N.J.

A. You will need a temporary support. If the span is less than 7′ when done, you can use a double 2x8 lintel but if larger use a double 2x10. This will necessitate cutting not only the two center studs but all the short studs above the present windows. It's a good idea to extend the lintel to the next adjacent studs in the wall and toe nail them to this, plus putting a short stud under each extended end.

Breakthrough

Q. I'd like to know the proper method of cutting through a frame wall. We want to add a couple of double-hung windows.
J.M., St. Paul, Minn.

A. Mark off the window inside and remove plaster or wall covering to bare studs. Provide temporary support of a double 2x10 along the ceiling against the wall, supported on 4x4 or double 2x4 props. Then drill holes or drive nails at corners of the marked area to be used as guides outside. Make

the opening wide enough to allow for double 2x4 studs at sides and a double 2x8 lintel. To cut siding and sheathing at the same time, bore 1/2″ or larger holes at upper corners and start a cut with a keyhole saw, finish with crosscut saw. Pry siding from sheathing and sheathing from wall studs.

Thicker walls

Q. Our home is built of cement blocks plastered on the inside. Now we find that in the winter our walls sweat and the paint cracks and mildews. We know we have made a serious mistake in not having the walls furred to provide an air space between inside and outside walls. We plan to do this ourselves with strips and wallboard panels, but how do you fix it at the windows?
N.A., New Bern, N.C.

A. To extend window frames the thickness of furring plus wall covering, use 1-1/2″ strips nailed to present window frames with finishing nails. To make an almost invisible joint, remove any paint from edge of frame, apply a waterproof glue and attach strips. Counterset nails. It would be better to remove and replace the door frames with wider stock.

Window conversion

Q. My home has double-hung windows, each section of which has six small panes of glass. I would rather have one large pane than the six small ones. Can these windows be converted easily?
E.B., Erie, Pa.

A. You can first remove the putty and glass, then carefully remove the mullion strips that divide the larger sash up into smaller units. Clean the groove that the glass rests in; the joint where the mullion strips come out will be clean already, serving as a guide. Check the frame for rot.

Purchase glass cut to fit the new, larger area. You will need heavier grade glass for this size. Lay down the frame, spread a ribbon of glazier's compound in the groove all around, press in the glass and then set in glazier's points—two at least per side or more—and reputty.

Fixing leaded glass

Q. **We have recently moved into a house that has leaded-glass windows that must be either repaired or replaced. I do not wish to replace them with panes of glass, but can find no information on them. Can you help me?**

J.M., Brockway, Pa.

A. It is possible to find a good glass craftsman who might fix your window, but it would cost you a fortune. You are better off trying the job yourself. If the glass

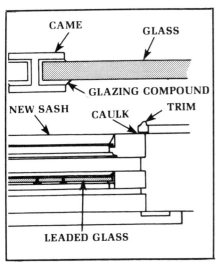

has been set in lead cames, individually puttied or caulked, you can try replacing the caulk with glazing compound, a very slow and tedious operation. Try making a good seal with the new glazing compound not only between the exterior surface of each piece of glass and the came it fits into, but around each piece and on the inside surface also. Each edge of glass is surrounded by the glazing compound in a U-shaped manner. Use black or grey putty and remove the sash if possible to work on the glass,

since you will have to force the glaze a little from both sides of the glass.

Another alternative is to use the leaded glass as a panel inside the regular glazed sash. If you have a set-in-place window, the easiest way to accomplish this is to install a permanent storm sash, keeping the sash members as small as possible so as not to interfere with the appearance of the glazed panel.

There is a third alternative, but it may not please you. Install plain, glazed sash and have the leaded glass reset in cames (either you do it yourself or else have it done) and hang this panel inside the window frame simply as decoration, free of its duties as a window. You may profit from writing to Whittemore-Durgin Glass Co., Box 2065, Hanover, Mass. 02339. Send a close-up snapshot of the glass that will disclose its condition and ask their advice. They may be able to help you.

Leaky windows

Q. **Our 20-year-old ranch home has two picture windows in front. We've lived here two years and each winter we have water dripping inside these window frames. This only happens when the gutters are filled with ice. What is happening and how do we repair it?**

J.C., Loveland, Ohio

A. Construction of your home may be similar to the detail shown. If previous owners did a good job of caulking at "A," it is possible for

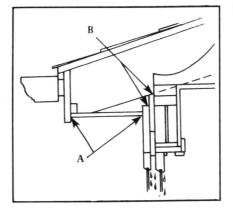

water to work its way onto the window frames at "B." Assuming this is what's happening, you can 1) use heat tapes to keep the water in the gutters flowing so no ice builds up; 2) install flashing under the shingles far enough up to divert the melted water, or 3) make sure the top of the gutters is well below the lower edge of the roof. Assess the damage that may already exist inside the soffit area and repair as needed. Also check attic ventilation.

Removing windows

Q. **I have an older house in which the walls are made of lath and plaster. I would like to remove a couple of windows and fill in those openings. Should I plaster the whole area shut or can I use gypsum wallboard and plaster the seams?**

D.P., Blencoe, Iowa

A. It's simpler to use gypsum wallboard. Begin by removing the

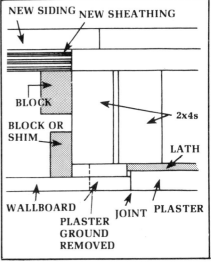

sash, then the window trim and frame. Expose the rough framed opening. You need to bring both interior and exterior surfaces of the new wall area up to match the surrounding areas. Usually you'll need one more 2x4 down the center of the hole where the window was (two more if it is wider than 32") to support the center.

Sheath and side the exterior surface, blocking as necessary to get old and new surfaces flush. Plaster on wood lath is usually much thicker than gypsum wallboard so you'll have to shim or block to bring the new surface flush with the old plaster. In old, quality-built homes, you may find a wooden strip, the plaster ground, is nailed to the frame right where you need to shim. It served as a guide for the plasterer. You can do without it, but remove it carefully to avoid damage to the plaster. With shim material the right thickness (you'll probably need a strip down the new center 2x4s, too) you can install the wallboard patch and tape the joints as in new construction.

You cannot do seams very well if either surface moves so it is important to provide ample support along all the edges. Install insulation in the new wall area, too.

Rotting window sills

Q. I find that the window sills (outside) on my house are rotting. Undoubtedly this is because I have a stucco exterior home and the only way moisture can get out is through the windows. The house is 45 years old.

Do you recommend that I put in all new windows or simply replace the sills? I can find no literature on replacing windows and wonder if you can suggest something that would be helpful?

N.B., St. Paul, Minn.

A. Window sills aren't easy to replace. You'd have to do as much work to get the sill out and replace it as to replace the whole window frame. If the sashes (the parts that move) are good, and you can get a frame to fit them, you might save something, but generally speaking your easiest out is to replace the whole unit. The fact that the house is stuccoed on the exterior might make it a bit more prone to rainwater entering between stucco and

window frame, but we doubt if you can blame the stucco for the rotting of the sills. This usually happens when maintenance is not kept up. Scraping, caulking and repainting is a continual process over the years, if the sills are to last.

Metal channels

Q. A friend told me that metal sides and guides are available for repairing windows that are worn and hard to open. Do you have the name of a company that makes replacement guides?

M.Z., Massapequa Park, N.Y.

A. The metal channels are made by Quaker City Mfg., 701 Chester Pike, Sharon Hill, Pa. 19079. Write them for literature and name of your nearest dealer.

Removing putty

Q. How do I get hard, old-fashioned putty out so I can replace broken glass?

Z.L., Toluca, Ill.

A. By soaking with linseed oil, you can sometimes soften it for immediate removal. By heating it with a soldering iron or your clothes iron tip a short space at a time, you can soften it for speedier scrape-away. If old and rotten, the putty falls out.

Putty leaks

Q. The windows on the south side of my house leak through the putty in a driving rain. The putty appears secure and not loose and I hesitate to reglaze. What would you suggest?

J.L., San Francisco, Calif.

A. Putty should be painted over completely with outside paint, so completely that paint touches the glass. Unless this is done, shrinkage of the putty is bound to occur, drawing it from the

glass and leaving a crack. If your putty is sound, simply touch up the paint. If not, better remove it and replace with glazier's compound, then paint over as outlined.

Broken sash cord

Q. One of the ropes on which a window sash is hung is broken. Could I put in a new one myself or is this a professional job?

G.M., Crestwood, N.Y.

A. You can do practically the whole job with a screwdriver. Remove the stop strip on the side where the cord is broken. Lift out the sash, holding the unbroken cord tightly. Remove it from the sash and put a nail through the knot (or clip a clothespin just above the knot, anything so the cord is

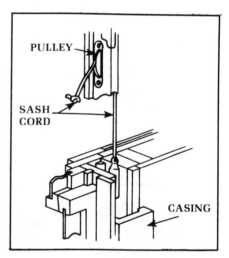

not pulled into the weight box). On the opposite pulley stile, locate the cover of the weight box. Take it off and fish out the lost weight. Remove the old cord and cut a new one to the same length. Tie a knot at one end and slip the other over the pulley into the box, holding the knotted end as before. Fish the cord out through the cover hole and retie the weight. Replace the weight and then the cover. Get the sash in a position so you can easily release the sash cords and replace the knotted ends in the sash. Replace the sash, check operation, then replace stop strip.

Window kit

Q. I have double-hung windows with ropes and weights. Some years ago a company came out with a kit that would replace these. It fastened to the present frame sides and the window sash could readily be taken out to wash, or moved up and down. A friend of mine had some installed in his windows but he doesn't remember where he got them. Can you help?

J.Z., Conemaugh, Pa.

A. Quaker City Manufacturing, Dept. FH, 701 Chester Pike, Sharon Hill, Pa. 19079 makes a repair kit that does away with the ropes and weights and permits both sashes to be completely removable. The kit consists of a pair of metal channels that fit into the window frame with very little fuss. Directions tell you exactly how to do the job. A spring arrangement is built into the metal parts which allows the window sash to move up and down snugly.

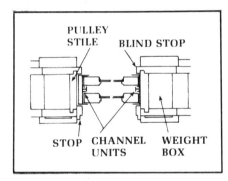

PULLEY STILE BLIND STOP
STOP CHANNEL UNITS WEIGHT BOX

Draft blocker

Q. At the wheel the sash weight rope goes over, we have a terrific draft. Is there any way this can be blocked off?

G.R., Rochester, N.Y.

A. At each side of the window frame remove the casing, exposing the pocket in which the weights move. Plug the bottom and top of this recess with mineral wool insulation, keeping it above the pulley and below the weights. You may notice some cracks on the

outer wall of the house into the recess. Plug these on the outside with caulking. Check window operation to make sure insulation is out of the way, then replace casing.

Worn wood sash

Q. Our double-hung windows look like burglars have been practicing on them. They are a mess across the bottom member of the lower sash from being pried open but when we tried to use plastic wood and level them off, the patches just fell out. Can you suggest another method, short of buying new sash?

A.C., Ithaca, N.Y.

A. Did you remove the paint before using the wood putty? That would help but even so you are working on a very vulnerable edge and stronger methods would be better. Take the lower sash out and plane the bottom. Nail and glue on a tapered wood strip to provide a stronger, straighter bottom edge. You can use wood putty to fill in unevenness above this strip with some assurance that it will stay. Check the sill for unneccessary roughness too. You may have a mangled metal weatherstrip that is the real culprit. Paint on a good wood preservative and return the sash to the window.

Rattling windows

Q. How can I prevent double-hung windows from rattling? I keep them locked but it does no good.

H.R., Revere, Mass.

A. Try resetting the window stops closer to the sash, both inside and outside.

Leaking window

Q. I have hinged windows that swing in on my back porch room.

The sills are flat and a driving rain seeps under the window across the sill. I fastened quarter-round to the bottom of the sash outside, but doesn't seem to help much. Can anything be done to cure this?

N.H., Albany, N.Y.

A. A weather strip along the bottom of the window would cure the trouble. Since it might prevent proper closing if attached to the sash, remove the quarter-round and attach the felt to the bottom of this strip, then replace it so the felt rests snugly on the sill.

Window moldings

Q. I recently purchased a brick veneer house with windows and frames made of wood. The caulking of the frames where they meet the brickwork is very amateurish and the bricks are smeared with excess compound. I tried scraping the compound from the bricks but this hasn't worked well. I am planning to use quarter-round, painted moldings on all four sides to hide the smeared caulking. What do you think?

D.F., Jamaica, N.Y.

A. The caulking is probably not nearly as messy as you think and would not be noticed except

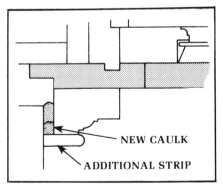

NEW CAULK
ADDITIONAL STRIP

by those who looked very closely. However, remove as much of the old caulking as you can and then apply some new acrylic latex caulking. There is no reason why the quarter round should not work if you like the looks of it. Paint each of the four pieces with a primer and follow up with two coats of latex finish paint. Countersink the brads or finishing nails and fill the nail holes with knife grade caulking. Then touch up the caulking with paint.

Window replacement

Q. How do I replace a large, metal window with a shorter wooden one of the same width?
H.T., Omaha, Neb.

A. Metal and wooden windows do vary, but not enough to cause you any difficulty in your project. Diagram A shows the parts in a

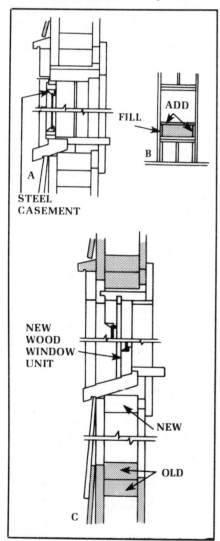

conventional metal window. Remove the metal frame and whatever wood parts will not be used for the new wood window. You should end up with a hole in the

wall framed by a header, trimmer studs and a 2x4 rough sill. You will need to put in the parts shaded in diagram B to make the hole the right rough opening size for your smaller window. Information on the proper size for this opening should be included in literature supplied with your new window. Put in the framing parts first, then patch up the sheathing and exterior siding. Install whatever insulation you want and apply the interior finish as indicated in diagram C. If you read the manufacturer's literature on the window unit you buy, you'll have no difficulty with your installation.

Jalousie windows

Q. I have a frame house with wood windows and wish to install glass jalousies but am not quite sure how to go about it.
W.L., Tampa, Fla.

A. Units are usually provided complete, the glass cut to fit a ready-made frame that resembles a stock window of any other type. You need only frame the opening to fit the measurements of this stock jalousie window. Unless you select a unit of a size other than the stock windows you remove, you can probably salvage and reuse any sound window casings now in service. The frame should be new and cut to a snug fit around the new windows.

Replacing casement

Q. I have steel casement windows and would like to remove them and install double-hung windows. The windows have plaster (wet wall) around them. Should this be knocked out and the window frames installed to the studs?
M.L., Woodmere, N.Y.

A. You will have to remove the plaster far enough to expose the original studs, header and sill of

the window openings. Then place the window frame inside this opening and nail the frame to the framing studs. Make sure the frame is plumb. If it turns out that the original stud opening is a little too large for the new window frame, you may have to fill the space between frame and studs with the kind of construction shown in jamb section of the drawing. The external caulking is extremely important and should be carefully applied all around the joint where the window frame meets the siding. Be especially careful of the caulking of the rain or drip cap above the top of the exterior window frame. Once this is completed, apply your window moldings, interior stops and window stool.

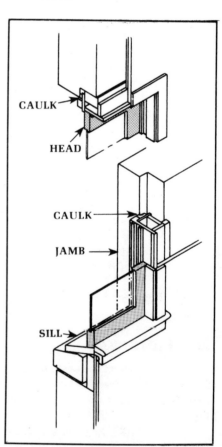

Stained glass

Q. I have several old leaded stained glass windows that I would like to install in a gambrel-type roof somewhat like a skylight. However, the windows are quite old and have some loose lead

strips. Since they will be somewhat at a slant, how can I seal them properly? I have thought of putting a pane of glass outside the stained glass which might be better than trying to get the old windows into their original condition.
S.G., Sayre, Pa.

A. You are quite right in thinking it will be easier to add an outer clear glass layer than to repair and

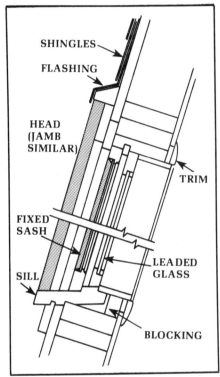

make weathertight the old units. The simplest thing is to make a matching frame for the clear fixed-glass sash and the stained-glass window. Set both sashes in this frame and place the new frame in the opening in the roof. Be sure to putty the outer sash properly to make it watertight.

Tight windows

Q. Our double-hung windows became difficult to operate so I took all paint from the wooden channels with paint remover. Inasmuch as the lower half is exposed to the weather, please advise me what I may use as a substitute for painting these channels in order to protect the wood.
C.N., North Arlington, N.J.

A. The lower half of the window frame which forms the groove for the upper sash can be protected against the weather with boiled linseed oil. Apply one coat daily for two days, wiping up the excess a half-hour after application. This makes a good lubricant for the sash but won't add to the appearance of the windows and may be unneccessary. Usually these exterior grooves are painted. Resetting the stop strips may permit the sash to slide down easily in spite of a coat of paint or two. If the sash are actually too tight for the frame with a coat of paint added, a stroke or two of a plane on each edge of the sash may permit them to slide over the painted surface.

Stuck windows

Q. The bottom sash of my double-hung windows work easily but the top sash are stuck by paint. What do I have to do to get them unstuck?
W.H., Syracuse, N.Y.

A. For tight fitting windows, you can cut the paint surface along joints with a sharp chisel point. Loosely fitting windows can be freed with a hacksaw blade forced in and drawn along the joint. As a desperation measure, apply a little paste paint remover along the joint which will wrinkle the paint free, then follow up with a knife inserted in the joint.

Sticking storms

Q. My aluminum storm windows are getting harder and harder to push up and down because they slide against more aluminum and a spring clip on the other side of the frame. The frames have grooves dug into them because each section rubs against the other.
P.L., Amsterdam, N.Y.

A. Aluminum becomes pitted and non-anodized varieties of

aluminum accumulate a hard, gritty deposit—both conditions caused by exudation from gases in the air where oil burners are working—and this does increase the abrasive action. Oiling should reduce these hazards somewhat. We think the main trouble lies in the spring clip. Investigate to see if the pressure can be reduced without causing the sash to fall out or slip.

Storm windows

Q. We have steel casement-type windows and would like to make metal frame storm windows for them. Where can I find information on this?
H.M., Denver, Colo.

A. You can obtain detailed information from the Reynolds Metal Co., D.I.Y.A., P.O. Box 27003, Richmond, Va. 23261.

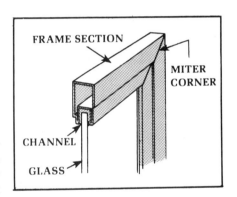

Storm window repair

Q. We have a bay window which is drafty and leaks in heavy rain. The panes measure about 17″ x 21″, and there are 12 in all, each of which is very expensive to replace. Can a storm window be made from Plexiglas or a similar material by a do-it-yourselfer?
H.K., Manassas, Va.

A. We think what you have in mind is the clear plastic film that is simply applied less permanently over the entire window area. This is usually polyethylene film and not as clear visually, but much cheaper. This is not meant to re-place necessary repairs but to keep out bad weather and prevent the excessive loss of heat. It works quite well, actually, if you take the time to do a neat job. On most windows, it looks better if you set in a back-up strip so that you have

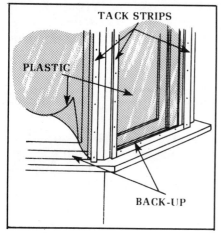

TACK STRIPS

PLASTIC

BACK-UP

something on all four sides to lay the plastic against; use tack strips all the way around.

However, I do believe you should first repair the leaks. Perhaps the putty or glazing compound needs attention. Also, a bay window often is not insulated at the floor, and a lot of cold is felt from that lack. We suggest that you do first whatever makes the most sense towards putting the existing bay window in the best possible shape, then consider what is the most reasonable way to improve it with a storm sash.

Large windows

Q. **We have two custom-made, multi-pane windows which are so large that we have been unable to obtain storm windows for them. Someone suggested that we get a sheet of Plexiglas for each window, but they didn't know where they could be obtained, or whether they would actually be suitable. One window is 63-1/4″ x 89-1/4″ and the other is 55-1/4″ x 77-1/8″. If we used Plexiglas we would like to make the installation permanent. Can you give us some advice on this problem?**

A.W., Malvern, Iowa

A. Plastic in that large a size is no easier to find than glass for your storm sash glazing. What you should consider is either vertical or horizontal divisions to break up the size glass that is required into two or three sections. If your window is equal-sized, multiple panes somewhat as shown, perhaps three vertical sections would be most attractive. It may be that you have some other arrangement of panes that would lend themselves to a different division of sash; your letter is not specific on this. The idea is to frame glass or plastic of sizes that are more economical than one large piece would be. The mullioned storm sash can still be one large and hard-to-handle unit whether you install it permanently or seasonally.

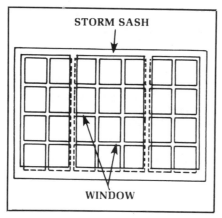

STORM SASH

WINDOW

Plexiglas scratch

Q. **For a fixed sash portion of a bay window, I made an inside storm sash, using Plexiglas for the glazing. It recently got scratched. What can I use to remove the white scratch lines?**

S.L., Hancock, N.H.

A. For a minor scratch on the surface alone, a bit of hard auto-mobile paste wax (not a cleaner-wax) will sometimes cure this problem. Buff lightly with clean cotton cloth (flannel or jersey). For a deeper scratch, you will have to try wet or dry 150-220 grit sand paper, followed with grits to 400 and buff with a clean muslin wheel, dressed with a good grade of fine-

grit buffing compound. Finish this up with a clean, soft cotton-flannel wheel.

Triple storms

Q. **I have outside storm sash at all my double-hung wood windows. For additional heat savings, I am considering adding one sheet of clear plastic to the inside of the bottom sash and another sheet on the outside of the top sash. This would allow for raising and lowering each sash without obstruction. I've never seen this done and am wondering if there is something wrong with my plan. I know the plastic might be more expensive than glass but should be easier to install without breaking. What do you think?**

K.E., Greensboro, N.C.

A. We think you're going to a lot of trouble to accomplish what might be more easily and more effectively done simply by in-stalling one inside storm sash at each window. This way you'd cut down infiltration between the sash too. Probably be less expensive, too, if you use one of the packaged plastic-and-frame kits available at your home center for just this purpose.

Home-made storms

Q. **Can storm sash be made? They are so expensive to buy that, since I am forced to do some things for myself, I thought I might be able to do this and save heat and money, too.**

M.R., Brooklyn, N.Y.

A. About the cheapest effec-tive storm sash would be made of 1x2 stock joined at corners with flat corner irons. Over this whole frame tack one of the many types of transparent plastic sheet mate-rials which cost only a few cents per square foot. Total cost per average window should be less than $1 this way.

Inside storm sash

Q. My sliding glass windows need storm windows, but there's no room on the outside of the frames. What types of storm sash are available for inside installation?

L.P., Glen Cove, N.Y.

A. It's easier to make your own inside storm sash to fit your windows, and do-it-yourself materials are available at any home center store. There's even a double-pane inside storm sash kit you can size to suit your needs. One company you can contact is Arco Polymers, 7001 West 60th St., Chicago, Ill. 60638.

Insider storms

Q. I've tried to find the "Insiders" storm windows, but can't find them in this area. Please help me.

H.S., Blue Grass, Iowa

A. Write directly to Plaskolite, Consumer Service, 1770 Joyce Ave., Box 1497, Columbus, Ohio 43216. They have their dealers listed in zip code sequence and can get the address of the source nearest you swiftly.

Thermal panes

Q. Do you have any books or information on how to replace thermal pane or insulating glass in windows?

J.W., Granite City, Ill.

A. Thermopane is a registered trade name for insulating glass made by the Libbey-Owens-Ford Glass Co., 811 Madison Ave., Toledo, Ohio 45695. Twindow is another name for a similar product made by PPG Industries, One Gateway Center, Pittsburgh, Pa., 15222. Write the manufacturer of whichever brand is available to you and ask for installation instructions and information. We have no books or printed material that would help you. It is not an impossible job for the home handyman (assuming the size you desire is not too large to handle), although it requires extra care and special glazing techniques.

Window insulation

Q. I have three very large fixed windows on the front of my house. I have severe inside condensation problems with them in winter, and a heat transfer problem in the summer. Can you recommend any practical method for adding storm windows—or other insulating materials—from either outside or inside?

M.S., Charlotte, N.C.

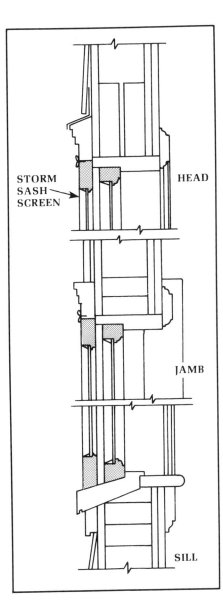

STORM SASH SCREEN

HEAD

JAMB

SILL

A. About the easiest way to add storm windows to a fixed sash is to build a wooden frame or frames, or else buy an aluminum one, glaze them, and then set the works into the existing window frame. You didn't say whether the sashes are wooden or metallic. We'll assume that they are made of wood. The sizes that you have indicated would not be done easily in one piece, but can be handled with three or four sections. Most window frames are built to take a 1-1/8" screen or storm sash stock, but you'll need one a bit heavier for the sizes you have. It's better to set the glazing on the outside of the window rather than the inside for the appearance. Double-glazing in this way will not help too much with summer sun heat unless you use a special glass. You should rely more on shades and awnings for that.

Storms and screens

Q. My home has full-length screens for all windows and I would like to know the best way to put them up after storm windows are taken down. If they are hooked on I believe these hooks will interfere with storm windows later and if they are nailed on the wood will be damaged.

J.L., Dorchester, Mass.

A. Standard hardware for storm sash and screens assumes both will be hung from the same hook. There are various styles with slight differences in shape and size but basically the idea is to use two hooks on the frame over which you hang screen or storm sash, both of which are equipped with identical eye plates that fit the hooks. Both may be held by a hook and eye fastened from the inside or held by a turnbutton from the outside. Naturally, each sash has the eye part in an appropriate location.

Flooring Problems

**Basement floors...Carpets...Concrete slabs...Linoleum...Painted
...Refinishing & repair...Seamless...Squeaks...Stains...Stone...
Structure...Subflooring...Tile...Wood.**

Cold basement floor

Q. I am contemplating installing a new floor in my basement to reduce the coldness of the present floor which is concrete covered with asphalt tiles. Should I install 1x4 sleepers on 12" centers and then plywood and new vinyl tile? I would then use some form of insulation between the sleepers. Or should I place plywood right on the present floor without sleepers?
A.A., Cedar Grove, N.J.

A. At first thought your proposal seems reasonable. Substituting 2x2 sleepers, 16" apart with 5/8" exterior grade plywood improves it some, but the major objection is still there: dampness. If there is any at all, you are inviting rot, lifting of tiles, odor and mildew. Tile manufacturers recommend strongly against this installation. Actually the problem you describe probably has other solutions. In the first place you can't insulate-in heat you are not supplying. Heat directed at the ceiling seldom warms the floor. Very little heat is lost downward anyway. Storm sash on basement windows will help some but supplying heat at floor level will help more.

Wood basement floor

Q. We would like to get a wood floor in part of our basement but have heard this is impossible as the concrete is below grade. What is your feeling on this subject?
T.W., LaGrange, Ill.

A. You need a waterproofed floor to begin with. Then there are at least three ways approved by the lumber industry to install a

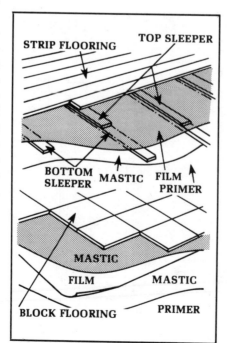

wood floor. You can use screeds set in asphalt or split-screeds with plastic film between them under a strip wood floor, or you can set blocks in mastic, following the individual manufacturer's instructions.

Warming concrete

Q. I want to finish my basement floor to make it warm so that my young children can crawl on it without getting cold. How can I go about laying vinyl asbestos tile over the poured concrete so that the floor won't be as cold as bare concrete? The floor would have to be relatively thin since the basement ceiling is only 6'10" high.
W.G., Milwaukee, Wis.

A. Regardless of what you use to cover the floor, the floor itself must be absolutely dry. An even easier method than laying tile is to lay indoor-outdoor carpeting which has a sponge rubber base and is soft and warm and ideal for crawling around on. If you still want to lay a tile floor, you'll have a little more difficulty. Some handymen say they have gotten good results using Styrofoam, between

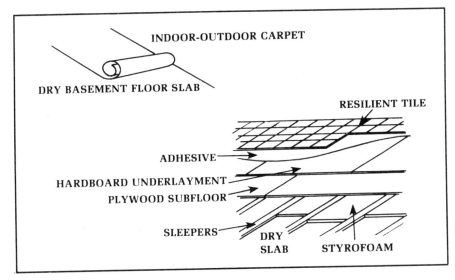

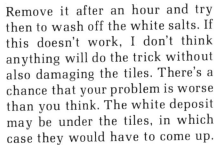

Remove it after an hour and try then to wash off the white salts. If this doesn't work, I don't think anything will do the trick without also damaging the tiles. There's a chance that your problem is worse than you think. The white deposit may be under the tiles, in which case they would have to come up.

Removing floor paint

Q. The basement floor in the house we recently purchased is painted. We want to tile but understand resilient tile cannot be laid over paint. Do you have to sand concrete to get the paint off?

M.A., Staten Island, N.Y.

A. Try dissolving 2 teaspoons of lye in a cup of warm water. Use this to test the paint. If it disintegrates within 10 minutes it is oil base and should be removed. Two pounds of lye in 1 gallon of hot water should do it. Then wash the floor with hot water and scrape if necessary. Otherwise we would suggest renting a floor sander. Use #4 or #5 open coat sandpaper. Paint remover can be used or you can burn it off but the first is expensive and the second not very safe. After such removal jobs are undertaken, it is a good idea to install a few tiles with the recommended adhesive, wait 2 weeks and try to lift them. If adhesive clings to both concrete and tile and you have quite a time getting the tile up, you'll know it is ok to proceed.

Tile over paint

Q. Can I put asphalt tile on a cement cellar floor that has been painted?

V.M., Baldwin, N.Y.

A. You can put this type of tile down on a dry floor painted with a chlorinated rubber-base paint which is in good condition. For other types of paint, either remove it first, or use the felt underlay method: Sweep the floor clean, coat with liquid asphalt, lay 15-

---

sleepers on the floor. Dow Chemical Co., which makes Styrofoam recommends an installation similar to that shown in the bottom drawing in which 3/4" sleepers (wood strips) and insulation are used as a foundation for 3/8" plywood, covered by 1/4" hardboard underlayment, and topped by resilient tile. You may want to put a vapor barrier under the Styrofoam and sleepers.

Subfloor needed?

Q. I would like to install a wooden floor in my basement right over the concrete. Can I do this without first putting down a complete subfloor?

H.H., Maspeth, N.Y.

A. You sure can install a wood floor in your basement without a subfloor of any sort. Prime the floor after sweeping it clean. After that dries apply a cold-type mastic over which a plastic film vapor barrier is laid. Then wood block flooring can be easily installed in more of the mastic. If you'll follow the recommendations of the manufacturer of the wood blocks, you'll have no trouble determining which materials to use where.

Clean floor tiles

Q. Last winter I had a leak in the foundation of my home and water got under the tiles on my recreation room floor. The water dried up but the edges of many tiles are white. Can you tell me how to clean them?

E.S., Colonia, N.J.

A. The white material is a mineral salt. Acid will remove it but a powerful acid will also destroy your tile. You can try saturating a cloth with white vinegar and laying it over one of the marred areas. Cover the cloth with cardboard and weight it down lightly to keep it in contact with the tile.

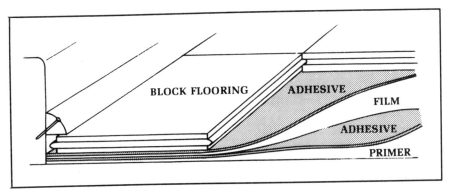

pound asphalt-saturated felt with butt joints, then tile. (It is only fair to add that tile manufacturers and some distributors insist this is not good practice, but we've yet to hear from a reader who was displeased with the results, which we have been recommending for years.)

To find out what kind of paint is on the floor, try this: Dissolve two teaspoons of lye in a cup of warm water and drop a couple of spoonfuls of the mixture on the paint at several places on the floor. If it is oil base, it will disintegrate in 10 minutes or less.

Tiling a rough floor

Q. Due to freezing weather at the time that my basement floor was poured, we couldn't make it smooth. We'd like to lay asphalt tile on it, but in addition to the unevenness it's chipping in spots.

I'd like to level it but I don't want to make a new pour that would reduce the ceiling height. Perhaps I should put down tar paper? How about sanding it?

N.A., Harrisburg, Pa.

A. The asphalt tile manufacturers have anticipated your difficulty. Major companies make mastic underlayment that can be used to bring rough floors level, and you can spread them as thin as 1/8" or as thick as 1/2". All these mastics require is that the floor be dry. Check the manufacturer of the tiles you're using for the specific formulation to use; what, if any, primer is needed; and the correct adhesive. It's important that all materials be chemically compatible.

Your statement "chipping in spots" causes some concern here. If you mean dust or flake-size pieces, you can clean them up with a vacuum, because nothing sticks to dust long. If you mean larger holes, repair with a latex cement patching mix first.

To answer your other questions: we'd recommend tarpaper only if the floor is smooth enough so it wouldn't poke holes or cause ridges

in the tarpaper. If it were just a ridge here and there, a sander could be tried—but it's too much work to do the whole floor.

Loose tiles

Q. I put asphalt tiles on my basement floor a year ago. Now the tile corners are coming loose. Is there anything I can do to keep the tiles from curling up?

U.D., Union, N.J.

A. Warm up one tile to over 70° and remove it from the floor. Check to see if you've applied enough adhesive. If it looks skimpy, use more adhesive and reinstall. If you find enough adhesive, then it is probable that moisture coming through the concrete is preventing a proper bond. In that case you need to waterproof the floor.

Basement floor tile

Q. Before we put the tile down in our basement family room, the floor was always dry. A few months after laying the tiles, water seeps up between them. What causes the problem and what can I do to stop it?

P.C., Hazleton, Pa.

A. Before laying basement floor tile, we suggest taping a piece of bright tin, rubber mat, plastic sheet or even aluminum foil tightly to the floor, no matter how dry it looks. Leave it there 72 hours. Then look. Water droplets on the surface indicate a condensation problem. If it is damp underneath (as your test would have been) you have a seepage problem. What happened was that the seepage was slight and evaporated before you saw it. Now the tile prevents evaporation. The solution is to remove the tiles and start again. Scrape off the adhesive and allow the floor to dry. Then mop on asphalt and lay saturated roofing felt in that, butting the joints; then lay the tiles. This works where there is a slight seepage problem such as

you describe. However, it will not hold together a disintegrating floor.

Tiles in basement

Q. I get conflicting advice on which type of floor tiles may be used in a basement. Could you clarify this for me?

R.R., Milford, N.H.

A. You get conflicting advice because not all manufacturers agree in this matter. Asphalt and vinyl asbestos seem to have unanimous acceptance in basement installations and some manufacturers add vinyl and rubber tiles. Recommendations for specific adhesives and primers for below-grade applications should be followed.

Tile trouble

Q. Three years ago I finished my basement and applied asphalt tiles to the floor. After six months a white crystalline substance raised the tiles off the floor. It was caused by an alkaline condition in the cement. There is no evidence of dampness. We've heard a number of suggestions. I'd like to hear yours.

A.H., Floral Park, N.Y.

A. Whether there is indication of dampness or not is debatable. The crystalline substance is a mineral salt brought up by seepage of moisture which evaporates and leaves the salts behind. You can still use the tarpaper method described above and re-apply the tiles.

Dusty cement floor

Q. Part of our basement floor has been successfully tiled, using your underlayment suggestion. The area around the furnace is still dusty enough to track onto the tiles, after 2-1/2 years. Do we have to tile it too?

F.H., Mt. Pleasant, Pa.

A. No, you do not have to tile a floor to prevent dust tracking. You can use a concrete hardener to advantage. Sweep off as much dust as you can and apply the hardener, a liquid which may or may not demand dilution in water depending on whose brand you use. Simply pour it on and spread out with brush, broom or mop. If the first application is readily absorbed, a second coat is indicated.

Leveling broken floor

Q. My basement floor is very rough and uneven and seems to be only about 2″ thick in spots. What can I use to build it up level and smooth?

W.G., Torrence, Calif.

A. With a floor this weak and probably cracked and leaking too, you will be far better off to break it up and excavate further. Use the broken concrete as part of the fill. You need at least 4″ of fill, tamped level, and 4″ of concrete. While you are at it, polyethylene film over the fill, under the new slab and turned up at the edges the thickness of the new floor, will give you the best job. Use an expansion joint at the perimeter.

Leveling concrete

Q. What is the best way to get my basement floor level so I can lay tile? It's thick enough I think, just bumpy.

P.G., Hackensack, N.J.

A. If the floor is not damaged or leaking you can paint it with a bonding fluid and apply 1/2″ of new cement at the shallowest spots; as much as needed to fill hollows, holes, etc. There are also prepared mixes, generally latex based, that can be used for skim coats in this manner, but the expense is generally more.

Buckled tiles

Q. My basement floor is quite a mess. The vinyl tiles buckled and cracked. Looking further, I found the former owner had put in a plywood floor and cemented the tiles over that and now that is buckling. How can I eliminate the problem?

E.L., Maspeth, N.Y.

A. You will have to take up the floor—plywood and tile—and start over. Lay a properly damp-proofed and reinforced concrete slab floor. Put your tiles directly on that. Read the label to make certain you are selecting a type of tile suitable for below-grade installation. If you feel a tile-on-concrete floor surface will not suit you, you have two choices: 1) Leave the concrete bare, use paint, select an indoor-outdoor carpet that can be used below-grade or 2) lay a wood block or strip floor following the manufacturer's directions for proper installation.

Springboard floor

Q. My recreation room is in the basement. Its floor is tongue-and-groove oak placed over 2x4s which rest on the concrete. They span the 12′ width. This floor buckles greatly, particularly during the summer. Thus it is a springboard. What can be done to correct this problem?

S.M., Maplewood, N.J.

A. It sounds as though your concrete floor wasn't adequately waterproofed and your wood flooring may not have been treated with a preservative before laying. The sleepers and the underside of the flooring have become wet and swelled. The fact that this condition is at its worst in summer suggests that seepage is likely but evaporates at all times except when the air is hot and moist. An underlayment of asphalt paint and tarpaper would probably cure most of the trouble and treatment of the wood with a preservative, the rest. Since it's too late for this without taking up the floor, here's a temporary remedy. Remove a board at each side and with a small fan aimed at the opening, force air to circulate beneath to dry it out.

It's hard to de-warp boards and sleepers but if drying them will cure the spring, this is the way to do it.

Removing old carpets

Q. I now have indoor-outdoor carpet in my kitchen and dining area and am interested in having wall-to-wall tile or linoleum put down. What is the best method to use in removing the carpet which is glued down?

B.B., Havre de Grace, Md.

A. The best method is the simplest—loosen one end and pull, preferably in the warped direction. You will have left behind a hard deposit of glue which can be scraped or sanded off with a rented floor sander. If the underlayment is a tempered hardboard it should come off readily; if it is a cheaper substitute, you may find that you are removing half the underlay too —in which case you have a job on your hands and may have to pry the carpet off, splitting it from the underlay along the glue line carefully so as not to disturb the underlay. If you know the type of glue used and there is a solvent available for it, you can, with considerable expense, use that to soften the glue and remove the carpet, letting the residue harden up again before sanding. Scrape off what you can while it's still soft.

Carpet shears

Q. I would like to lay some new carpet myself, but I can't find the type of heavy shears the professionals use. Do you know where I can get them?

L.M., Cleveland, Ohio

A. The Cooper Group, P.O. Box 728, Apex, N.C. 27502, makes all kinds of scissors and shears, and would be most likely to have carpet-cutting ones. Write to the attention of the sales department. You might at the same time ask them for a list of dealers in your area who carry their line.

We would suggest, however, that you go to one of your local carpet contractors, especially the place where you expect to buy new carpeting, and see if they won't rent or loan you a pair of their shears. You have nothing to lose with this approach, and you just might save yourself the considerable expense of buying a special tool you seldom would use again.

Carpeting concrete

Q. I am looking for information on the best way to apply wall-to-wall carpeting on an above-ground level cement slab floor. This is an area 50 miles north of New York City where there might be a temperature and humidity problem. Can you help me by suggesting one of your publications which would detail instructions on this type flooring?

J.C., Brewster, N.Y.

A. You will be able to obtain just the information you are seeking by writing to:
Consumer Services Dept., Armstrong World Industries, Lancaster, Pa. 17604

Carpet caper

Q. I am planning on taking a rug and cutting it to fit our hall. The last time I had occasion to try this, there was quite a bit of raveling along the cut edges. This rug is a better quality but is there anything else you could suggest to overcome this particular drawback?

J.R., Chillicothe, Iowa

A. Before you make any cuts in the rug, coat the back of the area to be cut with shellac. This will prevent a good deal of raveling and shedding of nap.

Fiber rug revival

Q. Two of our rugs, exposed to sunlight, have faded. One is a fiber rug, the other sisal. I'd like to brighten these. Can you suggest a method?

M.D., East Detroit, Mich.

A. Spray-on stain, any color you like, would be the most practical and can be quite attractive. Since the fibers are dry, you'll need quite a bit.

Wall-to-wall carpet

Q. We plan to have wall-to-wall carpeting installed. The floor isn't in bad shape but I believe I'd better cover it with something first. How about hardboard? Plywood?

H.R., West Newton, Ind.

A. Either plywood or hardboard would cost more than simple sanding. If the floor needs strengthening, use plywood at least 1/2" thick. Wall-to-wall carpeting calls for padding underneath. The screened side of hardboard, raw plywood or a sanded floor will hold padding in place with friction alone.

Floor under carpet

Q. I am finishing my attic and plan to use wall-to-wall carpet. Is there anything other than plywood that is suitable as a subfloor?

E.H., Peabody, Mass.

A. You can use 1x6 or 1x8 tongued and grooved pine boards but they tend to warp and curl. Plywood is preferable. Or you could cover this sort of subfloor with 3/16" hardboard for a smooth result but the plywood does the thing in one operation and it's easier to tack down carpet to plywood.

Flooring over concrete

Q. We live in a bilevel house with concrete floors on the main level. Can we put a wood floor over this?

G.Z., Baltimore, Md.

A. There are a couple of ways to do this, provided you have a dry concrete slab to begin with. You'll need more specific instructions then we can give here, but generally you can install block flooring in mastic if you first coat the slab with a special mastic, lay asphalt-saturated felt in that and provide a damp-proofing membrane. The block manufacturer can give you details. Another method is to apply a waterproof coating to the slab, attach 1x2 sleepers on 16" centers, lay polyethylene film over them and nail a second course of sleepers on top of the first ones. Then install a subfloor on the sleepers and the finish floor on that. Or you can install wood strip flooring directly to the sleepers, eliminating the subflooring. The National Oak Flooring Manufacturer's Ass'n., 804 Sterick Building, Memphis, Tenn. 38103 can send you the specifications for this method.

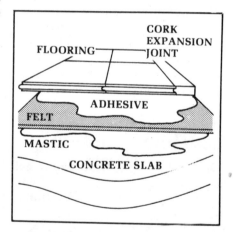

Oak over concrete

Q. We are starting construction on our own split level house and want to use the most economical method for ensuring a good strip oak floor in the living and dining areas which are on the on-grade level of the house. What method do you think is most economical?

L.F., Memphis, Tenn.

A. First, do the slab right. Use .004 polyethylene film over a 4" to

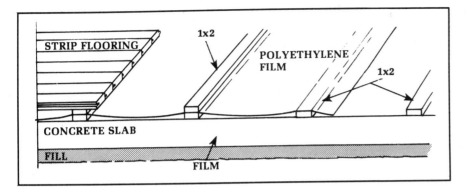

6" fill and then pour 4" concrete. Lay 1x2 strips treated with wood preservative in rivers of adhesive on 16" centers and also fasten to the slab with 1-1/2" long concrete nails 24" apart. Lapping the edges over, lay another barrier of .004 polyethylene film over these bottom strips. In line with them, nail down a second 1x2 with 4d nails. On these two-piece sleepers lay your strip floor.

Wood floor on slab

Q. I have heard of some method for putting wood strip flooring down on concrete with asphalt and screeds. We are finishing a shell house built on a concrete slab. Is this method something we could use?

P.G., Irvington, N.J.

A. We would think this a very good method for you to use. Prime the concrete floor with asphalt primer. When dry, spread asphalt mastic specially developed for bonding wood to concrete. Select flat, dry pieces of 2x4 stock, ran-

THIS METHOD WILL WORK WHEREVER YOU HAVE A DRY CONCRETE FLOOR

dom lengths up to about 36" long. Use only wood treated with wood preservative. Lay out these screeds in staggered rows on 12" centers at right angles to your finish flooring. Embed each one in the mastic flat side down letting the ends overlap at least 4". Install the hardwood flooring with each strip bearing on at least two screeds. Sand the floor and finish it as you prefer.

Cold floors

Q. I own a lake-front cottage with cement slab floors which are extremely cold. I don't heat the cottage during the cold months. I have been thinking about putting in a wood floor and indoor-outdoor carpeting. Is this a good idea? If so, what is the best and least expensive way of doing it?

E.M., St. Johns, Mich.

A. We don't have the information to say definitely that one way is the "best." For a while the screed (wood planks put on with an adhesive) was thought best. Then the wood industry developed a split screed method, sandwiching the vapor barrier between the screeding-material. Some homeowner variations use foamed plastic insulation with plywood surfaces, but we have nothing from the plywood industry to confirm this use. Indoor-outdoor carpeting can be put directly on concrete or can be installed on plywood and will make the floor seem warmer. The problem is in what is under the plywood. An enclosed, unventilated space that may become damp can damage wood or ply-

wood. The damp can exist unsuspected through condensation on the cold slab or by slow seepage through an imperfect slab. Walking on insulation panels may damage them and dampness can adversely affect the adhesives used, so there is no guarantee that using insulation as a base is a good idea. We wouldn't recommend insulation without hardboard or plywood over it. No rule says you can't carpet over hardwood block flooring installed over on-grade slabs, but this won't provide warm floors if you don't supply heat in the first place.

Settled concrete

Q. The floor in our family room is concrete at ground level, finished with 9" square asphalt tiles. The original room was 14' x 14', but was extended 19 years ago. When the contractor poured the foundation for the extension, apparently the new ground was not completely settled. The new area settled. A few years after that, we had a tapered ramp built and retiled the floor. After a while, the ramp broke down. The drop is still about 1/2". We want to tile over the whole floor with vinyl tile. What can I use (assuming I remove two rows of tile where the floors join) to fill in and taper the high side to the low? Or since I have a belt sander, can I leave all the tiles down and sand off the high areas?

M.G., Highland Park, Ill.

A. With the history of your floor slabs, we'd be inclined to say it is about time to start again from the concrete. Better remove all the old tile, clean off the adhesive and resurface the whole floor up to level. A good, sound, clean substrate is essential. Your dealer can tell you which brand of leveling mix he carries that will team well with the adhesive and tile you intend to use. In the long run, the extra removal work now should be worthwhile in extending the life of the new tile.

Sloping cement floor

Q. We enclosed a cement terrace for a play room, putting asphalt tile on it, and now are worrying about the slope of 3" in the 12' width. Can I build up the low side with layers of felt and finish with linoleum or would it be too springy?

S.P., Michigan City, Ind.

A. You can't build up a floor 3" with felt. It's too soft and won't hold up under chair legs or heavy objects. Without removing the tile, you can use tapered 2" wide sleepers secured to the old floor. Nail 5/8" exterior grade plywood on them and lay the new floor covering on that. For a less expensive cement floor, remove present tiles, then mix three bags portland cement with 9 bags of sand and add water. Spread and level off. You can bring in the two ingredients dry, then add water, mixing right on the floor.

Removing linoleum

Q. My kitchen has three layers of linoleum. I would like to remove at least two layers and lay down 12" squares of vinyl asbestos tile. How do I remove the linoleum?

B.D., Oceanside, N.Y.

A. With any luck you can just pull up the linoleum a layer at a time. It may not even be glued down. If it is, cut through it in many places and either use a commercial stripping fluid or pry up what you can with a wide bladed floor chisel. If the bottom layer has many holes in it and is torn or uneven, it is best to remove it. This is a good time to examine the old floor for rotten or damaged boards or to check out the hardboard underlayment and repair it if necessary. You can glue the tiles directly to the hardboard or plywood underlayment, or you can put down felt paper with staples and glue the tiles to the paper. The advantage of this method is that you will

later be able to remove the tiles very easily.

Covering linoleum

Q. I would like to put down a new inlaid linoleum floor covering over my old ceramic tiled floor in the bathroom. How do I do it?

F.D., Woodbridge, N.J.

A. First scour to clean the tiles. Then apply a thin layer of a latex based mastic underlayment, leveling and smoothing it to provide a suitable subfloor surface for laying linoleum. Cement down a layer of 15-lb. felt, then lay the linoleum. Following exactly the manufacturer's recommendation as to which-adhesives-to-use-where is especially important in this type of installation.

Linoleum tiles

Q. We are planning to install linoleum tiles in our kitchen and would like to know if there is any method other than the one we heard of—to lay felt, then cement the tiles to the felt. Can we lay the tiles without using felt?

J.M., Chicago, Ill.

A. It is best to use felt under the tiles. It helps smooth the floor and there is less chance of individual tiles coming loose. Should you wish to remove tiles at a later date the presence of the felt layer will make removal a lot easier and reduce damage to the wood floor.

Linoleum removal

Q. I would like to know how to go about removing an inlaid linoleum from the floor.

G.P., Woodhaven, N.Y.

A. You can take up old linoleum with a floor chisel, one with a blade about 3" wide. Drive it under the linoleum at a shallow angle and pry up, without gouging the floor.

Corrugated floor

Q. We took up old kitchen floor linoleum and removed the felt by soaking with warm water. New linoleum was laid without a liner. It's been down four years and every floor board shows. How can this warped condition be remedied?

P.J., Los Angeles, Calif.

A. The floor warped either from the soaking it received when you removed the felt or from a damp condition under the floor which should be corrected now. You can make the floor level by sanding it. While a liner is not absolutely necessary, heavy felt will prevent slightly warped boards from showing through.

Kitchen linoleum

Q. We want to lay linoleum floor covering on our kitchen floor. How does one cut around obstacles, openings, corners, to look neat without buckling?

M.C., Niagara Falls, Ontario

A. Make a pattern of stiff paper by joining strips of it with tape after spreading the strips out to cover the entire floor. Your pattern is then the exact size and shape of the floor. Cut out at obstacles to match them exactly. Where a pipe goes through the floor it is necessary to make a cut from the wall to the obstacle. Spread out the linoleum and lay the pattern on the upper surface. Cut the linoleum with a sharp, curved linoleum knife to follow the pattern. Fit down the longest edge of linoleum first. While inlaid linoleum is laid in adhesive the rug type can be laid on the floor loosely.

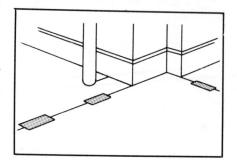

Ruined linoleum

Q. Recently the drain in our kitchen sink clogged and the plumber we called put something in that splashed our inlaid linoleum and took out the originally blue color. We have a set of sort of pinkish spots left. How do we set about restoring the original color?

J.U., Philadelphia, Pa.

A. Inlaid colors go through the linoleum and probabaly have been damaged deeply as the chemical was probably a form of lye. You can consider setting in carefully cut patches if scraps of the same material are available, replacing large square sections instead of trying small patchwork pieces; replacing the entire floor covering; painting the linoleum with deck enamel; spatter painting with contrasting colors over the entire flooring to disguise the fact that it is spotted.

Dull looking linoleum

Q. We have a large kitchen with linoleum on the floor. I used wax on it and for some reason can't keep it bright looking. It constantly appears to have something spilled on it and no amount of scrubbing or rewaxing corrects the condition. Please give us some advice.

F.T., Kalamazoo, Mich.

A. This condition usually follows the use of an inferior "hard" wax containing shellac. When damp the shellac becomes milky in appearance and gives a blotchy look to the floor. Remove the wax by scrubbing with steel wool and alcohol, then apply a dependable liquid floor wax or a first coat of paste wax.

Varnish off linoleum

Q. The linoleum that is down in this house now looks like it has been varnished. Can this be removed without wrecking the linoleum?

R.S., Kitanning, Pa.

A. Try sponging the surface with a solution of trisodium phosphate in water. Use it lukewarm, about three pounds of the chemical to a gallon of water. Let the solution stay on the linoleum just long enough to get the varnish soft enough to steel wool up. Then rinse immediately with clear water and rub dry.

Cutting error

Q. My husband was doing a fine job laying sheet vinyl in our family room but he over-cut one place right at a doorway and I'm afraid it will tear there in time. Is there some stickum or something that can mend this?

T.Y., Logan, Ohio

A. The adhesive used to lay the vinyl will help hold it together, but you can sort of weld the cut too if you are careful. Lay a strip of aluminum foil over the cut, dull side down. Use heavy duty foil about 1" wide. Run the point of your iron over the foil lightly. When you think you have it hot, going by the smoothness of the foil, rub foil with a cold damp cloth. Let it cool off and slowly lift the foil back. If you have scraps left, you could practice this a time or two to better gauge how long and how heavy to work with the iron.

Painted linoleum

Q. The kitchen floor of my 1892 house is covered with old-fashioned linoleum and I don't want to go to the expense of replacing it. Is there a special kind of floor or deck paint that would do the job of covering the surface and stand up to wear and tear, as well as be waxable?

J.M., New London, Conn.

A. If your present linoleum is waxed, the coating will have to be removed thoroughly with a commercial wax remover. Then, assuming enough wear has given the surface as good a "tooth" (degree of roughness) as you'd get sanding, use a good oil-based floor enamel. We'd suggest a two-coat job on the background color and then spatter-dash two or three more colors on top of that to give you a textured surface. Protect the walls well when you do it.

Painting floors

Q. I wish to paint my hardwood floors white to match the walls, but have been discouraged from doing so. Can I obtain a similar effect through bleaching, waxing and staining?

M.S., Pt. Richmond, Calif.

A. Painted floors are not the most lasting finishes one can find. A floor painted white will require attention quite soon if it is to be kept looking good. A reasonable compromise would be to bleach, whiten and protect with clear varnish. You would want to sand anyhow to remove the old finish, so you could bleach the actual surface. Neutralize this well and let it dry, then try (off in the corner somewhere) wiping on a heavy-bodied white stain. You'll need a bit of practice to get the effect and evenness of application you desire, but it can be done. If the floor is oak, you may wish to use a white filler on it first. Then when the "stain" is dry, sand lightly and use one of the urethane floor finishes in the clear color. You will have a handsome, off-white floor that still looks woody, yet is light enough to pass for white without showing every footprint or scratch as white paint would.

Painted patio pattern

Q. I am planning to paint my concrete cellar floor to resemble a flagstone patio. The floor has already been painted. Is there any place where I can buy a pattern to have a uniform marking for making these flagstones? Also, is there any special paint you would recommend for a long-wearing finish?

Q.R., Silver Spring, Md.

A. We've never heard of patterns for painting a floor to resemble flagstone. Perhaps you want to study a few photographs and stonelaying diagrams to see what you want. The pattern produced using uncut flags is apt to be quite busy. The pattern formed by cut stones may be too regular to suit

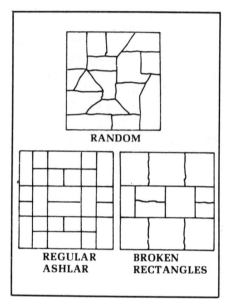

RANDOM

REGULAR ASHLAR

BROKEN RECTANGLES

you. We'd nominate an imitation of the rectangular flags broken on the job as being easy to duplicate and not too hard to follow through. You can use masking tape to mark off even-width "joints" if you want. We would recommend chlorinated rubber-base floor enamel, but you'd best stick with whatever is down now as long as it has given you no trouble.

Porch tiles later

Q. I'd like to know the simplest way to have a porch at the back of our house. We have sliding doors but they open out about 20" or more off the ground. If possible, could this be concrete and about 8' x 10'? We'd like to use precast patio tiles on it but probably won't install them till next year.

M.I., Lansing, Mich.

A. Patio tiles may be up to 2" thick on 1" of concrete. If you figure

the step down to that finished level at 7", you'll have a 10" step down till you surface the porch. This is uncomfortable but probably not disastrous and still leaves two steps down to grade. Make a foundation of 8"x8"x16" blocks on a footing 16" wide and 8" thick at frost level. Fill inside these walls with dirt, compacting it well to about 8" below the tops of the blocks. Then put in a 4" fill of crushed rock. If you slope the end foundation walls 1/4" per foot you can use them to level the 4" slab you pour within the walls. Fill the block voids too. Your porch will not be finished-looking this year but you can use it.

Tiled deck

Q. I have a wood porch or deck that I would like to tile but it will have to be the sort of tile that can be used outdoors. How is this applied?

E.B., Hermosa Beach, Calif.

A. If your porch is strong enough to take the 20 lbs. or so per square foot that tile weighs and is tightly jointed, you can proceed as follows. Nail waterproof building paper down and stretch reinforcing mesh over it. Nail in place 1/4" above the wood. You need a 1" mortar bed embedding the reinforcement. Use 1 part cement to 5 parts sand. Dust cement on the surface and set the tiles. Finish the joints the next day with a jointing mortar mix of 1 part cement with 3 parts sand.

Breezeway floor

Q. Is asphalt tile practical for a breezeway which is screened in the year round? The floor is subject to a certain amount of water and cold.

J.R., Newark, N.J.

A. Asphalt tile will not do for this as it shrinks and becomes extremely brittle at freezing temperatures. We suggest a cement floor which can be colored. At more expense, you could use quarry tile. Don't forget, whatever you choose, to provide a slight slope for drainage of the floor away from the building ends.

Concrete over wood

Q. I want to put a cement floor over my wooden porch floor. It is well braced and solid but won't be able to have more than 1" of concrete over the part under the doors. Is this enough?

F.N., Angwin, Calif.

A. It's not a good idea to put a concrete floor over a wooden one. The wood is slightly flexible and would give when walked on, breaking the concrete. Unless the wood is totally waterproofed rot would quickly develop. Temperature changes cause expansion and contraction at different rates in the two different materials which would quickly separate. In any case 1" of concrete is not enough. Since you have a solid wood floor, why not stick with that and refinish it properly?

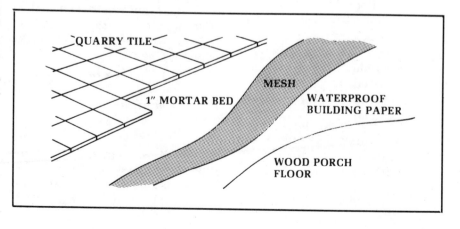

QUARRY TILE

1" MORTAR BED

MESH

WATERPROOF BUILDING PAPER

WOOD PORCH FLOOR

Level porch floor

Q. The newly built porch on my cabin was built dead level. When it rains, puddles of water stand on the surface. I don't want the extra expense of rebuilding the floor. Is it practical or feasible to apply floor tile on the plywood to protect it?

W.M., Gillespie, Ill.

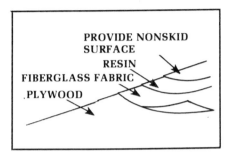

PROVIDE NONSKID SURFACE
RESIN
FIBERGLASS FABRIC
PLYWOOD

A. In our opinion it is not sensible at all to apply floor tile meant for indoor use. Tiles will do little to protect it and cannot be expected to last very long under exterior use. You should rebuild the floor right to provide the slope required. You might consider a fiberglass-reinforced resin deck topping, but whatever protective surface you use, some slope for proper drainage is most important; 1/4" per foot is about right.

Tile finish

Q. Can I wax exterior tile for an easier surface to clean?

F.G., Maywood, Calif.

A. Don't use self-polishing wax on exterior floors. I'd suggest after the tile has completely dried out, giving the surface a couple of coats of a colorless sealer.

Curved porch floor

Q. My outdoor porch flooring is badly cupped. There is no subfloor. It is exposed to sun and weather but it is only two years old. What can I do to avoid the cupping in the first place and what material can be used to fill the present cracks?

A.S., Bridgeport, Conn.

A. The underside of your porch is probably bare. It can become damp. This side swells while the top shrinks in the sun. Coat the boards with a wood preservative and a coat of paint. You can use wood putty or sawdust mixed with waterproof glue to fill the cracks. Sand when dry, then prime and paint. This should be protective deck-paint.

Leaky porch floor

Q. The floor of my front porch is made of single 3/4"-thick tongued and grooved boards which have warped and separated. Rain drips through. I don't want to go to the expense of making a reinforced concrete floor. What else can you suggest?

E.T., Kalamazoo, Mich.

A. One inexpensive solution is to cover the floor with asphalt paint, tar paper and a layer of 3/16" hardboard. Caulk the few joints in the hardboard surface with mastic caulking as the floor is laid. Fasten it down with counterset brass screws.

Floor refinishing

Q. Most of the wooden door thresholds in our house have been worn down to bare wood at the center portions, ruining the appearance of our otherwise beautiful wood flooring. Can the thresholds be refinished or must they be replaced?

J.R., Auburn, Maine

A. There is absolutely no reason to replace the threshold, unless it's worn down so badly that it has an obviously concave shape. Refinishing the threshold, or parts of any wood floor for that matter, is quite simple. Sand the worn areas smooth and then apply two or three coats of shellac thinned 50% with alcohol. If the shellac finish on the remainder of the threshold has yellowed or darkened with age, matching it will be difficult. It would be better to sand the entire threshold down to the bare wood before you apply the fresh shellac. Allow each coat of shellac to dry thoroughly before applying the next. You can also refinish the thresholds with varnish or urethane floor finish.

Cracks in floor

Q. Recently we replaced some damaged boards in the front porch. Some of these new boards have shrunk, leaving large cracks. What can I use to fill these cracks?

E.H., Santa Ana, Calif.

A. We assume you plan painting the porch. Therefore, plug the larger cracks first with oakum caulking which you can find in any boatyard or marine supply store. Push this below the surface into the cracks with a chisel or screwdriver. Then use regular caulking compound to level off the joints with the surface. You can paint over this at once.

Remove floor board

Q. I have some repair work to do on my floors. How does one get out just one badly damaged board without wrecking the place?

P.W., Elmhurst, Ill.

A. Take out one board in split pieces to avoid damaging adjoining boards. Use a power saw or a sharp chisel to make the necessary cuts. Cut a new length to fit and remove the underside of the groove so the piece can be dropped down into place and then surface nailed.

Floor sanding

Q. I have several wood floors with wide boards that are painted with several coats. I would like to sand them clean and refinish them, but the price of having them sanded is too high. Can you suggest a type of inexpensive sander I could buy for this purpose?

D.W., Keene, N.H.

A. For the job you have in mind, you would need a belt sander. However, trying to do several floors with a portable belt sander is quite a chore. It would be slow going and you would have to be on your knees for long periods of time. You could easily rent one of the large machines used for this purpose for far less than any belt sander will cost.

Seamless floor

Q. I am considering putting in one of the seamless floor-type coverings in our kitchen area. Do you advise this as a do-it-yourself project? If so, can the covering be placed directly over the asphalt tile that is now on the floor? Also, how can the old wax on the tile be removed?

E.M., Michigan City, Ind.

A. This can be a do-it-yourself project if the manufacturer's directions are followed carefully and you can keep off the floor long enough after the job is done. Most types of covering can be applied over asphalt tile. You should first build up any missing areas with wood dough, and the floor must be level and structurally sound. Use a wax remover recommended by the maker of the wax you have been using; rinse well after use. If you have a lot of patching to do, sand the whole floor after the wax removal.

Poured floor

Q. I would like information on a poured floor that looks like terrazzo.

P.D., Smoch, Pa.

A. You can get current information and how-to instructions from manufacturers of the materials. Dur-A-Flex, 100 Meadow St., Hartford, Conn. 06114 makes a seamless flooring system for homeowner installations. Basically, prepare the present floor surface according to directions, coat it with the base, and "toss" the color-

ful vinyl chips into the wet coating. When that is dry, additional coats are applied and sanded according to directions.

Second floor squeaks

Q. Our bedroom floors all squeak something terrible. Can they be oiled or something to quiet things down a bit?

A.M., Hinsdale, Ill.

A. Powdered graphite or talcum powder can be dusted between boards and allowed to filter into the cracks or you can wipe on and work in linseed oil but the excess turns sticky and can be quite difficult to remove. Surface nailing with finishing nails or spirally grooved nails with small heads will most often do the trick.

Squeaky floors

Q. We are being troubled with squeaky floors in our entry hall. It is wood strip flooring. Can you suggest some means of handling this situation?

D.P., Long Island City, N.Y.

A. If the underside of the floor is accessible from a basement or crawl space, you can cure the squeaks from that side by inserting small wedges between the subfloor and the joists to force the subfloor upward against the finish flooring which stops a lot of squeaking. Or drive screws not more than 1-1/4" long up through the subfloor into the finish floor.

Squeaky linoleum

Q. Our upstairs bath has inlaid linoleum over it but it squeaks. I have heard you can cure squeaks

by driving nails, but won't they show on linoleum?

E.D., Garden City, N.Y.

A. You've heard correctly and yes they will show. However, this can be minimized by countersetting the heads, concealing the small holes with melted crayon. Select wax crayon of the same color as the linoleum, melt it and mold it into holes. When it hardens, smooth off and protect with floor wax.

Squeaking floors

Q. My house is an older bungalow with five rooms. The problem is that all of the floors squeak. The house has a full basement. All but two of the rooms are carpeted. I would appreciate your advice on how to eliminate the squeaks.

S.S., Youngstown, Ohio

A. Where you can get at the underside of the squeaking floor, you can often use wedges to prevent the movement. Have someone walk about upstairs while you listen downstairs. With a supply of wedge-shaped pieces of scrap or wood shingles, try wedging between the top of the joist and underside of the subfloor where the noise originates. If the movement is between finished flooring and subflooring, rather than between joist and subfloor, screws can be driven in from below.

Stopping a squeak

Q. The floors in my upstairs hall squeak very badly. As the boards are not first quality, I was thinking of covering them with rubber tiles. Am I right in assuming that the adhesive used in laying the tiles will seep through the

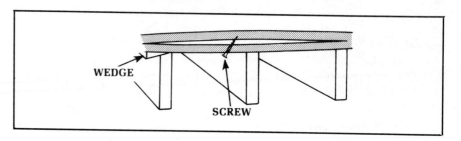
WEDGE
SCREW

cracks and bind the floor, eliminating the squeaks?

A.O., Brooklyn, N.Y.

A. There is not much chance that you can rely on mastic to do this job satisfactorily for you. If the floor is as greatly irregular as your letter indicates, it would be best to lay the tiles on a layer of 15-lb. felt anyhow. In either case, stop the squeaks first. Otherwise they will still be there—under the tile.

Ink stains

Q. Some ink stains have soaked into the pores of my hardwood floor. What can I get to remove them? The floor is prefinished oak with a wax finish. I have tried oxalic acid, milk and several types of soap and detergents, to no avail.

J.S., Waterford, Conn.

A. If the ink is below the finish of the flooring, there isn't much hope since it will have soaked in 1/4″ or more. Oxalic acid if given 15 minutes before rinsing, might reduce it. So also might 3% commercial peroxide. These call for some neutralizing after use. Sanding would have to go too deep. The alternative is replacement of the damaged pieces.

Durable floor finish

Q. My hardwood floors are a mess. We would like to sand them and put on something that will stand hard usage but look good. What can we use to gain this result?

R.T., Toronto, Ontario

A. The clear sealers and plastic finishes seem to stand up very well under hard use and greatly resemble varnish in color and gloss. They are applied like shellac or varnish but only on raw wood. Work at a room temperature of 70° when applying.

Whitish shellac finish

Q. I would like to know how to remedy a whitish appearance on

some parts of a shellacked hardwood living room floor. For nearly four years it has remained satisfactory but after repeated washing with detergents in water the whitish appearance has increased. This occurs in only a few spots.

R.N., Bethayers, Pa.

A. You can remove the effects of the "blooming" by washing the areas with alcohol. It is caused by moisture in the wood beneath the shellac finish. It is possible water penetrates the wood around the finished areas or from below. A paste wax coating over the entire floor would relieve the situation if the source of moisture is from too generous wetting when washing the floor.

Chipped floor finish

Q. Can you tell me what caused my varnished floor to chip? After removing the old finish and sanding, I put on stain, one coat of shellac and three coats of varnish.

H.A., Chicago, Ill.

A. Either the shellac was used straight and in too heavy a concentration which leaves it brittle, or the varnish was too thick and had no resilient base to keep it flexible. Shellac should be applied in two or more coats and when in 4- or 5-pound cuts should be cut about 50% with alcohol. Varnish should be thinned to a point where it does not "follow the brush" or bubble on application. Usually thinning 1/5 or 1/6 is adequate for varnish.

Up-to-date slate

Q. I am planning on building a house and installing a slate floor in the foyer and in a mud room off to one side of the kitchen. What size slate should I use? Will I need extra support under the subfloor? If so, how should I handle this problem? Can I use regular mastic such as is used for ceramic tile or will I have to use mortar and then grout?

S.M., Cleveland, Ohio

A. There are two ways to install slate. The old "wet" way, you use 3/4″ to 1″ thick slate set in mortar on a concrete slab. This obviously weighs a lot and would require considerable support if over a wood floor. The up-to-date way is to use 1/4″ thick ground natural slate installed very much like an adhesive application for ceramic tile. We suggest you use the latter. Sears carries it and many building and supply dealers have similar products. The sizes are usually 3″ x 6″ to 12″ x 12″. Colors range through natural greens, purples, reds, grays and black. If you use slate tile, you need not provide extra support but you will need at least 1/2″-thick waterproof plywood over your subfloor. One then uses the adhesive suggested by the producer of the slate tile, applying it as directed, and setting the slate in this. When dry, you grout the joints.

Dog damage

Q. The wood floors throughout my apartment were beautifully finished about two years ago. The problem is in one corner of my living room, where my dog used to wet in one spot. Lying there a few hours each time, it has penetrated the finish and turned the wood black. Is there an inexpensive way to get the stain out and refinish just this area or do I have to strip and redo the entire floor?

R.M., Bronx, N.Y.

A. You should be able to sand or scrape, bleach and patch almost invisibly without having to refinish the whole floor, provided no wood stain was used to color the whole floor first. (If there was, patching will be much more difficult.) Sand down through the finish to raw wood. Remove the black by brushing on a solution of oxalic-acid crystals mixed in warm water. Rinse it off well with clear water at the right time or the bleaching action will continue. Let the area dry thoroughly, then sand again and build up with repeated coats of finish, feathering out each one with gentle sanding. The final coat should be just about invisible.

Flagstone floors

Q.   We wish to put down a new living room floor in our basement-less house and have considered a flagstone floor. Do you have information on this project?

E.V., Bethlehem, Pa.

A.   On the present slab apply a bonding material following the manufacturer's directions. Spread a mortar mix of 1 part portland cement and 3 parts sand about 1/2" to 1" thick. Press the flagstones lightly into this mortar and set them with a spirit level. After about 12 hours they will support enough weight to allow pointing with the same mortar mix. To prevent stains, coat the top only of each stone with floor wax. Thoroughly moisten the inside of the joints with water. For an inside floor, fill joints full of mortar flush with the surface of the flagstone.

Marble over wood

Q.   I would like to install 1" thick genuine marble tiles in my entrance hall. Is it necessary to remove the hardwood flooring and embed these 1" square tiles in cement or can they be installed like asphalt tiles with an adhesive spread directly over the wood floor?

F.M., Edgemere, N.Y.

A.   You can install marble tiles with tile adhesive applied over hardwood flooring. The floor should be sanded first to get down to bare wood so the adhesive will adhere. Removal of the wax and floor finish can be done chemically but sanding is quicker and not too arduous in a small area. You probably realize that since the tiles are 1" thick, the floor will be raised by that much—creating a stumbling

block along any edge where the tiles don't butt against a threshold. It would be best to apply a molding to the floor to round off such an edge. This molding will also keep the tiles from sliding under pressure. It takes a while for the adhesive to dry.

Shellacked wax

Q.   There seems to be a powdery substance on our black marbelized tile floors which I can't remove. The floor looks fine when waxed but a day or two later the trouble recurs and water marks show. Would a machine waxer cure this?

R.H., Cleveland, Ohio

A.   Initial wax coat probably contained shellac which turns white and gritty when wet. Get it all off with alcohol and steel wool. Rewax with a high grade product. A machine waxer is easier than hand work but won't solve this problem.

Slate finishes

Q.   We just bought a house with a slate floor entry and outside terrace. How do we finish and care for it properly?

K.K., Gladstone, Mich.

A.   Slate is not a "shiny" material. Slate producers suggest it not be "finished" with anything, just swept and washed with water. Masonry dealers have matte finish sealers that can be used. "Futura" (from your supermarket) has been used with good results, and a pleasing patina builds up from using Murphy's Oil Soap. Or use the pre-cut shapes without grout, butting each piece against the next for a truly maintenance-free surface. The Building Stone Institute has a new folder, "How to Install Interior Slate Flooring," that includes a section on maintenance. It's $1 from Building Stone Institute, 420 Lexington Ave., New York, N.Y. 10017.

Remove slate stains

Q.   We have green slate in our entryway and hall on which I have used slate paste wax. Dark marks that resemble stains have appeared on it and we wondered if they are removable or if they're in the slate itself.

J.K., Sacramento, Calif.

A.   Green slate usually has dark or mottled areas in it, ranging from deep purple to near-black. It's the natural coloration. Your use of wax was a good idea inasmuch as it keeps the slate colors bright. But as you probably know, wax collects dirt which eventually hides the color. Start over. Remove all the wax. Stick to the paste wax only and the stone will show its natural color.

Removing spots

Q.   We just moved into our new home. The natural slate foyer has paint and varnish spots on it. How do I remove them? Is there some kind of sealer I can use after I get it clean?

J.A., Chicago, Ill.

A.   A paste type paint remover is the answer. Touch to each droplet. When the drop is wrinkled and soft, scrape up with old paper. A second application takes off all of it and the spot can be wiped off with soft steel wool. Once off, apply floor wax to the slate. A paste wax is best even though it calls for polishing. Once applied and polished, handle as you would any other waxed floor.

Soiled finish

Q.   Can you tell me what to use to clean oak floors, particularly at entrances where the floor is very dirty? I wish to clean and wax without refinishing the whole floor.

S.Y., North Grandy, Conn.

A.   The dirt referred to is probably grit ground into the softer oak grain plus the stains left by dirty water from wet shoes. A strong chlorine solution, a mild lye solution or cleaning ammonia diluted 50% with water would help to dissolve dirt and remove it and bleach the wood back to near-normal shade. It's going to be difficult to keep these patches exactly the same shade as the undamaged floor. Don't simply wax these spots as the protection will not be adequate. Apply at least two coats of thinned shellac as a protective coating. Then use a paste wax first followed by your regular floor wax.

Furniture marks

Q. Can you tell me what to use to clean my hardwood floors? The heavy furniture in my bedroom leaves black marks which detergents and water will not remove.
H.B., Riverview, Mich.

A. Since the grain is crushed and dirt ground in and perhaps some of the substance of the casters too, the finish is probably damaged. Use two tablespoons of ammonia in a quart of water and scrub with the grain across the marks with a fine wire brush. If the finish is not damaged, this is sufficient treatment. If the finish has been pulverized or brushed away, refinishing will be necessary. Touch up with several coats of thinned shellac, then wax. Deep dents from crushed wood can be raised some by laying a wet cloth over them, then running a hot iron along the line of indentation. Refinish when dry. Use broad glides on this type of furniture.

Flooring an attic

Q. I am finishing my attic, putting in two bedrooms. I have decided to use plywood for a subfloor and cover it with asphalt tile. The joists are 16" on centers and I'd like to know what minimum thickness of plywood I can use as a subfloor.
D.P., Bellmawr, N.J.

A. You can use 1/2" plywood nailed down with 6d common nails 6" apart on panel edges, 10" apart on intervening joists. Blocking is necessary along the joints at right angles to the joists so set in 2x4 pieces for nailing here. Use underlayment type plywood or any sanded grade of exterior type.

Bouncy floors

Q. I've been told my living room floor is "bouncy" because there is no bridging under it. What's bridging and do I need it?
E.P., Roslyn, N.Y.

A. If the joists are the proper size for the span and spacing, lack of bridging may well be the cause of the bounce. Cross bridging is 1" stock or 2x4s beveled and nailed to the top of one joist and the lower edge of the next with a second brace in the opposite direction, forming an "X" between joists. Solid bridging is simply stock the same size as the joists cut to fit between them tightly.

Solid bridging

Q. How is solid bridging installed?
R.P., McKeesport, Pa.

A. Establish a centerline across the joists where you want the row of bridging to go. Cut the pieces to fit snugly between joists. Set them alternately one side and the other of the centerline to provide access for nailing through the joists to the bridging. Keep top edge flush with tops of joists.

Floor load

Q. We have a ranch style home with a bedroom where we'd like to have a garage. The flooring consists of subfloor and a hardwood finish. The joists are 2x8s at 16" centers, one end resting on a central beam. Would the floor be strong enough to support the car and what would I have to line the room with to satisfy the insurance company?
L.M., Prospect, Conn.

A. Your floor won't hold the car in motion. I don't know what your local code requires for fireproofing an attached garage but safety demands cement stucco walls and ceiling, a concrete coating over the present wood floor and metal clad fire proofed doors if any open onto the house proper. We'd suggest you abandon this project.

Sloping floors

Q. I have some floors that slope to one side. I would like to put plywood over them and then tile. How can I make the wood floor level first?
A.B., Manchester, Conn.

A. If you'll use 2x3 sleepers across the present floor boards, tapering the sleepers to present a level surface, you can use 1/2" underlayment grade plywood on 16" spacing of sleepers or 3/4" on 24" spacing. This will raise the floor level somewhat. You'll have to reset baseboards and adjust door swings, of course.

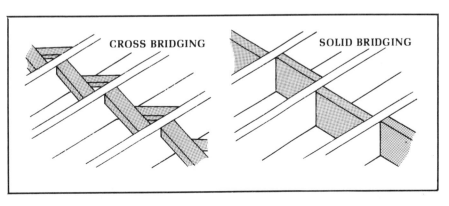

CROSS BRIDGING   SOLID BRIDGING

Leveling slab

Q.   The concrete floor slab in my house is not level. We want to lay wood floors in some rooms. Can you tell me what mixture of concrete I should put on or maybe there is another way to get a level wood floor in.

M.N., Greenfield, Mass.

A.   You can bring the slab up to level with a skim coat of cement. But as your purpose is to lay wood flooring which calls for sleepers laid on concrete, you can kill two birds with one stone by using tapered sleepers to bring the flooring level and no treatment of the concrete is needed.

Fastening joists

Q.   I am building a ranch house. How are 2x10 joists laid and nailed?
G.C., Long Island City, N.Y.

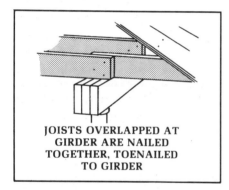

JOISTS OVERLAPPED AT GIRDER ARE NAILED TOGETHER, TOENAILED TO GIRDER

A.   Joists are laid on edge, toenailed with two 8-penny nails on each side to the house sill. Accepted practice is to overlap the joists on the central girder or beam, nailing them together with two 10-penny nails and toenailing to girder with one 10-penny nail on each side of the pair of joists.

Shaking floor

Q.   I have just bought a new home and every time someone walks across the floor, it moves. The floor was built with 2x10s on 16″ centers with 5/8″ plywood flooring. How can I stop it from shaking?
M.L., Sliver Springs, Maryland

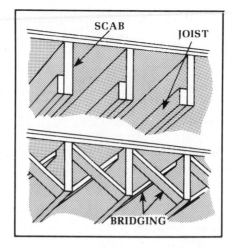

SCAB   JOIST

BRIDGING

A.   The use of hardboard or plywood underlayment as an addition to the subfloor would be helpful. Cross-bridging is another means of making a floor more solid. Probably the most economical method for you would be to attach an additional 2x4 scabbed on the sides of the existing 2x10s, assuming this floor is over a crawl space or an unfinished basement.

Sagging floor

Q.   Our floor slants as the beam under it has sagged approximately 1″ between the foundation and center posts. Is it possible to jack up this beam to level the floor without damage to the rest of the house?

A.B., St. Laurent, Quebec

A.   You can set a screw type jack under the lowest part of the sagging beam and raise the beam by a turn of the jack but not more than 1/4″, preferably less. After several days give it another 1/4″. Repeat at regular intervals until the floor is again level. Lock the jack in place and leave it there or substitute a solid post. You'll do considerable damage trying to raise the floor a full 1″ at one time.

Rising floor

Q.   My hardwood floor is of the tongue-and-groove type. Sometime ago I discovered that a container of water had been leaking and slowly seeping out onto the floor. I drew the carpet back from the area and allowed it to dry thoroughly. There was some slight warping, but nothing that the carpet did not cover, so I left it alone. Now, about two months later, I discovered a high ridge farther along the boards, perhaps 3′ from where I thought the water had stopped. It runs for about 3′ on the edge of two of the boards. How can I get the floor level again?

R.H., Los Alamos, N.M.

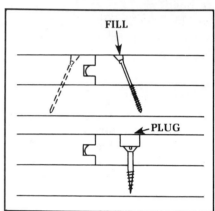

FILL

PLUG

A.   You can try forcing the boards back down level by weighting them, but you might break the tongue off this way. If the dampness that caused the warping in the first place has long since disappeared, there is little chance that they will break and it would be worth a try. Lay a 2x4 along the joint and weight it, increasing the weights until the boards lay flat. Then nail as shown. Use your nail set and fill the depressions for a neater appearance. You can also draw the boards down with screws and plug the pre-drilled hole as in the second diagram.

If the area is still rather damp, though, the weights might break the boards. About the only thing you can do in this case is a method that is both quick and easy, but tends to mar the floor's appearance somewhat. We only suggest it because you have carpeting over it. Using a circular power saw, angle a cut in between the two warped boards and cut lengthwise up the entire warped area. This cut is called a pocket cut (as opposed to a flat cut where the saw starts cutting at the end of the wood rather than in the middle and is held flat). When finished you will have made a lengthwise gouge in the floor about 1/8" wide in between the two boards. The results will be almost immediate. You'll find that the warped boards will probably go down to about half of their present height almost before your eyes. In a matter of time they should go down all the way, flat with the others without any other work on your part. If they do tend to stay a little warped, you can weight them after the airing has dried them out.

Filling floor cracks

Q. We have floors of 2x6 tongue-and-groove Douglas fir which we are about to sand, stain and finish. However, there are cracks between boards of various widths, some as wide as 3/4". We are considering the use of mahogany strips or a mixture of redwood sawdust and glue. We like the sawdust and glue method best but we are afraid that in time it will crack and chip out.

P.I., Ukiah, Calif.

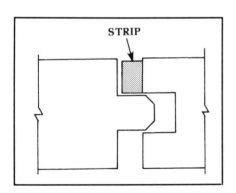

STRIP

A. It is most unusual to have tongue-and-groove boards as far apart as you mention. The purpose of T & G is to permit slight movement yet maintain alignment. In most cases the cracks between T & G boards are hardly more than 1/32" and 3/4" is certainly unreal. Yes, the sawdust and glue would ultimately crack and chip out. Whatever the width of the cracks in your floor, we suggest that you use mahogany strips toenailed to one side or the other.

Board cracks

Q. We have purchased an old Colonial home and before we refinish the floors will have to fill in some 1/2" spaces between some of the old 12" pine floorboards. This will take a lot of wood filler. Is there another way?

R.S., Angelica, N.Y.

A. There are two other ways at least, both more apt to work than filler alone. Tap oakum caulking into each crack to a depth of about 1/16" below the floor surface, then fill with wood dough filler. Let dry, sand smooth. Use a tinted filler to match the floor for an inconspicuous job. Or paint glue inside the cracks and drive a pine slat or lath gently into the crack. Taper the strips—thicker on top—and use a wood block to pad the hammer. Sand floor preparatory to finishing after the strips are in. They will take stain and finish about the same as the flooring.

Gaps in floorboards

Q. Our house is made of used lumber. There is a good subfloor over heavy joists, but the top flooring is of used wide boards which do not fit together exactly. Some of the nails tend to work up and there are rather wide cracks where the tongue and grooves do not meet tightly. I have wondered about running Tite-Bond glue in the cracks. Would that keep the boards from wiggling? We have vinyl glued down over the floor in some of the rooms, and now we would like to put carpeting down in the living and dining rooms, but we don't want nails working up under it. What do you suggest?

R.H., Dodge City, Kan.

BOARDS MOVE INDEPENDENTLY

A. Whether you want it or not, a subflooring or underlayment of some substantial panel material is needed over wide boards that are not tight together. Even Tite-Bond will not stop major structural movement such as you are getting, and your carpet will wear unevenly if it is not laid over something much smoother than wide boards. (So will the vinyl you've already laid down.) You'll likely get failure at the line of movement between the boards before you'll have major trouble with nails working up through, but eventually both will happen.

Wide board gaps

Q. The floors in our recently purchased 20-year-old house are 12"-wide pine boards. They have separated and in many places have wide, ugly gaps where the tongue-and-groove has split off completely. The appearance doesn't bother us as much as the possibility of the gap catching heels, breaking someone's neck. What could be used as a filler? Plastic wood putty does not stay put. A mixture of fine sawdust and glue has been suggested. Would that be practical? Our carpenter's advice is "Get rid of them old pine boards and put down a nice, new oak floor." We hope you do not concur with that.

E.J., Denver, Colo.

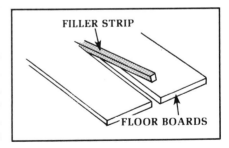

FILLER STRIP

FLOOR BOARDS

A. The carpenter has a point; a new floor would be an improvement. If tongue and grooves are not fulfilling their function you will have a problem keeping anything between two adjacent boards. If they move independently, your filler soon falls out.

Gaps wide enough to catch heels

had best be filled with wood strips. Taper the strips a bit so they are wider on top, and drive them into the cracks, coated with glue. But first do everything you can to firm up the floor underneath. Re-nail, wedge or split joists, etc. Fill, then sand and refinish the floor.

Wobbly floors

Q. My floors are very wobbly. When anyone walks across the kitchen or living room everything shakes. The house is 20'6" x 28'6" with the joists running the 28' direction and resting on a center beam. We have only single thickness floors but there is no visible slope. What can I do?

J.M., Erie, Pa.

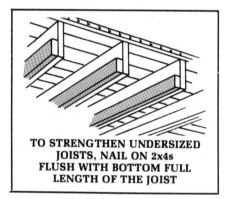

TO STRENGTHEN UNDERSIZED JOISTS, NAIL ON 2x4s FLUSH WITH BOTTOM FULL LENGTH OF THE JOIST

A. The floor joists should be 2x10s spaced 16" apart for this span. Smaller joists may be strengthened either by adding a second joist the same size along-side each of the present ones, spiking them together or by nailing a 2x4 flush with the lower edge of each joist the full length.

Damaged subfloor

Q. We started building but were interrupted. Now the subfloor is warped and uneven. We can't sand it due to all those nail heads nor can it be removed and replaced as the partition walls now rest on it. Could you suggest a solution?

W.S., Harrison, Mich.

A. Set the nail heads, then sand. Use only medium grit paper

in the sanding machine. With a layer of 15-lb. felt between the subfloor and finish floor plus the sanding, you'll have a level floor.

Subfloor not diagonal

Q. I'm finishing off two bedrooms in my attic and need advice on installing hardwood flooring. The subfloor is 1x6 square-edged lumber laid at right angles to the joists. I believe subflooring is usually laid diagonally and the finish floor is at right angles to the joists. Should I lay my oak strips parallel to the subfloor?

H.S., Arlington, Va.

A. Diagonal subflooring is preferred but quite often it is laid at right angles. You lay the finish flooring at right angles to the subfloor, that is parallel to the joists. This prevents dishing of the subfloor boards.

Dropped subfloor

Q. Can I cut off the tops of the joists to lower the subfloor so quarry tile will be level with wood tile in the finished floors?

L.R., Moorhead, Minn.

A. Cutting off the joists is apt to weaken them a bit too much. Far better to set cleats at the sides of the joists in the area to be tiled and lay 3/4" plywood subflooring on them, between the joists and flush with the tops of the joists. Then cover with 1/4" exterior grade plywood and lay your quarry tile on that.

Subfloor fungus

Q. One area of the subfloor of my home is covered with fungus and mold. I am planning to insulate it, but first I would like to find a product to apply to the wood that will prevent it from rotting. Can you suggest something?

J.D., Hillside, N.J.

A. Before you apply a preservative to the wood, you must get rid of the fungus and mold. Scrub the area with Clorox and allow it to dry thoroughly (if it's the least bit wet, your problems will continue). Then, use a preservative with mildewcide properties to prevent further decay. Be sure to remove any wood that is already decayed before you apply the preservative.

Tile over tile

Q. We have vinyl-asbestos tile on our kitchen floor with urethane varnish on it for easier cleaning. Now we wish to lay new pure vinyl tile over this. The varnish people write that this could be done if the floor is first sanded well—presumably to remove varnish and roughen tile. Is this true? What is the easiest and cheapest method to re-lay tile?

G.D., Reading, Mass.

A. You should indeed follow the specifications of the manufacturer of the tile you will use. While a few do admit to success in installing tile-over-tile provided sufficient sanding gives a clean, good tooth to the old surface, most suggest removal of the previous

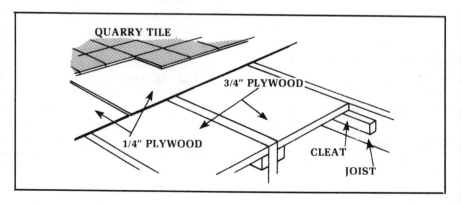

QUARRY TILE

3/4" PLYWOOD

1/4" PLYWOOD

CLEAT

JOIST

tile and proper repair of the underlayment as needed. An underlayment of hardboard over existing tile will increase the total thickness but you might prefer it to tile removal. It does add the cost of the underlayment but it also meets the requirements of most manufacturers for a sound, level, clean surface.

Moisture in subfloor

Q. The floor around my kitchen sink is positively soggy. It has vinyl asbestos tile on plywood. Is there some way we can take the bounce out when re-tiling?

D.L., West New York, N.J.

A. Over and over again we recommend the use of exterior grade or marine plywood where there is any danger of excessive moisture. First remove the tiles and see how bad the situation really is—look for dry rot. You'd be better off to replace the subfloor with the proper type of plywood, cover with 15-lb. felt and lay your new tiles on that. The difficulty is that all floor-based fixtures have to come up for this replacement job.

Removing tile

Q. The vinyl tile in our kitchen (over wood) and utility room (over concrete) is curled and buckled. We want to replace it, but don't know how to remove the cemented-down flooring.

P.H., Goodrich, Mich.

A. You can freeze and chip, or you can heat and lift. Either way you will have some scraping and clean-up work to finish the job. The easy way to handle the freezing method is a simple wood frame to contain and allow you to move the dry ice around. The best way to heat is with a heat lamp. You're working to provide a sound, clean surface, so sand any dried adhesive remnants. Try not to gouge when you scrape and make sure you get up all the loose material before you lay new tile.

Tar paper cure?

Q. I want to put some roll tile on the kitchen floor which is beech. The floor is smooth, but I've been told that on a floor like this there will be wear spots and roll flooring should be put over hardboard or plywood. I don't want to do that because of the doors, etc. Please advise if felt tar paper will solve the problem.

T.P., Jackson, Miss.

A. Modern floor coverings, such as vinyl tile, vinyl-asbestos tile, linoleum, sheet goods, etc., are flexible to a greater or lesser degree. They have little structural value, and their purpose is primarily to provide an attractive wearing surface. That is why you need a smooth, sound underlayment. Felt will not prevent the independent movement of one floor board alongside another.

Floor sandwich

Q. Some years ago vinyl tile was installed over the previous layer of tile in our home. Now there are two layers of paper and two layers of tile. New tile will now be needed and I am planning on using 1/4" plywood over the present installation. Is this practical?

C.D., Toledo, Ohio

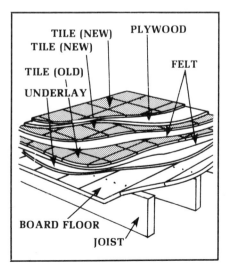

TILE (NEW)
TILE (NEW)
TILE (OLD)
UNDERLAY
PLYWOOD
FELT
BOARD FLOOR
JOIST

A. Eventually there comes a time when adding another layer of

floor tile is not the best option. You may have arrived at that point. If you are installing new tile now because the existing tile is not in good shape, we'd suggest you remove both layers and start new. Your plywood subfloor by now may not be in good shape and you might as well fix it now. The only way to find out is to remove both layers of tile and both layers of paper. When you find out what is there, follow the manufacturer's directions for properly preparing the surface. If you install plywood plus tile over your existing floor, you'll most likely have to trim some off the bottoms of doors and may have a threshold problem. Also if you tile-and-plywood the floor up to, but not under, built-in cabinets, then if you later change the layout of your kitchen, you've created a two-level floor.

Wet subflooring

Q. Our bathroom has vinyl asbestos tiles laid over a plywood subfloor. Moisture from bathing, etc., manages to work into the floor between the joints of the tile and this results in warping the veneer of the subflooring which raises the floor tile. How can we waterproof the existing flooring or install a new covering which would be waterproof?

N.J., Dearborn, Mich.

A. You will have to remove the tiles to start any renovation. If you can dry the plywood thoroughly and nail it down without any bulges, it can be left in service. Lay new tiles on a covering of 15-lb. felt which should be secured to the plywood with tile adhesive but without overlap. You could eliminate the between-tile joints using inlaid linoleum if you prefer.

Bulging tiles

Q. Our new home is radiantly heated. We covered over the old asphalt tile flooring with the vinyl asbestos that was highly recommended to us. However, a few of the present tiles bulge. Could this be trapped air or is it caused by heat?

M.M., Atwater, Calif.

A. It's not a good idea to have two layers of tile on a radiantly heated floor. You should have taken up the asphalt first, before laying the vinyl asbestos. It is probably the heat that is causing the tiles to bulge. There might be a bit too much adhesive in some places or, perhaps the top layer is trapping too much heat into the asphalt tile layer and your expansion rate is slightly different between the two kinds of tiles. Is the bulged area in front of a door or under a window, or in any sort of pattern that would indicate an additional common factor that would explain it? The ultimate solution, however, is having just one layer of finishing material.

Problem tile cement

Q. I have a problem with the tile cement on my floor which keeps coming up between the tiles. The floor was laid over painted concrete. Do you think too much cement was used? Can I cover the old tile over by cementing on paper and then laying new tile on top of this?

J.S., Fayette City, Pa.

A. The usual cause of tile cement coming up between tiles is too much cement. You may have an additional problem if the cement used was not meant to go over painted concrete (and few are). We would not suggest putting anything new over something old that is not properly affixed. It is almost always better to take off the misapplied stuff, clean it up and put down the right material in the proper way. In your case, take up the old tile, check the paint type and compatibility with the tile cement you want to use (which also should be right for the tile you will use). Of course, there may also be something wrong with the cement itself, which is the most likely cause of the problem. It may be that some further treatment of the painted surface is required. Your dealer should be able to advise you once you give him all the details. You could also write to the tile manufacturer.

Tile removal

Q. What is the best way to remove linoleum tiles from a plywood floor?

W.N., Taft, Calif.

A. The linoleum tile may be laid over felt, in which case you can ease the two up together using the pry power of a broad (about 3" wide) blade of a floor chisel. Do it gently so that you do not gouge the plywood underneath. If the tile is laid bare on the plywood, you can still use the chisel but you will have more work to do. Residue of felt and adhesive can be removed usually with commercially available chemical tile remover solutions. Follow those directions. Do not soak the floor with water as you will wind up with a delaminated plywood subfloor.

Rotted substructure

Q. Our floor beams and joists over a crawl space were full of dry rot. They will have to be replaced I know, but what can we do to prevent its happening again?

K.S., Jackson Heights, N.Y.

A. Ample height in the crawl space—no wood closer than 2'6" to the ground—is the first point. Use a preservative on all wood before cutting and all joints after cutting. Cover the ground of the crawl with a suitable moisture barrier. Provide sufficient ventilation. Proper grading for surface drainage is also important.

Preparing for tiling

Q. After removing old linoleum, is there a fast way to clean the remaining paste and felt off a hardwood floor to get it ready for asphalt tile?

J.P., Youngstown, Ohio

A. You can soften old paste with warm water, with turpentine or with a lacquer solvent followed up with a scraper. A floor sander equipped with medium coarse paper does the job quicker. A coarse grit paper on the sanding disc of an electric drill or on a belt sander will work if you're careful. Since the first step toward laying tiles is to cover the floor with tarpaper, the floor need only be made firm and level—appearance isn't important.

Tile in basement

Q. I want to use cork tile in our basement living room but the dealers we've spoken to say it is not satisfactory. If we put down wood first, could we use cork tile?

S.M., Lackawana, N.Y.

A. The dealers are right. If you put down a wood subfloor in the basement you'll invite some addi-

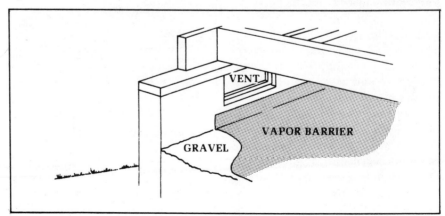

tional problems and still not have a satisfactory floor. We'd suggest you look at some of the cork-like patterns available in asphalt and vinyl asbestos tiles and settle for one of those.

Tile over tile

Q. My present floor is vinyl asbestos tile. It was of an inferior quality and has now commenced coming loose and in some cases the tiles have torn. The plywood sub-floor is in good condition, either 5/8″ or 3/4″ thick. I want to put down a new floor of all vinyl tile. Can I lay a new underlayment of plywood or hardboard over the present floor, then lay new tile on top? I have heard it may be better to pull up all the present tile and start over but this seems like an awful lot of work.

D.R., Florissant, Mo.

A. You can put down 1/8″ or 3/16″-thick hardboard over your present tiles and lay the new ones on this but every door swinging over these tiles may have to be trimmed for clearance. You should also fill any crumbled-away-completely areas under the hardboard first. Perhaps best is removal of all old tiles, sanding off old paste and getting back to the base. Which is really the most work depends a bit on how bad the present tile really is.

Painted floor

Q. Is there any kind of a paint for a concrete floor which does not have to be removed in order to install a tile floor later?

E.M., Long Island City, N.Y.

A. Oil base paints on concrete in contact with the earth must be removed completely. Good quality latex base paint is not affected by alkali and would not have to be removed, according to some resilient tile manufacturers. It is extremely important that you follow the specifications of the manufac-

turer as to primer and/or adhesive. Some epoxy resin paints could be tiled over but their cost is such that you probably would not consider tiling for some time. Any flaking or peeling paint must be removed and probably indicates a dampness problem which should first be corrected.

Cork tile

Q. Our cork tile floors are finally getting a bit run down in appearance. Is there some way they can be perked up to last a bit longer?

R.D., Hackensack, N.J.

A. You can use a floor sander on them but only the medium to fine paper should be used. After the floor is dusted you can use a coat of synthetic resin floor varnish or a floor sealer.

Hardboard over tile

Q. I am planning to put down a new tile floor. I want to put a hardboard underlayment over the old tile floor in order to make a smooth, even base for the new floor. Do I need a layer of felt lining between the two?

R.H., Mundelein, Ill.

A. You may lay the hardboard down over old tiles without an underlayment of tarpaper. We're guessing that the original floor is wood. For a good job use coated or spirally grooved nails to put down the hardboard.

Baseboard substitute

Q. How are those vinyl baseboards installed? We are finishing our attic and using vinyl tile on the floors. I'd imagine these baseboards would be easier to keep clean than wood ones, and also we wouldn't have to paint them.

E.E., Jackson, Tenn.

A. The top-set cove baseboards are cleaned the same as the floor tiles are and they do eliminate the

task of painting at that point. You need to have a smooth, dry surface straight down to the floor to which the strips can be cemented. The adhesive is applied to the back of the base with a notched trowel and the base pressed in place against the wall. Then roll the surface and push the floor edge against the wall with a piece of wood. Preformed corners are available or you can cut and bend the strips to form corners as you need them, heating with a torch and cooling in water to set the shape.

Too much adhesive

Q. I put vinyl tile on my kitchen floor using asphalt tile cement. It was my first job and I used too much cement and now it is coming up between the tiles and I don't know what to use to get it off the tiles.

J.D., Newark, N.J.

A. You don't have as big a problem as you think. There isn't that much difference between vinyl and asphalt tile adhesives. Denatured alcohol will soften the tile adhesive nicely so that it can be wiped up, without damage to the tile surface.

Cove bases

Q. I like the looks of those floors that just turn up at the edges, rather than having a different color baseboard. Is this difficult and how is it accomplished?

E.W., Topeka, Kan.

A. Most manufacturers of sheet goods make available a filler strip which is installed at the juncture of floor and wall for the flush type cove base you describe. Careful scribing is necessary to make the material turn up properly and fit into the metal binding strip that is first attached along the wall. The corner cuts must be made exactly right for a tight joint there. As for being difficult, if you feel confident of installing sheet vinyl at all, this additional step is not going to throw you.

New kitchen floor

Q. I plan to put vinyl tile on my kitchen floor. The present plywood floor has a wavy surface from being walked on for quite some time. Is there a product I can use to smooth this surface?

R.C., N. Sebago, Me.

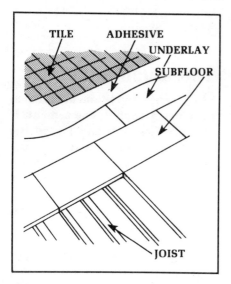

A. If the plywood surface is a subfloor, an underlayment (either hardboard or plywood) is almost a necessity, and it's certainly a better solution than using a filler to smooth over the worn plywood. Make sure the nails on the old floor are well set, then install the underlay according to the specifications for whatever kind you use. Proceed with tiling, following the manufacturer's directions.

Regrouting a tile floor

Q. I would appreciate your advising me if a ceramic tile floor can be regrouted. After having grouted it the first time a year ago, we find it is not as good a job as we would like it to be.

W.L., Montauk, N.Y.

A. To regrout a ceramic tile floor, it is necessary to have some sort of crevices between tiles into which the grout can be worked. Any loose grout must be scraped

out with a pointed instrument and wire brushed clear. When joints are opened up at least 1/16" deep, regrouting becomes possible.

Broken tile floor

Q. We just bought a 50-year-old house in which the ceramic tile bathroom floor is badly cracked and uneven. Would breaking up this tile floor and substituting asphalt tile be too big a job for amateurs?

A.D., Laurelton, N.Y.

A. You can break up the floor using a hammer and chisel. You'll discover cement under the tile in a house that age.

Soiled tiles

Q. About two months ago we had a tile floor laid in our new bathroom but it defies all my efforts to get it clean. I believe some of the trouble is due to the paper and adhesive the tile was stuck to. Can you offer a solution to this problem?

M.F., Bay Shore, N.Y.

A. Use an electric drill with a lamb's wool buffer attachment. Buy some powdered pumice at a paint store and mix with enough water to form a thin paste. Work over the floor with this and the buffer. Rinse with clear water.

Hardwood flooring

Q. In finishing the interior of our home, our present problem is installing oak flooring. We've never done any carpentry before and don't quite know how to get started.

T.M., Melrose Park, Ill.

A. Stack the flooring flat for two weeks at room temperature with spacers between to allow for shrinkage before laying. Sweep the subfloor clean, check for any protruding nails, then cover with 15-lb. asphalt saturated felt. Stretch a string to guide you in lining up

the first course. If you will run flooring parallel to long wall, set nails at opposite ends of the room at equal distances from that wall for the string. If you lay flooring at right angles to entrance, establish diagonal lines from opposite corners crossing at room center and measure from this point to each wall. Use a framing square on this line to draw guide line for flooring. Lay the first board with grooved side against one wall. Drive nails through upper part of tongue at an angle into the subfloor. On this first board only nail straight down through opposite edge and counterset these nails. Continue on across room a course at a time. Every three courses, hold a piece of scrap against a tongue and strike with a hammer to drive nailed flooring snug. Use cut steel nails or screw type flooring nails. Joints in adjacent rows should be at least 6" apart. You'll find it easiest to lay out loosely on the floor the pieces for the next few courses, a good job for the helper.

Lining felt

Q. Is there any right or wrong direction to lay the felt you put under tiles over a tongue-and-groove wood floor? What about the joints?
E.Y., Malden, Mass.

A. Lay lining felt so it runs across the floor boards rather than parallel to them. Always use butt seams. Lapping the joints would make ridges in the finished floor. Turn pieces upside down as you cut them so they flatten out better.

Short length oak

Q. I am going to have oak floors installed in my home. The contractor has suggested using 2' bundles. Would a floor made up of 2' bundles be as good as one made up of bundles of a longer length?
G.K., Brooklyn, N.Y

A. Those 2' bundles of oak flooring are not all pieces exactly 2' long but random lengths about 2'.

The ends are tongued and grooved as well as the sides. Properly laid, these strips interlock and make a fair type floor a good deal less expensive than the longer length. Your contractor's suggestion is sound.

Flooring at archway

Q. Small question on what happens when two floors meet. We plan oak flooring in one room that opens off a hall that is tiled. There is no door, just an archway. Which material runs into the doorway?

M.T., Maplewood, N.J.

A. Run the oak flooring through the archway to join the tiles which will end flush with the hall walls.

Wood block flooring

Q. What do you put under wood block flooring? I want to do our attic floors which are now just subflooring of 1x6 straight edge boards.

J.C., Winfield, Kan.

A. There are block floors and block floors, finished and unfinished, made up of solid wood flooring or laminated of plywood or fancy parquet tiles. Almost any of them would require at least 1/2" plywood over your subfloor, properly nailed around the edges and through the center to the joists. Some if not all require building paper. Some types of block can be mastic applied, others can only be nailed. Laminated blocks do not require as much allowance for expansion and contraction as solid strip blocks do.

Block flooring

Q. We have a fairly new house with a plywood floor in the attic which we want to cover with wood block flooring. I understand there is some way to use adhesive for wood tile applications. Can we do that here? The plywood is either 5/8" or 3/4" and the floor beams are the ceiling joists for the rooms below and they are 16" on center.

We would rather use prefinished blocks.

J.C., Winetka, Ill.

A. You are all set. Sweep the floor clean and check that it is level and well nailed. One type of flooring blocks that you can use is solid hardwood, 5/16" thick in 6" x 6" blocks held together by knurled wires in the back of the tile. Follow the manufacturer's directions and apply the recommended adhesive. Tile is set immediately in some types of adhesive, others require a waiting period so check instructions well. Mineral spirits of naptha is used to clean off excess adhesive but if you drop blocks in place rather than sliding them you'll not have this difficulty.

Block floor layout

Q. We've seen a kind of block flooring made up of strips of wood into squares. Can this be laid kitty-corner across a room?

A.T., West New York, N.J.

A. Assuming your subfloor is properly installed and you follow the manufacturer's installation directions as to nailing or adhesive application, there is no reason block flooring cannot be laid diagonally. Just make sure your starting lines intersect at right angles. You follow the same pyramid system of installation.

Finish flooring

Q. I am finishing my attic which has a subfloor laid at right angles to the joists. How should the finish

flooring be laid? Some say at right angles to the subfloor, others say in the same direction.

J.T., Cleveland, Ohio

A. Lay the finish floor at right angles to the subfloor. Otherwise warping of the broader subfloor will be indicated by a wavy effect in the finish floor.

Read the label

Q. About a month ago I put parquet tile on our living room floor which looked smooth enough not to use underlayment as per instructions. It must not have been as level as we thought as there are noticeable cracks of 1/32" to 1/16" where full rows join— the small blocks that make up each tile are tight. Is there some type of grouting filler that could be used to fill the cracks to match this light oak wood? I want the floor to look as nice as I have seen it in other homes.

C.M., Clifton, N.J.

A. Read the labels. Follow the specifications. We know of no special filler for floor tile cracks and can only suggest you try one of the commercial available wood-putty fillers. There is some variety in color available so shop around. It might even be worthwhile to take up the tile and try again, this time following the instructions. We suggest you contact the manufacturer on that possibility. He might be able to recommend the easiest solvent for removing the particular adhesive used.

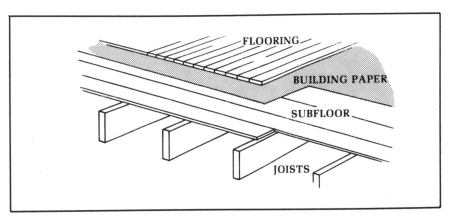

Ceiling Problems

**Basement ceilings...Beams...Dropped ceilings...Lighting ceilings
...Paneling...Repairs...Tiles.**

Basement ceilings

Q. What can be used to cover the ceiling joists to finish off a basement room?

J.H., Pittsburgh, Pa.

A. There is a variety of suitable materials, in sheet or panel form as well as tiles, plywood, gypsum wallboard, hardboard, insulation board in 4' x 8' panels and decorative or acoustical tile, in 12" x 12", 24" x 24" or even 24" x 48" sizes. All materials are best mounted on furring strips attached across the ceiling joists. Original cost, ease of installation and maintenance necessary are all points for you to consider in addition to appearance.

Covering pipes

Q. If I "box in", as they say, every cable and pipe in my ceiling so as to use tile on furring strips I'll have about six boxes and this seems like an awful lot of work. Two places the pipe runs parallel to the joists so notching them is not the solution. Can you tell me what is?

T.Y., Midland, Mich.

A. If these pipes and cables of yours project less than 1-1/2" or so,

see if double furring won't solve the problem for you. One set of furring strips across the joists on 2' or 2'6" centers over which you run the second set at right angles to them spaced to take the tiles. Nail through both sets at each joist.

Pipes in joists

Q. In finishing off the ceiling I would like to raise the copper hot water lines, notching into the 2x10 joists 1-1/8" for the 1" pipes. This would leave about 8-5/8".

J.V., South River, N.J.

IF CROSS-SECTION LEFT ABOVE NOTCH IS SUFFICIENT TO CARRY THE LOAD OVER THE SPAN YOU HAVE, GO AHEAD

A. Maximum span of 2x10 joists at 16" spacing is 15' 3" and that of a 2x8 joist system 12' 1". If the span of your floor joists is

between these limits you can safely cut them. Attach a steel plate across each cut. Line each recess all around with pipe insulation to avoid expansion noise.

Fitting beams

Q. We would like to use decorative beams on our ceiling, but two of the walls begin to pitch slightly about a foot or so below the ceiling. Can we run these beams to the pitched sides?

G.R., Reading, Pa.

A. There is no reason why you cannot run the false beams across the ceiling as you desire. Just miter them at the proper angle on each end to correspond with the slight pitch where they butt against the walls. To copy the exact angle of the pitch from the wall to the beam, use an adjustable square.

Cracked beams

Q. I moved into my ranch style home last spring. The living room has exposed oak beams, 4x6 and 15' long. Since I moved in they have developed some rather large cracks that have me wondering as to how the strength of the beams is affected. I have a floor above for storage only.

L.R., Harrisburg, Pa.

A. If the cracks are along the grain you have little to worry about. They are not abnormal in heavy timber exposed to hot, dry air. There would be little if any loss in strength. Only if the grain runs off the centerline to the edges between beam ends would there be any danger. Oak is unusually strong and straight grained.

Beamed ceiling

Q. My 80-year-old home has a 14' x 18' living room with an 8'4" papered ceiling. I want to install a beamed ceiling. Will you please give me information on the proper spacing of the beams and their minimum size, since I will build them myself?

M.S., Mills, Pa.

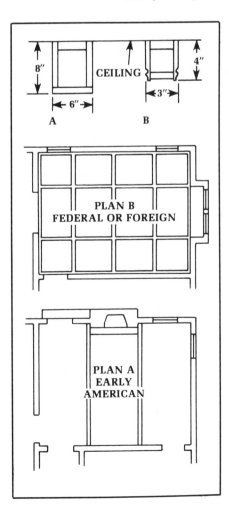

A. We assume you refer to natural finished wood beams to contrast with a light ceiling. You might want to think of how the room would have been built had it been framed with beams originally. For example, if you have a fireplace on one wall, you might have two 6" x 8" beams perpendicular to it, dividing the room into thirds. With a bay window, you might divide it in thirds again and divide the length in quarters across it using smaller beams. You might do a trial run using strips of brown paper in the proper widths. Just remember dark wooden beams will look heavier than the paper; if you paint the beams to match the ceiling, you can use wider ones.

False beams

Q. I want to make a beamed ceiling where no beams are. Can you tell me how to make false ones to fasten over plaster and how to hold them on?

T.S., Westfield, Conn.

A. You need an anchor board to fasten to the ceiling at each beam position, nailing through the plaster into the ceiling joists. The width of this must be exactly the same as the inside width of your false beams. Build the beam with one piece the full width for the bottom and two strips for the vertical sides. Glue and nail through the bottom piece into the two sides. Then nail through the sides into the anchor strips to fasten the beam in place. You may want to install a half-beam

around the perimeter, which is easy enough but you will need two strips or cleats inside the beam, one for the bottom and one for the side pieces to fasten to.

Ceiling materials

Q. We are finishing up a shell house and have a ceiling problem. Is it better to put up furring strips, then acoustical tile or to go ahead with gypsum wallboard and put up the tile with adhesive? The joists are 16" on center and this is in the living and dining area, under the bedrooms.

W.T., Paramus, N.J.

A. We'd vote for the gypsum wallboard. It eliminates the chance of error in measuring furring strips, is a good ceiling by itself should you wish to defer tiling. Tiles alone will not prevent noise transmission, and solid blocking for panel ends will strengthen the floor some. The cost is roughly the same but the installation somewhat simpler with the board.

Clean ceiling tile

Q. There are some pencil marks and a few fingerprints on our new ceiling tile. How do we get these off?

I.J., Poultney, Vt.

A. On many types of acoustical tile, art gum eraser (from your art supply or stationery store) will do it. Turn the eraser often to avoid smearing if it was very soft pencil.

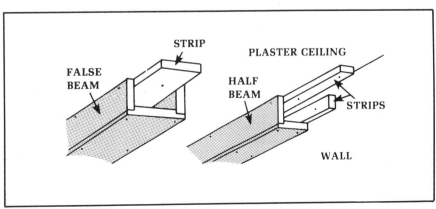

On larger smudges, try wallpaper cleaner with care. Either putty or paste-type works. Just make sure it is fresh and clean. Of course, if the tile is washable, use a mild soap and warm water. Use more suds than water and rinse with clear water, again as little water as possible. Wring out your cloth or sponge so the tiles are not soaked. The other direction is camouflage. A bit of chalk can often make a mark disappear. Here's a tip from tile manufacturers: To avoid getting fingerprints on ceiling tile, wash your hands and dust them with talcum powder before handling or installing the tile.

Ceiling height

Q. My problem is my living room which is about 18' x 26'. The rafters and studs of the wall are exposed. The roof has a steep pitch and I have collar ties 10' long tying the roof together. From the top of the plate to the inside of the collar ties is a distance of 8'. We want to do something about surfacing the ceilings and walls. It has been suggested to me that I put up a new set of collar ties below the existing ones. Would you recommend that?
B.M., Manchester, N.H.

A. Lowering the ceiling is a matter of personal preference. By lowering your ceiling beams 2' you would then have an 11' ceiling at the same time reducing the sloping portions and putting them further back from the center of the room. But you'll need at least 2x6 and preferably 2x8 stock for this purpose, due to the increased span. If 2x6s are used, vertical ties of 1x4 stock to the present collar beams should be added.

Compressed moisture

Q. I just dropped my ceilings in the living and dining rooms and now my walls are covered with moisture. Could it be the rooms are sealed off too tightly?
J.S., Chicago, Ill.

A. Your first move should be to trace the source of humidity and reduce it. Don't allow the humidity to build up in the area between old and new ceilings or it may condense there and stain the new ceiling.

Low ceiling

Q. I like the looks of the light-paneled (flourescent) dropped ceilings but to get the proper clearances I figure I'd have the dropped ceiling at 7'2" as our present kitchen ceiling is 8' exactly. Is this too low?

T.S., Muncie, Ind.

A. The 7'2" is not too low. Many are dropped to the top of upper cabinets usually 7'. You might consider the possibility of recessing the fixtures between present ceiling joists, gaining 2" or more. This does limit you to one-directional fixture placement which may not suit you, but it is worth considering.

High ceilings

Q. I am concerned about ceiling problems in several rooms of my home. The house is 70 years old; ceilings 12' high, walls not plumb or square. The options seem to be a hung or suspended ceiling or a false ceiling (rafters, furring strips, and 12" x 12" tile.) What's your opinion?

D.F., Wesson, Miss.

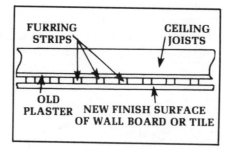

FURRING STRIPS — CEILING JOISTS — OLD PLASTER — NEW FINISH SURFACE OF WALL BOARD OR TILE

A. In the South, ceiling height of 12' or more was common in the days before mechanical air conditioning. High ceilings keep the rooms cooler. We'd suggest you retain the ceiling height. Apply 1x2 furring strips over the old ceiling, nailing them into the joists above the plaster. Just tack the strips to the ceiling, then shim them level with cedar shingles before nailing them tight. You should space the furring strips 12" on center for ceiling tile; 16" on center for wallboard. The wallboard can be taped and spray textured or painted flat. Installing the furring strips and either tile or wallboard would be your most economical solution, and would be an easy project to do yourself.

Level furring

Q. I don't understand how furring strips level the ceiling. I patiently put up about 14 rows of the things, tiled the ceiling in our basement room and find it is still bumpy with the tile corners never meeting flush. Does the tile thickness vary?

L.J., Chelsea, Mass.

A. The tile thickness probably doesn't vary much. Furring strips do not automatically level the ceiling when you run them across the joists. It is necessary to check with a level and shim with bits of wood shingle to bring the furring strips level first, after determining what is the lowest point you have to work to. The bottom edges of rough joists are seldom exactly level or true with each other.

Joist height

Q. How does one go about finding the lowest joist in the basement?

J.S., St. Louis, Mo.

A. Take a long string and fasten to the bottom of the end joist. Run across the joists to the opposite wall. Some joists will not touch the string when it is pulled tight, others will make it bend down. They're the low ones. Another method: Take a long piece of light wood (at least 6' long) and rest across as many joists as it will span, a straight edge of the board up. With it level, run until the end butts into a joist that is lower than all others touched. Do the same thing from the opposite direction.

Furring method

Q. **Could you tell me, please, about furring the ceiling which is open joists before tiling our basement family room? How do we start?**

S.C., Chicago Heights, Ill.

A. Select your tile first as the furring spacing depends on the tile size. Most often it goes on 12" centers but a few types use a metal strip which is furring and joint clip combined. Assuming you will use 1x2 or 1x3 strips, find the center of the ceiling joists and work toward the walls at either side. You need a strip along the edge of the ceiling though this may not be a full tile width. Use two 8d nails at each joist crossing. Check spacing often and do not drive nails home till you are sure each strip is level. Some will require shimming with thin wood strips driven in between furring and bottom of joist.

Sagging ceilings

Q. **I'm looking for a way to remedy sagging ceilings caused by the use of 2x4s for ceiling joists which I suspect are on 24" centers. I cannot use a beam across the two rooms in the opposite direction of the joists because of brick which separates the two rooms and because of the excessive length. I can't jack up the ceiling and tie to roof rafters because they also are 2x4s on 24" centers.**

I am not too concerned about the sag in the ceilings of the rooms below as we are lowering ceilings 6", but someday I want to finish off the upstairs attic and the attic floor now sags too badly to do this.

Can you give me some idea of what would be involved to correct this sag in the ceiling?

W.H., Webster, S.D.

A. To answer your last question first, quite a bit is involved.

You give the dimensions at right angles to the joists, but it is the span (the length of the joists unsupported) that determines how heavy they need to be. For a floor, assuming the proportions as you've indicated them gives a length of 18' or 20' for the joists, you would need at least 2x10s on 16" centers which is nowhere near what you have. If the joists are 11' and 13' long, 2x8s should do it as that arched wall would be a bearing wall in that case which is quite likely.

We hope you haven't already lowered the ceilings because if you want to do that you might as well take out the whole floor structure and put in the right size joists—carry the ceiling and the floor correctly, in other words. Done as two jobs—lowering the ceiling and shoring up the floor—adds a lot of unnecessary weight. The accepted method for strengthening too-small or cracked joists is to nail a second member alongside the first. You would be well advised to have a local builder who knows his business come in and take a good look at your house. The solution of tying the sagging ceiling to the roof rafters often results in a sagging roof so you are right in not pursuing that path. The direction of the joists and the room sizes indicated are a bit out of the ordinary and it may be that the building is framed differently. The real solution should be obvious to a good builder who is right there on the scene. Just pay for his information—you can still do the work.

Lighted ceilings

Q. **How does one hang a suspened luminous ceiling?**

M.D., Mount Pleasant, Mich.

A. Exact details depend on precisely which system you use. Generally, hanger brackets, adjustable in some fashion for height of finished ceiling, are mounted through the present ceiling to the joists. Main grid members are

fastened to these brackets and cross grid members fasten to the main grid, making a suspended framework into which the diffusing panels are set. Some systems combine acoustical tiles and diffusing material panels in adjoining squares. Others use only the main grid members and a roll type diffusing material that runs the length of the room, held by the grid pieces on two sides.

Crown molding

Q. **I would like to build a drop ceiling in my living room and finish the joints where the wall meets the ceiling with a cove molding approximately 6" wide. Is such a molding suitable for use in dry wall construction obtainable anywhere?**

W.B., Jasnen, Saskatchewan

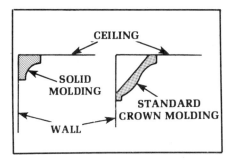

A. It is a normal practice to use such a molding for plaster or dry wall construction. It is a standard molding and should be available in most lumber yards.

Ceiling molding

Q. **We've bought a 40-year-old bungalow, in good shape and well built but it has those very heavy cove moldings and less than a foot below, a picture mold. Can I take these off, and if so what will I find behind? I'd like to have not more than a 2" molding at the edge of the ceilings.**

W.S., Oak Park, Ill.

A. You can take them off easily enough by prying them up carefully. You should find nailing grounds behind them and in a well built house, probably will. Remove these too and figure on a lot of plaster patching. It is not at all impossible but time-consuming and rather tedious work. You won't know exactly what is there till you get the moldings off and if there seems to be more wood than plaster, new lath and new plaster from the picture mold up may be simpler than the two rows of patching. On the ceiling, the plaster may continue further beyond the trim, giving you less of a problem.

Ceiling overhaul

Q. Since the plaster on my cove-edged ceiling is very bad, we decided to install plaster board and beams and fit a board around the edge to match the beam. We ran into problems, however, with the cove edge around the ceiling. I have seen an installation on a similar ceiling in which the ceiling tiles were slit in the back and glued around the ceiling to match the beams. Do you have any suggestions?

Y.M., St. Louis, Mo.

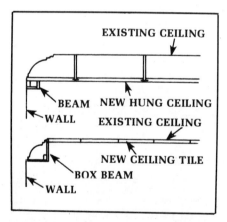

A. If your cove molding is small and located around the ceiling-wall joint, simply take off the molding, repair the plaster and add your beams, including one around the perimeter to cover the patches. If you have a plaster cove too large to be covered by the beams, install a dropped or hung ceiling as shown in the upper drawing. If you have 9'6" ceilings and the cove is, say 9", you can have an

8'9" finished ceiling wall height up to the curve by installing tile on the ceiling whose finished height would be only slightly less than the original as shown in the bottom drawing.

V-joint paneling

Q. I am using 8" tongue-and-grooved V-joint redwood boards to panel my ceiling. The joists are 16" on center and the boards are nailed blind. Is it necessary to cut the boards so they will join on a joist or will the tongue-and-grooved joint hold them tight enough where there is no joist?

L.K., New Concord, Ohio

A. Board ends should all meet on the joists. Flooring which is tongue and grooved at board ends as well as along the sides can be handled your way but you'd run the risk of warpage pulling those wide boards out of line and could end up with some rather unsightly gaps.

Damaged plaster

Q. We had a flood in the bathroom upstairs over our plastered dining room. The new paper was badly stained so we removed that but some of the plaster came with it. Now what is still there in the area that was wet is very crumbly.

R.T., Mayfield, Ky.

A. This plaster will never be the same again. If it does dry out more it will doubtless stay crumbly. You might just as well remove it and re-do the ceiling now. Damaged plaster just doesn't get well.

Old plaster

Q. I have an old house with cracked and sagging plaster on some ceilings. What is the best way to finish these rooms; is it possible to sand sagging cracks level and smooth and paint over them?

J.M., Great Falls, Mont.

A. Ceilings can be dangerous. If the plaster has pulled loose from the laths or if lath and plaster has sagged away from the joists, it would be better to tear this out and either replaster or cover with wallboard. Loose spots overhead can drop down all at once. Check all sagged areas carefully for this condition. If there are only cracks, they can be patched.

Repairing plaster

Q. As the result of a leak in my roof (now repaired) the plaster ceiling of one of my upstairs rooms has cracks, and there is a hole in one part of it where the plaster fell out leaving the wood lath exposed. How do I repair this ceiling? If plasterboard is used in the repair, how do you figure the angle at which the edges of the boards must be cut where they meet the sloping walls of this attic room?

D.R., Callender, Iowa

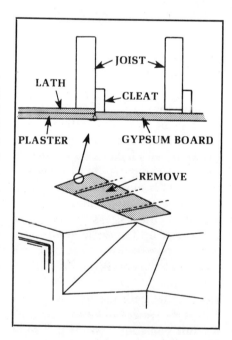

A. If more than half of the ceiling is badly damaged, it may be best to remove all the plaster and lath and replace it with plasterboard nailed to the joists in the usual way. On the other hand, if the hole is the main area of damage, cut a retangular area out of the

ceiling that includes the hole and the damaged parts around it. You can do the cutting easily with a keyhole or electric saber saw. Be careful not to cut through the joists (ceiling beams). Allow enough length for the plasterboard (used in patching the hole) to have solid support on a joist at each end. Choose plasterboard that matches the thickness of the plaster ceiling. If the lath and plaster of the ceiling are thicker than 5/8" (the thickest plasterboard you can buy), you will have to shim out the desired thickness with strips of wood applied to the joists.

Don't worry about the angle where the ceiling boards meet the sloping walls. The slight gap where they meet can be filled with joint compound, perforated paper tape and more compound.

Smooth ceiling

Q. A few years ago, an earthquake damaged the plaster ceilings in our 80-year-old house. Some plaster has fallen, while in other places it clings loosely to the lath. What can I use for repairs that can be painted and will appear to be one whole piece? (My wife does not like the looks of the square tiles).

P.R., Los Angeles, Calif.

A. The obvious answer is wallboard, properly nailed and with the joints smoothly taped and sanded. It may be possible to use the thinner wallboard meant for remodeling if enough of the plaster and lath still is in place to support it evenly. You'd install it over the old ceiling, nailing into the joists, and you would thus avoid the mess of plaster removal. Otherwise, remove all the old plaster and broken lath and install regular wallboard, as in new construction.

Open and shut case

Q. There is a crack in my plastered ceiling that will not stay mended. I've filled it after under-

cutting the plaster as you have described many times. The patching plaster always falls out. Is there no other answer?

R.E., Old Town, Maine

A. The other answer is a fiberglass repair tape developed for patching movable cracks in plaster that come and go with the weather changes. You apply the resin, press on the fabric tape, let dry and cover over with more resin.

Falling ceiling

Q. We have a bathroom with a plastered ceiling which has been papered several times. The plaster has let go in a number of places and must be repaired. Is there anything we can nail over it?

D.B., Staffa, Ontario

A. You can apply 1/2"-thick wallboard over the plaster. Before applying the wallboard, remove any plaster that is sagging, so your new ceiling will be level.

Cracked ceiling

Q. I'm having trouble with my ceiling plaster cracking over the living room. I had one man tell me the joists were not heavy enough. I used 2x6 joists, the room is 15-1/2' x 22' with joists running the narrow way spaced 16" apart. I used

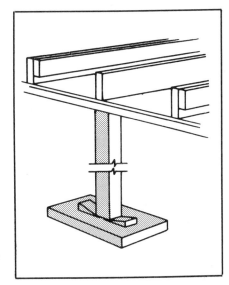

rock lath and plaster and did not bridge the joists. Above it is unused attic space.

M.J., Akron, Ohio

A. Maximum span for 2x6 joists with no added load overhead would be 15'4" which you exceed by 2"; no grave matter were it not for the heavier plaster ceiling material. You can add strength to the ceiling by nailing a 2x4 to every other joist, placing the 2" edge flush with the top edge of the joist, and spiking through both of them at 2' intervals. If there is any perceptible sag to the ceiling, prop it up before adding the 2x4s.

Ceiling cracks

Q. The ceiling in my older home has large, long cracks. The ceiling-to-wall joint is a large curve that I would like to retain. Is there an alternative to having a plasterer replace the entire ceiling? I've seen ads for spackles but wonder if they would expand and contract with the house. I also wonder if any ceiling tile exists that would conform to the curve.

D.S., Kenilworth, Ill.

A. Since you are specifically concerned with movement, a fiberglass patching system that bridges the cracks would seem to offer the best solution. Look for Krack-Kote (Pat. Pend.) and Tuffglass Fabric® packaged together with an applicator and instructions for making a pliable, permanent repair on interior walls and ceilings. You may want to write Tuff-Kote, 210 N. Seminary Ave., Woodstock, Ill. 60098 for specific information.

Oil on ceiling

Q. An oil-based substance ran down from my attic floor and stained the living room ceiling. The room has not been painted and I want to do this. What can I do to cover the oil stain when I paint the ceiling?

B.M., Baltimore, Md.

A. We're sorry to say there is probably no sure way to seal that oil into the plaster and woodwork above it so it won't continue to seep through and spoil paint. Apply a paste of corn starch and water thickly. Let dry to absorb as much oil as possible. Brush off when dry. Then apply two coats of glue size to seal the area as much as possible. Glue will adhere where shellac may not. This can then be painted over when dry. A rubber-base paint may prove of some help. It will depend largely on how much of the oily deposit remains in the wood overhead. In hot weather, it may seep through in spite of this treatment. The alternative is to cut out damaged plaster and patch it.

Insulated ceiling

Q. I would like to put a tile ceiling up. The present ceiling is plaster, badly cracked, and above the plaster is a layer of insulation. What is the best way to attach new ceiling tiles so they will adhere to the original plaster?
P.B., Muskogee, Okla.

A. On a cracked plaster ceiling you do not use adhesive to attach the tiles. Use 1x2 furring which will also hold up the plaster. Nail the strips at right angles to the joists, leaving plaster and insulation alone, spacing the furring to accommodate the tiles you select. Use a stapler to fasten the tiles to the furring strips.

Ceiling renovation

Q. The ceiling in my kitchen is plasterboard with vinyl fabric wall paper on it. Is there a glue or paste I could use to put up ceiling tiles right on the paper or could I staple them to the plasterboard?
A.S., Martinsville, N.J.

A. If you attach the blocks to the wallpaper it could pull loose and bring down the whole covering. Why not remove the wallpaper first? Wash off the old paste with

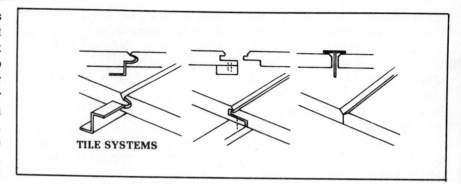

TILE SYSTEMS

warm water and if the ceiling is in good shape, go ahead with the tiles but use adhesive; staples won't hold in plasterboard.

Ceiling tiles

Q. I am planning on putting up ceiling tiles and would appreciate your advice. I understand there are a number of type blocks that can be used. Could you summarize their differences, please?
W.W., Linden, N.J.

A. Make the distinction between decorative tile which has a little thermal insulation value, may be pulpboard, may be predecorated and is less expensive generally than the acoustical tiles which are apt to be similar materials specially treated to add to their sound absorptive value. Most of the tiles are 12" x 12" but may be two units in one piece too. Most interlock in some way to conceal fasteners or have a spline joint or require a molding strip over the joints. Most can be put on ceilings in good shape with adhesive, or can be stapled or otherwise fastened to furring strips over a not-so-good ceiling or on furring on the bare joists. Some types are meant to go in suspended frameworks or to slip in specially designed metal channels.

Tiles over drywall

Q. My attic was finished off with 4 x 8 panels of a soft wallboard and painted and although the joints and nail heads were obvious, the job was adequate. As an improvement, I am thinking of gluing square ceiling tile to the existing ceiling. Is there a special glue for such a process or is there any other solution?
R.C., Ozone Park, N.Y.

A. If the present ceiling is rigid and not sagging, you might be able to do as you plan. The main trouble is that the added weight may cause both materials to sag together. There are a number of permanent adhesives that would do this part of the job. They are applied in gobs on the tiles and then pressed against the ceiling. Care must be taken not to get this on the surface as it can't be removed. As an alternate solution, you might consider texture paint which will conceal all the present cracks and blemishes and the weight would not be a problem.

Tile to tilted tile

Q. I am planning to tile the ceilings of several upstairs bedrooms. I am going to remove lath and plaster first, then install foil-faced insulation between the ceiling joists, fur across the joists and then tile. The problem is where the

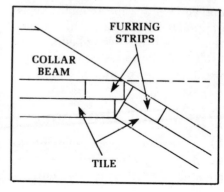

FURRING STRIPS

COLLAR BEAM

TILE

flat ceiling meets the sloped areas. What is the best way to make that joint? I thought of using a false beam at this point.

R.M., Spokane, Wash.

A. How neatly this joint can be made depends first on how your tile size works out and on the type of joint you work with. We've illustrated the easiest way to handle it. Your thought about the false beam whose size and position can be adjusted to utilize full tiles on both sloped and flat areas is a good one if you can work it out so that the beams are attractive.

Ceiling tear-out

Q. I intend to replace a ceiling, now plasterboard, with ceiling tile. When this house was built, loose insulating material was scattered over the plasterboard between all the floor beams. Is it practical to gather up this loose insulation and use it again over ceiling tile?

H.B., Oceanside, N.Y.

A. Why do you want to remove the plasterboard? If it is sound,

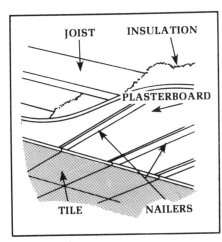

the tiles can be affixed to it with adhesive. If not, furring strips can be nailed through the plasterboard and into the joists above and the tiles stapled to the strips. Either way you eliminate the question of what to do with the insulation and have a better ceiling than just tile could provide.

Acoustical tile

Q. The living and dining room ceilings in our house are covered with acoustic tiles. We want to cover the ceilings without removing the tiles so as not to lose the benefits of noise reduction and heat savings.

At first we thought of lowering the ceilings, but decided against it because we wanted to keep the height. Now we want to cover the ceilings with natural wood, either paneling or individual pieces. How can we do this without removing the acoustical ceiling tiles? I don't think that they are strong enough to hold either paneling or pieces of wood.

L.Z., Brookfield, Ill.

A. The quick answer to your question of how to hold paneling to

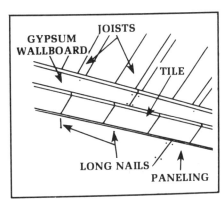

the ceilings over the tile is to simply use longer nails if the tiles are presently affixed to the underlying ceiling with adhesive, which seems most likely from your letter. If they are clip-attached you have a slightly different problem, in that you'll have to ascertain where the clips are to avoid these areas when you nail. You can only get the paneling to hold well enough if you nail into the joists, assuming the ceiling is as shown in the diagram. This takes a nail equal in length to the thickness of the paneling, the tile, the original ceiling and a good inch or more into the joist. If the ceiling tile is clip-applied on 1x2s at right angles to the joists (unlikely in your case), you would be better off removing it.

Tile replacement

Q. I have ceiling tiles measuring about 16″ x 31″. These are in a house about 40 years old. The roof has leaked and we need to replace some of the ceiling. I want to match these tiles, but I've checked with building supply companies here and they cannot help me. Where can I buy enough to replace four rows?

D.D., Cartersville, Ga.

A. We suggest you redo the whole ceiling. You'll probably find it more economical in the long run and depending on the house construction, it may also offer an easy opportunity to install insulation if you need that, too.

Ceiling cover-up

Q. I would like to install ceiling tile over a plaster ceiling, using adhesive. What type of edging or trim can be used between wall and ceiling, or can tiles be trimmed to fit flush?

J.S., North Augusta, S.C.

A. It's possible to put up ceiling tile and use no trim at the ceiling/wall joint. However, doing it neatly enough to look nice is diffi-

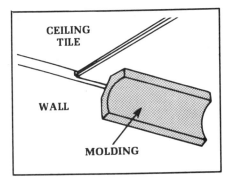

cult. The more usual solution is a cove mold of one style or another, though quarter-round can also be used. Exactly what profile you select will probably depend on what the rest of your woodwork looks like. Something small enough to be reasonably flexible works best in compensating for not-quite-flush walls. The diagram gives you the idea.

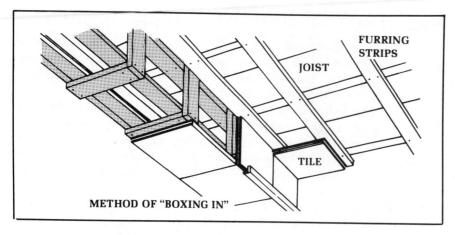

METHOD OF "BOXING IN"

Low ceiling for tile

Q. To save headroom, can I cement ceiling tile onto the ducts for our forced hot air heating system and if so what kind of cement is used?

B.A., Longview, Wash.

A. Ceiling tile cannot be cemented to hot air ducts. The expansion or contraction would quickly shed them off and besides what would hold up all the other tiles on the same level? Ducts may be flush with the underside of joists but even so joists alone won't serve for such tiles. You need furring strips here, usually 1x4 at right angles to the joists. This covers over the ducts as well as the joists. If ducts extend below joists, you might consider leaving them exposed to heat the basement or else box them in.

Pleasing pattern

Q. My husband put up 4' x 8' panels of hardboard on our dining room ceiling and covered the joists with 3/8" thick strips 2-1/2" wide of trim stock which we have painted white along with the hardboard but it still looks funny. I think the strips are too wide for one thing but it is the arrangement that bothers me most. It's three full panels down one side with one and a half cut 3' wide down the other. I don't know what to do to make it look good.

C.M., Las Vagas, Nev.

A. Get your husband back up there with some more strips. Have him use these extra strips to create a symmetrical, balanced arrangement. Narrower strips might still be preferred but it's up to you whether to take down those that are already in place or not. Using extra strips where they are not required is a decorative device that often comes in handy.

Attic tile

Q. In a past issue you recommended the use of ceiling tile in converting an attic with a kneewall into a room. Would you provide me with more details for this process? Specifically, how do you provide for the meeting of ceiling tiles at the angled joints of the ceiling and wall? Do you miter the ceiling tiles or cover them with molding? I know of no molding that will accommodate an angle other than 90°

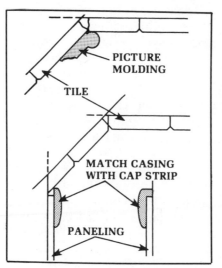

PICTURE MOLDING

TILE

MATCH CASING WITH CAP STRIP

PANELING

What do you recommend?

C.B., Fairfield, Conn.

A. The sketch shown should clarify the situation for you. The use of a picture rail molding with the rounded top is the easiest way out at the ceiling-slant-wall juncture if any molding is required at all. If you plan it correctly, the ceiling tile edges can just butt there with the normal bevel joint as shown. Drop or raise the ceiling height a bit to get even tile width across. Where the vertical wall paneling finishes, one usually needs a cap mold of some sort, anyhow. A little care in selecting this and the ceiling tile on the slanted wall will fit down behind it nicely, hiding the cut edges. An important question is how true the meeting edge of the tiled ceiling and the slanted wall can be. Mitering the raw edges of cut ceiling tile for this joint is generally not a good solution as the material does not usually take that neat a cut easily. The problem is common enough so that your local supplier will have the needed molding suggestions ready for you.

Refinishing ceiling

Q. My five-year-old house has settled somewhat and developed a lot of fine cracks in the ceiling of the living room. I wish to repair it myself and am in doubt how to fill the cracks. I would appreciate your answer.

E.F., Floral Park, N.Y.

A. Fine cracks can be filled with a spackling compound or plaster-of-Paris, either mixed to a paste. Cracks should be wet when patchwork is done so the new material doesn't dry too rapidly. Wide cracks can be cut out with the tip of a can opener and should be somewhat V-shaped. Wet the inside of the crack with a sponge just before filling with the patching material. Work into the crack, smooth off and let dry. Then sand lightly. Prime all patchwork before painting.

Chapter 9

Wall Problems

Basement walls...Bath...Ceramic...Concrete...Drywall installation, repair...Kitchen...Paneling...Plaster repair...Plastic & metal tiles... Structural problems...Wallpaper & fabric...Wainscoting.

Hiding a furnace

Q. I want to build a frame around my furnace the outside of which will be covered with knotty pine paneling to match the rest of the basement. Have you any suggestions on such a project?
R.B., Detroit, Mich.

A. Use 2x4s to make the frame. Check your local building code to see how near the furnace you can build. It may be necessary to use gypsum wallboard or cement panels on the inner side of the partition walls. You will probably want to include a disguised door for access too. You can use a batten or x-braced door of the pine paneling for this if desired.

Flaking cement

Q. I wish to recover my basement walls with new cement to replace that which is flaking off. What is the proper mix?
L.L., Woodbridge, Ontario

A. The mix should be 1 part cement to 2-1/2 parts sharp sand. Before you apply it, brush down the walls well to remove all the loose, flaking material. Dampen the surface and damp-cure the newly applied mix.

Basement partition

Q. The way our basement is arranged, I'd like to partition off the laundry room. Could you tell me how this is done?
P.J., Hartford, Conn.

A. Build a 2x4 or 2x3 frame which you surface with paneling materials. Attach the plate to the floor. With a plumb bob, locate the top plate directly over the floor plate and secure it to the joists above. You will have to plan your wall so it runs across at right angles to the joists or locate it directly under a joist to have something to nail to. Surface with the material of your choice, probably the same as you use on the rest of the basement walls. If you used a vertical paneling on these walls you may need blocking between the studs on 16″ centers you use in a normal frame wall.

Panel buckling

Q. About nine months ago I finished off my basement with plastic-faced hardboard sheets. As they fit together well, I didn't use

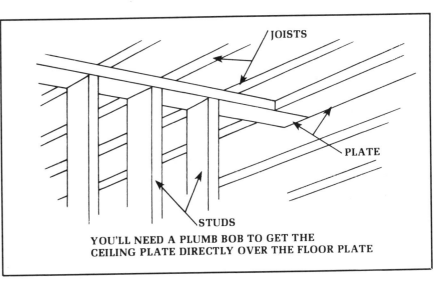

YOU'LL NEED A PLUMB BOB TO GET THE CEILING PLATE DIRECTLY OVER THE FLOOR PLATE

the metal trim. Now several of the sheets have buckled and bulged. Can you give me any help?

L.B., Troy, N.Y.

A. Apparently the material has absorbed enough moisture to expand or the sheets, butted tightly in a cool room, have expanded on being warmed. You should have used the metal trim recommended by the panel manufacturer. It's designed to hold the panel edges flat while allowing for expansion of the material. About the only solution now is to remove the panels, install the strips and replace the panels, trimming them as necessary. While you have them off, it would be a good idea to apply a waterproofing coating to the basement walls or at least protect the backs of the panels so they will not be affected further.

Pleasant playroom

Q. Our basement walls are made of fairly smooth rock. A year ago, I painted them light green as a step in converting it to a playroom for the kids. Now I'd like to panel, but I understand this would be difficult because of the uneven wall surfaces, and I don't want to pay a professional to do it. How can I brighten it?

R.S., San Diego, Calif.

A. It's not so difficult to panel over rock. You can build a frame of 2x4s and attach the paneling to that, avoiding the walls altogether. Just provide a sill and ceiling plate and attach the studs between them.

Coloring cement

Q. We've decided our basement walls need a troweled-on cement finish. We wonder if this can be colored in any way to save the cost of painting it.

L.W., Windem, Mass.

A. Yes, you can add color to the cement and sand mix by using mineral pigments. For a true white,

use white portland cement. For a slate grey, use manganese oxide mixed with iron oxide; for red, brown or tan, use various quantities of iron oxide; for blue, cobalt, and green, chromium oxide. You'll find them under these names as well as trade named coloring agents.

Crumbling walls

Q. I want to paint my cellar walls but they are crumbly in spots. What is a good filler? The walls are poured concrete and dry, not sweaty.

D.B., Staten Island, N.Y.

A. If the crumbly areas are simply a dusty surface defect, waterglass will seal them and form a good base for paint. If the defect is deep and sandy you'd do better to re-surface the wall. Brush away all loose material, then wet the wall. Apply waterproof cement about 1/2" thick, troweled on from bottom up, to smooth and level the whole wall surface. Wait three weeks before painting. Then use a portland cement paint.

Wall covering

Q. We plan to live in our cellar while the rest of the house is being built, but do not know what kind of material to use to cover the cement block walls. Is there anything that can be put directly on

the blocks without putting 2x4s up first?

D.S., Ballston Spa, N.Y.

A. Since you can still get at the outside, take the most important step. Waterproof this exterior surface and set drain tile. On the inside you can use colored or plain stucco applied directly to the blocks. Or, you can point the joints smooth as laid and then paint the walls. You can use 1x2 furring with a dry wall finish over that. If your cellar is appreciably above grade, insulation may be used between the furring strips to advantage.

Waterproof first

Q. While I do not have any problem with the basement walls at the present time, I am going to cover them with plywood and understand that the concrete must be sealed prior to attaching furring strips. What types of sealer are available, which is the most effective and durable and which is the easiest to apply?

F.H., Niantic, Conn.

A. For economy and ease of application we suggest polyethylene film applied with a plastic adhesive. Next in line would be tarpaper held on with asphalt which is very little cheaper, a lot more messy, and the plastic will outlast it. Furring may be applied over either. Paint-on sealers are quite effective when properly

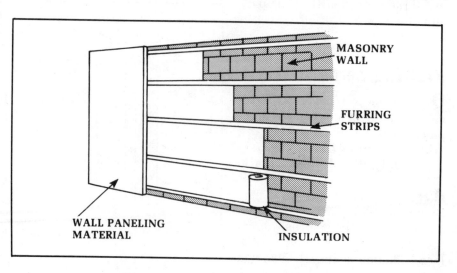

WALL PANELING MATERIAL — MASONRY WALL — FURRING STRIPS — INSULATION

handled but most good ones are expensive and they all have one drawback—it is too late when you discover you missed a spot.

Wait to finish?

Q. I just bought a new house and want to finish part of the basement in knotty pine. Some people say I should wait two years or more for everything to "settle" before doing anything. Is this so?
G.U., Wantagh, N.Y.

A. Some new homes are provided with finished basement rooms by the builder. Masonry shouldn't "settle" anyway. The only advantage in waiting is to determine if there are leaks or overflow of surface water into the basement during severest wet spells. You should waterproof the basement walls with a portland cement paint if the walls were not previously treated.

Over whitewash

Q. I want to finish my basement in cement over the present whitewash. Will it stick if I first chip the walls with an old hatchet or does all the whitewash have to come off?
J.R., Narberth, Pa.

A. It is hard to remove whitewash to a degree where cement will hold, even with a lot of chipping. Get around all this work by putting up wire lath with steel-cut nails driven into the present wall. Apply the new cement on that like a stucco job. As long as the lath is rigidly held in place, this method will solve your problem.

Jog in basement wall

Q. I look at all these nice pretty pictures of beautiful basements and wonder what to do with ours. It's dry and fairly light as basements go but the wall is poured concrete up to about 36" where it

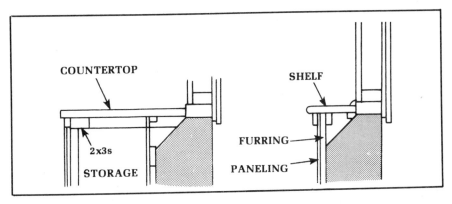

jogs in and up at an angle to a 2x2 and from there up it is plaster. Have you any suggestions for this situation?

R.S., Berwyn, Ill.

A. Depending on how your taste goes, you could easily use vertical furring strips up to the level of the 2x2 and panel the lower part of the wall with horizontal boards, predecorated hardboard, plywood etc. Cap the top of the wainscot with a broad enough shelf to conceal the difference in wall surfaces. You could run 2x4 framing from floor to ceiling and build a flush wall full height but this will set your windows deeper than they need to be.

Basement finishing

Q. In finishing the basement walls, how do I attach the materials I choose to the walls? Is studding necessary in attaching panel materials to the walls?
J.P., Hartsdale, N.Y.

A. You don't need studding (2x4 or 2x3 framing free of the walls) unless you have a very rough stone wall you wish to cover with panel materials. You will find furring strips give you an air barrier between your walls and your foundation which reduces condensation. If your walls are not perfectly perpendicular, furring strips can be shimmed to give you a level surface. You may use 1x2 stock or even 1x3 if your walls are not too bad.

Furring which way

Q. I want to make a family room in my basement. I plan to use 2x2 rather than 1x3 furring to allow space for insulation and wiring. I have been told by some to run furring vertically and by others horizontally. What are the reasons and advantages of each?
W.P., Crown Point, Ind.

A. Furring is put up in order to attach wall material to the existing walls. If the new wall material is vertical boards, the furring must be horizontal. If you are using a sheet material, furring can be run in either direction but vertical is better as the long edges of the sheets can meet on the furring strip. A center piece will support the center of the panel stock. It is a good idea to have a top and bottom furring strip too for sheet material. Horizontally placed boards require vertical furring strips about 16" apart.

Recess meter

Q. Our gas meter is huge and black and sticks out like a sore thumb. Can we recess it in the concrete block wall somehow and cover it over as we panel the walls? If we put glass on the outside, the meter reader could get his information without having to go downstairs at all. What is your opinion?
S.F., Riverside, Ill.

A. It is pretty simple to fur out before your wall surfacing materials go up so as to enclose the meter. You'd have to provide access but this is easily accomplished by hinging a section of your wall material appropriately. When you are planning built-ins, perhaps you can incorporate a place for the meter there. As an alternative, you can ask the gas company to move the meter outdoors.

Fasteners for concrete

Q. With what do I fasten furring strips to my basement walls?
J.P., Hartsdale, N.Y.

A. You can use steel-cut nails to anchor strips to the walls or drill holes with a carbide tipped drill and insert lead or fiber plugs. Drive screws through the furring strips into the plugs. You can also use adhesive.

Hole in wall

Q. How exactly do I go about making the hole in masonry wall to install a basement window?
A.M., Union, N.J.

A. For brick, stone and concrete or cinder block walls, mark off the area. By chipping away at the mortar joints, you can remove a central unit. With the opening thus started, break other brick or block out, working toward the edge of the opening. In the case of brick, remove whole bricks to the line but allow bricks extending beyond to remain protruding into the opening, then break them along the line with a chisel. With blocks, break them by blows near the voids and chip off pieces to the marked line with a hammer.

Concrete cutting

Q. What tools do I use to make a hole in a poured concrete basement wall?
P.C., Chicago, Ill.

A. Mark off the area first. Make an initial opening with a cold chis-

el. The remainder can be broken with a hammer to the center. A masonry drill can be used to make a group of holes to start the center, then continue with a hammer.

Frame in concrete

Q. I want to put a window in my basement wall but don't just see how to get a wood frame in there. Can you help?
A.M., Cicero, Ill.

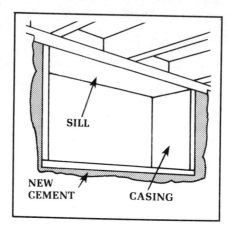

A. Determine the rough opening size needed to accommodate the sash you want to use. Break through and cut the opening as close as possible to size. Once the opening is completed, the inner surfaces are covered with cement to square them off as a base for the wood framing. It is best to make the opening up to the underside of the house sill so that the sill will serve as a lintel.

Remove old tile

Q. I recently purchased a home which has ceramic tile walls in the bathroom. The color combination is not the most desirable so I would like to retile but am at a loss as how to remove the old tile without damage to the walls.
H.M., Kalamazoo, Mich.

A. How you go at it and how successful you'll be depends on how the tile is put up, on what and how smooth you expect the results to be. If the ceramic tile is on plasterboard with adhesive, you might

as well remove board and all. If on plaster with adhesive, chip it off and sand down the plaster; tiles set wet, over plaster on lath, you'll probably break up the wood lath and have to redo it from the studs out. On metal lath you might fare better and only need to bring the rough results up level.

Door installation

Q. I am planning to install a sliding door in my shower stall. The wall is covered with ceramic tiles. These must be removed in order to install the sliding tracks. Is there an easy way to remove these tiles without breaking them?
A.L., Hollywood, Calif.

A. The ceramic tile may not have to be removed to install the sliding track surround for the door. Many assemblies are simply caulked and installed on top of the tiles. If screws are required, drilling tiles without breakage might be a problem. But the proper drill and a bit of care usually will prevent that. Check with manufacturers.

Loose tile

Q. Some of the ceramic baseboard and cap tiles in our bathroom are loose and coming off. We did have a water problem but that's been fixed. Is there a way to remove and replace these tiles?
E.A., Raleigh, N.C.

A. Ceramic tiles can generally be reused if you remove the present adhesive. Where tiles are off, check the wall underneath. You probably have a gypsum wallboard surface, most likely in poor shape due to the water damage. The section of wallboard affected should be replaced. Then look at the backs of the tiles. If the adhesive is dry, sand it off with coarse sandpaper. If it is still pliable, scrape off as much as possible. If paper is stuck to the adhesive, scrape that off, too. The tiles may then be reset with adhesive and regrouted. The Tile Council of America does not recommend using the adhesive solvent on glazed tile; it may cause uneven staining.

Covering ceramic tiles

Q. I have a shower stall that has a slate floor and is otherwise completely covered with ceramic tiles, including the ceiling in which there is a recessed light. The grouting between the tiles is badly mildewed, and it seems impossible to keep it reasonably clean. About two years ago I painted clear epoxy sealer over the whole of the interior in the hope that it would solve the problem. Now the sealer has started to peel in places and the joints between the tiles are dirty again. Have you any suggestions as to what I might do? If I were to rebuild, I would install a new unit molded out of plastic. Is it possible to line the walls and ceiling with a smooth covering such as Formica?
R.E., Chapel Hill, N.C.

A. You can try cleaning the grout again and resealing. You can also try removing the grout, re-grouting and then resealing that. Another suggestion would be to cover the entire floor with seamless flooring, leaving the slate, if you like, untouched. You can line the walls and ceiling as you suggest with one of the laminated plastics such as Formica. Depending on the condition of the surface the tiles are mounted on, it might be easier to remove that and the tiles before applying panel-type materials. If your ceramic tile is on ordinary gypsum board (not the vinyl-surfaced material that is used in showers) it should probably be removed first. Otherwise, drill right through the tiles to mount the moldings.

Wonder-board

Q. Some time ago, my uncle mentioned a substrate for ceramic tile called "Wonder-Board". Our local lumber dealers have never heard of this material. Where can it be purchased?
C.M., King George, Va.

A. Wonder-Board® is made for American Olean Tile by Modulars Inc., and would be found at tile distributors who carry the American Olean line. If you cannot locate your local distributor, write American Olean Tile, Consumer Inquiries, Dept. FH, 1000 Cannon Ave., Lansdale, Pa. 19446 for the name of the nearest dealer in your area.

Replacing grouting

Q. The grouting in between the tiles in the shower of my seven-year-old house is impossible to clean. Is there anything you can suggest short of replacing it?
B.S., Salem, Ore.

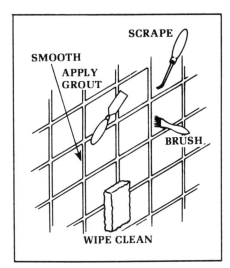

A. You can clean it with ammonia, rinse it off well, and then clean it with bleach. Do *not* mix the two, the fumes are poisonous. If this hasn't worked and you have ceramic tile in your shower stall, then the grout should be replaced. Scrape out the old grouting and brush away all of the loose pieces. Buy the best waterproof white grouting that you can find and mix a little at a time to ensure doing a careful job. It washes easily enough off of your hands, but once hardened is not so easily removed from the tile, so it is important that you apply it neatly. Once the grouting has set you may wish to use a grout sealer, but they very often give the grout a yellowish cast. Frequent cleansing will keep it from becoming mildewed.

Removing towel hook

Q. I bought an adhesive-backed towel holder for the bathroom; plastic with metal hooks for towels. The hooked prongs broke off the thing and now I find I am unable to remove the device from the wall tile. Can you help?
H.S., Winchester, Ky.

A. If the tiles are glazed ceramic, you can probably remove the towel holder with chemicals without damage to the tiles. Many adhesives yield to solvents such as acetone, nail polish remover, shellac solvent, etc. Trickle a small amount against the tile just above the offending device, let it run down and start action. If the solvent fails, try a very thin knife blade heated in a gas flame. Whichever method works, more of the same will remove the remaining adhesive from the tile surface.

Stained grouting

Q. We have some lovely tile that is held in place by stained, discolored grouting. We've tried every way we could think of to clean it, but to no avail; the grout is too old. Regrouting doesn't hold, due to lack of room between tiles and the fact that the old grout is so firm. What do you suggest?
L.W., Stamford, Conn.

A. Stained grouting is difficult to unstain, although some readers report good results with Amway's Liquid Organic Cleaner and a toothbrush, while others have had some success with paint remover. We've heard of wire-brushing out the grout with a mini-power tool (like a Dremel Moto-Tool), then re-grouting or wiping just the grout with a weak solution of muriatic acid. Both these last two solutions have to be handled with a great deal of care to avoid damaging any glazed tile surfaces.

Seal shower wall

Q. I need information on repairing and sealing a ceramic-tiled shower wall.

F.G., Chester, Ill.

A. Assuming the ceramic tile has been applied over a proper backer-board or wet-set on plaster or cement, repair usually means re-grouting. Rake out cracked and/or crumbly grout and clean the joints between tiles well. Regrout with a waterproof grout, properly mixed. Clean off the face of the tiles before the grout sets. If the job is done well, ceramic tile shower walls should not need further sealing.

Tile bathroom

Q. I am planning to modernize my bathroom and intend to install ceramic tile. Can I use plasterboard on the walls or do I need marine plywood?

L.Z., Newark, N.J.

A. There is a vinyl surfaced gypsum backer board which forms a waterproof base for installations of ceramic tile in showers and tub enclosures you might consider for this job.

Ceramic tiles

Q. I need to cut eight ceramic wall tiles to make them fit a place in my bathroom. What does one use and how do you cut them evenly? They are glazed tiles.

C.U., Lyndhurst, N.J.

A. Ceramic tiles are cut by scoring the glazed side with a glass cutter or sharp chisel corner, then breaking over a flat, broad edge with a sharp snap. Curves can be scored and small pieces nipped out with pliers.

Resurfacing shower

Q. I have a stall shower which has ceramic tile on its interior walls and ceiling and slate on the floor. The grout joints between the tiles are badly mildewed and it seems impossible to keep them clean. Is it possible to line the walls with some smooth, waterproof material like Formica or Marlite and if so how should the corner joints be treated?

R.E., Chapel Hill, N.C.

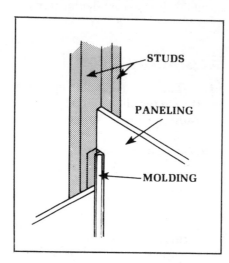

A. Both Formica and Marlite make laminated panels designed for use in stall showers. Attaching panels over ceramic tile is not an easy task but it is preferable to removing all the tile. The panels will have to be glued to the tile and since most glues will not stick well to glazed tile you will have to remove some of the glaze. To do this quickly and easily, rent a belt sander and some 80 grit sanding belts. The belts are 3″ wide, so sand a vertical strip of this width every 12″. Place a bead of silicone rubber cement (available in most hardware stores) in the middle of each sanded strip, then press the laminated plastic sheets against the walls. Brace the sheets for 24 hours until the cement cures. The illustration shows corner treatment when everything has been removed down to the studs. The same corner treatment should be used except that the moldings are cemented in place against both

walls with silicone rubber (instead of being nailed) and sealed inside the molding with the same adhesive

Remodeling bathroom

Q. I am planning to remodel and modernize the bathroom in my 37-year-old bungalow and would sincerely appreciate your suggestions on how to go about removing the old ceramic wall tile so I can replace it with new.

V.L., New York City, N.Y.

A. Your old tile is probably set in a heavy bed of plaster or cement. You can pry the tiles off this material; a cold chisel and hammer are the best tools to use. Also remove all the base material and expose the wall studs. If the plaster or cement is set on wood lath, which is fairly level, the lath can be left in place but it would be best to take everything off.

Dyes for grout

Q. Where can I find information on coloring grout for ceramic tile? I have been able to find colored grout but nothing that approaches the kind which is used on our kitchen sink tile. What kinds of dyes are used for mixing with white grout?

E.S., Anaheim, Calif.

A. Colorants for cementitious materials can usually be found where you buy the cement. Try your local masonry supply house. Dry powders for tinting cement should work for coloring grout, too.

Hardboard in bath

Q. The coating on the paneled walls in our bathroom is coming off. How can we remedy this unsightly situation?

M.M., Viola, Ill.

A. If the film coating of predecorated hardboard is penetrated, moisture can seep in and cause damage. You can try to extend the material's life with good enamel paint. Clean the surface, roughen it slightly but paint only when the panel is absolutely dry. If you can seal out moisture, there's a good chance you can postpone repaneling.

Shower wall covering

Q. We would like to use artificial brick on our shower/tub walls. We've checked into the styrene and ceramic (individual brick type), but can get no solid information on their use in wet areas (we use our shower a lot). Have you any information or experience with covering of this kind?

R.P., Columbia, N.J.

A. Ceramic tile is fine and it can be used on the proper backing board in wet (shower) areas. But so can a lot of other materials—predecorated hardboard, laminated plastic, etc. If you can't get sufficient information locally concerning installation, get the manufacturer's name and address and write for installation information on those products that interest you.

Molding or nails

Q. On those vinyl surfaced gypsum wallboards, do you have to use the matching moldings to hold them up?

F.J., Peterborough, Ontario

A. No, you can use the matching colored nails to fasten the vinyl surfaced board in place of the moldings. You'll just have a neat, rounded-edged joint at panel edges.

Wall options

Q. We would like to redecorate our small bathroom. Since the wallpaper in the shower area has begun to peel, we would like to avoid using paper there. What are our alternatives?

C.T., Benton, Pa.

A. You can use ceramic tile, decorative laminate, predecorated hardboard, structural glass or perhaps one of the prefabricated fiberglass reinforced plastic tub surrounds. You could also use metal or plastic tile, if available; wood if you finish it properly; waterproof wallcoverings if you can get a good adhesive bond; acrylic plastic sheets or mirrors, or a lot of other far-out things if you want to spend the money. If the wall is plaster, high-gloss enamel paint is fine. If it is gypsum wallboard, check for dampness and decay. Use the proper vinyl-surfaced backer board if you do select any of the tile finishes. Any panel material must be used in the channels designed to accommodate it properly, if you are to avoid future trouble.

Shower stall

Q. I want to build a shower stall in my basement which would be of larger dimensions than those on the market. I don't care for tile. What other materials can be used for the inside of a shower stall?

L.S., Arriba, Col.

A. More economical than marble and structural glass is predecorated hardboard which comes in 4' x 8' sheets so you need only worry about the corner joints. Metal moldings are available for application or you can use adhesive. Along the same lines but a bit more expensive are laminated plastics. With either, you'll have no trouble as long as you properly seal them to the base.

Wood-walled bath

Q. In a how-to magazine I saw a picture of a bathroom done in redwood. What other types of wood could be used and how do you prevent damage from steam and water?

A.B., Tulsa, Okla.

A. Besides redwood, we've also seen knotty pine and knotty cedar used to cover bathroom walls. To protect the wood, give each piece, including the edges, a coat of polyurethane. Caulk well where water could get behind the wood. Ventilate the bath generously after showers, baths, etc. In short, as long as you get the water off the wood quickly and eliminate places where it can soak in and stay, you'll be all right.

Over pulpboard

Q. I bought a home to which the former owner added a room which he finished in a brown, soft wallboard. I would like to install plasterboard but wonder if I should remove the wallboard first. The walls and ceiling are not insulated.

J.C., Dunellen, N.J.

A. Apply the gypsum wallboard over the softer wallboard, nailing through into the studs with 1-3/4" or 2" nails. You'll have insulation behind a surface firm enough to wallpaper satisfactorily that way.

Window openings

Q. How do you handle gypsum wallboard at window and door openings? I'd like to avoid a lot of trim if possible.

R.T., Niles, Mich.

A. You can butt the wallboard against window and door frames in the normal manner and conceal the edges behind casings and apron which is the easiest way or you can use metal trim which is probably what you have in mind. This is usually a strip of metal that covers the edge of the board and folds back on the face of it with a perforated flange through which you nail and over which you duplicate the point taping process. It leaves a metal edge and bead visible when you're done.

Trade secrets

Q. Can you offer any tricks of the trade that will ensure a satisfactory job of installing gypsum wallboard in an add-on room I have to finish this summer?

R.W., Spencerport, N.Y.

A. It is most important to be sure all studs are spaced right so panels meet on centers properly. Use spiral or screw-type gypsum wallboard nails about 1-1/2" long. Set the heads just slightly below the surface dimpling the board without tearing the covering. Begin your nailing from the center of the panels. Do your joint taping and filling by the book and feather out carefully to reduce sanding required. The trick is to follow the manufacturer's instructions. There are no short cuts.

Taped joints

Q. Are the recessed edges of gypsum wallboard done the same on the ceiling as on the wall and what about where the panel is not long enough?

P.C., Ottumwa, Iowa

A. The taped joint system is the same for ceilings as for walls. The bedding coat, the tape, the cover coat and the finish coat are all applied in that order and feathered out. Pick the longest panels you can get for the fewest end to end joints. Never try to join the recessed edge of a panel to the butt end of another. Butted ends are taped in the same way as the recessed edges but you will have further to feather for a smooth job.

Drywall application

Q. I plan to install drywall in a new home I am building using the recessed edged gypsum wallboard. Could you please tell me the proper

way of using that perforated tape?

M.R., Miamisburg, Ohio

A. Butter the joint first with the compound sold with the tape, properly mixed. A broad steel finishing knife is the best tool to use. Fill it even and full but not overflowing. With the knife wiped clean press the tape down over the center of the joint, picking up some compound as it comes through the holes in the tape. Then apply a skim coat and let this much dry. Spot the nailheads while it does. The second coat of compound is applied about 24 hours later, feathering out about 1-1/2". Let that dry and sand lightly. Apply a thin finishing coat, feathering the edges 2" or more beyond the previous one. Let dry, then sand lightly. Alternate steps with the nail-head work, as there too you need the three coats for a superior job.

Tiles over paper

Q. I want to put 4" square glazed ceramic tile in my entry which is now wallpapered. I have the tile but don't know how to go about the job or what materials to use. Do I need lath? The wall is plaster under the paper.

P.M., Bronx, N.Y.

A. If the wall is sound and the plaster firm and unbroken, the easy way to put up tile is with adhesive. First remove the paper. Wash down the wall to remove any remaining paste that might let go later. Prime the surface and spread the adhesive with notched trowel according to the recommendations of the manufacturer of the organic tile adhesive you select. Set your

tile, spacing evenly with toothpicks if yours are not self aligning tile. Wait at least 24 hours before using a latex base grout to finish up the job.

Cracked joints

Q. Thinking that excessive indoor dryness was the cause of cracking at the joints in our drywall, we installed a humidifier last year. While this was beneficial, the joints below one window and on both sides of the sliding glass door have reopened. Will using fiberglass strips or aluminum wire mesh on these cracks instead of the paper strips that come with the joint compound help?

T.S., Copley, Ohio

A. Dryness may have been a factor but you've remedied that. If the cause of continued cracking remains a mystery, try a "moving crack" cover. Tuff-Kote Co., 210 N. Seminary Ave., Dept FH, Woodstock, Ill. 60098, makes a bridging tape and mastic system meant for plaster that might do the trick. You should find Krack-Kote at local paint and hardware stores, or write the manufacturer for the name of the nearest dealer and specific instructions on application. If there's a build-up of joint compound, be sure you apply Krack-Kote to solid, sound material.

New stair walls

Q. The walls of my stairway are in such bad condition that they can not be painted or wallpapered. How can I cover them with wallboard or planks, how do I cut 4' x 8' panels to fit slopes?

M.D., Williamsport, Pa.

A. You can use wallboard nailed through the old wall to studs framing the stairway or you can nail 1x1 furring to the studs, then attach the panels to these strips. Whichever way, remove molding first. Use a perfectly straight 1x1 and a level, draw a straight line

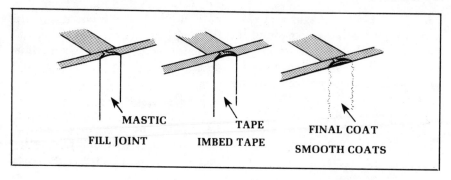

MASTIC
FILL JOINT

TAPE
IMBED TAPE

FINAL COAT
SMOOTH COATS

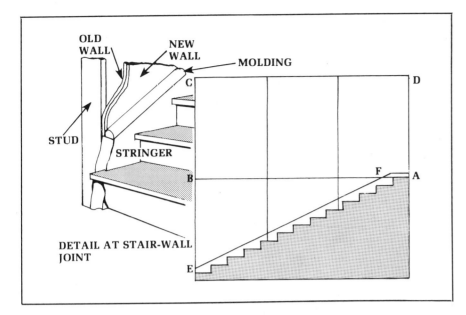

OLD WALL · NEW WALL · MOLDING · STUD · STRINGER

DETAIL AT STAIR-WALL JOINT

C · D · F · A · B · E

from A to B which is an extension of the top step landing shown in diagram. Cut three 4'x8' panels for the A—B—C—D area and nail in place. Using heavy paper cut three patterns for the panels below line A—F—B, cutting along a line 2" below slope E—F which represents the top of the baseboard. Put the patterns on panels, cut to shape and nail the cut panels in place. Replace the molding, nailing through new wallboard into old wall. Use 1/2" half round or astragal molding over line B—F to hide the joint.

Wallboard basics

Q. I am now building a home and want to make sure I fasten the drywall right. Where can I get information on installing Sheetrock from the start?

J.W., Thomaston, Ga.

A. Paper-faced gypsum wallboard (sometimes called "plasterboard") is made by a number of firms. "Sheetrock"® is the brand name of this product made by United States Gypsum Co. You could write them at 101 S. Wacker Drive, Chicago, Ill. 60606 for installation information. Your local building materials supplier should also be able to give you a brochure with this information. This chapter in this book also gives procedures and tips.

Half-inch ceiling

Q. I am paying my builder extra for the installation of 1/2" wallboard on all ceilings instead of 3/8". Now he tells me it is not advisable to have 1/2" on the ceilings because the weight is too great and eventually the ceiling will sag. I'd like your opinion.

R.G., St. Joseph, Mich.

A. Following the recommended nailing, installation of 1/2" board should be satisfactory. The only other way the ceiling could sag would be if the joists themselves are substandard for the load, in which case you should not be paying extra and had better check the joist size installed against the architect's plans right away.

Wall beneath hood

Q. We are looking for a practical and still attractive covering to use from the bottom of a copper-finished hood down behind the range. Would copper tiles be satisfactory here?

P.K., Cicero, Ill.

A. We suggest you install the tiles without any joint spacing between them for easiest cleaning. Otherwise metal tile to match the hood would be a most appropriate finish for this area.

Wet concrete wall

Q. I have a new house of cement block with brick on the outside. Recently a lot of water seeps through the walls in rainy spells and has ruined the inside plaster on the blocks. My contractor wants to stucco the outside but I don't want to. What can I do to remedy this and repair the damage already done?

D.N., Houston, Tex.

A. It is likely that water is entering the wall through joints around windows, at the eaves or where chimney passes roof. Sealing the outside would not cure this. It would be best to check thoroughly for leakage first. Once you have found and cured the cause, you will need new plaster inside as the damaged plaster cannot be restored.

Nails showing

Q. Could you tell me what causes nail heads to poke up under the wallpaper on my walls? I think it is gypsum wallboard. The condition is not general but appears mostly near the ceilings. What can I do?

G.W., St. Louis, Mo.

A. As green wood shrinks on drying it contracts around the nails too and they no longer hold as tightly. Vibration and expansion-contraction of the wall panel material work them out. About the only remedy is to counterset the nails slightly, cover the holes left and size the filler so paint or paper will conceal them.

Nail head bulge

Q. We have recently built a house and are slowly getting the inside finished, doing the work ourselves. We have gypsum wallboard walls and have filled the nail holes, sanded, filled again and sanded until we feel we have a nice, smooth wall. However, after painting some of the rooms, it

appears the walls were not as smooth as we thought. Since the walls look bad, we thought of wallpapering, but my husband says it is a messy, difficult project. He also says, when I decide to change wallpaper someday, it will be very difficult to get the old paper off. Can you give me any help?

M.M., Goshen, Ind.

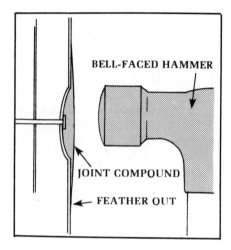

BELL-FACED HAMMER

JOINT COMPOUND

FEATHER OUT

A. With a reasonable job of nailing, taping and sanding, there's no reason why nails aren't well hidden. Tip: A bell-faced hammer will give you a better "dimple" to fill as each nail is sunk more easily and without damage to the panel surface. Using the joint compound the panel manufacturer recommends is next. Apply it properly, tapering it off to nothing (feathering). Then a gentle smooth sanding should do it. Proper painting procedures are a must, too. Exactly what to do depends on the finish coat you plan to use.

Papering, contrary to your husband's opinion, is not that difficult with modern materials. When the time comes to repaper, you need not take if off if it's holding well. A good plan may be a good painting first and then wallpapering when the time comes to change. That way, you've protected the surface of the drywall enough with the paint so that eventual removal of the paper is not as apt to cause damage. But don't give up on painting before you find out where you went wrong.

Metal corners

Q. My home has metal corners on the interior walls. While there was no heat in the house the corners rusted and the tape started coming off. I want to sand and retape the corners but how can I be sure the same thing won't happen again?

R.K., West Orange, N.J.

A. Since you now have heat, which will presumably be maintained, you can go ahead with the retaping. Peel off the paper and sand down to bare metal. Apply a coat of thinned shellac and retape. You'll get good adhesion and the tape should stay put.

Tiles over wallpaper

Q. My bathroom is partly metal tiles, papered above that on wallboard. We would like tiles on all the walls. How do I put tiles over wallpaper?

L.M., New Castle, Del.

A. Remove the paper. Let wall dry. Then apply tiles with the mastic provided with them. Metal tile over wallpaper would probably cause the paper to loosen.

Studs or furring?

Q. I plan on finishing our recreation room myself. It has walls that are brick on the outside and block on the inside. What determines whether one should use 2x4s or furring strips (1x2 or 1x3s) for the panel installation?

A.F., Washington, D.C.

A. The choice depends on if you are simply mounting the furring strips as a means of attaching the paneling to the wall or whether you are building a self-supporting frame wall of 2x3s or 2x4s. Furring strips are usually right for dry, modern walls where you do not have to accommodate bumps and other projections. You are more apt to need a frame wall, freestanding, in an older home where uneven stone foundations make furring strips almost impossible to mount. Another factor to consider early on in your plans is whether you wish to incorporate built-ins supported by the paneled wall. If so, it's generally wise to use 2x4s. Whatever you do, first make sure you have a dry wall and floor.

Wall behind range

Q. My kitchen is plasterboard and I have papered it. Grease has been spattered behind and around the stove. Is there any way of preventing it?

A.W., Monongahela, Pa.

A. You can put a protective covering of glass over this area, leaving the paper for decoration. You can use predecorated hardboard or plastic laminate panels over the paper held in place with metal molding. Or these two and also ceramic or metal tile can be adhesive mounted to the wallboard proper provided you can remove the paper satisfactorily. None of these prevent grease spatters but it is easier to clean them off. A range hood with fan and filter would help a great deal by carrying off greasy material otherwise deposited on walls and ceilings as well as offering the added bonus of removing cooking odors.

Hole in the wall

Q. We didn't even have the new gypsum wallboard wall painted when a tipsy pile of furniture went over, one of the chairs' legs poking a nice hole in the wall. We have scraps left but no full panels. Is there a way to fix it neatly?

U.G., Buffalo, N.Y.

A. You're in luck with the scraps and probably joint compound on hand. Cut out the damaged area in the shape of an equilateral triangle, slanting the edges inward at 45°. Make it at least 1" beyond the hole on all three sides. Make a similar triangle from the scrap and shape to fit with sandpaper, slanting the edges the same way. Butter the edges of the patch with compound. Set in place and scrape off excess compound evenly. You can apply joint tape and more compound the same way as you did at any butt joints in paneling the room in the first place. Sand smooth when dry. If patch is large, back the opening with a slat of wallboard cemented to the back of the panel.

Removing tile grout

Q. I put mosaic tile in our kitchen but left some of the white grout on the tile. We find it can be removed with a razor blade but have discovered no faster means. Can you suggest something?

A.B., Hicksville, N.Y.

A. You probably used a waterproof grout. If it can be scraped off with a razor blade, it can be scoured off faster with a mild abrasive which won't scratch the tiles. Powdered pumice or rottenstone or ordinary tooth powder will do. You make a thick paste with one of these and water and scour in a circular motion. If you can get an electric drill with a lamb's wool bonnet, wet that and add paste for the same effect with less effort.

Attaching paneling

Q. I want to remodel our bathroom which was half started by the previous owner. It now has wallboard walls. I want to cover the walls with wall paneling that has a smooth, colored, patterned effect on one side, looks like marble and comes in 4' x 8' sheets. How can I attach this paneling with nails and not have the nails mar the finished side or have the nail heads show? (I do not think the adhesive application is adequate or permanent as it "pulls away" after some time.) Should the paneling be applied over the drywall, or is it better to take the drywall down and put the fiberboard on the studs?

S.M., Mastic Beach, N.Y.

A. Whose paneling are you intending to use? We suggest that

you write them for installation instructions. If you expect to use nails to hold something on, the nails will show on the surface. What's wrong with adhesive? Provided the plasterboard is properly installed and receptive to the adhesive used, and you use the right adhesive, there's no reason why it won't hold. Unless you have some unusual paneling, the regular mastic panel adhesive (usually offered in cartridges) should work very well.

Sill and ceiling plates

Q. You mention building a frame of 2x4s and attaching paneling to it in those cases where a masonry wall is too rough to panel. Please explain what is meant by the sill and ceiling plates in this frame.

P.P., Brookline, Mass.

A. The sill plate is the horizontal 2x4 which is nailed to the floor. The ceiling plate is the horizontal piece which forms the top of the frame and is fastened to the ceiling. The studs are the vertical members that stand between the two horizontal plates with their front edges flush and equally spaced 16" o.c. "on centers"-from the center of one stud to the center of the next.

Paneling adhesive

Q. Is it possible to apply paneling directly to painted wallboard by using adhesive? We can't use furring strips because our rooms are too small. We are trying to eliminate as much painting and wallpapering as possible.

R.K., Glenview, Ill.

A. It is possible to use adhesive to install paneling, but the paint coat must be sound or it will come off with the adhesive. The wallboard needs to be solid and the surface flush, too. Scrutinize the manufacturer's directions for the panel installation. You may prefer to select a style with predecorated

trim to match. This elimates repainting, too.

Paneling high walls

Q. How can I panel rooms with walls 8'8" high when the panels available are only 8' long?

F.H., Mallard, Iowa

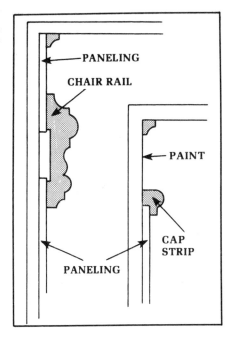

A. You may be able to order paneling in 10' lengths. If not, use an extra-high baseboard and wide cove molding. Split and spread the panels at chair rail height. Use 7' panels and top with a plate rail. Least expensive and simplest is to cap 8' panels with a simple ply-cap mold and paint the remaining wall the same as the ceiling. If you prefer paneling to the ceiling, some styles are attractive run horizontally.

How-to-panel books

Q. Where can I find a book on how to install paneling and how to cut molding in a miter box?

R.B., Bellmawr, N.J.

A. Your local lumber yard should have folders on paneling: how to estimate, lay out, cut and fasten. If you know what kind of paneling you want, you could write to the manufacturer for full installation information. Cutting moldings in a miter box would be covered in most "how to work with wood and tools" books.

Horizontal paneling

Q. Is there any reason why I cannot have bleached mahogany planking running horizontally on my wall? We only want to do one wall but I think making it vertical is the wrong direction to accent.
　　　　　　T.H., Newport, N.H.

A. No reason under the sun why wood planking must run vertically. You can put it horizontally directly on the studs, on vertical furring strips over an unsound wall or directly over a sound wall nailing through to the studs. A shiplap joint rather than tongued and grooved might be better in this application but is not critical.

Paneled kitchen

Q. I would like to wood panel my kitchen but find most woods run into too much money. Could plywood be used and if so what thickness would be required? Could I do this job myself?
　　　　　　P.M., Fox Lake, Ill.

A. The 1/4″ plywood is fine for paneling. There's no reason why you can't put up the panels yourself. You may find the 4′ x 8′ size awkward to handle but a good deal of the job is measuring and marking accurately, techniques that certainly don't demand heavy work.

When to finish

Q. We want to put up pecky cypress, just tinting it a bit on the greenish side. This is 6″ tongue-and-groove V-joint paneling. At what stage do we do which step in the finishing process?
　　　　　　P.G., Plainview, Tex.

A. Your best bet is to pre-stain the wood before putting it on the wall. Sand smooth first and be

sure you have enough. Once you've practiced up on scrap to see exactly how to get the "greenish" tint you want you'll want to do all the staining at one time to be sure of maintaining uniformity. Stain the tongues too. Then put in place, on horizontal furring strips if it is to run vertically. You can give it a coat of lacquer, rubbed down with fine steel wool. Follow with a good paste wax and buff to bring out the sheen and provide added protection. If this is to go on a basement wall or anywhere else dampness might possibly be a problem, back paint the boards to seal them completely before installing.

Wood paneling

Q. I want to panel one room myself using 1/4″ prefinished plywood 4′ x 8′ panels. Would furring strips have to be nailed on first?
　　　　　　E.G., Wadsworth, Ohio

A. If your walls are level and without breaks or bumpy spots, you can apply the panels over the wall without furring. You'd have to locate the studs first since nailing has to go into the studs. If the walls are covered with waterproof paint, you can put the panels right over them with mastic and avoid nailing entirely.

Plywood paneling

Q. We're pretty well set on plywood paneling for our living room but wonder if we may be missing something. What our questions boil down to is this: Is there any plywood as inexpensive as fir that looks more attractive?
　　　　　　E.W., Brockville, Ontario

A. Fir plywood 1/4″ thick is probably the least expensive plywood material for paneling. It can be treated so the grain is subdued yet still visible. Knotty pine is not too far out of line with fir in cost if you watch for the cheaper grades with some broad knots and centerline streaks. Fluctuation in ply-

wood costs makes it impossible to be positive on costs but some mahogany panels are inexpensive. Wire brushed or sand blasted or striated fir is also a relatively inexpensive material. When you include in your comparative costs the finishing materials you'll need, prefinished panels do not seem quite so expensive.

Walls too short

Q. I'd like to put up 4′ x 8′ prefinished plywood panels in my den. Unfortunately the walls are 9′4″ high. What can I do?
　　　　　　J.R., Queens, N.Y.

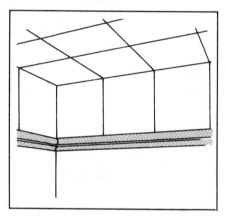

A. You can seek out the few manufacturers who offer 10′ long panels and use them. Or you can lower the ceiling to 8′ in the usual manner that project is done. Or you could gain a few inches with a high baseboard and wide, flat molding at the top of the 8′ panels, leaving you 12″ to fill above them. In a den you might well want acoustical tile and one row around the top of the walls would not look bad at all.

Plywood over plaster

Q. I wish to panel a plaster living room with 4′ x 8′ wood panels. My problem is how to do this without nails showing. Are there special fasteners available?
　　　　　　R.J., Kingston, N.Y.

A. You can put up the panels with adhesives if the plaster wall is sound and can support the weight.

This way you need no nails or panel moldings. You would have to remove and reset the baseboard and any crown or cove molding at the top, of course.

Trim removal

Q. To put up plywood panels properly, how much trim has to be removed? This is a solid plaster wall from which we've removed the wallpaper. I figure on using adhesive to hold on the panels.

F.R., Salinas, Kans.

A. If you plan on painting the wood, butt the panels against the door and window casings without removing them. Take off the trim molding on top of the baseboard, rest the panels on the baseboard and replace the trim. If you plan a clear finish on the panels, remove the finish from all the trim or take the trim off and replace it with material to match the panels.

Glue to studs

Q. Can predecorated hardboard be glued right to the studs? We're expanding the attic and I would like to do it as fast as possible.

C.V., St. Paul, Minn.

A. Use a panel adhesive applied to the studs. It is a good idea to fit the panels carefully first to make sure they are trimmed properly.

Cracked plaster

Q. We have plaster walls that are cracking rather badly. In view of the fact that it is rough plastering I understand patching is unsatisfactory. We have been advised to cover the walls with canvas, felt or paneling. Would you kindly give me your opinion?

W.T., Muskegon, Mich.

A. Canvas, heavy fabric such as burlap or grasscloth can all be applied to cover defects in plaster.

Panel materials applied on furring secured to studs right over the plaster, hold up the whole load. Panel materials can be painted, papered or what you wish. Paneling may be the most satisfactory as it is the most durable and can be almost as cheap.

Attic basics

Q. We would like to finish our attic and are thinking of putting up pre-finished plywood paneling. Does it go on the straight walls and the slanted areas with ceiling tile on the flat ceiling or should the ceiling tile come down the slope to meet the straight walls?

G.C., Royal Oak, Mich.

A. The usual arrangement is to consider the horizontal ceiling and the sloping portions as all part of the ceiling itself, and the vertical portions, called the knee-walls, as the only wall portion. To run the wall material up over the slanting portion makes the room appear smaller and leaves you with a tiny ceiling.

Pine over stucco

Q. I have a small room that I wish to panel in knotty pine or cedar planks. The room at present has stucco walls. Can I panel directly over this or must I use furring?

J.P., Crystal Lake, Ill.

A. The only practical way to avoid the use of furring strips would be to fasten the paneling with mastic adhesive. To do this the walls must be absolutely level and strong enough to hold the added weight. Of the two methods, furring would be preferred in this case.

Nailing hardboard

Q. All things considered, one of those textured or embossed hardboards seems like a good bet for our boy's room. Can these pan-

els be applied over a plaster wall that's been repaired a few places but is in otherwise good shape? Is furring necessary for nailing?

L.G., Quincy, Mass.

A. Hardboard panels can be nailed over a solid backing with nails long enough to go through the existing wall and into the studs at least 1". Nail 4" apart around panel edges and 8" apart on intervening studs. Remove baseboard, cove or other trim first. No furring is necessary assuming your wall is firm. A two-tone finish will bring out the texture you select.

Plywood on studs

Q. I am finishing our attic and want to put up mahogany plywood paneling. Could you tell me on studs 16" apart how thick the plywood should be and how to nail it?

R.Y., Price, Utah

A. On 16" stud spacing you can use 1/4" thick plywood. Use paneling nails of the same color as the paneling. Space nails 6" apart and nail down the center of the panel first. You should figure your panel layout so edges always come on a stud centerline. Keep back about 3/8" or more from the edge.

Removal of panels

Q. I am going to remove the old panel molding from my living room and dining room walls. I would like to know how this can be done without damage to the plaster and can it be done without leaving the outline of the panels on the walls?

J.D., Bronx, N.Y.

A. These molding strips are nailed up to studs as a rule with long finishing nails. You will probably find either paint or wallpaper around and, perhaps, even behind them. At the very least, the removal operation will leave a lot of nail holes in the plaster. There will definitely be an outline of the panels on the present wall finish whether paint or paper. If you remove them at all, you might as well look forward to a redecorating job.

Stone to wood

Q.   Our living room is wood paneling and we have a stone fireplace. There is a space between the two. How should it be covered?

R.Y., Andover, Mass.

A.   A good finishing job includes a wide strip of wood cut to approximate the stone contour with a coping saw. This overlaps the panel at one side, fits snugly against the stone at the other. It should be tried for fit, then finished, then nailed in place. To mark for the cut, place the wood strip against the stone. Take an ordinary scribing compass and run the pointed edge lightly down the stone face allowing the pencil side to trace the outline on the wood.

Wall to window

Q.   I am planning to install pine paneling in my home but find I will have to put up furring strips first. With the thickness of furring strips and paneling, the wall will be out beyond the window and door casings. What do I do about this?

G.W., Reading, Mass.

A.   You remove door and window casings, the baseboard and any trim moldings. The baseboard is replaced over the panels. For windows and doors rip pieces of

pine to the exact thickness of furring plus panel and attach these to the edges of the window and door jambs, flush with the inner surfaces. The panel stock is then cut to extend over the exposed grain end of these filler strips. Casing stock is then nailed onto the panel stock to frame the deeper openings. You may have to extend window sills too in the same manner after planing the nosing off flat. The apron under the sill is then replaced. If you plan finishing the paneling clear your biggest problem will be removal of all old finishes to expose the bare wood.

Knotty pine

Q.   I want to fasten knotty pine 3/8″ thick over the lower 5′ of plaster wall in my kitchen. Boards will be laid vertically. I'm concerned about how the boards will stay up since only every third or fourth board will be over a wall stud. Would you advise the use of adhesive?

J.J., Skokie, Ill.

A.   If the wall is sound and smooth you can use adhesive but you'd do better to provide additional anchorage with a baseboard nailed through to studs and an overlapping molding strip at the top, similarly anchored to studs. The usual method is to provide horizontal furring attached to the studs over which the boards are fastened.

Finding studs

Q.   I have recently purchased a house made with plasterboard

walls and would like to know a sure way of finding studs in order to hang pictures and mirrors. I've heard of using a magnet or pocket compass to locate the nails in studs and so find them, but it doesn't work for me.

S.B., Bronx, N.Y.

A.   You can locate studs in a plasterboard wall by sound. Tap along the length of the wall. The hollow spaces between studs sound hollow, the studs solid. You can sometimes detect the vertical line of panels joined over a stud and having found one, the others are usually 16″ but may be 12″ or 24″ away. If your outer walls are masonry, it's possible you won't find studs at all. Try the sound method in a vertical line as well as a horizontal one. You can find furring this way, even if it is horizontally applied.

Cracking plaster

Q.   We live in a 100-year-old house and are constantly plagued with cracking plaster problems. We've tried spackling and various tapes without satisfactory results. We've heard about felting of walls and ceilings but from the estimates we've had this would be an expensive solution. Is there something we can do to solve this problem ourselves?

A.   If the cracks recur in the same places each time, there is obviously movement in the wall behind the plaster. Unless you can find the cause of such movement you won't be able to solve the cracking problem. A network of fine cracks in one particular area may be the result of dampness which may mean condensation behind the walls. Here again, assuming there really is any dampness, the cause of the moisture must be found before you can solve the cracking problem. One company makes a patching system that bridges cracks with a gently flexible build-up of glass fiber-re-

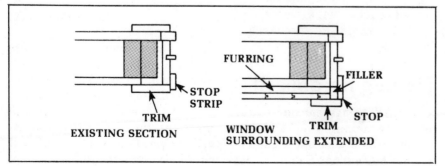

FURRING

FILLER

STOP STRIP

TRIM
EXISTING SECTION

STOP

WINDOW TRIM
SURROUNDING EXTENDED

inforcing tape and a special patching compound. You can try this system especially if the cracks are large and well separated. Write to Tuff-Kote, 210 N. Seminary Ave., Woodstock, Ill. 60098.

Plaster stick

Q.　**Some time ago a putty-like stick was available that was excellent for patching hairline cracks in plaster. Our local hardware stores don't stock it any more. Can you tell me the name of the manufacturer?**

J.G., Penfield, N.Y.

A.　This item is still being made. One manufacturer is Red Devil, 2400 Vauxhall Rd., Union, N.J. 07083. Old line paint stores might be more apt to stock the sticks than stores selling drywall materials.

Crumbly plaster

Q.　**The foundation of our house is made of stone. This has been plastered over on the inside walls of the basement, but now the plaster is crumbling. How can I remedy this?**

S.C., Catonsville, Md.

A.　First, remove the crumbly plaster. Repair any joints that require it and waterproof the wall. A plaster finish is best applied over expanded metal lath that is held slightly away from the wall. This will give a smooth, flat surface with less work than plastering directly over the stone.

Non-sizing of plaster

Q.　**I stripped paper from the walls and ceilings of two rooms and after making the necessary repairs proceeded to decorate with paint. I did this without sizing as the plaster is 25 years old. About 10 days after painting, in one area only, the paint formed bubbles and burst, taking off the paint and a skin of plaster as well, leaving the area rough. Could you advise?**

R.K., Belleville, Ontario

A.　You painted here before the plaster had a chance to dry thoroughly. Age of the plaster does not change its porous quality nor reduce the lime content to any extent. The moisture sets up a reaction which would blister off the finish coat with or without paint on it. Letting the plaster dry thoroughly, then sizing, would have prevented the trouble. Sizing is essential. You'll have to remove paint from the area, patch the rough plaster spot, let it dry, size with two coats of glue size, then repaint.

Repairing plaster

Q.　**I have an older home with blown-in insulation. Some of my plaster walls have developed cracks. I am planning to remove only the plaster, leaving the lath untouched so as not to disturb the insulation, and then cover the lath with plasterboard. I was also thinking of placing a sheet of plastic film between the lath and plasterboard as a vapor barrier. Is plastic film a good vapor barrier? Would such a film, in contact with the plasterboard, cause the deterioration of the plasterboard from moisture?**

G.E., Brainerd, Minn.

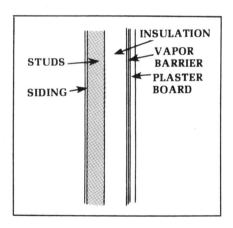

A.　You may find it impossible to remove the plaster without destroying a great deal of lath. We suggest that you patch the cracks in the plaster, cover the walls with plastic film as a vapor barrier and then install 1/4" or 3/8" gypsum board using nails long enough to go into the framing behind the lath. Plastic film makes an excellent vapor barrier and will not cause any damage to plasterboard. Certain types of plasterboard are available with a vinyl film or aluminum foil on one side, both of which make good vapor barriers. Ask your lumber dealer about them.

Soiled plaster walls

Q.　**I would like to know how to clean non-painted plastered walls. They are somewhat smoked and I would like to know what I can use to clean them without harming them.**

R.S., Owenton, Ky.

A.　You can clean the raw plaster with warm water into which a detergent is mixed until you have thick suds. Use a rough sponge or coarse cloth to wash them. Rinse lightly and let dry. If there is anything oily on the plaster, better use a tablespoon of household ammonia to a quart of warm water as a cleaner, then rinse. When plaster is dry again, it would be a good idea to apply a size coat of thinned shellac as a protective coating to avoid repetition.

Restoring plastic tile

Q.　**While using a strong solution to remove paint from the woodwork in our kitchen, we put tape along the edges where the wood and plastic tile meet. We must have left the tape on too long as the solution ate into and ruined the tile. I tried to touch it up but the tile is white and no matter what I use, it eventually turns yellow. How can I do a successful touchup job on it?**

J.A., Thompsonville, Conn.

A.　The color in plastic tiles goes completely through the material. In order to restore it simply scour off the various applied materials until you get down to plastic. Use the very finest grit garnet paper with a very light touch. Sand evenly until the white plastic is uniform. It will be dull, may not be perfectly even but it can be all one color. Then brush away all grit and rub further with jewelers' rouge on a pad or with plain tooth powder made into a thick paste with water to restore the gloss.

Papering a ceiling

Q. We have just purchased a new home and are decorating and would like to paper the bedroom ceiling. The room is 12' x 16' with 7' walls. Do you think papering would tend to shorten the walls?

E.J., Westport, Conn.

A. In selecting paper for the ceiling, the lighter the shade and the "quieter" the pattern, the less tendency to make the walls seem shorter. A contrast between lighter ceiling and darker walls, with a vertical stripe on walls, and a border paper complementing both wall and ceiling pattern will make the room appear higher.

Removing plastic tile

Q. My home was built about 20 years ago when plastic-tiled kitchens were popular. The walls and ceiling are covered completely. How do I take off the tile and the underlying glue so that I will have a smooth, paintable surface? The walls are plasterboard over standard stud construction.

J.A., Allison Park, Pa.

A. When you pry off the tile with a flooring chisel, the glue will either be dry and can be sanded or still sticky and can be scraped off. You could try a solvent for the glue which probably was a mastic which will yield or dissolve in mineral spirits. You are pretty safe with sanding or scraping since plasterboard or plaster can always be patched and made smooth. However, do size the plaster before painting.

Bathroom wall

Q. Our bathroom has plaster walls. About 10 years ago it was covered half-way up with aluminum tile. These tiles keep popping off in different places and we would prefer to remove all of them. How can we remove the adhesive that holds these tiles?

L.M., Nixon, N.J.

A. If the aluminum tiles keep coming off, the adhesive used was probably not waterproof. This suggests a means for removing it. Try using hot water first. If that doesn't work, use a lacquer solvent to soften the adhesive, then apply hot water and a non-sudsing detergent. Another approach would be to remove the adhesive with a power sander. It's a rather dusty but very effective method.

Covering tiles

Q. My bathroom is tiled in a very dark, drab grey tile which I would like to cover. Could you please recommend a paint or covering that will cover this and withstand the moisture of this area?

D.B., Rockaway, N.J.

A. Vinyl chip floor surfacing systems such as Dura-Flake, Torginol, DAP Seamless Flooring, etc., will adhere to ceramic tile. It is not hard work to get the flakes to stick on a vertical surface, but it does take a bit of doing. The results are more lasting than any paint and will simultaneously give you a good waterproof tub surrounding. If you have plastic tiles we suggest removing them and refinishing the walls.

Tileboard color

Q. We have plastic-finished tileboard in our bathroom in a color I dislike. Is it possible, without ripping the walls down, to cover it up with wallpaper or paint over it?

J.P., Chicago, Ill.

A. Wallpaper, no; paint, possibly. The surface must be absolutely clean, grease-free, dry and sanded lightly to provide a tooth for paint. One of the epoxy or polyurethane enamels is your best bet for a final coat. Follow the manufacturer's directions for the prime coat. Whether you can do a neat and even job may be debatable, but you can change the color. Flowing enamel onto a vertical surface is not easily managed without runs and sags. It takes a bit of practice.

Rough-finished walls

Q. Our living room walls are finished in a very rough plaster. Can you tell me how to make this surface smooth so it can be papered?

G.G., Brooklyn, N.Y.

A. Sanding is almost out of the question as you'd have dust all over. And since it is usually painted over, plaster filler cannot be expected to adhere. About the only way to prepare the wall for paper would be to remove the plaster entirely—or leave it there and build out the walls with furring—then apply drywall panels to form a smooth surface for paper.

Wall removal

Q. I would like to remove a wall to make a large living room. I have been advised removal will cause the ceiling joists to buckle. Is this true?

J.M., Niagra Falls, N.Y.

A. Depends on whether the wall is a load-bearing wall (often referred to simply as a "bearing wall"). A bearing wall is one that supports weight from above—in this case, your roof. Walls that are not load-bearing are curtain walls, serving only to separate one space from another. Curtain walls can be removed with no problem. A bearing wall must either be left in place to carry the load above, or supports can be substituted to take the place of the bearing wall.

In new single-story homes that have truss roofs only the exterior walls are load bearing and the interior walls can be moved. If your roof and ceilings are conventionally framed, you can still open up the room by replacing a load bearing wall with a beam or a large cased opening or archway. If you plan to do it yourself, check with your local building inspector on the size beam or proper framing needed to carry the load. If you're not an advanced handyman, you'd be better off to hire a contractor to remove the wall and install new supports.

Temporary brace

Q. **We have a two-story house and I want to make a hole in the front wall to install a large window. I imagine there is some simple way to brace this opening while it is being finished off to contain a new window but I have no idea what. I've been told the opening size, 6′8″ long by 4′8″ high, will necessitate a double 2x8 lintel if that information will help you tell me how to hold up the house till I get the lintel in.**

S.B., South Bend, Ind.

A. You definitely need to "hold up the house" temporarily and you need to do it before you open the wall. One good system is to use two 2x10 planks, one on top of the other, against the ceiling, tight up against the front wall. Support these at both ends on 4x4 posts. Rest the posts on planks on the floor with wedges driven under to fix them firmly. You had best tack down the wedges to prevent skidding. Mark your opening on the wall first so you will not block it locating the posts.

Uninsulated walls

Q. **I have a very old house with about a 1/4″ of plaster over wooden lath. Much of the plaster is cracked and in some rooms it has fallen off**
and left gaping holes. All walls are covered with many layers of paint or wallpaper. There is no insulation between the lath and the outside siding which consists of asbestos sheets held by metal strips. I hope to paint the walls which are in fairly good shape and panel the others. If I paint or panel, do I have to pour in insulation too?

M.T., Lancaster, Pa.

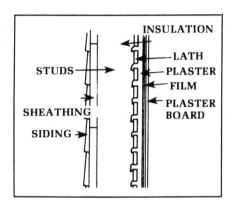

A. Your walls are obviously in very bad condition and you must be losing much heat because of the lack of insulation. Since your outside walls require insulation anyway, remove the plaster and wood lath and install batt insulation which has a vapor barrier facing. Then nail on 1/2″ gypsum board which you can paint or paper. The interior partition walls which are in good shape can be patched and papered or painted. Those in poor condition can be covered with 1/4″ or 3/8″ gypsum board and finished as you see fit.

Bearing wall

Q. **I wish to expand two rooms into one but the wall between is a supporting wall and I do not wish to remove the supports entirely. Is there some treatment for the space between studs that will give an "open" effect?**

T.F., Mt. Carmel, Ill.

A. Once you realize you can't remove the supports entirely, your problem is going to be selecting which treatment you will find most attractive. Filling and smoothing the rough studs is the hard part.
Once they are presentable you can set in lightly framed panels of perforated hardboard, metal grille, even tautly stretched fabric. Or you can set shelves between the studs, build in storage units encasing the lower portion of the wall. You can add more studs, leaving space between for an airy look or set in louvers or fixed louvered doors or shutters. As long as you leave the studs undiminished you should be safe. You can even remove every other stud, doubling up the remaining ones, a good solution for passage at the ends of your new "open" wall.

A-frame rot

Q. **I have an A-frame cottage which has several of its outside rafters rotted. Since they go from the base of the cottage up to the ceiling, I can't replace them. How can they be repaired?**

N.K., Warmleysburg, Pa.

A. Without knowing the specific detail at the lower end of the rafters, we must be rather general. A "splint" might be cut to run from the lower end to as far beyond the rotted section as possible. Cut a second piece, the "closer," to match. Scab on the "splint." Cut out the rotted section carefully and make a "patch" to piece it out, matching the rafter in cross-section. Scab on the "closer," sandwiching the cut end and the "patch" in between. If you do one rafter at a time this way, it should be possible to work without harming the roof. Needless to say, use treated wood.

Fabric-type covering

Q. **I want to apply fabric-type wall coverings on gypsum wallboard. We understand that if we want to remove this later and apply paint, we'd ruin the wallboard. I am anxious to go ahead with my plan in at least one room and would appreciate any information you can give me.**

A.R., Union City, N.J.

A. Go ahead and apply the fabric-type material you selected. It's waterproof, so it can't be soaked off like paper but it can be removed by taking an upper corner and carefully pulling it downward. The paste will remain on the walls. This should be lightly washed with a damp cloth, allowed to dry then brushed to remove any loose paste scale before painting. The alternative is to give the fabric material a coat of shellac and paint right over it.

Wallpaper remover

Q. Is there any product you know of which will remove wallpaper that has been covered with latex paint?

E.O., Hatboro, Pa.

A. A wetting agent called Fast, manufactured by the Savogran Co., in Norwood, Mass., may be of help. Or try your local paint dealer. He may have something similar. Scratching through the surface of the paper with coarse sandpaper on a sanding block should help, too. The idea is to get the wetness behind the paper where the glue is, so the paper will slip off as you scrape. That's why steamers help.

Steamer substitute

Q. We want to get paper off gypsum wallboard walls without steaming. Is there a reasonably good second choice method?

O.F., Sun City, Ariz.

A. If you can't borrow or rent a steamer and don't want to buy one you can soak off the paper, handling only small areas at a time. Soak with warm water to which either vinegar or alum has been added. Liquid paint removers also do a good job of loosening the paste but run into money on an area of any size. Some vacuum cleaners have attachments whereby a warm misty spray of water can be directed at the wallpaper. This works as well as soaking.

Using steamer

Q. Please tell me how to remove wallpaper from gypsum wallboard. We have no idea whether the walls were sized beneath the paper or not. We intend to paint.

M.H., Hawthorne, N.J.

A. The best way to remove the paper is with a steamer. This softens the paste behind the paper without too much moisture penetrating the drywall material. In most places the paper can be slipped off the walls following the steaming operation. Be careful to handle the scraper carefully so as to avoid gouging the softened surface of the panels. Let dry thoroughly and size with a thinned shellac coat before painting.

Removing adhesive

Q. Upon removing fabric-backed wall covering, large areas of the wall retained what appeared to be the backing of the fabric coating. Dry scraping and soaking in hot water followed by scraping again did not remove it. Can you tell me of a solvent that might remove this dried adhesive from the walls?

C.N., South Ozone Park, N.Y.

A. Fabric wall coverings are applied with regular wallpaper paste as a rule. Some pastes include a glue powder that takes a lot of softening to remove—but hot water eventually does it. Where that does not work, we suggest a lacquer solvent which will usually soften most such materials to the point where they can be scraped smooth enough to be resized for painting or repapering.

Texture trouble

Q. We used texture paint on our walls. Now I want to paper the walls. How do I make them smooth again?

E.S., Muscatine, Iowa

A. Some types can be softened with paint removers, some with heat. Others can be sanded down with a power sander which is a fast but dusty job. Fill the cracks, sand smooth and size before applying paper.

Wallpaper paste

Q. A short time ago I repapered a room and have discovered that in several places I got paste on the front side of the paper. What is the best way to remove it now?

A.M., Wellesley, Mass.

A. Most paste can be softened with warm water if soaked for a few minutes. Apply warm water by patting it on with a clean sponge, let it remain a minute or two and add more. After 1 or 2 minutes, a dry cloth can be run gently over the spots to pick up the softened paste. Don't rub hard. The paper will dry again.

Waxed wallpaper

Q. I have heard you can wax wallpaper. Is this so?

J.B., Cicero, Ill.

A. You can but not with floor wax. Use a white liquid wax made for waxing wallpaper. Clean the wall first and if the colors are fast, apply the wax with a soft cloth. Allow to dry thoroughly and apply a second coat.

Greasy wallpaper

Q. Our "guaranteed grease-proof" kitchen wallpaper isn't. There are grease spots here and there. Can I apply new paper over these and how can I prevent this grease from bleeding through?

J.B., Weehawken, N.J.

A. If you can't remove the grease with a good detergent, then it would be better to remove the old paper entirely, size the walls and start over. Shellac size in two coats might seal in the grease but why take a chance?

Papering panels

Q. I have painted grooved fir paneling in my den. I am considering papering it. Can this be done? The grooves are 1/2″ wide. Would they need to be filled in?

N.S., Karnack, Tex.

A. Do continue painting the grooved fir paneling in your den. Papering over 1/2″-wide grooves is not going to work, and filling them in would be neither economical nor particularly successful. If you really want an unusual texture-color combination, perhaps you can try painting and then mounting some decorative molding down the grooves in a contrasting color.

Resticking wallpaper

Q. My wallpaper is becoming unstuck along the seams. I have dampened the paper and squirted paste under it with an ear syringe but it hasn't helped. I want to avoid replacing it. Would diluted white glue do the job?

H.J., S. Penobscot, Me.

A. There are wallpaper adhesives designed specifically for this problem often packaged with dispenser tips for easy application. There is no other way except to try to get glue under the edges where it is needed. Trouble might occur where you have already squirted glue because another, stronger glue might not be compatible with the first. Trial and error is the only way to be sure. Rolling the joints with a roller wheel after gluing should help significantly.

Removing wallpaper

Q. The home I am buying has a plasterboard interior. The walls have been papered over and later (latex) paint was applied over the wallpaper. In applying the paint, some of the paper started to peel. I could glue down the paper, but if this doesn't look right, is there any decent way to redecorate, short of new wallpaper or paneling?

A.W., Jersey City, N.J.

A. It is possible to remove paper from properly sized plasterboard surfaces if you are reasonably careful. Your stop-gap measure (tape cement) might also work fairly well if you shellac the patch and the edges of the torn paper before painting over them. The really right way to do the job is to remove the torn paper and then paint the walls properly. Use one of the wetting agents such as Fast or other commercial wallpaper remover and work gently. The object is to soften the paste so that the paper will slip off rather than having to be vigorously scraped off. Steaming does not remove the paper facing of the plasterboard. It's a good idea to round the corners of your putty knife or whatever tool you use for scraping in order to avoid gouging the gypsum wallboard.

Wallpaper on panels

Q. At present, I have inexpensive wood paneling on the walls of my basement and wish to wallpaper them. Can the wallpaper be placed over the paneling without any sealer? What would you recommend I use to fill the grooves in the paneling so that they won't show through on the paper?

S.G., Brooklyn, N.Y.

A. On inexpensive wood paneling (if you mean plywood), wallpaper put up with water-based paste will warp the 1/4″ thickness quite a bit. Also filling in grooves in the panels or between them would be a problem as anything you might use would either not adhere and fall out or shrink at a different rate and show cracks.

A chancy procedure would be to remove any wax on the paneling first. Shellac and then let dry. Use a fabric-backed supporting vinyl or other "wallpaper" (such as Sanitas), and hope for the best.

The gauge of the paper might bridge the cracks sufficiently well to hide them.

The safer procedure is to clean the paneling well, sand lightly to provide a better "tooth" (depending upon what finish is on the paneling and whether it is plywood and not hardboard), and then paint.

Burlap wallcovering

Q. We wish to cover a wall with burlap and would appreciate any help you can give us relative to its application.

R.S., Don Mills, Ontario

A. You can apply burlap plain and paint it later or buy it already dyed. You can use thick wallpaper paste, applying it to the wall in a strip floor to ceiling just wide enough to hang a strip of burlap over. Brush downward to press the material into the paste. Another adhesive is clear shellac bought in 4 or 5-lb. cut and diluted 50%. Apply with a wide brush and brush on the burlap as soon as the shellac becomes tacky. If the wall is new or just cleaned, you may have to use two coats. Joints are always butted, never overlapped. Burlap once hung may be painted but use a paint that can be thinned down considerably.

Paper over paper

Q. We have one coat of wallpaper on gypsum wallboard on our walls. New paper is to be applied over the old. Some of the first coat is applied with butt joints and some overlapped. What should be done to the walls to prepare them for the new paper?

P.L., Brooklyn, N.Y.

A. Nothing need be done to the walls where the paper was butt-joined, as long as the paper is tightly stuck to the walls. Where the paper was overlapped the ridge over the overlap would show. Take a straight edged board or piece of metal and a safety edge razor blade and slit down the side through the overlap. Then soak this extra layer with a sponge and peel it off. Leave the one underneath and the finished job will be smooth.

Wainscot basics

Q. How is wainscoting applied over drywall and what are the variations of the material and design of wainscoting?

L.D., East St. Louis, Mo.

A. In common use wainscoting is generally taken to mean a material that faces or finishes off only the lower part of a wall. The variations of material might first include paint, wallpaper or other treatment applied directly to the drywall surface. Any paneling material can be used as wainscoting, too—wood, plywood, hardboard, etc., applying it only part way up the wall. The only difference is you'll have a cap molding at the top of the wainscot instead of where wall meets ceiling. Design considerations would include color, texture and scale. Note too that a strong horizontal line, carried all around a room, usually makes it look lower. With careful color consideration, it can also serve to unite a lot of different details.

Wainscot over tile

Q. We have ceramic tile both in the kitchen and in the bathroom half way up the wall. I want to cover both up but do not want to have to remove the tile. In the bathroom we want to cover the tile with one of the vinyl wallcoverings meant for bathrooms. Can you do that? In the kitchen we want to use Z-Brick half way up with the vinyl covering above it. How can we finish off the upper edge where the brick would end? If we do have to remove the ceramic tile, what is the best—and the least messy—method?

S.M., Steubenville, Ohio

A. There is no easy way. The tile should come off if both cases, though you might get away with leaving it in the kitchen. Finishing off the top edge could be simple. You can check with the manufacturer of the artificial brick to learn of any special preparations or specific adhesives needed. Then select a molding that can be attached to serve as a cap strip as shown in the sketch. If the tile in the bathroom is on plaster walls, you can be a bit rougher in prying it off since the inevitable gouges can be patched with reasonable ease. On wallboard, it is often simpler to remove the wallboard with most of the tile still on it and just install new wallboard.

Pine wainscoting

Q. I want to put knotty pine paneling around my dining room walls about 36" high. Do you have any information available for this type of project?

H.Z., Syracuse, N.Y.

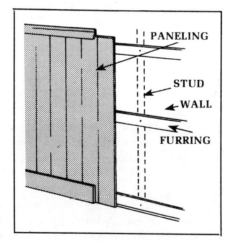

PANELING

STUD

WALL

FURRING

A. First remove the shoe-mold quarter round at the bottom of the baseboard. Nailing into the wall studs, fasten a 1x2 around the room keeping it level at the 36" height. Starting at a doorway, place the pine boards against the baseboard and this 1x2 strip, nail through the tongue side at top and bottom of each board. The groove on the next board covers the nails as you continue right around the room. Across the top of the paneling and strip, apply a chair rail mold and if you wish, a new shoe mold at the bottom of the pine boards.

Lower wall protection

Q. The walls of my hall are plastered and have an 8" baseboard. This hall has heavy traffic, including children on bikes and scooters and sometimes plaster gets knocked loose. With what can I cover the lower 3' or so of wall as a protection against these bumps?

A.P., Pittsburgh, Pa.

A. A simple and inexpensive answer would be to cover the lower 4' of the wall with predecorated hardboard. This is sold in 4' x 8' sheets and can be cut in half to make even size panels. Nail up or put up with metal molding strips between sections and along the top. This material is available in a number of patterns and solid colors. Even more child-proof are the laminated plastics but they are more expensive. Least expensive initially but requiring your time and effort in finishing would be textured or embossed hardboard. It is almost indestructible over a solid backing and has one advantage over the prefinished materials—it can be finished over again when they outgrow the destructive stage.

Gluing hardboard

Q. Can embossed hardboard that I want to use for a wainscot be applied without nails?

T.P., Providence, R.I.

A. Provided your existing wall is firm and dry, hardboard can be applied with waterproof tileboard adhesive or waterproof linoleum cement. Spread the adhesive over the back of the panel with a saw toothed trowel and brace panels as necessary until the adhesive sets. You'll want a baseboard and some sort of cap strip to make a neat job of it.

Chapter 10

Masonry Problems

Adobe...Asphalt...Brick—cleaning, construction, repair, veneers ...Concrete blocks—construction, repair...Poured concrete—driveways, walks, slabs, walls...Stonework.

Brickwork help

Q. I have been trying to find a book (or pamphlet or plans) on bricklaying that contains, in addition to general information on the subject, more specific instructions on how to clean and reuse bricks, how to clean up a chimney and especially instructions and plans for installing a small brick-floored porch or stoop. Can you help me find the information I want?

D.T., N. Pembroke, Mass.

A. Probably the best all-around source for helping you with the various questions you have is the Brick Institute of America, 1750 Old Meadow Rd., McLean, Va. 22102. They have quite a bit of consumer literature that would be of help to you.

You might also consult *"America's Handyman Book,"* published by Scribners and compiled by FAMILY HANDYMAN editors. There are a number of entries on bricks, including pointing up brickwork and general instructions on installing brick. Plans for a brick floored porch are the one thing we do not have a ready-made source of information for. There is plenty of information of footings and foundations, but we don't know of any place you can get actual plans, tailormade for you. You should be able to get enough information from BIA to plan your own brick-floored stoop or porch and enough information from the FAMILY HANDYMAN book mentioned above to do the job yourself.

Brick patio patterns

Q. Is there any difference in one brick pattern over another? I mean does one way of setting them in sand hold up any better than another?

J.L., Jackson, Ohio

A. If you set brick tightly, running bond is best as other patterns show up discrepancies in brick sizes more. With open joints it doesn't matter so much. Basket-weave with the bricks laid flat is about the simplest, next to running bond, to keep even. Herringbone is attractive but will require numerous cut bricks if laid between parallel sides or in a grid.

New stoop

Q. I want to build a brick landing and steps at the rear of my home. I tried to find a set of plans but met with dismal failure. Where can such information be found?

M.J., Cedarhurst, N.Y.

A. Brick stairs are usually built over a concrete or concrete block base. You will find the Sakrete project book, "How To Do Your Own Cement Jobs," helpful. It should be available where Sakrete is sold in your area. Another source of information (with excellent illustrations) is the hard cover

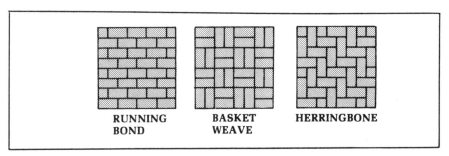

RUNNING BOND BASKET WEAVE HERRINGBONE

"Masonry" book in the Time/Life series which shows block steps with brick veneer. (About $10.95 at your bookstore or $9.95 plus $1.58 p&h from Time-Life Books, 541 N. Fairbanks Ct., Chicago, Ill. 60611.)

Still another source, better for design than for construction information, is the paperback "Walks, Walls and Patio Floors" by the editors of Sunset Books and Sunset Magazine. It's available for $3.95 from Sunset Books Customer Service, Menlo Park, Calif. 94025 or at your bookstore.

Driveway repair

Q. My asphalt driveway has a 3"-deep depression across it and many cracks. These imperfections were here when we moved in 14 years ago, but the depression has become deeper and the cracks wider over the years. I've tried various caulking materials to seal the cracks but they reopen. If it can be avoided, I don't want to go to the expense of replacing the entire driveway. Any suggestions?

D.D., Melrose, Mass.

A. What you are doing now is most likely the best that can be done, though you could attempt to fill the depression with cold mix. Chances are, however, that would break down rather soon. The difficulty lies beneath the surface, either in lack of fill or in uneven compacting of what fill there is. You don't mention any problem with washout (water getting under the driveway) which might speed the disintegration. Suggest you get a local opinion. It may be that redoing the edges and depressed area from fill-up, then adding a good top coating would postpone replacement for years.

Brick laying

Q. Both my friend and I are planning to brick the outside of our homes. We noticed professional brick masons using a steel pole standing off of all four corners from top to bottom to hold the line. What purpose does it serve? Will we need to use this in our own brick work?

L.A., Smithfield, N.C.

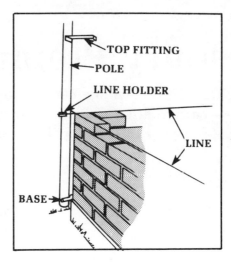

A. What you saw was likely one brand of story pole being used to hold the cord for aligning brickwork. They still have to be plumbed and the fittings that hold the line and hold the pole away from the building are all very expensive. These are meant to be time and energy savers for the professional brickmason rather than a handy gadget for the home handyman. Perhaps the sketch will help.

Building with adobe

Q. Where might I find some plans for building a "slump stone" or "mission stone" storage room? Both are similar to adobe. This store room would be either 10' x 10', 10' x 15' or 12' x 15', and about 8' high. The roof would be flat and covered with tar and gravel to match our home.

P.S., Sierra Vista, Ariz.

A. Adobe and stabilized earth methods have been written about in the past, often by the U.S. Government. We suggest that you start your search in your local library, particularly in the pamphlet files. Ask there, too, for the address of your local county agent, or the Ex-tension Service of the State Agricultural College. These people should be good sources of further information. It's unlikely that you'll find a step-by-step plan for exactly what you want. However, USDA Leaflet No. 535 "Building With Adobe And Stabilized Earth Blocks," published in 1965 by the Government Printing Office, Washington, D.C. 20402, has the information.

Brick in mortar

Q. I have heard there is an easy way to lay brick with mortar joints without doing it like a wall. Could you tell me about this?

R.G., Hastings, Mich.

A. The dry mortar method is not as easy as it looks. It's pretty easy to get messy results from a little cement left on the brick surfaces. The bricks are laid on a bed of 1 part portland cement to 6 parts sand, grading and leveling the bed as for plain brick on sand. Lay the bricks with about 1/2" joints in the pattern you want and level them carefully. Mix 3 parts sand to 1 part cement for the joints. Sweep or brush it into the joints. Tamp bricks and make sure the dry mixture is packed tight into the joints before you wet the patio down with a fine spray. Smooth joints with a piece of pipe so they are slightly rounded for best drainage.

Brick bar in basement

Q. I would like to build a 12' bar faced with brick in my basement recreation room. Would the weight load require ripping up the floor and pouring a footing under this area?

P.M., South Amboy, N.J.

A. If your floor is the standard 4" concrete on 4" fill which most all plans specify you could make an 8" brick wall and still be all right as far as weight goes. A brick facing would be only 4" thick and not very high. Go ahead.

Brick molds

Q. Is there a company which sells molds for decorative bricks?

E.C., Elmont, N.Y.

A. The address you want is Bric-Mold Co., 152 Rim Lane, Hicksville, N.Y. 11801. They also sell molds for fieldstone facings. Write for information and prices. The shapes you mold can be used to surface a planter as well as a wall.

Brick floor in barn

Q. I am redoing part of my connected barn into a family room and wish to use old brick on a 9-1/2' x 14-1/2' section of the floor. I plan to lay 1/2" exterior plywood over the existing 2" wooden plank floor and then use a mastic cement to glue the bricks onto the plywood. Then I would sweep a dry mix of cement, lime and sand between the bricks and spray this down with water similar to the laying of an outside brick patio. What is a suitable mastic compound for me to use and do you foresee any problems I might have?

P.B., Wolfeboro Falls, N.H.

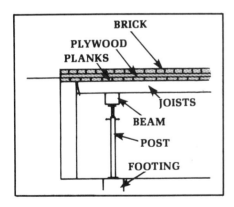

BRICK
PLYWOOD
PLANKS
JOISTS
BEAM
POST
FOOTING

A. Assuming that the concrete pads underneath the jack posts are sufficient your plan looks good. We would favor setting the bricks in mix rather than the dry and spray method you outline simply because that's a lot of water to have running loose inside. There are a number of suitable mastics to use under the bricks before you

use the cement. Check your local masonry supply house and ask them which is strong enough, yet less messy indoors for grouting. You may find, however, that the weight of the bricks is too much for your raised barn floor. In this case artificial floor bricks would be better.

Painted bricks

Q. I recently acquired some used red brick which I venture to say are over 100 years old. I plan setting these in dirt at an angle to divide my shrubs from the lawn. Before doing so I want to wire-brush them and paint them. Some folks say use flat oil-base paint, others say mix dye with gasoline and paint this on. What advice can you give me?

R.R., Bayonne, N.J.

A. Whatever paint you use will have to be waterproof so that no moisture can get inside the brick and blister off the paint. The bricks will have to be thoroughly dry when painted. The dye would work but does not seal them and our guess is that the color would fade rapidly. For best results, try a colorless masonry sealer first, then use waterproof enamel or a plastic base paint.

Disintegrating brick

Q. I have an 80-year-old Victorian style house with red brick foundation walls. In several areas, an extensive amount of brick has turned to dust. I am concerned about the structural safety of these load-bearing walls. What's the best way to correct this problem and is it a job I could do?

D.B., Maplewood, N.J.

A. We'd suggest you get a recommendation from a good masonry contractor in your area, preferably one experienced in restoration work. What is to be done depends on what the specific conditions are. What you describe is indicative of a moisture problem of long standing that has resulted in spalling and then dusting away of the brick material. There is nothing that will reconstitute the missing material.

Applying a waterproof coating now (or a water repellent) is not the answer. You can trap water inside the brick, resulting in even more extensive damage. You may want to send a check for $1 to the Superintendent of Documents, U.S. Government Printing Office, Washington, D.C. 20402, for a copy of the No. 1 Preservation Briefs. "The Cleaning and Waterproof Coating of Masonry Buildings," by Robert C. Mack, AIA, Interagency Historical Architectural Services Program, Office of Archaeology and Historic Preservation, National Park Service. Other titles in this series might also be of interest to you.

Re-set bricks

Q. We now have a patio of brick set in and I want to enclose this patio with a screened porch. Can I take up the brick and re-lay them in cement? Which is the best way?

W.M., Ridgewood, N.J.

A. Take up the bricks. Make a standard concrete slab on gravel or crushed stone fill, 3" thick minimum for both. Lay the bricks in 1/2" of mortar cement on top of the slab. Strike the joints a bit rounded for best drainage. Make sure pitch of 1/4" per foot is carried out, both in screeding the concrete slab and in the final brick surface.

Cleaning solution

Q. I've heard repeatedly "clean with a dilute solution of muriatic acid, but be careful". Just how careful?

M.U., Richmond Hill, N.Y.

A. Muriatic acid solutions are often suggested for treating various masonry wall surfaces. Sounding a warning note is necessary as the stuff is very corrosive, can cause skin burns, eye damage and is harmful to plant life. Always add the acid into the water—slowly, constantly stirring to avoid splashes. Old clothes, rubber gloves and goggles are advisable for working gear. Always wet the surface first and rinse extremely well with clear water. Use the proportions suggested for the job at hand. If you cannot insure safe run-off for the rinse water, better not use the acid at all.

Repairing cracks

Q. There is a crack between the bricks in front of our house that runs from the window sill to the foundation. Can you advise us on how to clean and repair this crack?
B.S., Richmond, Ky.

A. First, remove all the mortar you can from the cracked joint, using a nail, a beer can opener or some similar sturdy, pointed scraping tool. Try to get in about 1/2" from the face of the brick, and use a wire brush to clean the joints of any remaining crumbs of mortar and dust. Then you start repointing (filling the joints with fresh mortar). Using a ready-mix compound and a trowel, pack the joints tightly and smooth off your work, trying not to get any mortar on the brick facing. Use either your trowel or a rod or a rake, which is a special tool for shaping joints, to achieve an even effect with all of your joints.

Cracks in brick

Q. I want to build front stairs of concrete covered with brick but have been told these will crack and I'll have to point them every year. Is this so?
J.S., Cohasset, Mass.

A. Concrete or brick-on-concrete steps won't crack with an adequate footing underneath. If the concrete settles by being undermined, it will crack and break the mortar joints between bricks. Make the steps complete of con-

crete first but lower than the finished steps are intended to be by the width of the brick you will use. Then cement bricks to the risers of the concrete steps, finally adding the tread bricks.

Spalled bricks

Q. Some of the bricks on my 10-year-old house are spalling quite badly. This is especially evident in the chimney. Is there a coating which can be applied to the spalled bricks to prevent further damage?
E.G., Ft. Wayne, Ind.

A. Spalling occurs when moisture gets behind the face or surface of the brick where it alternately freezes and melts. The solution is to stop moisture from penetrating into obvious cracks found in mortar joints that are in need of repair. Neither we nor the Brick Institute of America know of any coating that will prevent already spalled bricks from spalling more. Also, the existing water-repellent coatings won't take care of the moisture that has already penetrated, nor will they seal across spaces where mortar or brick surface is missing.

Brick over old cement

Q. I have cement front steps and have considered covering them over with brick. Can you tell me what is the correct procedure?
J.W., Rockfort, Ill.

A. First measure from top step to door sill to see if you have the necessary 3" or so extra room to raise the steps. You're going to have a short step someplace. Soak the old cement well before starting the addition. One part mortar cement and 2-1/2 parts sand makes a strong mortar. Soak the bricks before use. Lay risers first, cementing them to the old concrete with a minimum of 1/2" mortar then add tread bricks. After two weeks apply a silicone water repellent if desired.

Fireplace mortar

Q. The mortar between the bricks on the inside of our fireplace has disintegrated. We tried to use fire clay mixed as directed but it was not satisfactory. Have you a suggestion as to what we should do now?
S.B., Cincinnati, Ohio

A. You used the right stuff to repair your fireplace and probably mixed right, too. The difficulty may lie in not having raked out all loose material first, as it takes a lot of raking, brushing and clean-up—a vacuum cleaner is handy. Some people mix a bit of loose asbestos fiber with fire clay and it does seem to stay put a bit better, but don't go overboard with the fiber addition. We'd suggest you clean it all out and try again, as you were on the right track before.

Repointing brick wall

Q. I wish to waterproof the front of my house, the walls of which are 8" thick. Are there any products on the market that could be sprayed on or must it be repointed?
J.H., Whitestone, N.Y.

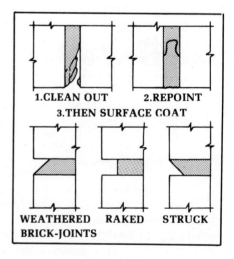

1.CLEAN OUT   2.REPOINT
3.THEN SURFACE COAT

WEATHERED   RAKED   STRUCK
BRICK-JOINTS

A. Your brick wall must be at least partially repointed. First rake out and repair any obviously leaking or cracked joints. Then repoint wherever it appears to be needed. After it has set you may spray or paint on a clear, masonry water repellent designed for this type of an exterior surface. This does not waterproof your wall, but it does cause the water to run down the wall rather than to soak into the masonry and the mortar joints. The three types of brick joints are shown in the second diagram. We suggest using the weathered joint.

Reclaimed brick

Q. **Our 16-year-old home was built of reclaimed brick. The line of bricks just above ground level is deteriorating. If this damage is due to freezing of absorbed moisture, is there any waterproofing method to prevent further damage?**

R.B., East Point, Ga.

A. Known as spalling, this problem is due to the absorption of moisture and subsequent freezing as you observed. If the old brick was not meant for exterior exposures, other factors may be complicating the problem. Once spalling starts, not much can be done. Provided the brick affected is not contributing to the structural demise of the wall, try brushing out the loose stuff. Then build a patch with waterproof cement. Give the whole area a good coating of masonry waterproofer. It won't look like brick any more, but it may not disintegrate further either. You will want to write The Brick Institute of America, 1750 Old Meadow Rd., McLean, Va. 22102, for information on using brick.

Brick efflorescence

Q. **My house has red brick walls which have developed a sort of white frosting. Can you recommend treatment?**

E.B., Toronto, Ontario

A. That's efflorescence. It is caused by mineral salts brought to the surface by migrating moisture, left there when the moisture evaporates. Usually muriatic acid in a dilution of 1 part acid to 5 parts

water will soften it to a point where a wire brush will remove it. Unless preventive measures are taken, it will return. You have to rinse the wall well to get the acid off and that starts the process again. You might try brushing it away with a dry wire brush on a power drill, then coat the walls at once with a transparent silicone water repellent. In a dry wall, where there is no seepage of water from within and no penetration of water from rain, no mineral deposit is brought out. In time the condition is self-curing without other treatment.

Repairing joints

Q. **Our new old house is in need of tuck pointing, some of the old mortar being soft as deep as 1-1/2″. What mix should be used to fill these joints with a white mortar?**

W.L., Granite City, Ill.

A. It is necessary to clean out all loose material in the joints. Then wet down the areas to be repaired. Use 1 part white portland cement and 2-1/2 parts sand. Work from the top down so you can immediately rinse away any splashes. Try to match the old sound joints so all will be uniform.

Repairing brick walls

Q. **I recently bought a brick house 30 years old, the brick in need of attention. Besides just plain dirt, these are remains of mortar stains and some mighty messy patching jobs. What methods can you suggest?**

H.W., Ottumwa, Iowa

A. Brush away as much of the mortar stains as possible. A solution of 1 part muriatic acid and 8 parts water will soften the mortar enough so you can brush away the remaining stains. But take care with the acid. It is dangerous. Immediately after the work, wet the whole wall, soaking it well with a hose to rinse away all the acid solution and the dirt. When

you're satisfied and any necessary repairs have been attended to, a coating of clear silicone masonry water repellent is a good idea and will make future cleaning easier.

Removing brick

Q. **My husband put up Z-Brick a couple of years ago. We now want to change it to a different color brick. Is there any way to remove it?**

J.R., Williamstown, N.J.

A. Z-Brick is intended to be a permanent installation. According to the manufacturer, there is no chemical which will soften the adhesive to make removal of the brick easier. The only way to get them off is chip and pry, piece by piece. But you don't have to remove them to change the color. Paint the brick and adhesive with a good, quality flat latex paint.

Shelves on brick

Q. **Could you advise me on how to put screws into brick walls that are plastered on the inside? I want to hang pictures and put up some shelving.**

M.G., Toronto, Ontario

A. The quick way is to nail up wood blocks with steel-cut nails set into the mortar joints. Then put the screws into the blocks. This is satisfactory if a shelf can be put up to conceal the blocks. The other method is to drill holes into the masonry walls with a masonry bit and set in a lead or fiber expansion plugs. Screws driven into the plugs expand them and they grip the sides of the holes.

Surface bonding

Q. **I plan to put a walk-out basement under my 14′ x 30′ mobile home. The cement bonding process using a mortar and fiberglass mixture troweled outside and inside the stacked-up blocks interests me. Where can I get information on**

the amount of mortar and fiber-glass to use?

H.J., Dayton, Minn.

A. Agriculture Information Bulletin No. 374 "Construction with Surface Bonding" by the USDA, Agricultural Research Service might be what you want. It's available for 45¢ from Superintendent of Documents, U.S. Government Printing Office, Washington, D.C. 20402. Order Stock No. 001-000-03340-9. The March, 1980 edition of the FAMILY HANDYMAN carried an article on surface bonding, too. You'll need a footing under those walls, however you build them.

Removing veneer

Q. I have a one-story, no-basement, brick-veneer house. I would like to remove a double window in the dining room and install sliding glass doors which would lead to a redwood porch outside and also serve as the rear entrance to the house. How do you cut the brick below the original window so that the sliding doors can be installed?

J.C., Marion, S.C.

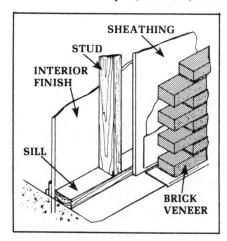

A. You don't exactly cut the brick nice and even for the new opening as your letter implies. First, you should remove the window frame. Then break out the bricks down the center of the area underneath the window, chunk by chunk. After you have done that, loosen the projecting bricks, remove them, and trim with your

bricklayer's hammer. Re-set them to provide the opening you seek, meanwhile having taken saw and other necessary steps to removing framing, sheathing, interior trim, etc., from the frame wall behind the masonry. In fact, you'll probably have to go a bit beyond the opening all the way up to get the new sliding door set into place properly.

Home-made blocks

Q. I plan a simple patio of concrete blocks to be laid directly on existing sod. I plan to make the blocks about 3' x 4' using 2x2s as sides for the form to give an actual thickness for the blocks of 1-13/16". Will such blocks shift or break up from frost? I want the easiest method.

H.L., Kansas City, Mo.

A. Your blocks are too big for their thickness unless reinforced and would probably crack up and break from weight put on them. If you cut out the sod to size and put about 4" of sand under them, setting them flush with the sod, you might be all right.

Casting patio blocks

Q. I would like to make concrete patio blocks from molds. How do I go about doing this?

E.P., West Babylon, N.Y.

A. If you want plain surfaced blocks they should be at least 1-1/4" to 2" thick up to about two square feet in size, depending on whether set in cement or in loose sand. Use a piece of plywood for the bottom if you taper the sides of the mold so the cast block can fall out when set. You can also make a form that you can open to release the cast block. The inside of a form is always oiled. You can buy ready mix or make your own concrete from one part cement to 2-1/2 parts sand and enough water to make a stiff mix that won't run. Pour in forms, level after compacting and

let dry for 24 to 48 hours, remove from form and let set five days before laying in patio.

Coloring patio blocks

Q. I am interested in making my own colored patio block of concrete. I would appreciate any information you can give me as to the type of dyes or coloring that is commonly used.

C.C., Bronx, N.Y.

A. The most easily obtained coloring material for cement blocks would be the metallic base colors sold in powdered form. Density of color is controlled by quantity used. For economy it is often best to cast the blocks 1/2" short of filling the mold. Then apply pure cement sand mix and scrub the color into it with a stiff brush, moistening as your work requires. Glaze with a steel float.

Textured patio blocks

Q. I have seen some concrete patio tile that had kind of a texture on top that looked a bit like slate. Could you tell me how this is done?

R.T., Knoxville, Tenn.

A. This was probably done by lining the forms the blocks were cast in with polyethylene film. Concrete poured over this does have an interesting texture which in reasonable colors might be taken at first glance for slate.

Fragile retaining wall

Q. I contemplate building a retaining wall 42" high in front of my home. Can I do the job with one row of common brick?

G.P., Deer Park, N.Y.

A. You will need a wall at least 10" thick for this height, built on a solid footing twice as wide and started at frost depth. For economy you can use concrete blocks on the backfill side and use brick on the exposed side.

Retaining wall crack

Q. My husband has built a fine-looking cement block wall 3-1/2' high in the front of our lawn. Rebuilt twice, now it is cracked again. Could you please explain what he should do to eliminate this trouble?

C.K., Collingdale, Pa.

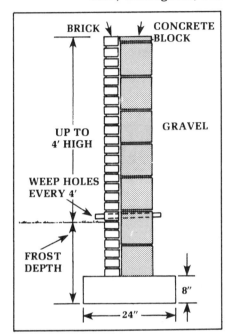

A. Your retaining wall is probably too weak and not properly based. The footing must be at frost depth and twice the wall thickness in width and at least 8" thick. Standard 8" blocks are not enough to hold back 3-1/2' of earth plus the water load. It is important there be weep holes along the base at grade so your wall does not become a dam holding back water too. The wall should be at least 16" thick at the base if it is to hold the full 3-1/2' high volume of earth. If single block thickness is used then reinforcing bars must be set into the footing and run up through the block voids to the top. These cores are then cement filled from the base to the top. Wire reinforcing at all mortar joints is also a good device to assure greater strength.

Cabinet mounting

Q. I am making a record cabinet but the project depends on how the unit is mounted on the wall. The wall is cinderblock behind plaster-board. Could you please advise as to whether toggle bolts or lead anchors are stronger?

A.A., Silver Springs, Md.

A. The plasterboard is probably on furring strips attached to the cinder blocks. Toggle bolts would fit behind the plasterboard only; not good with any great weight. With lead anchors you would have to drill through plasterboard, empty space and into the blocks 1". You'd need very long screws, but they'd hold well. Compromise: Attach a molding to furring with wood screws. Rest cabinet bottom on this strip. Run two or more screws through top of cabinet back into the blocks with lead anchors to keep cabinet from tilting forward.

Wall footing

Q. What sort of footing is needed for those attractive open-work concrete walls? We feel a screen-wall of this type would be more suitable for our house than a fence.

J.K., Joplin, Mo.

A. If you use lightweight pierced blocks you can go about 6' high without a footing. In fact some blocks are so light you can set them on a rail the same way a fence is built. Heavier blocks and drain tile constructions should have a standard 8" concrete block foundation wall on an 8" thick, 16" wide concrete footing at frost level for best insurance against frost heaving, if they go over three courses high above ground.

Bulging block walls

Q. I bought my home partly completed. The concrete block walls bulge outward. Now that the house is finished, is there some way I can straighten the walls?

B.D., Sinclairville, N.Y.

A. Those walls bulged while the mortar was still plastic. There is nothing you can do now to restore them to plumb. You can disguise the bulge with brick veneer applied directly to the block wall, using a heavy coating of mortar to bring the wall plumb on the brick surface. You could also apply furring as needed then wire lath and stucco or furring and siding shingles. In both cases, shim the furring to make a flush wall.

Concrete wall cracks

Q. I have a concrete block house which has developed a number of cracks. Those I repaired with grout have reopened and the grout falls out. What grout should I use?

E.K., Nashville, Tenn.

A. First of all, cracks should be opened to at least 1/2" width and 1" depth for best results. Use a grout consisting of 1 part portland cement to 2-1/2 parts of clean, sharp sand with enough water to make a stiff mix that stands without sagging. Wet the cracks with a hose and force the grout in deeply, then smooth off. Keep the patches damp with a fine hose spray for three days to cure them properly.

Breaking through

Q. How do I make a neat hole through a cinder block covered by stucco? I want to install a sillcock faucet.

E.M., Eau Claire, Wis.

A. First, figure out where the center of the block is. With luck, the block will be exposed inside the basement. Then measure from the corner of the basement to the center and take this measurement outside and mark the stucco where the center falls. If the block is the type with three voids, go through the center one; if it has two, go through either one. At any rate, don't try to cut through the solid part of the block.

Gently chip away the stucco with a chisel, removing only as

much as necessary. Then use a star drill to penetrate the face of the block, going inside to break through the block's interior face.

Finishing foundation

Q. Will you please tell me the mix formula for the stucco-type finish used to conceal the joint and course lines in cement block foundations and the method of application?

K.D., Westerville, Ohio

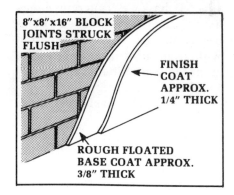

8"x8"x16" BLOCK JOINTS STRUCK FLUSH

FINISH COAT APPROX. 1/4" THICK

ROUGH FLOATED BASE COAT APPROX. 3/8" THICK

A. In most areas of the country, you can finish a concrete block wall above grade with a two-coat system directly applied. Use 1 part by volume of portland cement to not less than 3 nor more than 5 parts of damp, loose sand. Hydrated lime is usually added as a plasticizer but never use more than one quarter the volume of the portland cement. Apply the first coat over concrete block with flush joints which has been dampened, not soaked, first. You can use more of the same for the finish coat or you can use a prepared stucco mix, in which case follow that manufacturer's directions carefully. If you are planning a second coat, the first should be left rough, and dampened before the final coat is applied.

Installing a shower

Q. I am planning on building a shower bath in my basement which has cement walls and floor. I have already installed drain line with 2" extending above floor. My problem is where do I go from here?

H.H., Manchester, N.H.

A. Considering the location, you might as well make a cement floor in your shower, pouring it on the present concrete floor. It should be 2" minimum thickness at the drain and slope up to the outer walls with at least 1/4" rise per foot. The shower needs a wall around the base at least 4" high to handle any drain stoppage and avoid overflow. Simply continue the base up this high. Considering location again, why not make the walls of 4" concrete block right on up? This is simple, waterproof and fast and may either be glazed with mortar to a slick finish, may be painted or tiles may be attached.

Weep holes

Q. In a concrete retaining wall, how many and how large should I make the weep holes?

L.O., Irvington, N.J.

A. With a pad of gravel or crushed stone at the back of the wall for proper drainage, you need a weep hole every 4' to 6' along the wall. Using 2" galvanized pipe or 3" vitreous drain tiles in the forms is the easy way to make a hole and line it at the same time.

Patio drainage

Q. I have two problems with my concrete patio. Originally it was graded well and I had no problem with puddles after a heavy rain. Two years ago, I had the patio extended and the construction company was unable to maintain the same grade, with resulting puddles. I installed a drain at a low point, but it can't handle run-off from a heavy rain. Puddles still form. I want to level it with a long-lasting surfacer to establish proper grade. Can you recommend something inexpensive and easy to apply?

Also, I want to construct hollow brick walls, with 3'-high flower boxes on them, on the perimeter of the patio rather than on footings. Could a 4" steel mesh-reinforced

slab withstand this load year around? Would the brick wall crack or crumble due to expansion and contraction of the slab?

C.K., Paramus, N.J.

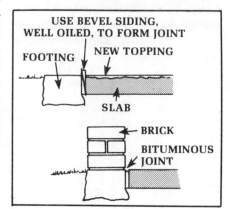

USE BEVEL SIDING, WELL OILED, TO FORM JOINT

FOOTING   NEW TOPPING

SLAB

BRICK

BITUMINOUS JOINT

A. You can level a patio with a latex or vinyl concrete mix. These mixes are more expensive but easier to work than the other alternative, a sand mix topping used with a concrete adhesive. For the latter, you spread the adhesive, such as Weld-Crete, over the old concrete before applying the topping. This prevents spalling and chipping. You can't apply sand mix topping as thinly as latex.

On your second question, we would not advise building brick walls on the patio. There will be an uneven distribution of weight and the material may crack. We suggest you build the walls on footings. Use an expansion-type joint between slab edge and wall footing, as shown in the sketch. To avoid adding to your drainage problem, make an opening in the low side of the wall for water run-off.

Pebbles in concrete

Q. I would like to finish the top of the cement squares with small aggregates. The effect is very popular today. What is the procedure for doing this?

R.P., Minneapolis, Minn.

A. Briefly, the routine is the same up to the final screeding of the poured concrete. Then broadcast the aggregate over the surface and tamp it in. Use rounded stones, 3/4" to 1-1/4", and wet them first. If they sink out of sight, wait; but don't wait too long. When the concrete sets up too much, you'll have to force them down in. When the surface water has disappeared, put a wide board or piece of plywood down. When you can stand on this without sending the stones still further down, it's time to brush. Use a stiff bristle brush and prepare for spatters. You want to leave two-thirds of each stone in the concrete, with only the top third seen. With a hose, on fine spray, you can remove the concrete particles as you brush them away. When you're satisfied, cover the concrete and let it cure a couple of days, then wash down again with a very weak solution of muriatic acid (1 part) and water (10 parts), following the necesary safety precautions when dealing with this material. It will take another five or six days to cure. If you're new to masonry work, you may want a copy of the Masonry volume in the Time/Life Home Repair and Improvement series. It's a good source for how-to information on masonry.

Step-by-step forms

Q. I can only handle a small amount of concrete at a time with the tools at hand. Is there some way to make porch steps of concrete in stages?

E.W., Teaneck, N.J.

A. There sure is a way. Build the form for your footing and get that in and cured. Then build the form for the lowest step but extend it back to the porch foundation, just the one step high. Pour full and level off. Build a second form to fit above this but set back one step and repeat the pouring on top of the first step. Continue this process until all the steps are poured. Remove the forms in each case after 48 hours. If you figure the steps to use a 7-5/8" or 7-3/4" riser you can easily use 1x8 stock for the various levels, setting back 9-1/2" to 10" each time for the tread. Use 2x8s if the stairway is wider than 3'.

Rich cement

Q. What is meant by "rich" cement?

S.F., Canton, Ohio

A. This term usually means a mix containing 1 part portland cement to 2 parts sand with the addition of a water-proofing agent.

Forms for steps

Q. I have the footings in for two sets of five steps each. Is there some way to build the forms so that the whole works can be done in one pour? I'd like to hire a truck load of ready-mixed concrete for this and a couple of other little jobs if I can get them all ready at one time.

H.J., Great Neck, N.Y.

A. You can cut stringers for form sides and set them in place. Nail on the risers. Anchor the form in place to the house or whatever and board up the sides beneath the stringers securely. Pour through the tread openings until the form is level full at each tread. Tamp concrete firmly into all corners of the form as pouring continues. Level off treads with a block of wood or a steel trowel. If you can, borrow or rent a mechanical or electric vibrator to compact the concrete in the form.

Fieldstone steps

Q. I'm laying out a 4-1/2' wide walk of fieldstone and have to include steps somewhere as there is a 3' slope between my front door and the sidewalk. I would like to make this a very good-looking job. Perhaps you have some ideas that could help me.

H.F., Pittston, Pa.

A. To make the steps all at one end or the other of the walk would be the ordinary method and grading would have to be done accordingly. You'll need a total of six risers at 6" or five risers at 7-3/16". It's a good idea to make one step up at the sidewalk to keep your walk above that level, avoiding excess water from that source. Make one or two steps at the house end for effect. Break the length of the walk with the others, about at the center. This will avoid too much grading and yet emphasize the slope. Make all steps of concrete on adequate footing but figured so that you can cover the surface with fieldstone set in 1" of cement on top of the concrete and still maintain the desired level. Build all steps first, then the walk between them. Figure a slope of 1/4" per foot away from the house for drainage of the walk.

Cement joints

Q. In building a cement or concrete driveway, I am wondering what and how they use between blocks as separators to take up the expansion and contraction and heaving.

L.C., Cleveland, Ohio

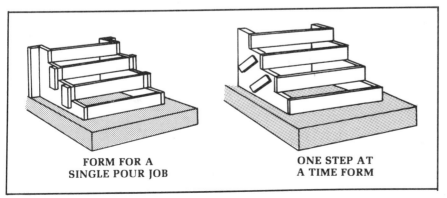

FORM FOR A
SINGLE POUR JOB

ONE STEP AT
A TIME FORM

A. Between sections any impregnated felt expansion strip will serve. This is about 2″ wide, 1/2″ thick, placed against one section when it is poured and the next one poured against it. Since it is hardly smooth enough to use as a guide to leveling, some builders insert a 1/2″ x 3″ strip of wood as a guide in screeding the drive level. This is removed and the expansion strip inserted, then the gap filled with poured asphalt.

Steps on slope

Q. I want to build three concrete steps on a dirt bank. The sides have to be built up so the dirt won't roll back into the steps. Could you give me some instruction on making forms for these sides?

B.A., McKeesport, Pa.

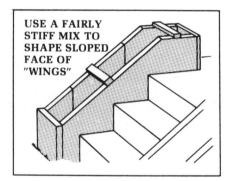

USE A FAIRLY STIFF MIX TO SHAPE SLOPED FACE OF "WINGS"

A. An easy way to handle this job would be to make the steps first. Then make the inner sides of the form in the shape of a stringer, one on each side, resting on the steps and cross braced to each other. This and the outer surface of the steps make up the inner form surface. Excavate as needed for these side "wings" and use vertical planks for the outer sides of the forms, driving them into the ground and cross bracing them to the stringer forms. Box in at the front and pour in the concrete. After removal of the form, back-fill against the wings as required.

Resurfacing

Q. The concrete drive running along the side of my house has settled about 3″, and every time it rains, the water from the driveway runs against the house basement wall and stands there. Can I resurface the driveway with blacktop, having it built up higher near the house so that rain water will be diverted away from the house?

J.C., Mexico, Mo.

A. Your thought about having the drive built up to drain away from the house is a good one. This is a job that must be done with hot asphalt, poured and shaped by a professional. However, it will only work if your present concrete driveway is suitably constructed and in good shape. If it is not, then nothing you put on top will keep it from disintegrating at an early age.

Mixing cement-dirt

Q. Please tell me how to mix cement with dirt to make a walk? Is this practical and lasting?

H.L., Isle, Minn.

A. You can mix portland cement with earth provided the earth is fairly free of vegetable matter. You strip off top soil, churn up the sterile subsoil to a depth of 4″ to 6″. In the churning process, mix in dry portland cement. After dry dirt and cement have been well mixed, add water until the whole thing is muddy. Then level off and let it drain and harden. With fair drainage the length of the walk, it sets up quite hard and serviceable. The difficulty is in the initial churning of the soil.

Heated driveway

Q. I am planning to put in a concrete driveway in the spring and have been thinking of installing heating cables in it to melt ice and snow when the cold weather comes. Can you give me any information about the installation of such cables?

L.Y., Pulaski, N.Y.

A. Write to Wiegand Div. of Emerson Electric Co., 7598 Thomas Blvd., Pittsburgh, Pa. 15208. They make the cable and usually supply information and literature on how to lay them.

Sunken walk

Q. My sidewalk has sunk in and cracked where a new sewer line was put in. Would a new layer of concrete poured to fill this depression hold or will I have to remove the old concrete and repour?

J.V., Niagara Falls, N.Y.

A. Since the walk has been undermined, there is no assurance it won't fall in further and crack any new surface applied. It would be better to pry up the damaged section and make a new base under it. Cut the sunken portion into squares and lift each in turn with a lever onto one edge. Lay at least 6″ of crushed rock fill under it. Lower the sections back into place. When all are in position, cement the joints between them. If you experience too much difficulty in raising sections, break them up and use the rubble for fill under a newly-poured length of walk.

Low walkway

Q. The cement walk between my house and garage is badly cracked and too low, so water settles in parts. How can I repair it? I have room for at least 3″ of topping. Should I break up the cement and start over or can I just top with the cement. Can I top it with asphalt?

R.C., Danbury, Conn.

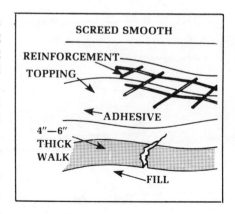

SCREED SMOOTH

REINFORCEMENT
TOPPING

ADHESIVE

4″—6″ THICK WALK

FILL

A. If the cause of the low-lying area is the lack of thickness of the original work, breaking it up for fill is the better answer. If it is 4″ to 6″ thick and in good condition, you might take a chance on the 3″ topping. Use woven wire reinforcing in the new work. Pay attention to screeding the final surface for good drainage this time.

Frozen drive

Q. We have a problem with our driveway. We live in a corner lot located on a slight hill. After a period of freezing temperatures, our drive rises in the center, making it impossible to close the garage door. This allows cold air to get into our house. What is causing our concrete drive to rise and what can be done to correct it?

J.O., Orlando Park, Ill.

A. Water takes up more space when it is frozen than when it is liquid, and this may be what you are witnessing. In time, the freeze-and-thaw cycle will indeed completely crack your driveway. The drive probably does not have as good a provision for subsurface drainage as it should have. You will have to study the surface drainage pattern of your lot. See if there is any remedy you might take to lessen the amount of water getting under the driveway. You will probably conclude that you will have to do it over to see what is underneath. There should be a good fill of gravel or crushed rock so that there is not a lot of water held under there to expand when it freezes. Even on well-drained areas there will be some heave, but not this much.

Patching colored walk

Q. My walk has cracked and I want to repair it. The walk is in red color which I added to the mix in powder form but much of it has faded where I repaired the cracks last year and you can hardly tell it was colored at all at this point.

How do I add the color to the mix to match the rest?

J.I., Union, N.J.

A. The color fading is probably due to the use of mortar cement containing lime which bleaches out the color. Use 1 part portland cement, 2-1/2 parts sand mixed dry. You can add the coloring up to 10% of the proportion of portland cement or scrub the color into the surface while the cement is wet. The dry ingredients are wet just enough to form a stiff mix which is pressed and tamped into the cracks. Water forced to the surface is used to glaze the surface with a trowel tip. Feather out lightly into areas just beside the cracks.

Oil on concrete

Q. Can you please tell me what I can do to get car motor oil stains out of a concrete driveway?

M.P., Hackensack, N.J.

A. First soften old oil stains with gasoline and while still moist, sprinkle heavily with portland cement. This will soak up a lot of the softened oil and the cake formed can be knocked off easily and the area swept clean. If the stain persists, repeat one time. Then wash with a strong detergent and a stiff brush. Take great care with gas fumes.

Grease on concrete

Q. Last spring, I installed a concrete patio at the rear of my house with a gas grill in one corner. Some grease dripped from the grill and made stains on the concrete—this in spite of using care to avoid it. Can you recommend a cleaner for concrete that will take up the grease as well as berry stains? We would also like to know if there is a material that could be applied to make the concrete surface less susceptible to flaking and staining. We find that we track a white powder from the terrace onto a dark-colored indoor-outdoor carpet on the porch.

R.G., Baltimore, Md.

A. There are a couple of driveway cleaners on the market, but we'd first see if TSP (tri-sodium phosphate) won't get off the oil and berry stains. You may have a hard time finding a small amount of TSP. However, you can use Spic-N-Span or similar cleaners containing TSP that you find in your grocery store. Make a paste of the material and let it stay on the concrete for a while before washing it off. Sometimes such cleaning leaves too clean a spot; so try it out in an inconspicuous area first.

The sealer-hardeners we know of are all meant for interior floors and may not hold up outdoors. You might write to Anti Hydro Co., 265 Bodger Ave., Newark, N.J. 07108 and/or Watco-Dennis Corp., 1756 22nd St., Santa Monica. Calif. 90404 for more information. A concrete paint or stain might also be a good answer to your problem.

Creosote stain

Q. While I was painting my trellis with wood preservative, a youngster tipped over the can and spilled creosote liquid on the concrete walk, leaving a large brown stain. Is there any way to remove this stain?

C.M., Closter, N.J.

A. There's very little hope that the stain can be removed entirely. It may have penetrated as much as 1/4″ in the porous concrete. You can chip away the stained cement and resurface or break up the damaged piece and replace it. You could try neutralizing the stain with muriatic acid which softens the cement momentarily and must be rinsed off at once but our guess is that this treatment will leave a smeary looking stain. Or you could hide the stain by covering the entire walk with cement paint.

Driveway drain

Q. Rain gets inside the garage because the concrete driveway pitches toward the doors and the rubber weatherstrip along their bottom edges does not seal out the flow. How can I prevent water from seeping into the garage?

D.L., Detroit, Mich.

A. You can prevent water running into the garage by intercepting it. Run a concrete lined trench about 4″ to 6″ wide and deep across the full width of the drive with a metal grille recessed at the top to support the weight of the car. Either end of the trench should empty into a tile pipe line to conduct the water away from the garage area.

Crumbling concrete

Q. I put in a cement sidewalk last year and now the whole walk is crumbling. What made it crumble?

F.S., Thompsonville, Conn.

A. It may be the concrete froze before it was fully cured. Too much sand in proportion to the cement or incomplete mixing of the two before the water was added could have this effect. If too much water was used or if the cement was smoothed too much with trowel or float the same condition could result.

If only the surface is crumbling, remove all loose material and wet the surface thoroughly. Apply 1/2″-thick layer of rich cement. Carry this down the sides of the slab. If the entire walk is crumbling it will have to be broken up and removed.

Paint stained cement

Q. I accidentally spilled some green enamel paint on my cement driveway. Can you tell me how to remove this paint. Methods I've tried all failed.

A.Z., Ferndale, Mich.

A. Try one of the rinse-off paint removers. Apply and let stand about 15 minutes keeping the spot covered with a damp piece of canvas. Then rinse off with a hose. To conceal the remaining stain which

has soaked into the cement, mix a quantity of portland cement with water to a thick paste and paint over the dampened area.

Rusty concrete

Q. We have a very nice patio with a trowel finish and rust stains from garden tools left outdoors during a rain. Is it possible to bleach the rust out without harming the smooth finish on the concrete?

F.H., St. Louis, Mo.

A. While muriatic acid will bleach out rust stains, it will also etch the smooth surface finish. You might try this household remedy with a good chance it will dim the stain a good deal if not remove it all. Make a fairly thin paste of lemon juice and salt. Spread over the rust stain carefully and not too thickly. Allow to remain about 5 minutes, scrub with a brush and rinse off with a lot of water. If you want to take a chance, apply kerosene or penetrating oil to dissolve the rust. Then use a strong detergent solution AT ONCE to remove the oil and its rusty collection or you'll have a worse spot than before.

Concrete repair

Q. I noted a masonry repair firm's crew working on a commercial building with what appeared to be a circular power saw using an abrasive wheel to widen cracks for repair. If this is the most practical way to do the job, what size saw should I use and what sort of abrasive disc?

E.F., Newton, Iowa

A. This is a quick way but unnecessary where only a bit of repairing is contemplated. A cold chisel is a lot cheaper. If you have a portable power saw with a 7″ or 8″ diameter blade, an abrasive disc of the same diameter will fit the arbor. Larger sizes would be hard to handle. You need a fairly coarse grit to cut concrete. Many hardware stores stock abrasive discs or can get them for you.

Crumbling steps

Q. Can you tell me how to repair our inside back porch concrete steps? They are only three years old but there seems to have been too much sand in them. They break off and are truly a mess.

G.J., North Platte, Neb.

A. It is possible that there was too much sand in the original mix or that the surface was troweled too heavily leaving nothing but sand on the surface. It may be the concrete was frozen before it cured. You can add a new surface not less than 1/2″ thick after thoroughly brushing ALL loose material from the present surface and soaking it. Use a mix of 1 part portland cement and 2 parts sand and to make adhesion certain add a waterproofing chemical to the water used in mixing.

Resurfacing concrete

Q. Three sections of our patio were poured with too little cement in the concrete mix. Consequently, they are practically sand in which weeds grow. Is there any way these sections can be resurfaced?

K.H., Los Angeles, Calif.

A. If the surface is that bad, start over; you don't "resurface" sand. We suggest that you remove the loose material until you reach something solid, or are at least 4″ below the finished grade. Rake smooth and tamp down solid, then pour a new slab in that area. You will probably need to rebuild the forms first, just as you did originally.

Concrete porch

Q. I have a front porch and stairs that are physically falling apart. It is made out of solid concrete that I poured myself. Is there some way I can face this crumbling mess with brick, use this brick as a form and then repour concrete? I would like to finish it off with flagstone treads on both the stoop and the stairs and do not wish to remove the entire structure.

C.T., Conklin, N.Y.

A. On the porch and stairs, pouring concrete over a crumbling mass of it is not going to give you a very good job. Building brick surfacing inside a form is not exactly the right way to do it either because you chance cracking the brick surface when you pour the concrete, pushing the brick against the form. The best thing to do is to break up the present crumbling concrete, discard the really rotten parts, saving the rest for rubble fill, and then build the form right, pour ample footings first and then finish it and surface it with brick later (if you wish).

Sharp technique

Q. I applied a coat of cement to our back steps last year and it seems to have stuck all right. I figure on doing the same thing to the front steps this year. The only trouble is I never discovered how to make a neat job of it. Have you any suggestions?

B.A., Winnetka, Ill.

A. We imagine it is the edges that you are concerned about. To make them sharp, straight and true, finish off the vertical work first. Run the flat surfaces over to these edges. By holding a thin straight board against the vertical surfaces as a guide, you can strike a neat edge. If necessary, you can use the same idea on all the edges that give you trouble.

Leveling concrete

Q. What is the best way to get my basement floor level so I can lay tile? It's thick enough I think, just bumpy.

H.P., Brooklyn, N.Y.

A. If the floor is not damaged or leaking you can paint it with a bonding fluid and apply 1/2" of new cement at the shallowest spots; as much as needed to fill hollows, holes, etc. There are also prepared mixes, generally latex-based, that can be used for skim coats in this manner but the expense is generally more.

Repair of steps

Q. I would like to repair my concrete steps which are covered with a 1/2" cement coat which has cracked and partly broken away. I want to replace this with a cement coating about 1/2" or 3/4" thick. Can this be done in a form or is it put on with a trowel (I hope not)?

G.B., Winnipeg, Manitoba

A. Sorry to dash your hopes, but the cement finish is applied with a trowel. Chip away all loose, cracked and broken cement possible, then soak the old surface thoroughly. Make a dry mix of 1 part portland cement and 2-1/2 parts sand. Use a waterproofing additive in the water you add to the dry ingredients. Add slowly till you have a smoothly flowing mass which can be wadded into a ball that will hold together without cracking or crumbling. Use a steel float and apply with upward strokes, starting at the bottom of vertical surfaces. Press into place and smooth off. On flat surfaces, simply spread out like thick butter and smooth off.

Settling concrete

Q. Both the front and side concrete stairs of my house have settled from 1-1/2" to 3" below their original level. Both consist of three steps but the top step of the front is wider. Is there any way I can stop this settling and return the steps to their original level?

G.M., St. Paul, Minn.

A. Apparently these steps are solid masses of concrete. The difficulty is inadequate footings. There is little hope of salvaging them so that the trouble will not recur. It is not too difficult to lever the steps back into place as a single mass if long and strong levers are used. The problem would be holding this mass up in the air while excavation is made underneath and an adequate footing put in. The footing should be 12"-thick poured concrete extending from 8" to 12" beyond the dimensions of the steps on the three exposed sides. Doing the job yourself it would probably be best to break up the steps with a sledge and use the rubble as a major part of the footing material for a new set of steps.

Crumbling shower

Q. Our stall shower was completely concrete. It began to crack and crumble so we had it paneled. Three years later, the paneling is rotting away, starting at the bottom, and exposing the already-crumbled concrete. It gets moldy even though we open the small window. Four people use this shower daily. What can be done now?

B.T., Shinnston, W. Va.

A. Covering up the problem isn't going to make it go away. You'll need to brush, chip, and clean away loose material until you reach sound concrete. Then patch and provide a smooth, waterproof surface, ready to be covered. You may want to consider suitable paints or other coatings, ceramic tile, or a pre-fab shower enclosure as possible ways to improve the looks of the facility.

Leveling steps

Q. My cement steps have become concaved from wear. I want to level them. What type of material should I use and how do I use it?

E.R., Liberty, N.Y.

A. Pick a day for the job when the temperature is above freezing. To level the steps, use a latex patching and floor leveling mix or one of the newer vinyl mixes. Directions for use will be found on the box.

If your steps are deeply or unevenly concaved, you should attach a form board across the front of each to contain the mix. For best drainage either pitch the steps lower in the front or the sides, if they're open.

Cracking joints

Q. Our poured concrete patio (approx. 56' x 40') is formed into 2' squares with white cement grouting about 1/2" deep and 5/8" wide. Periodically this grouting cracks, loosens and breaks out. Why? What can we do about it?

C.S., Miami, Fla.

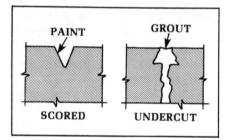

A. Please take a look at the two sketches shown. Those joints you are trying to get to hold the grout are not designed for that purpose. We suggest you give up grouting and use paint if you insist on white lines. If there are actually cracks or spaces between adjoining sections of the patio you can make the grout stay in place by undercutting in a sort of inverted keystone shape, as shown in the other sketch. First brush out the loose material and then dampen the joint before packing in the grout.

Caved-in basement

Q. Our summer cottage suffered a badly cracked and bulging basement wall from two sub-zero winters. Moisture-laden clay backfill is the culprit, pushing the walls inward. With no visible way of pushing the wall back into place, should I tear out the cement block wall and totally rebuild? Would jackposts crack the basement floor slab if I hoisted the one-story house temporarily? I'll continue

digging from the outside while I wait for your answer.

L.N., Xenia, Ohio

A. Stop digging. From your sketch, it seems unsafe. You'll have a cracked and caving-in foundation wall unsupported on both sides and could make matters worse as you dig. There are some questions that just can't be answered long distance. Best bet is to find a reputable masonry contractor and pay him for his recommendation after he has inspected the house thoroughly. Generally, you would probably support the structure and excavate in 4' to 8' units, repair and rebuild the wall in sections, backfilling as each one cured.

Sealing cracks

Q. The house we bought recently has a concrete stoop with brick steps. There are cracks between the concrete and the front wall of the house. I am anxious that rain freezing in these cracks may widen them and damage the stoop. What can I do to seal these cracks?

E.D., New London, Conn.

A. Freezing moisture will undoubtedly make the cracks worse. But you can easily solve this problem by using some of the excellent caulking products made by DAP, Stay-Tite Products and others which you can obtain at hardware and building supply dealers. These are ideal for sealing cracks against weather. Get the type which comes in a cartridge and can be used in a caulking gun. Observe the application instructions on the caulk cartridge.

Red concrete

Q. My house is 10 years old and the front porch is red concrete. The color comes off on the childrens hands and feet. Is there something I can get to paint or seal the porch to keep it from doing this?

H.B., Decatur, Ala.

A. Results can be unfortunate, as you've found out, when the base mix for concrete or a cement topping is affected by improper addition of pigment. One of the magnesium fluorosilicate treatments might help reduce the dusting and harden the surface. Suggest you describe the problem to your local masonry supplier.

Window close-up

Q. I have a basement window that I want to close up. The foundation walls are concrete with waterproof coating on the inside. The basement is dry now and I hate to tamper with it if it would cause a problem. The window sill is right at the ground. How do I make sure the filled-in area will not leak along the edges?

W.B., Lake View, Iowa

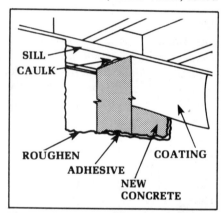

A. You should be able to wall up a window without creating any serious difficulties. Remove the window completely. Depending on the construction, you may want to make an even larger "hole" to provide a better mechanical bond. At least roughen the surfaces of the opening. Then clean thoroughly, brushing out all loose material.

If you are going to pour concrete you will have to build a partial form to retain it until set. Use a cement adhesive according to the manufacturer's directions for the most secure bond of new concrete to old. (Anti Hydro Co., 265 Badger Ave., Newark, N.J. 07108 is one manufacturer.)

Duplicate as near as possible any waterproofing or other coatings that may have been used inside or out on the rest of the wall, lapping over the newly finished joint. Make sure you've treated the top of the finished wall the same as the rest.

If there's oakum or caulk at the joint between wall and floor framing, don't neglect it over the new wall area.

Stone walk

Q. **I am having a new home built. The builder is putting in a conventional sidewalk. We want to cover it with flat stones. I want this to be a permanent, trouble-free installation. Are there any options for the setting bed or is a conventional sidewalk a good start?**

E.C., Provo, Utah

A. Assuming the "conventional sidewalk" is laid over a properly prepared base, there should be no problem, though setting the stone immediately would be preferred. Your builder should be aware of your intended topping when he determines the finish grade of the walk. You can get additional information on using stone from the Building Stone Institute, 420 Lexington Ave., New York, N.Y. 10017.

Film on stone

Q. **Recently I cleaned my stone-faced porch with muriatic acid diluted with water. It left a white film. Is there anything that will remove the white film?**

M.S., Wampum, Pa.

A. You didn't mention what kind of stone you have. If you know where the stone was purchased, you could go back and ask the company the procedure for cleaning your particular kind of stone. You may have used the acid in too strong a solution; always follow the proportion of acid to water suggested on the acid label. The film may be either calcium carbonate or calcium chloride.

Try using a strong detergent such as trisodium phosphate or dishwasher detergent on a small area. Scrub the film with the detergent solution and a stiff brush, and rinse thoroughly with clear water before the spot dries. If this removes the film, use this procedure on the entire surface.

If this is not successful, wash the stone again with a very dilute solution of muriatic acid, and be sure to flush the acid away immediately with a heavy stream of water. If the water you rinse with has a high mineral content, it may be the culprit. Always use acid in the proportion recommended; flush immediately with clear water to be sure no acid residue remains, and be sure the water supply is not high in mineral content.

Sidewalk stones

Q. **I have a sidewalk made of large flat stones with mortar between them. The cement has begun to break up between the stones. I understand there is an adhesive cement mixture which I can use to make a 1"-thick topping over the walk. I saw it advertised on television twice and the only thing I remember is the name "Campbell."**

C.S., Frenchtown, N.J.

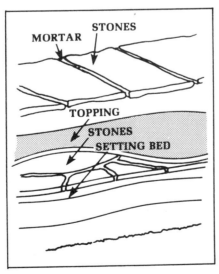

A. If the top sketch is about what you have now, a 1" topping is not a good answer. If the stones are moving independently of each other now, enough to crack the mortar, they'll crack the topping too. If your walk is like the second sketch shown at the bottom, there's a chance a 1" topping would work, provided you are able to correct the erosion problem that may have caused the initial joint failure. "Campbell" used to be Campbell Products of Towson, Md. 21204. They were a manufacturer licensed by Sakrete to make their line of ready-mixes. Use Sakrete products or ask your local masonry supply house for suitable topping mix.

Stone foundation

Q. **The foundation of my house is made of cinder block and looks ugly. I would like to put fieldstone on it. I have been advised that I must go below the frost line of 3-1/2' for new footings. Is this correct? Would gravel be suitable for new footings?**

P.D., Kearny, N.J.

A. Covering the foundation with real fieldstone poses a number of difficulties you could avoid by using imitation stone. Real fieldstone is very heavy and will require new footings to support it. Such footings have to be made of poured concrete. Gravel cannot be used for this purpose. The footings, as you have been correctly advised, must go below the frost line of 3-1/2'.

Real fieldstone makes a heavy, thick wall and will give you a rain-collecting ledge just under your siding which may cause its deterioration from excessive moisture. On the other hand, there are imitation "stones" which are very light in weight, do not require footings and do not protrude enough to create a ledge. Some are made of portland cement and pumice and look like rough-faced fieldstone. They are light in weight, look fairly realistic and usually do not require footings. Check with your building supply dealer for the kind of imitation stone facings he carries.

Chapter 11

Moisture Problems

Basement floors...Drain tile systems...Faulty foundations... Joint leaks...Humid basements...Stairwell seepage...Waterproofing.

Wet basement floor

Q. We do not have any leaks in our basement, but the floor is always damp under the rug. Is this condensation?

H.W., Riverdale, Md.

A. More likely it is seepage. A simple test will determine which. Tape a square of aluminum foil down on the floor, sealing the edges. Check it the next day. If there is moisture on the surface, your problem is condensation. If droplets cling to the underside of the foil when you lift it (or if the area of floor under the foil is visibly damp), you have a seepage problem.

Dry basements

Q. We are going to build a new house. I do not want to repeat the constant round of basement patching we do here, still without getting it dry enough to use. What steps should be taken to insure a sound, usable basement is constructed?

J.G., Akron, Ohio

A. Footings of sufficient size to carry the load is the best insurance against cracking from settlement.

Check surface draining and roof water so it is discharged away from basement walls. Run a line of drain tile properly installed around the house. Give the exterior surface of the walls a waterproof coating. Membrane waterproofing under the floor is a good investment in most situations. Slab at least 4″ thick with expansion joint properly filled around the perimeter is also considered good construction. The first step to take is in lot selection. Try to pick out something that has good natural drainage.

Basement seepage

Q. Could you please give information on water seepage in the basement? I have a fairly new home and would like to put a recreation room in the basement but it gets so damp down there I hesitate to try it. What causes this and what must I do?

R.P., York, Pa.

A. Yours is possibly the most common problem of the modern homeowner. Seepage is due to faulty construction and the fact

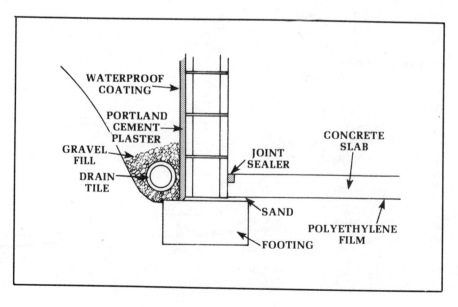

that concrete is porous unless treated. You need to waterproof the walls—preferably from the outside but failing that from the inside—before installing furring for finishing materials. The floor will probably need attention too; just what remedy depends on how bad the situation is.

Waterproof cement

Q. What do I mix to get waterproof cement?

P.A., Chicago, Ill.

A. You mix 1 part portland cement to 2-1/2 or 3 parts clean sand together first, then add the water to which a waterproofing additive has been mixed. You can also get pre-mixed cement where the waterproofing agent is mixed in the dry ingredients.

Perimeter space

Q. There are drainage ditches around the footing and criss-crossing under the basement floor, filled with stones. Two drainage lines carry the water away. Now I want to finish the basement but there is a 1" gap between the edge of the basement floor and the poured concrete walls. Should this be filled and with what?

A.B., Short Hills, N.J.

A. Tap a strip of oakum caulking into the gap, a thick enough strand to drive—not fall—in. Push to a point about 1/4" below the surface. Then pour in fluid asphalt. Sprinkle on dry sand if you are apt to step in the asphalt.

Open and shut case

Q. In our basement there is a fairly good-sized crack opposite the point where the garage wall joins the house above. I have filled it repeatedly but it seems only to get bigger and bigger and every spring it gets wet. Is there some way to fill it once and for all?

D.S., Muskegon, Mich.

A. You can make a project out of this and probably do the job just once. Chip out the crack to a T-shaped slot leaving the sides rough but clean of loose particles. Apply a mortar liner of a quickset compound to form a neater slot. When that is completely dry, apply a primer and let it dry. Then pack with a joint sealer for almost the full depth of the stem of the T. This is the elastic part of the repair that can absorb the movement that made the previous patches fall out. Finally, apply a mortar cap, filling the cross-member of the T slot. Score it down the center so movement can occur without cracking.

Pitching the ground

Q. In an article on wet basements in your column I noticed the expression "Pitch the ground away from the house." Would you please explain what this means?

J.A., Piqua, Ohio

A. The expression simply means to slope the earth downhill, away from the house so that some rainwater will run off and there will be less to soak into the ground around the foundations. What we were trying to tell our readers to avoid in our original statement is the all too common practice of digging foundation planting areas so that they are lower than the grass beyond them. This causes rain to collect in the planting strip and seep down along the foundation and often into the cellar.

Water repellent

Q. Would you please settle an argument for me. Aren't waterproof coatings and water repellent coatings practically the same? We're speaking about masonry surfaces generally, though I suppose the terms should apply to other things too.

G.H., Bronx, N.Y.

A. The two terms are often confused, sometimes with disap-

pointing results. A water repellent coating causes water to ball up and run off vertical or sloped surfaces without being absorbed. Water vapor can still pass through. Waterproof means a coating or film through which water will not go. With masonry materials, which are porous, this distinction is very important. You waterproof the inner side of basement walls so water does not come through them. You use water repellent on the outside above grade so rain water is not absorbed into the wall material.

Slight seepage

Q. My basement walls seem only a bit damp. I've been reading those advertisements for painting out dampness and wonder if this would do the trick. Can you advise?

P.O., Rumson, N.J.

A. Good to excellent results follow proper application of the waterproofing paints you've seen advertised, provided you do not try to repair a cracked and leaking wall with paint. Used as directed by the manufacturer to solve the problem the coating was designed to handle, they are fine. Make sure you cover the walls completely.

Perimeter drain tile

Q. We are just starting to have our new house built. I've been watching what goes on. The builder has laid some pipe around the foundation, outside the house, without fitting it together. What is this for?

E.T., St. Louis, Mo.

A. This is concrete drain tile which should be laid around the foundation wall with open joints covered on top by building felt. It serves to intercept and carry off ground water that would otherwise collect where wall meets footing, and could eventually seep inside. Your builder should have applied a waterproof coating to the outside of the foundation wall first, then laid the drain tile, covering it over with about a foot of coarse gravel or crushed stone. The felt pieces over the joints serve to keep the loose fill from blocking the pipes.

Seepage in wall

Q. **There is considerable seepage through my concrete block walls. I want to finish the basement. What should I do first?**
Y.P., Rochester, N.Y.

A. You can use asphalt paint and tarpaper strips to waterproof the walls under the furring or you can use polyethylene film applied with its own adhesive. The latter costs a bit more, goes on with a bit less mess and lasts longer. Either method can be used with even better effect if you can do it to the exterior surface of the walls.

Damp basement floor

Q. **My basement walls have been painted with a waterproofing paint and seem to be quite dry all year round now but the floor is another story. We would like to lay tile but fear to go ahead. It is constantly damp; the tiny cracks seem darker each spring. What would be the most reasonable treatment?**
P.R., Youngstown, Ohio

A. You need to fill any obvious cracks, of course, and then a minimum of 1-1/2" of hydraulic cement over the entire floor is your best bet.

Basement awash

Q. **We just moved into our house last fall and all was well. Now this spring with all the rain, we find the basement we planned to use for a summer living room is practically awash from a number of only moderate size cracks. Can they be fixed right this minute or must I wait till they dry up, if they ever do?**
S.A., St. Louis, Mo.

A. You can fix them right away and probably should. Use a hydraulic setting mortar or quickset patching mix. These are sold as premixes to which you add a little water or as additives which you use with ordinary mortar. Either way, clean out the crack first of any loose particles not washed away yet. Get set to work fast as the mortar hardens in a minute or so. Shape it a bit and force it into the hole or crack you have to fill and hold it there till it gets hard.

Flooded floor

Q. **My basement floor seems to be getting worse. Last summer it was just damp but this spring there are actually puddles a couple of places. At the front end of the house a couple of cracks have reopened and look dark along the edges. After I fix the cracks again, what should I do? We'd like to be able to move furniture down there and use the area this summer.**
W.O., Totowa, N.J.

A. This sounds like fairly heavy seepage to us and if so you might relieve the situation with a layer of polyethylene film on top of the present floor topped by 2" to 4" more of concrete.

Foundation opening

Q. **I have trouble with rain blowing between the foundation**

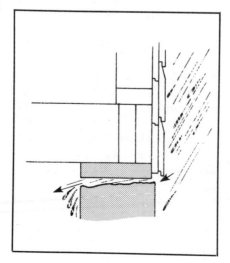

and frame of my house. Would cementing up the space between shingles and foundation stop this?
B.D., Bethpage, N.Y.

A. Cement would probably fail to stick in that space as the wood shrinks and swells. A better way would be to apply caulking compound with a caulking gun, squeezing the semi-elastic material into the space where it will stick. It will not be affected by wood expansion or contraction; it is waterproof, never dries completely. You could also use oakum caulking, driving it into the space with a cold chisel and hammer.

Glue for poly film

Q. **I have a damp crawl space under my house and intend to lay polyethylene film on the ground but there are five concrete piers and block walls that I would like to glue the vapor barrier to. Can you tell me what to use?**
R.K., Hot Springs, Ark.

A. When you buy the film you can also obtain an adhesive to seal it down with. If you can't find it locally, even caulking compound is sticky enough to hold.

Stand pipe

Q. **I thought we had licked our damp basement problem, having mended the worst crack so it held through last spring. But this year it's reopened and we again have water in the basement. I've heard of a way of solving the problem with a pipe run from a hole in the floor up to the ceiling, leaving the top uncapped. Will this work?**
L.S., Pearl River, N.Y.

A. The method of pressure relief you describe is called a stand pipe, in common use around Chicago. Usually it is a 4" diameter pipe and it should be cemented into a hole in the floor and run up to grade or slightly higher. It in no way reduces basement dampness but should stop the floor from lifting and cracking.

Outside treatment

Q. A local salesman claims his product will cure my very leaky, damp basement. I must dig all around the foundation and apply it to the outside walls. Will it do the trick?

G.K., Coal Valley, Ill.

A. That outside-the-foundation treatment is a lot of work but it is the best method since it prevents water from reaching the foundation at all. Two coats of portland cement base paint or two continuous coatings of hot bituminous material applied at right angles to each other over a suitable priming coat or polyethylene film laid in mastic are all considered good waterproof coatings when properly applied to the outside of foundation.

Basement on spring

Q. I am building my own home and have found a spring coming up in the basement. We kept the excavation pumped out when making the foundations. Do you think when the floor is poured it will hold back the spring?

F.J., Montreal, Quebec

A. It would be best to set up a drain tile system to carry away water either to a down-hill point or to a catch basin away from the house. Any water present, when pouring the floor, will ruin the concrete. Fill under the floor with crushed rock to about 4″ deep with a layer of sand on top. Then lay polyethylene film and pour on 2″ of concrete, add wire reinforcing and a second 2″ of concrete. Coat the surface of the floor and the basement foundation with 1/2″ of waterproofed cement as a final protection.

Cure leaks outside

Q. I have tried several ways to seal bad cracks in my cellar wall from the inside. This summer I plan to dig down to the spots outside and stop the leaks once and for all. What would you advise for this outside wall treatment?

A.G., Niagara Falls, N.Y.

A. Brush the wall free of dirt after you've dug down outside to the top of the footing. Coat with asphalt paint, cover with horizontally run strips of tar paper. Then apply a second coat of asphalt paint and apply the tar paper vertically. All joints should lap 2″.

"Sweating" concrete

Q. Moisture "sweats through" the concrete floor of my basement and keeps the floor wet in hot and humid weather. The walls do not seem damp and the drainage is good. How can I correct this condition?

T.S., Weymore, Neb.

A. Most concrete slabs poured on bare ground without waterproofing below will sweat in this manner. The concrete is porous and water penetrates from below by capillary action. In dry weather it evaporates; in humid weather it can't evaporate fast enough. You need to waterproof the floor.

Wet walls

Q. The hollow concrete blocks in my basement walls fill up with water as high as 2′ above the floor. I believe the tile outside the wall is broken but I can't dig to find out as the concrete drive runs alongside the foundation. I have already paneled the interior. Removed some panels to plug leaks but they just broke out someplace else. Is there any way of draining away this water, short of an open drain trench?

R.B., Flint, Mich.

A. There isn't any practical way you can drain the collected water out of the voids in the blocks. Even if you did succeed in making a hole into each of the voids, you'd have a whole line of waterfalls and an open trench couldn't handle that load. It is possible your tile line is intact but has no outlet to drain to. You could investigate and correct this with a dry well. The safest solution is no half-way measure. Remove the paneling and waterproof the wall completely. Assuming it is now untreated, unpainted blocks, the best would be 1/2″ of waterproofed cement applied over the blocks from the floor-wall joint up.

Basement dampness

Q. In spite of three windows kept open all the time (except winter) our cellar is very damp. It has an earth floor, stone walls, no furnace (we have stoves upstairs) and there are no eaves troughs. Even so, there is no water in the cellar.

H.E., Pittsfield, Mass.

A. No doubt there is a good deal of moisture coming up through your floor and through the foundation as well, but ventilation takes care of it to the point where no actual water is evident. A cement floor would seal out all moisture from below but you may have to seal the walls with cement over the stone. Sealing the floor may divert the water so it penetrates through the walls instead. Once you've sealed the basement, it would be a good idea to put up gutters to carry water away from the house.

Cracks in wall

Q. There are diagonal cracks running down from the corners of our front basement window. The wall is poured concrete and there is a concrete window well on the outside, flanked by two planters. We intend to paint the basement walls and I am concerned about staining should these cracks ever leak.

O.S., New Ulm, Minn.

A. Why not fill the cracks and paint over them? You have a choice of patching materials: easy to use but expensive latex cement compounds or fairly easy to use, less expensive sand-cement mortar with non-shrink additive which lessens the need for undercutting and the least expensive, patching mortar made of 1 part cement to 2-1/2 parts sand but you need to rake out and undercut the crack for a good bond. In fact in any case the crack must be cleared of all loose material. When the patch has set, you can use a prepared sealer over the whole wall if seepage is a problem or portland cement paint if it isn't.

Damp brick house

Q. I have a problem with my new brick house. It seems that it was built in a low spot, and now I find that it is very damp under the house. I've left all the vents open for three months, and it's still wet. The subsoil is clay. Can you help?

R.B., Conway, S.C.

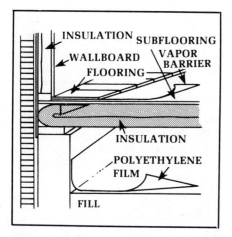

INSULATION SUBFLOORING
WALLBOARD VAPOR
FLOORING BARRIER
INSULATION
POLYETHYLENE FILM
FILL

A. If the spot you've built on is so low that the foundation is below the water table, you really are in deep water. We doubt that, but where good surface drainage (getting the rain run-off away from the house) is not sufficient to make a

dent in crawl space dampness, there are other steps to take. You are quite right to keep the vents open, but don't expect that to dry up an area where more dampness is being supplied all the time. Trapping the dampness below the crawl space will help, too. The diagram suggests 4 to 6-mil. polyethylene film be laid over the fill and brought well up the walls of the foundation. You'll find that insulating the floor helps, but be sure to include a vapor barrier on the warm side of the insulation, preferably between the finish and the subflooring (difficult in a house that is already built). While you are at it, if you insulate, get that cold strip between the ends of the floor joists.

Joint leaks

Q. Water comes seeping through the seam where wall and floor join in our cellar, usually during the spring thaw. How can I stop this?

E.L., Tyngabro, Mass.

A. You can construct a cove of waterproof cement. Carry it up the wall about 2″ and 2″ out over the floor. Use one of the pre-mixed putty-like quick-setting patching compounds or make your own with a mixture of hydraulic cement plus 2-1/2 parts sand. Chip out the cement enough to form a good mechanical key, clean off any paint, etc. on floor or wall and wet the area. Then tamp in hydraulic cement and shape it for a good appearance. If floor and walls are sufficiently well waterproofed and your joint is successful, you should have no more trouble. If floor and walls are not well waterproofed and strong, you may have moved the problem without ending it.

Floor wall joint opens

Q. I have repeatedly filled up the joint around our basement floor where it meets the walls, but

it continues to crack and water comes through every so often.

T.M., Eastlake, Conn.

A. You neglected to say what you used to fill up the joint. Plain cement will crack again and again. The walls set firmly on their footings but water pressure under the floor slab tends to lift it up like floating a boat. First relieve the pressure—with a sump pump if necessary. Diverting surface water to a dry well will also help, sometimes curing the problem. Then fix the joint.

Joint fixed

Q. I cut out and repaired most of the perimeter crack around my basement floor. Did a good job too—it doesn't leak there but now the floor is going to pieces. What happened and what do I do now?

F.J., Indianapolis, Ind.

A. Water denied entrance one way will seek it another. You did such a good job on the floor-wall joint repair that the slab is now the weaker barrier and water pressure, building up beneath it, is causing cracks, etc. You will need to waterproof the floor equally well.

Spring water

Q. Our basement is tile, inside and outside, with a sump pump pumping the water out to a ditch in front of the house. With the exception of a dry spell two years ago, this pump runs 24 hours a day, all year 'round. Is there some way to use this water?

S.W., Earlville, Ill.

A. In some situations, a spring can be capped and the water piped. Its use would depend in part on whether it met health standards. It is sometimes possible, if this is not a true spring but simply the closest outlet for a natural reservoir, to pipe it away without having to run a pump. In this case, you'd have to intercept the water and deliberately divert it around to bypass the house safely. You will need local professional help to see what is best (and least expensive).

Crack filling

Q. We are getting ready to finish out our basement for a playroom and have made a tour of inspection. While we've never been troubled with much water in our basement there are a few places where the mortar between the concrete blocks is cracked. Should these be fixed before coating the walls with a prepared sealer?

W.W., Rouyn, Quebec

A. It would be a good idea to make these repairs. Any crack you can see should be filled. You can use a sand cement patching mortar, undercutting the crack for a good mechanical bond. Where the crack is in the mortar joint, you'll often find the mortar rakes out easily and should be replaced with a pre-mix mortar or 1 part cement to 2-1/2 parts sand.

Foundation space

Q. While checking the walls of a basement rec room prior to finishing it, I noticed gaps between the foundation and the plate resting on it which are large enough to admit light from outside. The builder says the house must not be airtight and must breathe. Should I caulk these gaps?

A.D., Santa Ana, Calif.

A. It is true that a house needs to breathe but why count on a crack that shouldn't be there to supply the breathing space? By all means seal the cracks with caulking before you get water in your cellar from windblown rain.

Waterproofing first

Q. We have nearly finished making a recreation room in part of our basement—hardboard on the walls, electrical work in and tile on the cement floor. I am now confronted with the problem of water in this area, which was visible before construction only by beads of condensation. Water seeping down the walls has started forcing up the tile. We've spent over $400 so far. Is there any way my problem can be alleviated?

B.D., Hackensack, N.J.

A. It is always painful for us to have to answer a letter such as yours because the damage has already been done. Advice given now can't prevent trouble you already have. "Beads of condensation" probably was seepage. You need to start at the beginning and waterproof floor and walls. All your paneling materials should be taken down carefully and can probably be reused. You'll not save much of the floor tile unless it is quite loose all around. The electrical work is probably mostly confined to the ceiling and likely has not been harmed.

Basement leaks

Q. My basement leaks badly whenever it rains. Water seeps through the concrete block and brick veneer, which is underground. Is it possible to stop this by applying a waterproofing paint from the inside only? If this isn't possible, what's involved?

S.T., Toledo, Ohio

A. A badly leaking basement isn't going to be fixed with a brush-on masonry waterproofer, which is what you're talking about. This stuff is best for exterior above-grade masonry to keep rainwater, not groundwater, out. What you should do first is pitch the ground away from your house so rainwater drains off. Then repair the walls inside, filling in missing mortar and patching cracks. This done, apply a heavy-duty, pore-filling waterproofer followed by a coat of portland cement paint.

Basement crack

Q. A crack has developed in the corner of my cinder block basement wall. The crack is located at the level of the basement slab and it is visible by about 4", although it could conceivably start at the footing. The soil is clay and the house is 20 years old. During and after a heavy rain, a "spout" of water develops, starting about 2" above the slab. How can this be corrected?

J.L., Colonia, N.J.

A. To get a "spout" of water there must be considerable water pressure. If it comes only after a heavy rain, it's possible the soil does not allow water to run off quickly enough. First make sure you are doing all you can to divert run-off from collecting near this corner. Make sure downspouts are directed away from the house. Also correct any grading that funnels water into the area. After doing what you can to prevent water collection, fix the wall and waterproof.

Basement walls

Q. We wanted to use those striated gypsum wallboard panels in our basement but a local materials dealer says they will absorb moisture and create a disagreeable odor. He recommends this panel be used only above grade. I would appreciate your advice.

W.B., Greenfield, Mass.

A. Before you do anything at all to the walls, they should be completely waterproofed. Without stopping the dampness, there are not many materials that could be used successfully. Once this is properly done, you can use the striated wallboard.

Basement seepage

Q. We have a 10-year-old brick house; the front faces east. For the last three or four years we have been having a problem with rain seeping into the basement when there is a heavy rain from the east. The water comes down from the top of the basement wall where the wood and the plaster wall meet. At that point the plaster is falling off, and the water streaks the walls all the way to the floor. We have had the whole east wall and south portion of the house waterproofed, recaulked, and tuck-pointed. This didn't solve the problem, so we had the front of the house dug out and drainage tile put all across the front, but the same thing still happens and no one seems to know why or how. Someone suggested that the house is simply set too low—it does not have a foundation built up in the front, only at the sides and back. Do you have an idea on where the problem is coming from?

E.M., St. Louis, Mo.

A. From your letter, the construction at grade at the front of your house would seem to be part of the problem. Perhaps there is a heaping up of the grade at the flashing, so that it no longer serves its purpose. This is a very vulnerable joint, as it is so near grade, and it can be easily disrupted, letting water right in under the flashing that is supposed to keep it away. Inspect it carefully to make sure that all grade slopes away from this point. A puddle at a downspout could easily rise high enough to work under the flashing.

Putting in the drain tile across the front should have cured the difficulty, but if it was done sloppily it could have made it worse. On-site inspection and trial remedies are about the only solution we can suggest from here. A good roofer could inspect inside and out at the roof/wall joint to determine whether that location is a possible source of the water. Is there any localization of the damage to the plaster that suggests any source? That is, does it occur, for example, in three spots—directly below your front door and the two windows on that wall? Something like that might clue you onto the point of entry of the water.

Humid basement

Q. During humid weather, we get a lot of dampness and mildew in our basement. The bottom row of concrete blocks and the floor (five feet below grade) becomes very wet after the outdoor humidity is high for several days. One day of dry air and the basement usually dries up. Will a dehumidifier make it worthwhile to partition the area and finish off a playroom?

R.H., Brewster, N.Y.

A. First, make sure you are dealing with condensation rather than seepage. Tape a square of aluminum foil or plastic film securely to the floor and another to the wall before the problem shows up. Let them stay in place while the dampness appears on the uncovered surfaces. Then look at the test squares, and beneath them. If it's wet underneath, you have seepage and you need to take steps to waterproof the area. If it's wet on the surface of the patches, it's condensation and a dehumidifier would be a good idea.

Wet basement tips

Q. Do you have a booklet on solving a wet basement problem?
G.S., New York, N.Y.

A. Two of the reprints in the Family Handyman Information Bank should answer your needs. No. HM102 "What You Can Do With Wet Basements-I" (50¢) and No. HM103 "What To Do With Wet Basements-II" ($1) can be ordered from The Family Handyman, 1999 Shepard Road, St. Paul, Minn. 55116. Add $1 for postage and handling.

Water leak

Q. I have a rather frustrating problem concerning water leaks in my basement. The second floor of my Colonial house has aluminum siding, and the first floor is entirely split-rock brick. The leaks are on the east wall and occur when the rain is blown against the wall. The leaks are located between the basement window frames and floor joists that run parallel to and adjacent to the window frames and the basement wall. There are three windows; yet, strangely enough, only two windows leak. I have caulked the window frames but it has not helped. I suspect that the water is weeping through the brick and mortar and that the tar paper underneath is deficient or torn. I would like to know if there is a solution to this problem and if the builder would have an obligation to correct it. The house was built in 1970.

M.G., Lathrup Village, Mich.

A. After these years it's unlikely you would get far with the builder's obligation. It seems most likely that the water is running down the siding and creeping back in under the slight overhang to gravel across the top of the brick and between the window frame and floor joist. This would be due to a lack of window head flashing rather than a weep-through of the masonry area proper. You may want to run a test. Try slipping a piece of aluminum flashing a bit up under the siding, letting it extend out from the wall, long enough to carry beyond the width of the window. If this "drip cap effect" prevents a leak at that window while you still get water from the other leaky one, you will know what to do.

Basement seepage

Q. My house is situated at the bottom of a hill. My problem is that water is constantly seeping through the walls of my basement. What can I do about this?
M.H., Grundy Center, Iowa

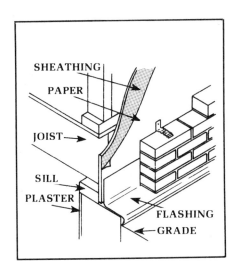

SHEATHING
PAPER
JOIST
SILL
PLASTER
FLASHING
GRADE

A. It may be that some combination of actions could help you solve your problem. It is easier to keep water out of a basement than it is to get it out once it's in. Therefore, any water you can prevent from getting under your house is water that won't later come in through the basement walls. Drain tile set in the area between your porch and driveway and extending as shown will help collect subsoil water before it reaches the house. However, your house may be sitting in an underground pool, in which case the above suggestion would not help. Check with your city building or zoning department. They may have a water table study that would be of help to you. In any case, your problem is best tackled by first checking with local authorities and experts.

Porch floor

Q. Recently I put a new basement under my house and the open porch floor. How do I keep rain and snow from seeping through the porch floor without enclosing the porch? It has a roof over it but the wind still blows some rain and snow in on the floor.
V.J., Wess Spring, S.D.

A. A porch floor is not a roof and it's not generally expected to act like one. If you want it to be a roof over part of the basement, then you'll have to make it more

like a roof. Consider covering it with canvas as you would a boat deck, or lay exterior grade plywood over it and fiberglass the surface after taping the joints. You'll also have to provide for drainage from the porch floor the same as for a roof. It might be simpler to enclose the porch.

Crawl space odors

Q. My three-year-old house has a ventilated crawl space within its cement block foundation. Last winter we were bothered with a musty smell arising from this area. What's the best way to deal with this?
H.R., Bronx, N.Y.

A. Covering the earth floor of the crawl space should solve your problem. Use large sheets of polyethylene plastic film. Overlap the seams or seal them with polyethylene tape and also seal the outside edges of the sheets to the foundation.

Vapor barrier

Q. We have been told covering our crawl space with a vapor barrier would relieve condensation problems. What is a vapor barrier?
A.B., Clinton, Iowa

A. Generally sheet materials that are highly resistant to the flow of water vapor can be called vapor barriers. Such materials suitable for use in a crawl space would include asphalt impregnated felt with a shiny surface, 55-lb. coated roll roofing, duplex papers with a continous asphalt coating sandwiched between the layers, polyethylene film (6 mil) or polyethylene film combined with heavy paper. All must be suitably lapped and sealed so as to provide continuous coverage.

Floating slab

Q. To avoid dampness, we were going to build a crawlspace on a floating slab but find it is much too expensive. Is there a cheaper way?
B.N., Westport, Conn.

A. Yes, you can settle for a standard foundation on footings set below frost. Give these walls a suitable waterproof coating, install drain tile around the perimeter and seal off the ground surface of the crawl space with a properly installed vapor barrier. Provide means of ventilation according to area of space enclosed.

Water seepage

Q. I have an older home and water leaks through the basement floor cracks. Also the partitions were built before the concrete floor was put on and we have leakage through the partition walls.

What would you recommend to solve this problem? The house is situated on heavy clay. Also, the floor is rough and pock-marked.
A.S., Scottville, Mich.

A. You obviously have quite a problem. The right way to fix it all is to lay damp-proofing over floors and up the walls now and then pour a new slab on top of that, carrying it on up the walls as a waterproofing over the barrier. A basement is like a bathtub set into the ground. If the drain is open, (the cracks in the floor), water will come in at the lowest point. If the drain is plugged, water will come in at the overflow (up the walls by capillary action). If you fix both cracks and wall and still set in a goodly wetness—high water table—the whole basement tends to "float" upwards—cracking and shifting the floor and walls. We are not saying that your house will float away, but merely trying to explain the reaction stresses set up within the structure due to the presence of water under pressure. Now, if the pressure is not too great, filling

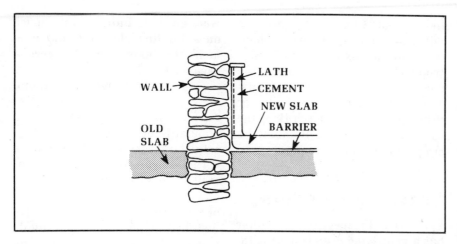

WALL

OLD SLAB

LATH
CEMENT
NEW SLAB
BARRIER

the cracks and waterproofing the walls may well prove successful. You'd need to clean out all existing cracks, undercut and fill them with latex or epoxy cement patching compound.

The partitions you mention are probably foundation and may well be stone. You need a lath of some sort in any case. How you attach it and what you use will depend somewhat on the material of the walls. Over that put your scratch-and-finish coat of waterproof cement. You can get good complete authoritative information for this kind of project from The Portland Cement Association, 5420 Old Orchard Rd., Skokie, Ill. 60077. They offer a free publications catalog.

Damp crawl space

Q. The ground in the crawl space of my two-year-old home is very damp. There are vents on the back, front and sides that are kept open in summer and closed in winter. I have been told that the moisture will encourage termites in the floor joists. How can I get rid of this dampness?

F.V., Bronx, N.Y.

A. Our suggestion is that you install a moisture barrier over the earth in your enclosed crawl space. This can be polyethylene film, laid with the edges lapped and run up the sides of the foundation to keep moisture in the earth from traveling upwards. Ventilating

above this barrier as you are now doing should lessen the dampness reaching your floor joists. You should also check the area around your house to be sure you are doing all you can outdoors to keep rainwater running away from the foundation walls. As for the termites, dampness does not attract them. Termites eat wood, damp or dry. However, dampness does encourage rot and should be eliminated for that reason alone.

Stairwell seepage

Q. I have a ranch-style house with a walk-out basement. My problem is that after a hard rain, water runs in under the door and accumulates in the outside stairwell. There is a drain at the bottom of the stairwell, but it does not seem to carry away any water. I suspect that the drain only goes down a few feet, as it is filled with coarse gravel. The basement is fully tiled and bone dry except at the door area. How can I prevent or eliminate this accumulation of water without spending too much money?

K.R., Iowa City, Iowa

A. It would be nice to know whether the drain stopped a few feet down. What might work is a drain to a drywell somewhat removed from the house. Whether or not it is worth digging all the way down to use this existing pipe is another matter. It probably is neater to do that than to break in

the outer edge of the areaway to install another drain to a drywell. The other method you may wish to investigate is a cover or awning of some sort to prevent such an accumulation of water from getting so far ahead of the drain. There is not much point in putting the drain tile in the yard and sloping the ground away from the house when the problem is a too-efficient built-in collection basin. The idea of keeping the rainwater out of the areaway in the first place is the easier of the two suggestions we could make on the basis of the facts you supply. How it would look is another matter. Designed correctly, it could be an asset.

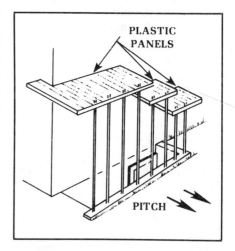

PLASTIC PANELS

PITCH

Cellar seepage

Q. My cellar floor is half-covered with concrete and water seeps in upwards from the uncovered part. I have a sump pump in the lower corner of the existing floor with a channel following the wall to carry water to the pump. Will putting concrete over the uncovered part of the floor stop the seepage? If not, how should I carry the water over the floor to the sump? Also, I have one wall of the cellar that is buckling inward. It is old and made of some kind of flat limestone. Is it correctable?

J.S., Amsterdam, N.Y.

A. There is no easy way to solve the problems you describe. The right way to make a basement floor watertight is first the proper fill, then a dampproofing course and then a 4" to 6" slab. The surface drainage around the house needs to be considered, too. There's no sense putting a basement in a puddle if you can move the puddle first. We suggest that you seek reputable local advice. The problem of the buckling wall just makes it that much more difficult. It probably needs a better footing under it, which should be done before fixing the floor. You may be able to do the entire project yourself, but should obtain some professional advice first.

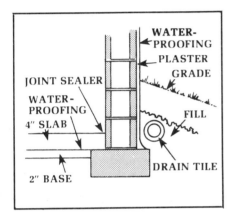

Conditioning water

Q. A year ago I installed a concrete walk and patio and since then the area under the house near the crawl space stays quite wet, especially after a heavy rain. There is also a lot of water draining into the area that comes from the central air conditioning unit. The water from the condenser is carried away on a separate line. Can you offer any suggestions on getting the water away from the house.
R.E., Tullahoma, Tenn.

A. The easiest thing to do is to collect the water setting in the gravel area adjacent to the crawl space and move it away from the house. Drain tile or pipe is one solution. The problem is how to get it under the concrete and off to another area where it can go more slowly into the earth. You have not given enough information to figure out where that might be. If

it has to be in the gravel area, try a catch basin of whatever type you choose.

Damp crawl space

Q. We have an unheated crawl space under the main living area of our split-level home. The space has a soil floor, and the flooring above it is insulated with 3-1/2" thick glass fiber, foil side up. The entrance to the crawl is through the wall of our playroom, on the lower level of the house. The problem is that the playroom is generally musty and damp. I assume the problem lies in the crawl space which does have a few vent openings. I've been told by neighbors to 1) put plastic tarpaulin over the soil; 2) put down a concrete floor in the space, and 3) buy a dehumidifier. What do you recommend?
B.S., Hartsdale, N.Y.

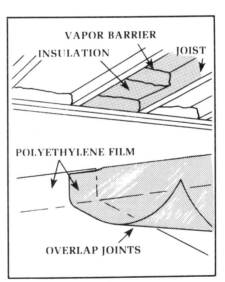

A. Start with a vapor barrier over the earth. You can use 4-mil. polyethylene film available at your building materials supplier or lumberyard. Overlap the joints and run the plastic up onto the foundation walls. Other suggestions: Check to see if size of the vents is adequate for the area they serve. Also check the wall between the playroom and crawl space. It should be insulated with its own vapor barrier on the warm side. Make sure the access door fits

well and is insulated at least as well as the wall.

Damp floors

Q. Our home has a 3-1/2' crawl space covered with 4" of cinders. Our kitchen and living room floors are always cold and damp. Is there a cure?
C.P., Peekskill, N.Y.

A. Insulate the underside of the floor. You can lay batt insulation on chicken wire or boards fastened to the bottom of the joists. Cover the cinders with 1" of sand. Spread a suitable vapor barrier over that to prevent further moisture from the ground reaching the floors. This will certainly relieve the dampness problem and help with the coldness. If you are not supplying enough heat to warm the floors, solution to that problem will be incomplete.

Chemical dehumidifier

Q. We have a very damp and musty basement. Someone told us of a certain substance that is contained in sacks and hung up in corners to absorb the humidity. What is the dehumidifying agent and under what product name is it sold?
M.Z., Bellmore, N.Y.

A. One substance used is diatomaceous earth to which a hygroscopic chemical has been added. This is packaged in a muslin bag for hanging up as you describe. De-Moist is one tradename. Follow the maker's (Coughlan Products Inc., 1011 Clifton Ave., Clifton, N.J. 07013) directions to regenerate the material by drying in your home oven. Your hardware or home center store should have such chemical dehumidifiers.

Chapter 12

Heating & Cooling Problems

Additions...Air conditioning...Attics...Baseboard...Basements...
Boilers, pipes...Ductwork...Electric...Furnaces...Gas heaters...Heat
pumps...Humidification...Oil tanks...Radiators...Reducing heat
losses...Solar heating...Thermostats.

Added rooms

Q. I am adding two rooms to my house which is heated by a central furnace without ducts. Is there any way to install the furnace without tearing up our concrete slab foundation for ducts to the new rooms?

R.P., Chicago, Ill.

A. There are so many variables to consider—construction, insulation, number of windows, capacity of present furnace, etc. You should get the opinion of a reliable heating contractor before you do anything. The first thing to find out is whether or not your present furnace has the capacity to heat the additional two rooms.

There are gas furnaces that can be installed in the attic and connected by ducts to registers in the ceilings. These work fine if properly installed. You might also consider leaving the present furnace as is and installing an auxiliary gas heater of the through-the-wall type for the two rooms.

Air conditioner

Q. I am getting too old and tired to keep installing and removing my air conditioner every year, so I would like to install it permanently. The wall is frame, with regular 2x4 sheathing, lath and plaster. Can you tell me how to go about this?

F.R., South Holland, Ill.

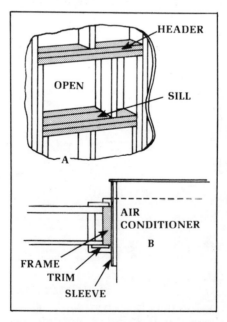

A. If you know how a window frame is put into an existing wall, you have the basics for your project. Open the wall, cut the unneeded framing out of the way, beef up the header, and double the sill. Set in a jamb where the size of the air conditioner demands it and slide in your frame, sized to fit the sleeve or other surround that houses the conditioner proper. Write to the maker of your unit and ask for installation details. Chances are that if it is recommended to install that unit through the wall, he will have the details available. You will need to know if there is a special sleeve or alternate brackets, etc., for this type of mounting.

Baseboard heating

Q. We are planning to convert our heating system from radiators to baseboard heating. Where can we find information on the subject so we can do the job ourselves?

J.M., Yorktown Heights, N.Y.

A. "Heating and Cooling" from the Time/Life Home Repair and Improvement Library, has three pages which do a good job of explaining how to make the conversion. Other sections of the same book on estimating needs, sizing, etc., should make it worthwhile for you to read. The whole series is very well illustrated, too. Other information is scarce, technical and buried in plumbing and heating trade books. It would be a good idea to secure specific instructions for installing those units from the manufacturer.

Heating attic rooms

Q. We have a 1-1/2 story house which we have just started finishing into rooms. We plan to heat the second story too with our gravity gas-fired furnace and any necessary auxiliary heat. Will heating by gravity be possible?

H.B., Columbus, Ohio

A. Gravity heat can be used to heat upper floors adequately if the furnace has the added capacity. Most of them do have. In all probability you'll not need auxiliary heat if ducts are the right size and insulation ample.

Hot air principle

Q. Last summer, I built a recreation room in my basement, and put a duct into it from my gravity-feed hot air furnace. I got so little heat out of it that I removed it. Can you recommend a method whereby I can use the furnace to heat this recreation room?

G.B., Fairlawn, N.J.

A. The principle is warmed air is lighter and rises while colder air falls. You could restore the duct and use a tiny motor and fan inside the duct, if you wish. Gravity feed will not deliver hot air on a level with or below the point of origin. There are also ceiling-mounted fan-equipped heaters which can be made to direct the flow of warmed air to selected spots. You might try this type in conjunction with some kind of portable electric heaters.

Basement heating

Q. Last summer I bought an oil furnace and partitioned it off from the rest of the basement where I built a recreation room. Now I find I can't live there comfortably because it is damp and chilly. I have three different ceiling outlets in the recreation room. A friend advised me to install a cold air return. Would that make a big difference?

A.L., Detroit, Mich.

A. A cold air return would probably help a lot since it would provide a circulation of air now impossible in the confined area. Place a return duct as near the floor as possible and the warmed air will be drawn downward to take the place of cold air removed to the furnace. You will not be able to fully warm the floor, but you can make the recreation room liveable.

Window conditioner

Q. We have a permanently installed air conditioner in the lower half of our dining room window. We would like to add some shelves in the upper half of the window. Could it be done so that a shadow box frame could cover the whole window? Also, is it possible to build sliding doors over the air conditioner to be opened only when it is in use?

J.W., Garden City, N.Y.

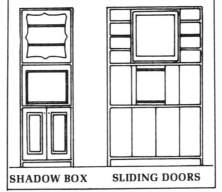

SHADOW BOX   **SLIDING DOORS**

A. There are so many ways you can add shelves in the window above your air conditioner, it is hard to know where to start. If the air conditioner projects into the room quite a bit and there is no need to see out of the window, you can build what amounts to a piece of furniture with a hole in the back for the air conditioner to stick through, "shadow box" if you want to. If you want to see out the win-dow, keep it simple and light. Cleats on the window casing will support knick-knack shelves. It is possible to put sliding doors in front of the machine, of course, but consider the width—two doors, each 12″ wide, will close off a 24″ unit—but each door needs 12″ more to slide into when you want it open. The simple sketches may give you an idea or two. Almost any "how to build furniture" book will have a few ideas you can adapt.

Cold cellar floor

Q. We have an older home with a stone foundation. We have had the cellar floor and foundation, 3′ up from the floor, cemented. Drainage trenches under the floor and outside the house have relieved a previous water problem. During wet periods, however, water runs under the cellar floor. I have lined the walls with 4-mil. polyethylene and covered this with 2x3s and Homasote. The cellar is still very cold and damp, especially the painted floor. What can I put on the floor under a rug to keep it warm? What is used in a raised ranch home on the lower level floor? We hope to be able to use a Franklin stove for heat in the cellar this winter. Forced hot air just doesn't heat this area.

W.C., Taftville, Conn.

A. Most raised ranchers have vinyl asbestos tiles of on-grade variety on the floor not because they make the floors warmer (supplying heat does that), but because they are relatively inexpensive. You could use wood block flooring under a rug with somewhat more insulation value, and somewhat more cost. The fact remains that if you aren't able to warm up the area with your Franklin stove, the floor will not be warm, even though a rug usually makes it seem warm-er than it really is. Forced warm air would have to have the system de-signed or altered to supply enough heat to the cellar to heat it properly. A system designed to supply heat to the regular heating quarters should not be expected to waste enough heat to heat the cellar of an old house.

Basement heat pipes

Q. Why should it be necessary to insulate heating pipes in the basement, as is so often recommended? I was considering taking the present insulation off mine and covering with metal fins to provide a source of heat in the basement. Could I do this and possibly increase the heat even more by putting reflector type insulation behind these pipes?

J.W., Toronto, Ontario

A. Insulating the pipes is done to prevent heat loss into the basement and to deliver all the heat to upstairs radiators. Removal of insulation and substituting fins will produce warmth in the basement but at the cost of heat normally delivered upstairs. If there is no loss of comfort above, your plan is OK. Reflector type insulation along the foundation side of pipes laid close to the foundation would be practical.

Anti-freeze

Q. I would like to install a hot water heating system in my summer home. The trouble is, I have water only from a brook and would have to fill the system by hand. Therefore, I wonder how to keep it from freezing-up without draining when the place is closed up. I have thought of adding the anti-freeze I use in my car, which does not evaporate, for this purpose. Do you have a better suggestion?

E.K., College Point, N.Y.

A. In a hand-fed system, it would obviously be an open type with an expansion tank located above the highest radiators. This means a frequent check to determine that water isn't below radiator level. In the open, evaporation could take place. When you considered anti-freeze, you may not

have calculated the system's capacity. This could be as much as 40 to 50 gallons—and you need 2 quarts for each 3 gallons of this water for protection down to -10°. Under these circumstances, we'd suggest you consider some other type of heating.

Open vs. closed

Q. I have an old house with the original coal furnace and hot water system and an expansion tank in the attic. Some of my neighbors have moved similar tanks to the basement. My question is do I lose out on the efficiency of my furnace if I do this?

L.S., Philadephia, Pa.

A. You can't just move the expansion tank to the basement. It has to be a sealed tank and all outlets on the system sealed as well except the overflow or relief valve. Otherwise your system would quickly drain out of the open tank. The purpose of the sealed system is to provide water at higher temperatures without creating steam since water under pressure can be handled in this manner. We'd say that if your system is providing adequate heat at present, save yourself the expense. If you want more heat, then make the change-over.

Insulating pipes

Q. I have a five-room bungalow of brick veneer with a hot water heating system. Foundation is 24′ x 34′. On cold nights, I can't get temperatures above 72°. I was wondering if this is due to the circulating pump which is only 1/12 hp-1725 rpm. I have also been toying with the idea of insulating the heating system pipes but, as yet, can't seem to make up my mind about this. Can you help me?

H.S., Staten Island, N.Y.

A. Don't blame the pump. It's delivering water as it should but the heat of the water is lost

before it gets to the rooms it should heat. Insulate the pipes by all means. Use sleeve-type asbestos insulation and fill in at joints and elbows with loose asbestos fiber mixed with water to make a hand-molding paste which is plastered over these irregular areas. The pump is only there to deliver water. It cannot change the water temperature.

Covering steam pipes

Q. In my living and dining rooms I have steam pipes going up to the floor above. I was going to box these in to cover them but they are too far from the wall. I want something that looks neat and will help deliver more heat to the upper floor. Any suggestions?

C.G., Brooklyn, N.Y.

A. To deliver more heat use a sleeve-type insulation. This will make the pipe still look like pipe though bulkier. The surface is paintable but about 4-1/2″ to 5″ in diameter. For neatness we'd have to say box them in, insulating them first. Another idea is to move the pipe closer to the wall with 45° elbows top and bottom of the pipe length. This will not interfere with delivery of steam, sometimes permits tighter furniture arrangements and still can be insulated and boxed in.

Cracking cement

Q. The asbestos cement used to cover fittings on the mains of my steam heating system cracks and pulls away from the asbestos air cell coverings. Can the cement be applied so it will stick?

B.K., Maspeth, N.Y.

A. Loose asbestos mixed with water to form a thick paste can be applied in thin layers to steam pipes. Each layer is covered with cheesecloth and another layer is then applied and so on until the proper thickness is built up. Let dry 12 to 24 hours before running heat through the pipe.

Noisy pipes

Q. I have a hot forced-air heating system. The heating ducts which are supported by metal straps, make a loud banging noise as they expand and contract due to heating and cooling cyles. How can I minimize the noise?

A.V., Dubuque, Iowa

A. Some of the noise is the metal itself which is expanding and contracting, and some of it is the movement of the ducts against the straps. It can be quieted by using a sound-absorbent pad between the duct and strap. Insulating the ducts proper will lessen the other noise and at the same time save you some heating expense.

Moving ductwork

Q. Ours is an older home with an oil-fired counterflow furnace I believe to be about 20 years old. Would I get better heating by moving my heating vents to outside walls and the cold air vents to inside walls?

A.G., Wilton, Iowa

A. What you are talking about is redesigning the whole heating system. A perimeter system is usually able to deliver more comfortable heating. The question is, will your present furnace have the capacity to deliver heat to the new locations in sufficient volume to make the cost of change-over worthwhile? Unless you plan on installing a whole new system—furnace, ductwork and controls—we'd be inclined to advise you to put your money in insulation and weatherstripping.

Heat registers

Q. I have a wood stove in my basement and baseboard electric heat upstairs. In fixing up the base-ment, I'd like use a ceiling material that heat can easily flow through so the floor upstairs would be warmer. What is best?

W.M., Westhope, N.D.

A. You might consider making a hole in the floor for the heat to go through. The Reggio Register Co., P.O. Box 511, Ayer, Mass. 01432, advertises a cast-iron floor register. It's a nice design if you have an older home. You can also check around in your area for forced warm-air heating registers that can be used in a floor installation.

Noisy ducts

Q. I have forced warm-air perimeter heating with square ducts for heat and cold air returns through the center of the house. We are annoyed by the ticking noise when heat is passing through the pipes and wondered if you could tell us how to stop this noise?

H.B., Utica, N.Y.

A. Wrapping the pipe with impregnated paper would reduce the sounds. Tape the joints first, then look into chances of reducing noise by using padded hanger straps, using felt lining between the ducts and the straps and also felt-stripping the connections, if loose, between ducts and registers.

Smelly heating ducts

Q. Our furnace is 19 years old, and for the past four years or so it has been emitting a foul smell when we turn up the heat. Neither the gas man nor the heating man found anything wrong with the system. The odor comes from the heating ducts only when we turn up the heat manually; when the furnace turns on and shuts off automatically, there is no odor. A friend suggested that dirt in the ducts is causing the problem and that we have the ducts cleaned by professionals. What do you say?

G.P., Villa Park, Ill.

A. Your friend is probably right, both in his analysis and in his suggestion. There could be dust and dirt in the ducts, and a professional cleaning is more efficient and effective than anything you could do with a household vacuum.

If you suspect that it may be a mouse (you did say a *foul* smell) that has sought refuge to die, setting up mirrors and lights to inspect the interior might reveal something, but the root of your problem is most likely dust.

Dusty house

Q. I have a great amount of dust throughout my house which is heated with a gas-fired forced air furnace. Is it possible to use some type of filter at the register in each room to trap a lot of this dust but still permit heat to enter the room?

J.M., Clifton Heights, Pa.

A. Have you ever cleaned your furnace filters? You already have filters, you know. A forced hot air system always has them. Of course yours might have been installed without filters but there is a place for them. They go by size and the largest costs around $2 each. If cleaned with a vacuum when they become dirty, they last a full heating season—if not banged to pieces in cleaning. They should trap a lot all the dust that might be distributed through the ducts.

Electric heat panels

Q. Will you kindly advise on the feasibility of installing electric radiant glass heating panels in my country home that is not fully insulated?

L.B., New York, N.Y.

A. The important factor here is the cost of operation. Any electrically operated heat generating equipment consumes a great deal of current. The local rate governs operation cost. Without insulation, heat loss will be considerable. Generally, it costs more to make up the heat lost than it would to insulate. Other points to consider are room size and panel placement must be figured correctly to avoid hot and cold spots. You may have to increase the current potential and rewire the house for the panels. For spot heating the type of electric units equipped with a fan are ideal, providing quick, clean, silent heat.

Smoke with hot air

Q. **We have trouble with smoke from the furnace getting into the house. It comes out of the registers. On the advice of a sales agent for the furnace, we had it reset, without helping this condition. I thought there might be leaks around the smoke pipe where it fits the chimney but after sealing this joint, conditions did not improve.**

W.H., Green Springs, Ohio

A. There should be no connection between the fire chamber, smoke pipe and flue system and the hot air distribution system which originates in a jacket around the furnace but is sealed off from the first mentioned. Improperly sealed joints in the smoke pipe, where it passes through the hot air chamber, are the usual causes of this trouble. It usually pays to have a single longer length of pipe run through here, even if there is a bend in that direction.

Balanced heating

Q. **I have a gas-fired, forced warm-air heating system. I'm told that opening a register in the basement would make the heating of the other two floors in my house inefficient. Now I'm considering an area heater. Do you think I can use my existing furnace to heat the basement without a prohibitive loss of heat to the rest of the house?**
B.F., New York, N.Y.

A. Your forced warm-air furnace is part of a system designed to heat your house. The furnace size,

duct size and layout, registers and their locations, are all balanced to provide efficient heating. If you alter the system (as you would in adding a duct) you may easily have to do some rebalancing to take care of the change. Proper placement of the take-off is essential. If in doubt, contact a local heating specialist.

Capped duct system

Q. **I have difficulty heating my second floor which has been duplexed into another apartment. Two hot air ducts lead to this second floor, but there are no return pipes. Furnace is gravity, oil-fed. I installed a door at the bottom of the steps and this seems to have stopped the return flow of cold air. I thought of installing a grill in the bottom of the door, and perhaps adding fans to the ducts leading upstairs. I would like your comments on this procedure.**

F.C., London, Ontario

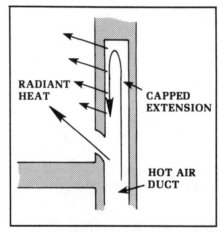

RADIANT HEAT

CAPPED EXTENSION

HOT AIR DUCT

A. In adding the door you also closed off the warmed air that went up the stairs above the cold layer of air that came down so there is now less heat rising to the second floor. A good system to use would be to extend the ducts of the second floor several feet higher than the registers and cap them off, thus creating warm air pockets on the second floor. This has a tendency to bring up more heat without fans. While you can put small fans in the ducts to push heat along them, it is almost impossible to control these fans thermostatically.

Stairway down-draft

Q. **I have a Georgian brick house with gas-fired hot air furnace. Thee are no return ducts upstairs and there is a sweeping cold air current down the stairs into the living room. I have to put up a curtain to keep the draft out but it is still chilly. I have high ceilings and the stairway bends about half way up with a closet under it in the hall. What is your idea?**

F.M., Chicago, Ill.

A. The best solution would be a cold air return duct with the opening as near the head of the stairs as possible. One method is to remove the riser of the top step and use this as a stair-width duct opening, running the duct under the stairs and through the closet to the basement. This duct can be as little as 3" in one dimension. If need be, remove a strip about 3" wide in the floor just above the top step the full width of the stairs. In either case, you will take up most of the cold air at this point, rather than have it flow down the steps.

Furnace maintenance

Q. **I have an oil furnace with a circulating hot-water heat system. I'm seeking information on maintenance, cleaning and adjustment of the unit. Can you recommend a book or manual? I've just recently bought the house.**

D.W., Asheville, N.C.

A. As a rule the manufacturer knows best how to maintain a given product. We suggest you take the manufacturer's name and address from the furnace name plate and write to him for a maintenance manual. Give him the model number and any other information you can copy. It's a wise practice, when buying a house, to get from the owner all maintenance material for any appliances included in the sale. A number of helpful guides on furnace maintenance and similar semi-technical subjects have been published in recent years. Your local library will be able to help you here.

Cracked furnace

Q. I just purchased an old home which I plan to remodel. The upper feed chamber of the furnace has a crack 3″ long that shows a thin line of light through it and several others showing no light. Can these be repaired for even one season without danger and, if so, how?

J.S., Chagrin Falls, Ohio

A. It is possible to patch this metal. It is quite possible there is no danger present even now, if the draft is good. There are several iron-patching materials, applied like paste, that harden into actual metal and are not injured by heat. Your hardware dealer possibly handles at least one of them. Apply exactly as directed to a rust-free surface.

Heat pump

Q. I'm planning to move to Florida in the near future. Being retired, I want to keep the bills as low as possible. Have been considering installing a heat pump for heating and air conditioning as I understand this type is less expensive than regular electric heat and air-conditioning systems. Where can I write for more information and folders on heat pump systems?

L.V., Melrose Park, Ill.

A. One of the manufacturers of heat pumps is Carrier Air Conditioning, Carrier Parkway, P.O. Box 4808, Syracuse, N.Y. 13221.

Unvented gas heater

Q. I've been shopping for a couple of new room heaters, gas fired, and find one line that insists no flue is required. How can this

be as I thought one always had to have fresh air to replace the oxygen consumed?

J.T., Picayune, Miss.

A. Your understanding is correct but there are some units that are built into an exterior wall where combustion air is kept completely separate from heated air, in effect a flue is built into the unit itself. Here, while you may wish to renew room air simply because you prefer it that way, no oxygen is taken from the room air for combustion so no safety precaution is necessary.

Dual furnaces

Q. I wish to install an oil burner in a 13-room, 2-1/2 story house in which, at present, there are two furnaces—one for the first floor, one for the second. The second-floor furnace has a 22″ diameter firebox. The heating contractor tells me this furnace can supply heat for the entire house. I have my doubts. Before I proceed, I would like your opinion.

N.G., Newark, N.J.

A. We can see no reason to doubt your contractor's statement since there are many installations of similar proportions functioning adequately. The type of heat and quality of insulation are important factors not included in your letter.

Humidity in the home

Q. Would you please help with my problem? Situation—apartment of 700 sq. ft., hot water-heated, very dry in winter, to the detriment of furniture. Can you suggest a method of humidifying other than buying a regular unit?

E.H., London, Ontario

A. There are thin metal cans with arms for hanging on the back of radiators where they are unseen. Kept full of water, enough moisture is released into the air of the average room to offset abnormally dry conditions.

Humidify or?

Q. I have a two-story brick building in which a forced-air furnace furnishes heat. I wish to install a humidifier. I have asked the advice of friends; many have warned me against a plate-type humidifier and have recommended a spray type; others have stated this would not be good. Please advise what type I should install, whether it should have a thermostat, how many gallons of water should it dispense, etc.

G.C., Northbrook, Ill.

A. You've probably been told "plate-type humidifiers cake up and do not deliver the proper amount of moisture," while the spray types are often accused of spreading mineral "dust" from the water throughout the house.

There is a certain amount of truth on both sides but reputable manufacturers take steps to overcome the objections through improved design, filters, demineralization, etc. A dealer who considers the indoor climate of your home as the end product—the results, not the machine—as the thing to sell, will give you the best service. He will want to know the type of heat, size of unit, size of house, and evaluate the type of construction as loose, average or tight, etc. On the specific questions you ask, a humidifier system doesn't need a thermostat, most require a *humidistat* to measure the relative humidity and control the humidifier. The number of gallons of water depends on the factors outlined.

Oil leakage

Q. I have a 275-gal. upright fuel oil tank in my basement. There is a small pin hole in the center of the bottom which leaks part oil, part water. Is there any simple way I can repair this leak?

J.H., Floral Park, N.Y.

A. You have to empty the tank first. The fuel feed line is not at the bottom so there would be about 2″ of oil and water left to drain out the clean-out plug. Remove rust scale, oil and water from the area around the hole and then use one of the metal mending products on the market. Mix according to manufacturer's instructions but be sure the surface is clean and dry for application.

Oil tank installation

Q. I have an oil burner tank stamped "Underwriters Laboratory Inspected, Inside Tank for Oil Burner." The tank is outside on a concrete platform. Is this all right?

G.H., Plattsburgh, N.Y.

A. The UL listing indicates that it is safe to put the tank inside the house. It may also be kept outdoors but does need protection against the weather.

Frozen filter

Q. I have a 275-gal. oil tank inside with an exterior oil filter. The filter freezes up in severe cold weather, and a wooden box around it hasn't helped. How can I eliminate the problem?

D.R., Worcester, Mass.

A. Why not move the filter indoors where it won't freeze? Your fuel oil supplier will help you on this one. Wrap the supply pipe with heating tape.

Whistling oil tank

Q. When I built my garage and breezeway, I thought I was doing the oil man a favor and put the oil inflow pipe inside the garage. Now he has difficulty telling when the tank is full since he can't hear the telltale gurgling sound in the air vent that warned him before. What gimmick can I apply to the filler pipe to indicate when the tank is full. It is 12′ from the tank laterally.

F.S., Schenectady, N.Y.

A. We don't know of anything to attach to the filler pipe—but there is an inexpensive whistling gadget that can be attached to the vent pipe, operated by a small float inside the tank, which cuts loose with a shrill whistle when oil is within a few inches of the tank top. This warning is enough to cause the oil man to shut off the oil before the tank overflows.

Radiator cover

Q. I would appreciate it if you would send me detailed plans for building radiator covers if you have such plans.

R.N., Cleveland, Ohio

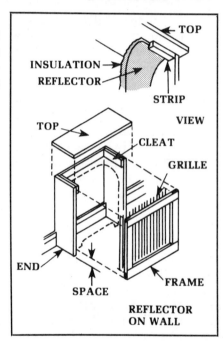

A. Radiators are usually located along exterior walls. When possible, even if you do not build in the radiator, providing an insulated back-panel behind it will aim some of the otherwise wasted heat back into the room. Enclosing the radiator must be done without unduly impeding its operation.

Essentially most radiator enclosures can be thought of as a box. The back is the room wall, the bottom the floor, and the front a more or less decoratively open area. One can easily "build in" simply by repeating this "box" on either or both ends of the radiator.

Depending on materials you have on hand, construction can be quite simple. A solid top supported by solid or framed-panel ends is the usual start. The front is usually a frame to the backside of which is affixed the screening (expanded or perforated metal, grille material, etc). The choice needs to be based on cost, appearance and heat transmission considerations. Stretched fabrics can be used though fuzzy surfaces tend to get dirty rather quickly.

Be sure to provide for room air to enter at the bottom, become warm and get out again into the room. A frame supported at the sides but free of the floor is the easiest solution, as shown in the sketch. A cleat on the wall at the back will support the top. A cleat at either end can be used to anchor the ends if desired. Or front, ends and top can be built as a removable unit should that be desirable. One of the simplest ways to provide the back wall reflector is spring a sheet of Do-It-Yourself® aluminum into place with batt insulation behind it. This can be carried on shaped blocks or simply retained by a strip as indicated.

Enclosed radiators

Q. I am thinking about enclosing my radiators. Would this change my heat production at all?

E.L., Altoona, Pa.

A. There is as much heat put out by an enclosed radiator as by an open one. The difference occurs in where the heat goes. If you waste it all heating an enclosure, you haven't gained anything over heating up the exterior wall behind the bare radiator. The idea in an enclosed radiator system is to provide circulation—cold room air in at the bottom, up around the radiator and reflecting it off the back wall of the enclosure, directing it out into the room better than is done with a bare radiator. An open grill material is a must for the radiator, and an insulated metal sheet reflecting back is an excellent idea. Aluminum foil or aluminum-faced insulation pasted to the wall makes a good heat reflector. The style and construction ideas of the enclosures should suit the room decor.

Conceal convectors

Q. I would like to box in my radiators. I am lining the boxes with foil insulation, but could you recommend some sort of fabric or screening which could at least partially conceal the radiators without impeding the flow of heat too much? I live in a small city so please recommend a commonly available material.

T.N., Greenwich, Conn.

A. Perforated metal is obviously the first choice that meets your requirements. Reynolds Do-It-Yourself aluminum is probably the easiest to find. Avoid fabrics as they soil and sag easily. You can use perforated hardboard if it is set far enough from the radiator and you seal *all* the edges carefully. You could build up a screening device with vertical wood dowels or strips in a frame (stay vertical; more dust collects on horizontal surfaces.) You can use the expensive woven brass often seen on cabinet fronts; or nice, bright, shiny, new copper insect screening will do, too.

New radiator

Q. I want to put a hot water radiator in my attic. Is it possible to cut into the feed lines of the radiator on the floor directly below instead of cutting into the main feed line? These feed lines are copper tube and are easily cut into for sweat fittings but I'd need reducer T's for cutting into the rigid pipe main feeds.

L.R., Oceanside, N.Y.

A. To get proper pressure up to the radiator in the attic, it would be best to cut into the main feed

lines. You would be reducing feed to the first radiator by half with your method. Both ends would be improperly provided with hot water. You can place T's on the main lines next to present T's by use of close nipples but the better arrangement is to space these feeds farther apart on the main feeds.

Making covers

Q. I would like to try my hand at making radiator covers. Do you have any instructions for this kind of project or any past issues that cover the subject?

S.J., Newton, N.J.

A. The diagram will give you the basic details you need to know. You can build either of two types— built-ins or removable "boxes."

The built-ins usually look better and permit you to include shelves and storage space. The box type is smaller, costs less and can be removed, if desired. What you use for the front or grille area is up to you. Almost any material that will not be adversely affected by heat is acceptable, provided it is open enough to permit heat to get into the room. It can be perforated metal sheet, expanded metal lath, wire screening, hardwood dowels or wooden louvers.

Cracked heater

Q. My elderly house has an oil-fired hot water heating system with cast-iron baseboard heaters. While painting, I scraped several layers of paint off one heater, uncovering a crack that had sealed itself over the years, and have been

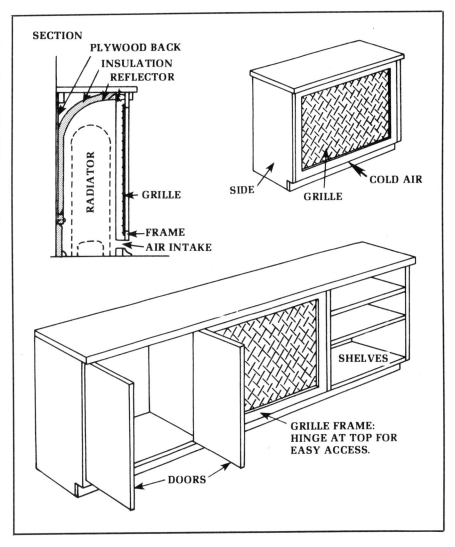

SECTION
PLYWOOD BACK
INSULATION
REFLECTOR
RADIATOR
GRILLE
FRAME
AIR INTAKE

SIDE
GRILLE
COLD AIR

SHELVES

GRILLE FRAME: HINGE AT TOP FOR EASY ACCESS.

DOORS

unable to reseal it. How should I go about this? Must I drain the water from the entire heating system, or just the one heater? How do I do this? There are shut-off valves in each room.

E.M., Farmingville, N.Y.

A. Shut off the supply to one radiator by turning off the valve to that room. Open the drain and be prepared to catch the water from that radiator. Make sure the area around the leak is bare metal by removing any paint or any of the stuff you used to reseal it. Repair it with an epoxy-based metal repair product, following the manufacturer's directions carefully. Allow it to dry and turn on the heater, after refilling, to make sure it works, before repainting.

Basement radiator

Q. Our three-year-old home has half the basement walled off as a recreation room and since the furnace is in the other half the recreation room is quite cool. We have hot water heat and I would like to put a radiator in this new room. I could use capped off connections which were made in the main feed pipes for possible attic use at a later date. I'm wondering if the circulator could handle a floor level radiator.

E.G., Ridgewood, N.J.

A. You can use the connections satisfactorily but we'd advise against a floor level radiator. While a circulator could probably handle the load, the radiator is apt to be at least partially cold most of the time. You'd do better with a radiator suspended sideways just below the joists and by adding fins to the pipe passing through this area.

Air-bound radiator

Q. I have one radiator which requires bleeding of air almost daily while the others in the house do not need this attention. Why is this?

H.W., Montgomery, N.Y.

A. The air-bound radiator may be nearest the feed line and get all the air present in newly heated water. You may best solve this problem with an automatic bleed valve which automatically releases air but closes when water reaches it. Make sure that all radiators are properly sloped slightly toward the end opposite the intake valve.

Aluminum painted

Q. I just bought a house which has hot water heat and all radiators are painted with aluminum paint. Someone told me I am losing a lot of heat because of this. Please advise me how to paint them.

W.S., McKees Rocks, Pa.

A. Remove the aluminum paint with liquid paint remover and steel wool. Then paint with flat paint in lighter shades, preferably with an alkyd base. You'll salvage about 15% of the heat you are now losing.

Banging radiator

Q. I have an oil-fired water heating system and wish to know what causes a banging noise in one radiator and a part of the copper pipe in the basement. It is not constant, just periodical.

C.J., Syracuse, N.Y.

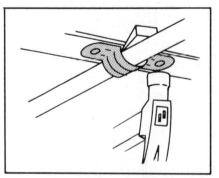

A. The noise may be due to loose pipes banging against hangers. This can be remedied by tightening the hangers or using wedges to keep pipes from contact with nearby rigid surfaces. It could also be due to a partially open radiator shut-off valve or defects in this

valve. Loss of packing in the valve stem is often responsible.

Noisy radiators

Q. Every time steam hits radiators in my home a loud banging noise results. I checked the pitch and it is OK. I drained the radiators and put on new valves. Still get the same noise. Why?

R.I., Dudley, Mass.

A. When you state you drained the radiators, you put your finger on the most likely cause of the trouble. The return flow of condensed steam in the form of water is interrupted. When steam hits water, you get a bang. If you have a one-pipe system, where water flows back through the same pipe, it may be your radiators aren't sloped toward the intake pipe or that the steam inlet valve is not turned on fully or is periodically shut off. In this type of system, the valve must be fully opened when no steam is rising to permit water to flow back to the furnace. If it can't there will certainly be a noise when the steam is turned on again. In a two-pipe system the radiator is sloped toward the end opposite the intake valve which again must be left open to drain the radiator properly.

Reducing heat loss

Q. I have to find a way to close off portions of my home during the winter. The floor plan is open with much of the living area connected by arches, so that I can't merely close the doors and lower the thermostats.

In my hall entry to the living room and kitchen areas, for example, the only thing I can think of to do would be to rip off the baseboard by the stairs and from the area at the right, install a header against the ceiling across the stairs and kitchen entrance, install three vertical pieces to serve as framing at the sides and in the center, and hang bifold doors as draft-proof as possible, one pair per opening.

I would probably have to make the doors myself as they would be too narrow for the standard width (with two per opening) and also would be just short of 8' in height. What wood should I use and how should I make them?

Is there any one type of hinge which would be best?

Can you suggest what size boards would be suitable for the framing?

I've been told my proposed doors wouldn't amount to much savings in heating bills as they would not be insulated. A decorator suggested I 'line' the back side of each door by tacking on a decorative, fabric-covered sheet of rigid 1/2" insulation of the foam type. It sounds practical, but how do you compensate for an extra inch of thickness when you want to open the doors?

M.P., Troy, N.Y.

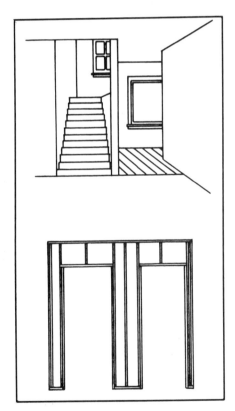

A. Your proposal of the bifold doors is not the easiest solution to your draft problem. Framing, against the wall, two normal door openings in which you can hang normal interior doors would present no particularly unusual problems. Use 2x4s for the framing and

the new wall can be built as a self-supporting unit. The framing is sketched into your floor plan as shown. Surface to match the walls and trim out to take the doors. You'll find details in any book on building houses to help you install the door frames.

Lining the backside of a pair of bifold doors is, as you suspect, not a practical idea. You'd have to consider the total thickness of the lined door to install your bifolding hardware, and it would not be very draftfree anyhow as you have five vertical cracks per opening instead of two with a normal swinging door. Ordering doors with weather-stripping at the bottoms should keep out drafts.

A very simple solution is insulated draperies to be ceiling-hung over both openings. This would certainly be the easiest to manage and easily removeable for summer which none of the door proposals are.

Reflection

Q. We have hot water heat with regular cast iron radiators. I was told to put a piece of plywood behind each radiator to save a lot of heat. Is this correct?

M.Y., Manville, N.J.

A. Plywood alone behind radiators won't do much. If you covered the plywood surface with aluminum paint or aluminum foil it would reflect heat now passing through the walls behind the radiators, throwing it back into the room.

Poor heating

Q. I have a steam furnace converted to gas from coal. It seems the radiators get almost cold before the heating goes on again. Could you suggest a way to get adequate heat from this system?

J.R., Cedarhurst, N.Y.

A. Chances are good there is nothing at all amiss with the sys-

tem. Check your thermostat. If it is located in the warmest area, naturally no additional heat will be demanded of the furnace until even that area cools off.

Escaping heat

Q. Recently we had installed an iron stairway leading from our den to our finished attic. This involved cutting an "L-shaped" opening that is 4'8" at the widest part. Now we are losing most of our downstairs heat to the upstairs. (The attic is well insulated.) Is there anything we can do to help alleviate this?

J.G., Memphis, Tenn.

A. The obvious answer is to put a trap door on the opening. Heat is going to rise and now you have given it a hole to rise through. Without a layout of your home we can only guess at other remedies. Try closing the den's doors, if the den is a separate room that can be shut off. You might consider relocating or resetting some of your heating. Your entire heating system needs rebalancing to provide uniform heat in this newly created situation. Remember, you are heating essentially twice the area you heated before, assuming the square footage of the attic equals that of the downstairs.

Lowered ceiling

Q. We live in a rented house with natural gas floor furnace in the small hallway that measures 52" x 70". Doors lead off all four sides of this hallway. There is no attic insulation and I would like to know a practical way to prevent heat loss through the ceiling directly over the floor furnace.

H.S., Princeton, Ky.

A. A practical method here would be to put in a false ceiling lower than the present one. Use 2x4 joists and cover with gypsum wallboard or similar panel stock, placing the new ceiling as low as possible for convenience. Install 2″ of insulation above it. This will conserve all heat and also help to direct it into the adjoining rooms with higher ceilings.

High heat costs

Q.   What steps can I take to save heating oil? I have a four-room house that is heated by forced hot air. I have had insulation blown in the house. The floors in crawl spaces are also insulated. This house was built in 1961 for summer living. I just added another room (12′ x 18′) which is well insulated; top, sides and bottom. My nephew has a house up north with five rooms and his costs are $100 lower than my own. Will it help to cover the metal ducts with insulation?

G.B., East Falmouth, Maine

A.   A house built for summer living is likely not to have any stormsash or weatherstripping. Adding insulation was a good first step. Now check out your heating system. Inspection by the oil supplier's maintenance service is usually the best place to get this service. You may not be getting the best possible from the equipment. Insulating the ducts would help, too. If you live in a particularly wind-exposed area, it will also cost more. And when you compare your total costs with your northern nephew, you should also compare costs per gallon.

Home energy

Q.   We will be building a new home in the future and are planning to do most of the work ourselves. We are very interested in energy-conserving ideas. How can we obtain information on these ideas, and is there any information available on do-it-yourself systems for homebuilders?

T.W., Newton, Ala.

A.   There are many possibilities in alternate energy sources and conservation. Much available information is quite technical. For basic understanding and insight into the many facets of alternate energy possibilities, plus real think-it-through-yourself help, we'd suggest "Energybook No.1" and "Energybook No.2," both edited by John Prenis. If you are generally curious and of a tinkering nature, both will be worthy of your attention. For price and ordering information, write to Running Press, 125 S. 22nd. St., Philadelphia, Pa. 19103.

While you're browsing at your local bookstore, look at "Producing Your Own Power," an Organic Gardening and Farming Book edited by Carol Hupping Stoner, published by Rodale Press, at Emmaus, Pa. This also has detailed how-to hints. "The Solar Home Book" subtitled "heating, cooling and designing with the sun" by Bruce Anderson with Michael Riordan published by Bride House Publishing Co., Andover, Me. 01810 is also most helpful. It covers fundamentals more thoroughly and is extremely well organized. The book includes do-it-yourself information on some aspects of the owner-built home as well as owner-built solar energy devices.

Solar heat

Q.   We live in an older home. How can we make a "Solar House" out of it to save money on fuel bills?

M.E., Westtown, N.Y.

A.   There's no reasonable way to make a truly solar house, one entirely dependent on solar energy, out of an existing house not designed for solar. There's a limited relationship between how much you can spend to save. While the experts debate the cost effectiveness of retrofitting, the handy homeowner can take advantage of some ideas discovered so far.

Many of these ideas are outlined in "The Fuel Savers: A Kit of Solar Ideas for Existing Homes." This booklet shows solar energy applications that can be built at moderate cost, as do-it-yourself projects, for existing houses. It contains practical steps you can take now to lower your utility costs. The booklet was prepared for NORWESCAP (a private non-profit organization primarily funded from state and federal agencies to serve Northwest New Jersey), but the information is applicable to other areas. To get a copy, write to Total Environmental Action, Church Hill, Harrisville, N.H. 03450. The suggestions are generally well within the capabilities of most home handymen.

Solar mobile home

Q.   Has the design shown in "A Home Built Solar Heater" in your past issues been tried in a mobile home? I would like to have one built but wonder if the air exchange would work in my 14′ x 70′ home.

J.N., O'Fallon, Mo.

A.   At a quick glance, it seems that the lack of a proper basement might present a problem in using this particular design for a mobile home. You could write Mr. Roger N. Perry, Jr., Worcester Polytechnic Institute, Worcester, Mass. 01609 and inquire. Don't rule out solar in any case. If your home is oriented properly, the window units should work very well. Since air is warmed and circulated back in a simple box at each window, circulation of warmed air within the house should be greatly simplified. This type unit is also relatively easy to build.

Solar by mail

Q.   I am interested in solar heating for the home I plan to build. Can you help me with sources and manufacturers of equipment or plans for projects?

J.S., Dallas, Tex.

A.   The most recent SUN Catalog ($5 ppd.) makes solar available on a mail order basis. Write, Solar

Usage Now, P.O. Box 306, Bascom, Ohio 44809. You'll find it lists materials, equipment, systems, kits, instrumentation, novelties and a number of related energy-saving devices. It's also a one-stop source for most of those popular solar books you meant to read but now can't find.

Solar sources

Q. I'm interested in receiving information about solar heating systems for homeowners. Can you help?

B.B., Jefferson, La.

A. You might get basic as well as technical information by writing the National Solar Heating and Cooling Information Center, Franklin Research Center, Twentieth and the Parkway, Philadelphia, Pa. 19130. The center is jointly run by the Department of Housing and Urban Development and the Department of Energy.

Fuel-less heat

Q. I have a seven-room, tri-level house with an upflow highboy gas-fired, forced-air furnace. What can I add on, build in, or attach to heat this home without relying on natural gas or electricity?

B.C., Columbus, Ohio

A. You might consider a solar collector with rock storage a feasible add-on for your house (see Dec. '77 FAMILY HANDYMAN). You also could install a piggyback woodburner to your existing forced-air furnace. Or, consider using wood-burning stoves, properly installed and maintained, in various locations in your home. There are a number of other steps you can take to cut heating costs without going whole hog into solar energy, though. A very good book on that subject is "The Fuel Savers: A Kit of Solar Ideas for Existing Homes." It's from Total Environmental Action, Church Hill, Harrisville, N.H. 03450.

Thermostat problem

Q. I have a fireplace I like to use quite often but every time I do, the hot water furnace circulator seems to run for hours. I try closing the fireplace damper nearly all the way but it does little good. When the fireplace is out, the circulator returns to normal and so do room temperatures. It seems that all the heat from the furnace and the fireplace just go right up the flue. Is there any way I can correct this problem and still use the fireplace?

V.M., Baltimore, Md.

A. It may well be when the fireplace is operating there is a strong draft of cold air toward it which is drawn across the area of the thermostat. As long as the fireplace operates, your thermostat would be in a cold spot and would cause the circulating pump to operate. Relocation of the thermostat may solve the problem.

Dirty thermostat

Q. I have a floor furnace with an automatic temperature control. Lately it seems to have lost its sensitivity. I can turn it on or off by hand but it will not perform automatically. Can I remedy this myself?

B.S., Long Beach, Calif.

A. The control may simply be dirty. Shut off the electricity to the furnace. Open the case of the thermostat and look it over. Blow the dust out and pick up wads of lint on a rough wood toothpick. Try the unit. If it still doesn't function, a replacement is probably needed.

Furnace failure

Q. Last spring our furnace just died. I'm wondering if you can tell me how to fix it?

A.L., Fresno, Calif.

A. Forced-air heating systems need periodic maintenance and adjustment. Most emergency-type repairs become necessary when the furnace simply quits providing sufficient heat. See if you can correct no-heat problems yourself before calling a serviceman. First, see if the electricity to the furnace has been turned off accidentally. Then make sure the controls are properly set. Check the thermostat for correct location and calibration, and see that it is the correct type for the controls used. Check for loose wires and connections. Sometimes insufficient heat can be the result of dirt on heating surfaces or insufficient return air (check baffles on all registers and remove dirt from ducts). Also make sure filters are clean. Check the blower for a slipping belt, a too-tight belt causing an overloaded motor to cut out, a motor that's running backwards, a defective motor, or improper blower speed.

No-heat radiator

Q. We have one radiator that doesn't heat. What's the procedure to find out what's wrong?

A.M., Watertown, S.D.

A. First make sure the radiator valve is turned on. If it is, the trouble is almost sure to be in the air valve. This valve does two things: it allows the cold air in the radiator to be pushed out by the steam coming up from the boiler, and when the steam hits the valve, the rise in temperature automatically closes the valve to keep steam from escaping into the room. If the air valve is stuck (because of rust, grit, or corrosion), no air can escape, steam cannot enter, and the radiator is airbound. To remove rust and grit, first close the radiator shutoff valve, and manually unscrew the air valve by turning it counterclockwise. Shake the valve vigorously—this may loosen rust —then try to blow through its threaded end. If air passes through, reinstall the valve; it not, boil it in a strong solution of washing soda and water for about twenty minutes.

You can put the valve back on the same radiator to see if it works, but a better test is to put the valve on a radiator that is heating well. If this radiator continues to heat, fine; if not, obviously the valve is defective and will have to be replaced. (If the first radiator still does not heat—and you know now that the air valve is all right—the radiator is probably waterbound.)

Frozen boilers

Q. The boiler in our summer home has frozen up. What should I do?

M.C., Detroit, Mich.

A. A frozen home-heating boiler can be a serious problem. Don't try to start a fire in the boiler until all the ice has melted inside it. First thaw the boiler intake pipe. Next open the drain and thaw the drain pipe and its fittings. Finally, apply warmth to the boiler. If it was completely filled and has frozen, it probably has been split open. You will find out as the ice begins to melt. If so, call a professional.

Rumbling boiler

Q. Our furnace boiler is making strange sounds. What's the reason, and can I fix it myself?

E.J., Chicago, Ill.

A. A rumbling noise in the boiler itself, surging noises in the pipes, or an unsteady water line in the glass are all signs that the boiler water is dirty. Drain the boiler. Let the fire go out and the boiler cool so that rust and sediment in the water can settle to the bottom. Turn off the cold water feed valve to the boiler. If you're not sure which valve it is, find where the cold water pipe enters

your home and trace it to the boiler. Probably you'll find a shutoff valve just where the cold water pipe is attached to the boiler. Keep one eye on the water gauge on the side of the boiler. There is one with all systems except a closed hot water heating system using an expansion tank. When water in the glass gauge shows the boiler is half full, shut off the feed valve. If you have a hot water heating system with an expansion tank, close the valve from the system to the tank. Then open the drain valve on the bottom of the tank and let the water out. Leave the drain valve open for an hour or two and then close the drain valve and reopen the valve connecting the system with the tank. Remember, open this valve when you're finished draining the tank; it must be open before you start the system working. While draining a rust-filled boiler is always recommended, excessive draining and refilling is not.

Noisy blower

Q. Our furnace blower was making a screeching sound, and our furnace man replaced it. Now I'm wondering if we could have had the old one fixed. What do you think?

P.B., Appleton, Minn.

A. Some homeowners regularly find themselves getting tricked into buying a whole new forced-air furnace because the blower on their old one is making strange noises. The truth is that, with a few adjustments or replacement parts, you may easily be able to eliminate the noise source and save yourself from an extra financial burden. Parts are usually available for everything in the blower mechanism of your furnace. A careful examination of the blower will usually tell you what's wrong, and what you have to do to correct the problem.

In checking the blower, first turn off the power to the furnace. Do not assume because you have turned

down the thermostat that the furnace will not come on. Often someone else will come into a cold house and turn the furnace back on by adjusting the thermostat. Remove the door(s) to expose the blower area of your furnace (you may also have to remove filters). Now you are ready to start troubleshooting. The best tool you have is your common sense or reasoning. For example, the softest material in your blower mechanism is the drive belt. It stands to reason that this has a good potential for wear, causing a noise problem. Check the the belt, removing it to check it thoroughly. To remove the blower belt follow these three simple steps: 1) grab the belt with your hand half way between the two pulleys, 2) pull the belt outward, away from the blower, and 3) at the same time rotate the belt toward the big pulley. The belt should pull free. If the belt cannot be removed in this fashion, it may be too tight. Now, with the belt in your hand, grab it with both hands and flex it back and forth. It should feel flexible, not stiff and dried out. Turn the belt inside out. Put a very sharp bend into the belt; the belt should not crack. If the belt cracks, you have an old belt that might make noise and should be replaced.

With more reasoning, you can see that the second cause that might create a noise problem is the pulley on the motor. This pulley does the pulling. And because it's smaller, it goes around faster than the larger one on the fan and wears more. With the belt off, use a flashlight to check to see if the pulley grooves are worn. If it is dirty, clean it out and sand it down. A pulley that has grooves in it or is dirty can make noise. (Note: If you need to replace the blower pulley, remember to measure the shaft size as well as the over-all size. Also check to see if the pulley is loose on the motor shaft. If it is the adjustable type, check to see if the set-screws are loose.)

In the same manner, check the pulley on the blower fan. See that it's tight on the shaft and that its set-screws are tight. You usually won't find much dirt or wear in this pulley. Give the pulley a spin and see what the blower sounds like. If you hear clicking noises, check to see if something is inside the blower. Even one small piece of paper inside the squirrel cage can make a noise.

A noise can also result if the squirrel cage is not centered in its housing and one side is rubbing against the housing. Recentering the squirrel cage is a major job if the cage's set-screws are hard to get at. In this case, you may have to pull the blower out of the furnace. Further check the blower by pulling out and pushing in on the blower pulley to see how much end-play there is. If you hear a banging noise there's too much end-play. To correct end-play, move one of the shaft collars in or out, whichever is needed. Between the collars and blower bearing brackets there should be some thrush washers (they may be made of leather). If these thrush washers are old or worn out, the metal collars will rub against the brackets and cause noise.

Some blowers never came with thrush washers and noise can be eliminated by installing them. You can make your own thrush washers out of leather (the tongue of an old shoe works well; it is soft and about the right thickness). However, before you install them, soak them in oil. If the blower has oil cups, oil the blower. An un-oiled blower, it stands to reason, will also make noise. But if your blower has a label that says it needs no oil, you probably have oil-less bearings. These can sometimes dry out and make noises. If so, replace them with the oil type; most good furnace companies can get you bearing replacement kits for your blower.

You can check the wear of the blower even more by pulling up and pushing down on the blower pulley. There should be no up-and-down play at all. If you find play, the bearings on the blower are starting to wear and may need to be replaced. Blower bearings wear for two main reasons: 1) lack of oil, and 2) the belt has been too tight. In time, worn blower bearings will make a lot of noise. However, there are kits you can buy to replace bad bearings.

A very small thing in the blower area that can make noise is a worn-out rubber bumper on the end of the motor adjustment screw or bolt. You can look right at this and perhaps still not see that the bolt has worn through the rubber and is banging against the blower housing to make noise. You can make a new rubber bumper out of almost any kind of rubber. Just some tape wrapped around the bolt end will stop most noise until you get a better bumper made.

If you have an old blower, chances are that you might have rubber bumpers on the blower legs. Most old blowers just set inside the furnace. Some new ones slide and come out like a drawer. Others are bolted to the furnace. Depending on which blower you have, there is a possibility that your whole blower has shifted over to one side and the blower housing is touching the furnace and the blower noise is transmitted through the furnace. To stop this from happening, there is usually an asbestos boot between the blower housing and the furnace.

Another check to make is the alignment of the two pulleys. Use some kind of straight-edge to check this; a dowel works well as it will lie in both grooves and you can see if they are lined up or not. When one pulley is to the side of the other pulley, the belt will rub on one pulley and make noise. The last thing to check is the motor itself. You cannot tell if the motor makes noise without running it. Leave the belt off and turn the furnace on just long enough to cause the blower motor to kick on. While the blower motor is running, listen. If you have noise that goes away after you put in a couple of drops of oil, the motor bearings might be starting to wear.

There is not much you can do for motor noise other than getting a new or rebuilt motor. Noise in the motor bearings does not mean the motor is bad and will stop running; a noisy motor may run for years and years. Caution: Do not run the furnace too long with the belt off; just long enough to hear what the motor sounds like. If you oil the motor, put in just a few drops. An over-oiled motor will be damaged sooner than one that's under-lubricated. The extra oil eats the coating off the field wires and shorts out the motor.

If you decide you need to replace the blower belt, use this technique before you install it. Flex the new belt back and forth in your hands as much as you can to work out some of the stiffness. A new belt will sometimes produce noise; flexing it helps cut down on that possibility. To install either your new belt or your good old belt, do this: 1) loop the belt around the small motor pulley first, then 2) start it around the blower pulley, while 3) you turn the blower pulley in the direction you want belt to go on. If the belt will not go on in this manner, loosen the adjustment screw until the belt will go on. Then adjust your belt so that you have an up and down movement (between the two pulleys) of about 1/2" to 3/4". A too-tight belt will wear the blower bearings out, and make noise too. A belt that's too loose will also make noise and might even come off the pulleys, especially if they're not lined up properly.

Finish the job by re-installing the filters, door or doors and turning the power back on.

Stove & Fireplace Problems

**Chimneys & flues—cleaning, construction, removal, repair, safety
...Fireplaces—construction, repair, troubleshooting...Gas grills, logs
...Stoves.**

Chimney cleaning

Q. **Where can I get round and square metal brushes for cleaning chimneys? I'm not interested in this as a profession, though how-to information would be helpful, too.**
R.D., Carthage, Ill.

A. Black Magic Chimney Sweeps, Dept. FH5, Stowe, Vt. 05672 offers brushes and free details, plus a guide to chimney safety and maintenance for $1. Clean Sweep, 418 Collegiate Dr., Marietta, Ohio 45750 and C & D Marketing, 342 Middlesex Turnpike, Old Saybrook, Conn. 06475 also sells chimney cleaning supplies. Clean Sweep offers free "how to" information.

Chimney fires

Q. **I need some advice on chimney cleaning. Five years ago we moved into this house, which was about 17 years old then. We've used the fireplace every day in cold weather. The chimney is clear but the sides are heavy with soot. Is the chimney in its present condition in any way a fire hazard?**
R.B., Pittsburgh, Pa.

A. Your chimney should be cleaned once a year to be safe.

Burning dry hardwoods efficiently is the best way to avoid excessive accumulation of creosote. It is the cooler flue temperatures that cause creosote to be more of a problem today plus just plain not knowing how to handle a wood-burning fireplace well. A check with your local fireplace accessory dealer or wood stove retailer might put you onto a good sweep.

Chimney sweeping

Q. **We just installed a wood burning stove which we use nearly every day. Is it important for us to have the chimney cleaned? Should we call in a professional sweep?**
R.S., Farmingham, Mass.

A. According to the Fireplace Institute, over 40,000 chimney fires occur each year, most of them caused by the build-up of creosote, the blackened residue of wood combustion. The best prevention is to give your chimney an annual check-up.

Although a professional chimney sweep is a good investment for a detailed chimney inspection, you can handle any minor look-overs yourself. Here are the potential troublespots that should be scrutinized: damage to the flashing where the chimney meets the roof; cracks in the chimney above and below the roof line; cracks in the liner within the chimney; blockage resulting from birds and animals nesting or from other foreign matter; creosote or other debris build-up on the smoke shelf, and properly functioning damper.

Heavy deposits of creosote or soot in a fireplace chimney are bad enough, but the build-up inside a woodburning stove should be watched even more. A few millimeters of soot on the walls of a woodburning stove can cut heating efficiency by more than 10%.

Construction

Q. **I am in the process of building a house, and need information on chimney construction. I would like to try to put up a fieldstone chimney with a 32″ fireplace opening, and I would appreciate any help you could give me.**
E.H., Kittery, Maine

A. If you want to build a fireplace opening of stone, you need to build not only a chimney but also an ash pit and a hearth. The shape of the interior of the fireplace is also critical. We've sketched the major parts of a fireplace so you

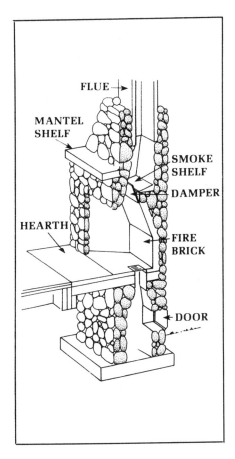

FLUE

MANTEL SHELF

SMOKE SHELF

DAMPER

HEARTH

FIRE BRICK

DOOR

will see quickly all that is involved. You'd be a lot better off building around a pre-fab fireplace circulating liner to take care of all this finicky detail work for you. The manufacturer will have figured out how to make the damper fit the throat and how to slant the smoke shelf without your having to become an expert mason overnight to be able to do these things in stone and mortar. You'd have your stone precisely where it should show, the working parts properly proportioned for the opening, and the correct flue liner size. Do look into this possibility.

Chimney building

Q. **I wish to read about chimney installation both through a wall and a flat roof, since I'm planning to install a chimney. Also, I need to know what type of fireproof surfacing should be applied over a gypsum wallboard wall behind such a prefabricated unit.**

P.G., Nova Scotia, Canada

A. On chimney installation, check with your local supplier or write some of the manufacturers of prefab chimney systems. Try Hart and Cooley Mfg., Holland, Mich. 49423 or Majestic Co., 721 Erie St., Huntington, Ind. 46750. Majestic carries the Thulman chimney, and all three should be able to offer you literature. If you're thinking of masonry construction, there is a very good, clear section on that subject in "Simplified Concrete Masonry Planning and Building," second edition, J. Ralph Dalzell, revised by Frederick S. Merritt. Write McGraw-Hill, 1221 Ave. of the Americas, New York, N.Y. 10020 for current price. As for backing, you'll find recommendations with the fireplace unit you select. Asbestos cement is about the least expensive sheet material to use.

Adding chimney flue

Q. **We plan an addition on our summer cottage and want to add a flue to the chimney at the same time. The Heatilator has rusted out due to dampness, salt air and rain getting in. We are considering closing the fireplace and using a Franklin stove which would need the flue. The present chimney is the "catsup bottle" shape and we want another flue for use on the other side—presently the outside. Is it possible to add the flue on the side—either to the projection for a free-standing fire cone or all the way if we should decide on an underfloor heater?**

H.C., Franklin, Mass.

A. You have to realize first that the weight added to the original footing may be too much. The second problem is the work involved in tying new masonry construction to existing work. And the third thing to consider is how you will incorporate the larger outside dimension of the chimney with an additional flue when you get to the roof structure, which is further complicated when you are adding

onto the roof, too, at this point.

We think you'd be better off all around if you'd just use a prefab flue/chimney unit. You may be able to surround both old chimney and new stack above the roof in a fake enclosure if you like the looks of it better. Many of the unitized chimneys have such structures available, or you could build imitation stone if the looks of two chimneys bother you too much. Also consider the location of an additional heat source. There is no reason, assuming you elect the easy way out, to locate the chimney right next to the old one.

Chimney liners

Q. **Who makes "Vitroline" chimney liners?**

J.F., Saugerties, N.Y.

A. Bow & Arrow Stove Co., 11 Hurley St., Cambridge, Mass. 02141 distributes "Vitroliner" available in heavy gauge metal coated inside and out with vitreous enamel or in uncoated stainless steel.

Prefab chimney

Q. **Does the prefabricated chimney for a prefab fireplace need a foundation?**

S.K., Perry, Okla.

A. No, a prefabricated chimney is generally supported at ceiling and/or roof. The chimney housing, visible from outdoors, is always roof supported.

Materials for chimney

Q. **I want to build a chimney but have never done any masonry work before. What would you suggest as the easiest material to use for this—block or brick? This is for a summer cabin so appearance is not the main factor.**

L.M., Watertown, N.Y.

A. You need first of all a poured concrete or solid masonry footing on which to construct a chimney. The size of the chimney will determine the size of the footing. Standard chimney blocks are the easiest material. Some types are glazed inside to form a complete flue when joined. Other blocks in various forms, most common being square or rectangular, completely surround a flue liner. Still other block forms are a square U shape, the two halves joining around the liner. These may be extended with standard blocks to include more than one flue. They are simply stacked and mortared together around the terra cotta flue liner.

Attaching chimney

Q. I would like to build a chimney of cinder blocks against an outside wall. The house is frame, covered with insulating siding. The blocks are regular chimney blocks. How do I attach them to the house, yet keep the chimney intact?
E.P., Philadelphia, Pa.

A. You may either cut away siding to the chimney shape and cover the sheathed wall with tar paper or simply apply tar paper to the siding. The masonry can be laid against it either way. The footing comes first, size dependent on size and height of chimney. At each tier, attach corrugated masonry ties to the building wall with rustproof nails. Extending these ties between the mortar joints ties the masonry to the wall. The joint between liner and blocks is mortar filled, mortar joints between blocks are from 1/2" to 1" thick, the mix 1 part portland cement to 2-1/2 parts sand. When chimney is complete, you can recut siding to butt against it, sealing that joint with caulking.

Chimney past roof

Q. I was going fine building an outside chimney against the end wall of my house. Now I'm almost to the roof and suppose it has to be cut somehow to let the chimney pass but then what? I've seen flashing details for chimneys completely surrounded by roof but don't understand how this applies to my situation.
D.D., Sterling, Ill.

A. The same principle applies. On the uphill side, the flashing goes under the shingles. On the downhill side on top of them. You will have to cut the roof to permit the chimney to pass any overhang. Then run metal flashing up the chimney side 8" and onto the roof 12". Apply asphalt to all flashing joints.

Inside chimney

Q. When building an inside chimney is it necessary to place anything between the brick and the wall?
I.F., Nassau, N.Y.

A. The chimney should not be in contact with flammable materials at any point. There should be at least 2" clear between masonry and house materials, though this space may be filled with fireproof insulation if desired.

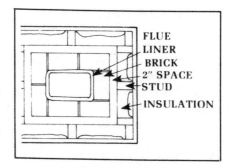

FLUE
LINER
BRICK
2" SPACE
STUD
INSULATION

Chimney insulation

Q. Should I insulate my chimney? I know there is supposed to be 2" between the outside of the chimney and the house structure but do not know if this has to be filled up with insulation or not.
H.M., LaGrange, Ill.

A. The space around a chimney does not HAVE to be filled but may be if you desire and use fireproof insulative materials. You may want to use the radiant heat from the chimney to provide additional free heat to the house in which case do not insulate. Where the chimney runs through a closet, insulation would generally be a good idea.

Chimney cap

Q. Could you tell us a simple way to make our own chimney cap, one that would look well on a brick chimney?
D.C., Irondequoit, N.Y.

A. A chimney cap is a flat stone or concrete slab erected over the chimney top on corner supports. It can be ornamental as well as useful. On a brick chimney, brick corner supports would be the simplest solution though there are other ways to do the job. Erect the corner posts two bricks high and cement on the top piece which should be at least 1-1/2" thick and the same outside dimensions as the chimney.

Removing chimney

Q. The chimney in our old house is directly in the center of the roof. I want to do away with it but don't know how to close the opening this would leave in the roof. Can you help me?
M.S., Clay, N.Y.

A. Removing the chimney is the hard part; closing the hole is relatively simple. First, piece the ridge board. Use the same size lumber cut to a snug fit and toenail to both ends of present ridge. Your roof rafters presently stop at a header. Cut short rafters the same size as these and long enough to bridge the space between header and new ridge piece toenailing at both ends again. Cut roof boards or substitute plywood same thick-

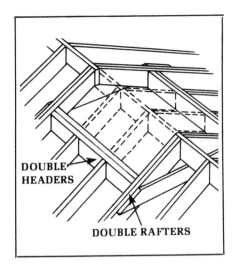

DOUBLE HEADERS

DOUBLE RAFTERS

ness as existing roof boards to fill the gaps on both sides of the ridge. Cover these with tar paper tacked flat, cut off vertical sections of any metal flashing you find. You can now run shingles up to the ridge on each slope and match the present ridge peak treatment. As an extra precaution against leaks, coat the joints between old and new material with a liberal application of roofing cement.

Smoke-filled cellar

Q. I have a hot air furnace which seems to back up constantly. Smoke comes out the fire door. There is a hole cut in the chimney about 4″ wide and 2′ long which has no purpose to my knowledge and I wonder if it interferes with the draft. I only recently bought the house and do not know what the chimney hole is for.

M.G., Colonia, N.J.

A. The hole may have been intended as an ash clean-out, but the 4″ dimension is small for that purpose. Try sealing the hole to see if that improves the draft. If so, brick it up permanently. Other possibilities: your chimney may need a cap to prevent severe downdrafts, or furnace smoke pipe too large for chimney flue size. One other possibility is the smoke pipe damper is kept almost closed when the furnace is firing and smoke is not able to escape.

Crumbling base

Q. Some of the bricks at the base of my chimney (in the cellar) are deteriorating. Can these bricks be replaced or repaired?

H.F., Middleboro, Mass.

A. Remove all loose and crumbling brick along one side at a time, wet the exposed surface, and apply a cement mix of 1 part portland cement and 2 parts sand. Extend this out 1″ to 2″ beyond the present face of the chimney. Repeat on the next side. If necessary to cut away crumbled brick more than an inch or two on any one side, let the first side dry 48 hours before tackling the next or you may undermine the chimney. This cement base may be tapered at the top for neatness. Replacing bricks entirely is not recommended unless the chimney can be braced up on scaffolding.

Cementing a chimney

Q. My home is only two years old but I notice the cement between bricks of the chimney is poor and sandy. It can be removed with the fingers. What am I to do? Shall I make a rich cement mixture and sheath the present chimney?

E.K., Paterson, N.J.

A. Your idea is sound. Make the mixture 1 part cement, 2-1/4 parts sand, wet the bricks thoroughly, and spread with a steel trowel. Once this has dried, apply a masonry sealer paint to prevent further water penetration. While you're about it, excavate down to the footing on which the chimney rests and treat this area also as it would appear the mortar was at fault from the beginning. Use a waterproof additive in the coating below grade.

Insulating a chimney

Q. The chimney in our home runs up through my kitchen on one side and dining room on the other, and is causing a problem. I cannot keep wallpaper on the kitchen side; the heat from the chimney drys the paste. Also, the plastered dining room wall cracks from the heat. Can you suggest a remedy for these two problems?

G.S., St. Paul, Minn.

A. A need for insulation between your chimney and the surrounding walls is strongly indicated. If there is not at least a minimum of 2″ between the chimney surface and any combustible member of the surrounding walls, the walls should be moved out at least a 2″ distance and fiberglass insulation installed in those spaces. Insulation should also be placed between the joints and the chimney where the chimney intersects with the floor and the ceiling. If the walls are already 2″ from the chimney surface, nail furring strips to the studs of the existing wall, insulate between the strips, and plaster over or nail plaster board to the furring strips.

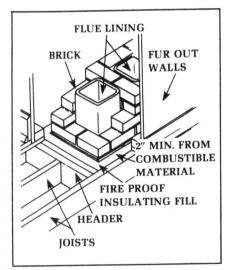

FLUE LINING

BRICK

FUR OUT WALLS

2″ MIN. FROM COMBUSTIBLE MATERIAL

FIRE PROOF INSULATING FILL

HEADER

JOISTS

Leaking chimney

Q. Every time it rains, water comes in the clean-out at the bottom of the chimney. It's a brick chimney, outside the house. We can't find any place where water is leaking in. What's the solution?

F.K., Staten Island, N.Y.

A. If you have no chimney cap, water can come down the chimney when it rains. You might construct a simple "roof" of noncombustible materials or you can purchase a ready-made chimney cap. These are often designed to improve the draft and/or prevent down drafts, too.

Chimney streaks

Q. My chimney which contains the flues for the oil burner and fireplace has become discolored. There are long, dirty streaks of soot on the outside. What is causing this and how may I remedy it?
M.W., Newtown Square, Pa.

A. If those soot streaks come straight down, they are being spread by rain washing down the side of the chimney. For rain to get at soot, it would have to be deposited in some cracks around the top of the chimney. We suggest you examine the top of the chimney for signs of loose mortar or cracks. Any defects should be mended with fresh mortar, applied with a small pointed trowel. Best results are achieved by wetting the old mortar first.

Cracked chimney

Q. We have a crack in our fireplace chimney from the top to the foundation. Quite a bit of water gets into the fireplace and runs down the wall and into my living room. We have now put a den on the other side, and the cracked wall is in the den. When it rains the whole chimney back wall gets wet. How can I fix it?
M.W., Weymouth, Mass.

A. The situation is more serious than you seem to think. It implies a weakness in the footing under the chimney and stresses strong enough to crack the masonry to this extent could be bad enough to cause the chimney to fall. You need an expert to examine

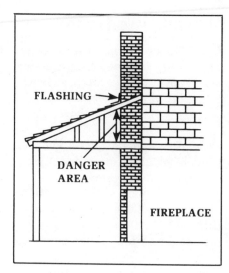

this, preferably your local building inspector. Where water comes through, smoke and sparks can go out. This is a very definite fire hazard if you use the fireplace at all. The cracks can be sealed with fresh mortar squeezed in deeply. Waterproofing will then stop the leaks. Check the flashing where roof and chimney join. Don't use the chimney until you can seal the cracks at the point where roof timbers and chimney meet for here is where sparks can get in to set fire to the house.

Chimney seepage

Q. I'm having a problem with the chimney I built for my woodstove. From the small door at the base of the chimney, there is a seepage of a black liquid I've been told is creosote. I built the chimney outside the house wall, 34' high, 4' above the house roof. I have to clean the stove pipe and around the chimney hole quite often. What can be done?
J.M., Ludlow, Mass.

A. The black liquid most likely is creosote. You get it as a result of burning softwoods or green wood, having an inadequate chimney and/or mismanaging your fire. You can minimize the problem by using seasoned hardwoods as fuel. Have your chimney inspected for proper size, design and safe con-

struction, too. Refer to the material that you should have received with the stove for the manufacturer's suggestions on how to use it most effectively, or write to the company. The airtights take a bit different management than fireplaces do.

Leaky chimney

Q. We have an 80-year-old house that has been remodeled, but have a problem with the chimney that goes through the center of the house and then through an unheated attic. The chimney sweats in the attic and water runs down through the upstairs ceiling, leaving large brown stains on the wallpapered walls.

We are using an oil furnace for heat and wonder if wrapping the part of the chimney in the attic with roll insulation will cure our moisture problem. The chimney is made of brick, unlined and is offset, rather than straight, to prevent downdrafts. Can you help us?
V.V., Proctor, Vt.

A. The situation you describe with the unheated attic space is backwards for condensation, or sweating, which is usually caused by warm air on a cold surface, not vice versa. We think the cause is more likely seepage. You have an old brick chimney, unlined, and it is generally wet on the outside. If the chimney were the coldest surface in the attic and the air in the attic was warm and contained considerable moisture in vapor form, your prescription of insulating the chimney would be answer, but the chimney can hardly be the coldest surface in the attic (especially when in use).

Have you looked at the part of the chimney above the roof? Is it in absolutely perfect shape? Are all joints filled in well and is the brick surface nonabsorptive? Is the top of the chimney coped well for draining off rainwater? When these repairs are made—take a look at the flashing where the chimney goes through the roof, too. Give the outside part of the chimney a coat of a clear silicone masonry sealer. The damp on the chimney inside the attic will not automatically disappear overnight, but by next summer you'll find it has become dry as no more water is being absorbed by the brick outside, seeping through the old, porous brick and mortar only to reappear as a stain below. Old bricks get a bit like sponges and if you prevent absorption of more water, they will eventually dry out.

The fact that the chimney has no lining is not unusual in homes of this age and area. The offset is seemingly an outgrowth of the builder's desire to make a symmetrical-looking house and get the chimney through the ridge of the roof so it will be at the highest point with the least masonry exposed. You don't say yours goes through the ridge but most old offsets do. By getting the chimney top higher than the roof ridge, downdrafts are prevented.

Water in flue

Q. I have a warm air furnace with a stoker sitting 3' from the chimney and joined to it by a smoke pipe. Water runs down inside the chimney every time it rains and into this pipe which rusts out. I have to replace it every fall. What can I do to eliminate this?

P.M., Omaha, Neb.

A. You can repoint the top of the chimney to close gaps between bricks which is very likely the main reason why water gets in. A cement peak from flue to outer edges of the chimney will direct water down the outside. If the flue is large, rain may be coming into it directly in sufficient quantity to cause the trouble, in which case a chimney cap would prevent the trouble. Smoke pipe should not extend into the flue far enough to permit water running down inside

the flue to contact the metal. Cut pipe to extend 2″ to 3″ inside the opening and cement it in place with asbestos paste, then cover with a metal ring. It's possible that some of the rust is also due to condensation in the pipe during the "off" season.

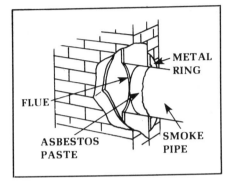

FLUE — ASBESTOS PASTE — METAL RING — SMOKE PIPE

Rain in chimney

Q. I have a home with a two-flue chimney. Water comes down the chimney. I thought this might be just one of the bad features of being a homeowner but friends tell me it's unusual. The clean-out doors in the basement fill up with water, particularly the furnace clean-out, yet no water comes out the fireplace. I checked the chimney top. The mortar is gone in places and a knife blade can be slipped through even between the two flues at the top. I am puzzled about why I get water in the cellar but not in the fireplace. If pointing doesn't help, would a cap do the trick?

M.R., Fairhaven, Mass.

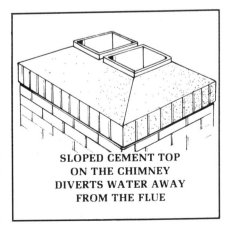

SLOPED CEMENT TOP ON THE CHIMNEY DIVERTS WATER AWAY FROM THE FLUE

A. The mortar must be very poor quality to be in this condition. Repointing is definitely necessary. The flue to the furnace goes straight down and to the clean-out with a hole for the furnace smoke pipe cut into it. Water goes right on down. The fireplace flue angles upward to cut into the second flue and water could not get past this point. It probably stands until it seeps through to the other flue and so on down. Repoint first, and build up a cement cap or at least an angle to divert water down the outside of the chimney only. Make this taper at least 30°.

Ghosts in fireplace

Q. If there is any wind at all, our fireplace howls like a banshee. Is it poor construction that causes the sound? The fireplace opening is approximately 28″ x 30″. The noise tends to diminish when the damper is fully open and is just terrible when the damper is closed.

J.D., St. Joseph, Mich.

A. Your banshee noise is caused by drafts plus a narrow opening. It might be that you are in a location where strong overhead wind can blow horizontally across the top of your chimney making a noise like that caused by blowing over the neck of a bottle. If the flue liner extends above the masonry a bit it can be corrected with a cement wash sloped up from the masonry to the liner. It might also be the downdraft narrowed in the chimney throat that brings on the wailing howl. If this is the case, a chimney cap will stop downdraft.

Chimney flue deposits

Q. I have trouble with a chimney. It is a patented one with a terra cotta lining inside tin and fills constantly with black pitch, hard and slick as glass. This may catch fire any time and roar up the flue. The flue serves a trash burner which includes coils for water heating so we can never stuff the stove with wood. The fires are not too hot. We can see nothing that could interfere with the draft as the flue extends above the house and there are no trees within 30'. Can you help us?

A.G., Fort Bragg, Calif.

A. This pitch is actually an impure form of creosote, usually deposited from the slow burning of wood and in combination with pitch from pine wood. It is inflammable. The trouble is probably due to a low fire and a quickly-cooled chimney. Apparently you load the burner and bank it so low insufficient heat travels up the chimney. If it were warmed enough, the draft would be better and the deposits would be carried outside instead of condensing on the cool lining. There's an old home remedy for this—a chunk of zinc in the fire. If at all possible, open the drafts wide when you first fire the burner so as to heat up the flue at the start of the fire.

Chimney hole

Q. Where can I get information on how to make an additional hole in an existing chimney to accommodate a new wood-burning stove in addition to the present oil-fired furnace?

C.G., Grand Forks, N.D.

A. It's dangerous to have a furnace and a wood-burning stove share the same flue. You need an additional flue for the stove.

Unsafe vent idea

Q. I have a single-flue chimney that vents the oil burner in my basement. I would like to install a wood stove in the basement on a back-up system and also to supplement the burner. Would it be safe to vent both the oil burner and the wood stove through the same flue? If so, how?

C.I., Rhodesdale, Md.

A. It is never a good idea to vent two burning installations into the same flue, even though you do not expect to use them at the same time. It is a very definite fire hazard and would be frowned upon by your local fire department. Functionally, the two would not be able to operate efficiently together, due to the peculiarities of flues and drafts. Use a separate flue for the wood stove.

Adding a fireplace

Q. We bought an old and drafty farmhouse with a comfortable lay-out. Because of high heating costs, we are planning several revisions and additions to the house. We would like to build a fireplace which is open on both sides, each facing a different room and one side open into the planned room addition. Would this type of fireplace be efficient? Also, could it be blocked off if the room addition is not completed by the winter?

M.P., Wellsboro, Pa.

A. Several companies do make forms for the type of fireplace you describe. Just how they could be blocked off temporarily might be explained by these companies. From your plans, the double-faced fireplace does indeed make sense though we note one thing that is questionable. The door from the heated garage is shown in the middle of the end wall, thus making an aisle of the whole area. Perhaps it should, instead, be placed near

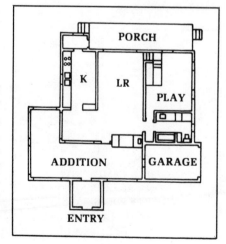

the outside wall or toward the fireplace wall.

Installing a fireplace

Q. I wish to install a wood-burning fireplace in the second floor of my house. Can I use the present chimney or must I install a new one? I wrote to a fireplace company and their recommendation was a chimney for each unit, but they did not answer me with a yes or a no. Can I use the present one?

R.F., Laurium, Mich.

A. The fireplace company has given you its recommendation and in effect said either yes or no. You can use the present chimney if it is

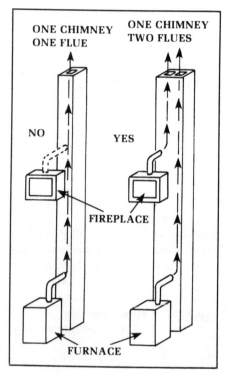

not used for anything but the fireplace. You can't use it if you intend to add the fireplace to a flue that is already in use. This assumes, of course, that the present flue is of sufficient size and in good enough condition for the fireplace. To clarify, a flue is the lined "smokestack" within the chimney. A chimney of brick, etc. can contain more than one flue. It is the flue that is important. Only one burning unit to a flue is the rule for safety.

Adobe fireplaces

Q. Can you tell me where I can obtain information on how to build pueblo and Mexican fireplaces?

G.C., Santa Fe, N.M.

A. You will find a good deal of help in the Sunset book on fireplaces. Check your library or local bookstore where paperbacks are sold. There is also a chapter on fireplaces in *Adobe, Build it Yourself,* a fairly new book by Paul Graham McHenry Jr., published by the University of Arizona Press, P.O. Box 3398, Tucson, Ariz. 85722. This is an excellent book, but may not be that helpful to you if you wish a plan to follow in detail on the fireplace alone. There have been a number of government publications that included Mexican and pueblo fireplaces, but they are all out of print. In your locale, the local library and the county Extension Service agent would be helpful. If you want something not as traditional and more mechanically built we suggest that you write to The Majestic Company, Huntington, Ind. 46750. They will provide free information on fireplace installation giving the details you would probably want, although not necessarily in the style you seek.

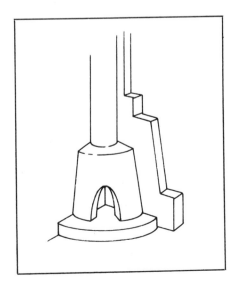

Fireplace foundation

Q. I want to put a prefab fireplace on the outside wall of my living room. I would like to install it so the face of the fireplace is flush with the inside of the wall, so it doesn't take up floorspace in an already small room. Will I need a foundation?

W.R., Lanexa, Va.

A. You can install the fireplace so that it sets on a platform extended out at floor level from the existing floor. Tie the extension joists into the existing joists so the resultant platform is as strong as the floor. Install the fireplace with the face flush to the inside of the wall, install the metal chimney, then frame the fireplace/chimney extension with 2x4s and cover the new framing with plywood. You can apply Z-Brick or similar material over the plywood to make a brick chimney. Seal to protect it from the weather. Insulate between the joists of the platform and staple batt insulation between the 2x4 framing to get a weather seal.

Electric log fireplace

Q. We are planning to build our own fireplace and expect to use electric logs in it for heat. We want to use either firebrick or some pretty rocks on which we would imprint arrowheads. We know little about this type of construction so would appreciate learning about any plans that we could obtain. Can you help us?

P.H., Jonesburg, Mo.

A. Lane Publishers, Menlo Park, Calif., publish the Sunset paperback on fireplaces which your local bookstore should have or be able to order for you. Your library might also have it. We have no plans, but some of our advertisers who run plan services include fireplaces among their offerings. Most of these include flue and chimney specifications which you

won't have to be concerned with. You should, however, follow the clearance specifications recommended by the electric log manufacturer.

Fake fireplace finish

Q. I have made an imitation fireplace using plaster of Paris "bricks." They are white now and we would like to keep them that way without repainting every year. Is there a coating that will seal them from dust?

J.L., Minneapolis, Minn.

A. It is possible to wash plaster of Paris about once—gently—but any transparent coating would yellow in time. Why don't you size, prime and enamel them in a washable paint? Vacuuming would keep off the worst of the dust and you'll be able to wash it a number of times before repainting becomes necessary.

Open-sided fireplace

Q. I would like to build a fireplace with two or three open sides on an enclosed porch using stone or brick around one of the prefabricated steel units. Could such a fireplace be successfully built by an amateur?

S.S., Columbus, Ohio

A. Makers of these open-sided units have types with two sides open but most suggest the use of a corner post of iron or steel to support the lintel along these two sides on which masonry rests. Three open sides would require two corner posts, quite heavy, to support the masonry above. Your floor may not be adequate to support this. Since the units contain all the necessary fittings except masonry and are built in proper proportions, a nonprofessional would have only the masonry to worry about. Have you considered a hearth with a metal hood as a substitute for the fireplace?

Double-duty flue?

Q. I live in an area where logs are plentiful. I would like to build a fireplace in the basement of the home I am building and hook it into the forced hot-air furnace so it could be used as a source of emergency heat. I'd like to use one flue for this and the furnace as the two will be right near each other. What is the smallest dimension I could use for the chimney for this flue?

A.A., East Patterson, N.J.

A. You need two flues, not one. Connecting fireplace and furnace to one flue would ruin the draft for both. Using the smallest flue size, 8-1/2" square, and putting the two together and using the usual 8" brick around them, you'd have a chimney about 26" x 35". On the fireplace, we'd suggest using a prebuilt unit around which your masonry is built. These units provide almost instant heat. The ducts are part of the unit and could be constructed to provide gravity heat through household hot-air ducts. Adding forced draft devices would needlessly complicate the situation.

Pre fab fireplace

Q. We'd like to install a fireplace in our cottage. Could you tell me how the prefabricated ones are built in?

E.O'B., Wausau, Wis.

A. Generally, the prefabricated fireplace consists of a finished firebox unit which may be set on the floor (properly insulated) raised off the floor on some sort of base or legs or hung on a wall. It may or may not have a section of smoke pipe to link it with a prefabricated fire-safe chimney section. This usually runs from the ceiling through the roof where it is protected from the weather by a chimney housing of some sort. In some models, the chimney construction comes down to the top of

the firebox. Exact installation procedures depend on the type and style you select. Most only require a hole for the chimney, possibly fastening to the house structure but seldom necessitate much "building in."

Damper installation

Q. I have a fireplace in my summer cottage that has no damper. It is brick construction. Could you tell me if it's possible to install a damper in this already-constructed chimney? Could I do it myself or do I need a mason?

W.T., Westmont, N.J.

A. If the fireplace is of usual construction with a smoke shelf at the back to constrict the opening just above the fire chamber, then you can probably install a damper yourself without too much trouble. Measure the opening at the narrowest point, and buy a ready-made damper to fit as nearly as possible. The damper unit is held with metal pins or screws set into mortar joints on each side which can be drilled with a masonry bit in a drill or cut with a short star drill and hammer. The joint, if any, between damper and flue can be best sealed with fireclay.

Fireplace heating unit

Q. We have an old-fashioned fireplace about 250 years old. It has no damper so we can neither control the fire nor keep drafts out. We have thought of installing a heating unit of iron inside the fireplace but it does seem rather expensive. Isn't there an easy way to put in a damper?

H.S., High Falls, N.Y.

A. You would have to practically dismantle the fireplace to install a heating unit. You can put in a damper which would involve only drilling small holes to sup-

port it in the throat of the chimney and possibly a small hole in the face of the fireplace through which a control bar or handle can be run. In some fireplaces, this can be totally concealed.

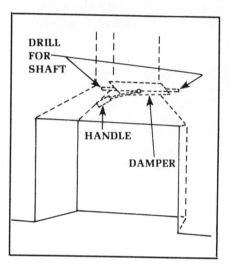

DRILL FOR SHAFT

HANDLE

DAMPER

Fireplace completion

Q. My fireplace has never been finished. The rough masonry is flush with the plasterboard wall. I want to use brick up to about 10" above the opening. What support is needed over the opening for the brick directly above it?

C.E., Nehalem, Ore.

A. You will need a steel angle as a lintel over the opening, preferably 2" x 3" minimum with the 3" leg laid flat.

Fireplace update

Q. I have a fireplace, ceiling-high, made of very ugly brick. It is 5' wide with a shelf sticking out about 5" half way up from the floor. It has a heating unit in it with four ugly registers in front of the fireplace. The whole fireplace is flush with the wall. I would like some advice on it. I have thought of removing the unit but I am afraid I might crack my other flues. What can I do?

G.H., Independence, Mo.

A. It would be extremely difficult to remove the entire unit. The shelf can be removed easily by cutting it off flush with the surface of the fireplace, using a chisel and hammer. It cannot be taken out as it supports masonry. The face of the fireplace may be made more attractive. The duct outlets and intake registers can be disguised with black iron or brass silhouette figures or filigree work, in keeping with room decor. It is possible to seal these openings but this destroys the function of the fireplace.

Stone fireplace

Q. We would like to modernize our old fireplace, making the lower part of that wall all stone. The present facing is what I would call ornate to say the least, all marble panels and curly wood carving. From what we learned closing up another fireplace in this house, it is just common brick behind. How can we support the weight of a stone facing?

Z.S., Akron, Ohio

A. Use thin stone, about 1" thick, grooved top and bottom to receive anchors that hold it against the wall surface. No special foundation or floor reinforcement is necessary as a steel starter strip supports the bottom row of stone. We suggest you remove the present facing first, see what you have to work on and build out the adjacent wall flush with it so the surfaces are flush for the effect you want. After the stone is applied, any mortar can be used to fill the joints and you have a stone wall.

Fireplace connection

Q. We are planning to install a wood-burning fireplace, but because of the layout of our home, we cannot put the chimney directly behind the fireplace. How far can the chimney be from the fireplace and how do we connect the two?

R.H., Abbottstown, Pa.

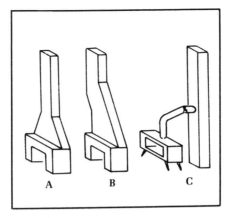

A. There are several different types of fireplaces and they have different requirements as far as chimneys are concerned. The chimney section of a masonry fireplace is part of the fireplace (drawing A). Although it is not a separate item that can be located far away from the fireplace, it can be offset somewhat and still work (drawing B). If your space problems are such that the chimney must be at a considerable distance from the fireplace, the best solution would be a prefab fireplace that is placed in a room and then connected with a free-standing chimney (drawing C).

Fireplace helper

Q. In the May/June '78 issue, a Leyden Hearth was mentioned. Please send me the address.

M.C., Philadelphia, Pa.

A. Write Leyden Energy Conservation Corp., Brattleboro Road, Leyden, Mass. 01337. The unit fits in a fireplace opening no less than 22" high and 24" wide. Self-contained, it's said to offer wood stove efficiency without sacrificing the charm of an open fire.

Flue size

Q. I am building a fireplace with an opening 32" wide x 28" high. It will be about 15" or 16" deep to the back wall. How large a flue do I need?

D.G., Denver, Colo.

A. You need a rectangular flue of the 8 1/2" x 13" size or a 10" diameter if you use a round one.

Fireplace repairs

Q. I have a two-way fireplace that leaks rainwater from the flue pipe directly into the fireplace. The leak is not caused by flashing or caulking conditions but results from rainwater that enters the flue pipe. I have thought of drilling holes in the fireplace floor to allow drainage into the fireplace foundation. Is this feasible?

G.M., E. Brunswick, N.J.

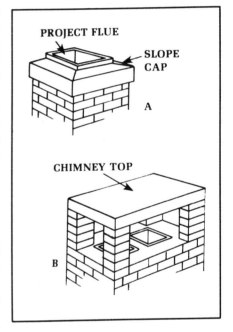

A. Correcting a leak by drilling holes in the fireplace floor is no solution. The most likely place for correction of leaks is up at the top of your chimney. (drawing A). If the cap on your chimney is cracked, water could run down between the flue liner and the masonry. Or the flue liner is cracked or not properly jointed and seepage is collecting. If, as you suggest, the problem is caused by rainwater entering the flue, the problem can be solved by building a cap on the chimney as in drawing B.

Offset chimney

Q. Would it be possible to install a pre-packaged fireplace with an offset in the chimney?

J.W., Butte, Mont.

A. You may offset the flue from the fireplace into the chimney proper if necessary. From the fireplace damper upward to the outer chimney flue the angled portion should be at a 45° angle or nearer to the perpendicular.

Fireplace patchwork

Q. Some of the bricks in the rear of our fireplace opening are chipped away. What do I use to repair them?

H.G., Reading, Pa.

A. The bricks are generally of fire brick and any replacement should be of this material. A badly broken brick should be replaced. Use fire clay instead of cement for repairing chipped ones. Wet surface thoroughly, then press in fire clay mortar. Keep surface moist as you work and let the job dry 48 hours before starting a fire in the fireplace.

Glass screen

Q. We are considering a glass fireplace screen as it seems to offer all the corrections our fireplace stands in need of. My husband believes the glass will get sooty and smoked just like the back of a fireplace. Is he correct?

L.B., Holbrook, N.Y.

A. Since one of the features of the glass screen installation is correction of smoking of the fireplace then it would follow that the glass itself would not be smoked up. The screen puts the draft at the bottom, across the fire and upward toward the flue where it belongs. About the only way you could smoke up the glass at all would be to close up the damper entirely and for a while the fire chamber would fill with

smoke, then the fire would be smothered out.

Opening too high

Q. My fireplace never did work just right. It would burn all right but we never seemed to get much heat from all the wood it consumed. I checked it lately with one of the dimension tables and find there for a width of 48″ and a flue size of 13″ x 13″ it should have been only 33″ high in the opening while ours is closer to 38″. Would this discrepancy make enough difference to be worth correcting?

R.T., Peekskill, N.Y.

A. A difference of 5″ in height could matter enough to make correction worthwhile. You can make a trial by setting a board temporarily over the top of the opening to see if installing a hood would help. If so, permanent installation of a suitable metal hood at the top of the fireplace opening is one answer, raising the hearth level another way to accomplish the same end.

Fireplace problem

Q. I have a fireplace in my home that has never been used. I would like to have a fire during the winter once in a while but also want to have it look clean and "unused" in summer. Do you have any suggestion as to how this could be accomplished?

C.R., Boston, Mass.

A. Cut three sheets of 1/2″ plywood to fit the sides and back of the fireplace and a fourth to fit the floor. Then cut "bricks" out of 1/8″ hardboard, mount them on the plywood and paint them to look like bricks. You can also get plastic bricks or Contact wallpaper at a paint store which can be put on the plywood. Join the three sheets for the back and sides of the fireplace with hinges of cloth tape like Mystik tape. In summer, slip your ply-

wood liners into the fireplace and it will look clean and unused.

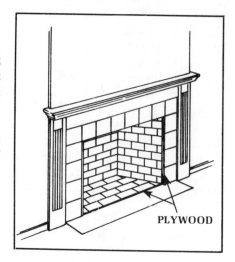

PLYWOOD

Problem odor

Q. Four years ago I added a living room to my house and had a fireplace built by the reputedly best fireplace builder in this city. I burn wood in the fireplace and this winter, although no smoke came into the room from the fireplace, the rooms would smell like a smokehouse for days after we had a fire. This part of the country is very humid and the more humid it gets the stronger is the smell of smoke. The chimney is on a one-story building and it has double flues with a long, glazed tile flue in it. Can you suggest any reasons for this smell and give me some ideas on how I can correct the condition?

W.T., Vicksburg, Miss.

A. From your letter we gather that you did not have the odor problem until this year. Therefore, the fireplace must have been properly constructed. Some other factor must have changed to give you this new problem. Have trees near the house grown enough to make a difference in the draft you now get up the chimney? Also, do you have the damper fully opened? (It should be.) Have you recently installed storm sash or a ventilating fan? (Your fire needs some air to work right.) It's also possible that the excessive humidity may tend to hold the odor. In this case you might consider a dehumidifier.

Bricking up fireplace

Q. We live in an old house with two fireplaces back to back, opening into separate rooms. We would like to eliminate one of these fireplaces. How is this done?

H.F., Flushing, N.Y.

A. If you are sure you want to eliminate one fireplace completely the first step is to remove the mantle and anything else that protrudes into the room, cutting it off flush with the fireplace wall. Then you have a deep hole which may be bricked shut and covered with plaster or other wall surfacing. The damper left in closed position shuts the concealed cavity off from the flue. If you have to remove the damper controls to get the wall flush, cement up the damper outlet before bricking up the wall opening.

Closing openings

Q. Since I hope to be able to discontinue the use of my oil stove when my rooms are insulated, I would like to know how to close off the chimney openings. Our chimney has no lining and all the wind and rain comes down it and the walls around the holes are always wet and stained.

W.B., Cohoes, N.Y.

A. The best way to close off a chimney hole permanently is to cement scrap brick and pieces of brick into the hole. Recess these pieces slightly in the hole, then coat the whole thing with a layer of mortar that can be smoothed off. All traces of the hole vanish. The job can be handled a little at a time, giving the first portion time to set before adding more—and thus avoiding the whole mass falling out. Also be sure the sides of the chimney are tight. Re-mortar any cracks between bricks, and inspect the flashing.

Resetting tiles

Q. Our fireplace hearth is covered with 4"x4" tiles which have come loose. What caused this and is it necessary to remove all the tiles to have a neat job?

W.W., Burtonsville, Md.

A. Tiles might become loose if the base cement becomes excessively dry, if the original mixture of cement was too sandy, if the reverse side of the tiles was too smooth when set and if the tiles were not soaked before setting them. It would be best to remove them all to do the neatest job.

Wrong tiles

Q. Our fireplace hearth has the glazed blue and white tiles continued down onto the hearth where they are badly scratched and unsightly. I want to remove and replace these with something a bit more attractive and practical. How to do this is the problem.

B.L., Canton, Ohio

A. First chip away with a hammer and cold chisel enough old cement to allow a new bed at least 1/2" to 1" deep. Wet the old cement thoroughly. Make a new mixture of 1 part portland cement and 2 parts sand, spread evenly and set the tiles on it spacing them properly. Level them by resting a broad board on top and tapping it evenly all around. Repoint the joints after the first layer has set about an hour or two. Wipe up excess cement while still damp.

Tile fireplace

Q. The facing of our fireplace is of common red brick and it has become discolored. We would like to cover it with glazed ceramic tile but are uncertain about what sort of mastic to use. We do not want to use mortar since this would involve too much work and skill.

J.F., St. Louis, Mo.

A. The organic tile adhesive used to apply ceramic tiles can withstand the relatively low heat of the fireplace but this is not your real difficulty. You need a level, smooth surface on which to spread the adhesive. Brick and mortar won't do. You'd have to apply a plaster leveling coat to the brick surface first, let it dry and then spread adhesive, set tiles and grout. You'd do as well to apply the tiles with dry-set cement mortar spread over the brick and while it is wet, press tiles into it and level them up.

Stone hearth

Q. We have a stone hearth which extends on to the hardwood floor. The cement has cracked out between the bottom layer of stone and the floor leaving a 1/2" space. The masonry is only seven months old and not cracked anywhere else. Cement doesn't hold. Is there something else I could use to fill in this space?

J.P., Wanaque, N.J.

A. Take a very small paint brush and paint the wood and the stone inside the crack with fluid asphalt. Then apply new cement mortar. It will stick to the asphalt readily which expands enough to allow the joint to remain filled. You could also pack the crack with oakum caulking and then apply a plastic type joint filler. This will stick to anything and remains semi-pliable inside but hardens enough on the surface to remain clean and dust-free.

Repairing fireplace

Q. I have three fireplaces built about 50 years ago. They were originally lined with large slabs of some material—probably firebrick, then stuccoed or coated with fireclay to present an unbroken appearance. This has broken and some bricks are showing. Some of the mortar is crumbling away. A friend tells me he used cement, lime and fireclay but has forgotten proportions. Could you advise me about this mix?

L.H., Louisville, Ky.

A. The danger in these fireplaces lies in the chimney, the joints of which may be assumed to have opened also. Check the flues with a mirror to be sure they are sound. The fireplace itself can be renovated by removing loose firebrick and repointing joints between bricks and behind them with cement. Use a mix of 1 part portland cement containing 10% lime (called mortar cement) and 2-1/2 parts sand. Replace the firebrick, cementing to the other brick with the same mortar, and to each other at the same time. Leave about 1" open between them for application of fireclay. Use a mix of 20% fireclay, 80% mortar cement or use fireclay mixed with asbestos fibers or iron filings without cement. Work into a thick paste with water, then fill the open joints with it, and plaster over the brick with it to a thickness up to 1/2". Do not build a fire for 48 hours after application.

Burned gold

Q. Our woven wire-mesh brass fireplace screen was sprayed with ordinary gold spray paint, which has burned off. Is there any type of refinish for brass, or any cleaner that would remove the sprayed gold and get us back to the original brass screen?

R.S., Leoti, Kan.

A. It's unlikely that there's much brass left under the charred paint. Solid brass wire mesh would not have needed gold paint in the first place. Paint removers probably won't touch the baked-on coating. Mechanical removal (abrasive cleansers, wire brushing, etc.) probably will leave patches of brass plating and bare wire. Considering the time, cost and safety factors involved, you'd be best off getting a new screen.

Gas log fireplace

Q. I have inherited a beautiful set of gas logs and thought of building an artificial fireplace for them. I note a label on the log states "For use in fireproof fireplace only". What exactly does this mean?

H.G., New Iberia, La.

A. A firebox lined with metal-backed asbestos sheets with at least 2" and preferably 4" of rock-wool batt insulation behind that and between the logs and any woodwork should meet the fireproof fireplace requirement. The unit should be placed on a well-insulated base. Metal-backed asbestos is suitable since most heat will be directed upward, not down. Observe local rules regarding such devices. Your gas company or supplier should be able to advise you.

Flue for gas logs

Q. I'm told I must have a vent or chimney for my gas logs. I cannot understand this since I have other gas heaters in the house without vents. Can you clear this up?

N.L., Big Spring, Tex.

A. The suggested use of a vent is a safety precaution since the gas consumption is such that oxygen could be quickly exhausted from the air. A vent need not be a chimney. A permanently opened window would do as well.

Indoor charcoal grill

Q. I would like to install an indoor charcoal grill so we can enjoy the benefits of this method of cooking during the cold months. Do you have any suggestions on building such a unit?

K.J., Franklin Park, Ill.

A. The most important requirement for using a charcoal grill indoors is that you must have a vent hood complete with fan and about a 6" outlet duct to carry away smoke and cooking fumes. Building such a hood into the basement play room makes it feasible to use your portable patio grill there. For a kitchen installation the firebox should be set into a brick or masonry counter to assure adequate insulation. If it is to be installed in a coventional wood counter, we suggest you use one of the units designed for counter installation that include some sort of a metal shell properly insulated for just this type of installation.

Install franklin stove

Q. I should like information on how to install a Franklin stove in my basement recreation room. Would it be possible to have the stove pipe lead into my existing chimney, off which my oil burner is working?

R.D., West Haven, Conn.

A. Installation of a Franklin stove is no more difficult than installing any other type of stove. It needs only a chimney connection the same size as its stove pipe. If your chimney has a spare flue, then use it. Do not connect two burning units to the same flue since the draft may be inadequate for both together and exhaust gases from one might work back through the other into the house due to downdrafts occasioned by weather.

Stove at fireplace

Q. Our summer house has fireplaces but they just don't seem to throw enough heat into the rooms. Would we be better off enlarging the hearths and setting Franklin stoves farther into the rooms and is there any reason for not doing this?

E.G., Stowe, Vt.

A. Assuming each fireplace can provide a sound flue for each stove, your idea should improve the heating considerably. You can close the fireplace openings temporarily or permanently, closing the dampers too, and make an opening above the damper for the stove pipe or you can brick up the opening partially and set the pipe into the fireplace at that point. Choose your unit accordingly.

Oil drum stove

Q. Last winter we saw a wood-burning stove made out of an old oil drum. Where does one find a used-stove lot to pick up parts? The door on the stove we saw was a cast iron part and the legs looked like they might have come from an old boiler of some sort. There was a fitting between drum and stove-pipe, too, that must have come off something rounded.

We bought a cabin up here in ski country last summer and now with the oil shortage, we wonder how we are going to get it warm enough to use. Is there a book about recycling stove parts? Can I have castings like these parts made up somewhere? Do you have any other ideas as beautifully simple as a stove made out of an oil drum? Please help us if you can.

J.A., McAfee, N.J.

A. What you saw was probably the Drum Stove assembled from parts made by the Portland Stove Foundry, 57 Kennebeck St., Portland, Maine 04104. You supply a clean 55-gallon steel drum and a stove pipe. The package includes flue collar, hearth, door assembly and two pairs of legs. If you can't do it, a sheet-metal man or a blacksmith can cut the necessary openings in the drum for you. The Portland Stove literature will tell you

how to assemble it all, but it is pretty simple once holes are cut. (Also see below.)

Drum stove kits

Q. I would like to heat my workshop with wood. I have seen door/draft control fittings that can be fitted to a 30-gal. drum for burning scrap wood. Who makes these kits?

G.S., Des Moines, Iowa

A. Country Craftsmen Co., Box 3333, Dept. FH, Santa Rosa, Cal. 95402; Fisher's, Rt. 1, Box 63, Dept. FH, Conifer, Colo. 80433, and Sotz Corp., Dept. FH, Columbia Station, Ohio 44028, all offer barrel stove kits to fit various size steel drums. Send SASE. (Also see previous answer.)

Stove shield

Q. The instructions with the Franklin stove we purchased suggest the nearest a combustible wall should be is 36″ or, with a shield, 21″. Since the room is small, I wish to place the stove closer. What can I do to make the wall safe (it's drywall on wood studs), short of replacing it with masonry?

R.G., Twinsburg, Ohio

A. Simply follow the recommendations of the manufacturer. Also ask your local fire department if they have an inspection program. Generally, masonry is the best bet though metal backed with asbestos or a panel of asbestos cement may sometimes be used. But be sure to avoid a faulty stove pipe connection.

Enclosing a stove

Q. We would like to enclose the Franklin stove in our summer cottage to make it look like a fireplace and are thinking of using cedar planks for this purpose that match

the walls. How close can we build to the stove without risk of fire?

C.E., Providence, R.I.

A. A Franklin stove enclosed in anything will lose its efficiency as a heater and is unlikely to look like a decent fireplace. Furthermore, it is practically impossible to enclose a Franklin stove with wood without creating a serious fire hazard. If you want a fireplace, we suggest you find another place for the stove and get a prefabricated fireplace with an insulated, jacketed stack.

Sawdust furnace

Q. Do you know the name of a company that makes a furnace that burns sawdust and wood logs? In Virginia, maybe?

E.M., Wilmington, Mass.

A. Here are two places that make wood-burning stoves that might be able to help you, though none are in Virginia. A reader of the *Whole Earth Catalog* describes using sawdust as a fuel in the following manner: "The stove can be any one but should load from the top. Make the loader of a gallon can with both ends cut out. Place a 3″ pipe down the middle and set can and pipe on a level surface. Press sawdust between can and pipe tightly. Remove pipe. Lift can and sawdust (without it falling out) and set into stove. Lite with kindling or starter at the center. A can of sawdust is supposed to burn an hour or so. Reuse the can. Use widely spaced grating so ashes can fall out freely. Have plenty of room at top of can, inside stove." We don't guarantee it will work, but that is the only reference we've found recently about using sawdust as a fuel. Stove manufacturers you can write to are: Atlanta Stove Works, P.O. Box 5254, Atlanta, Ga. 30307 and Fatsco, 251 N. Fair Ave., Benton Harbor, Mich. 49022.

Stove hood vent

Q. The metal pipe that goes up from our stove hood (which has a fan) runs to the attic where it stops about a foot below the plywood roof sheathing. The roof is about 15 years old but it is wet and soft in this area, between the rafters. What would you recommend doing to correct this problem? We can't seem to find a solution.

B.P., Franklin, Ind.

A. Your setup takes warm, moisture laden air in the house up that vent and aims it at an extremely cold surface. The moisture condenses on the cold plywood, and the heat may be enough to soften the shingles. The solution is to duct the vent to the outside. Insulate the duct where it runs through the unheated attic space. Make sure you flash properly where the pipe penetrates the roof surface. Usually 15 years is about the limit for asphalt shingles so you'll have a good chance to do the duct-installing properly as you reroof. Check the condition of the sheathing at the same time, and replace rotted or soft sections.

Oven parts

Q. We have a Tappan gas oven which requires two radiant screens. Tappan does not have them available any more. What can we use instead?

J.C., Woodmere, N.Y.

A. Don't give up yet on trying to get replacements. All Appliance Parts of New York, 1345 New York Ave., Huntington Station, N.Y. 11746 stocks parts for a number of major appliances including Tappan. They might have the part you need or a similar part from another line that would work. Give them model and model number when inquiring.

Chimney use

Q. We live in an older two-story house with a floor furnace as our only heat. We would like to put a wood-burning stove in the basement. There is one chimney in the center of the house. The flue for the gas-fired furnace is in it. Can we pipe the wood stove flue out the same chimney?

B.K., Meriden, Kan.

A. One chimney can contain one, two, three or possibly more flues. Each flue is completely separate from the others. You can vent the stove out the same chimney the furnace uses, provided that chimney has at least two flues—one for the floor furnace, a second flue for the stove.

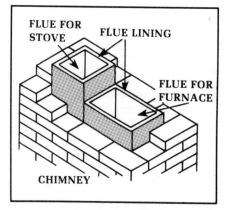

Burn creosote

Q. I have some cedar posts that were creosote coated in places. Would it be o.k. to use these as firewood in my wood stove?

F.M., Kiel, Wis.

A. This isn't a good idea for two reasons: Burning creosoted wood would create a terrible smell, and it would add to the build-up of creosote in your chimney, increasing the danger of chimney fires.

Chapter 14

Insulating & Ventilating Problems

Insulating—attics & roofs, ceilings & walls, floors...Soundproofing ...Ventilation...Venting exhaust fans.

Attic insulation

Q. I am finishing my two attic rooms, one of which will have storage space behind the kneewalls. I would like to know where to put insulation so the attic rooms will be warm in winter, cooler in summer.

A.D., Elgin, Ill.

A. We assume the storage area is to be kept warm as much as possible which would mean insulating all the way down to the eaves in that area. If no heat is supplied to this storage area, the kneewall itself will be colder than the rest of the room. This can be offset somewhat by use of a louvered door to the area which will also provide ventilation for it.

Insulation choice

Q. We want to add more insulation to our attic floor but aren't certain which type to use. I'm sure rock wool is fire-safe, but not so sure about pour-in cellulose fiber. Any suggestions to help us decide?

R.H., Knoxville, Iowa

A. You're on the right track in considering loose-fill for use over existing insulation. Most likely you already have a vapor barrier on the warm side of the present insulation and should not add another one. Read the labels on any insulation you are considering. Make sure the cellulose fiber meets the federal specification HH-1-515C; HH-1-103A is the spec on mineral wool. Such information must appear on the bag. You will also find a table showing how thick a layer of fill is needed to reach a specific R-value and the coverage per bag in square feet. If you will make an allowance for the R-value of the insulation you already have, you can then determine the additional amount needed.

Insulation needs

Q. We have just opened up the access to the formerly sealed-off space above the second floor in order to install an exhaust fan in the gable louver. We laid 1/2″ plywood on the rafters over the existing insulation which seems adequate. The fan seems to be doing a good job of keeping the upstairs cooler, but we are wondering if installing additional insulation on the ceiling of this attic would be even more beneficial. Or would it create a moisture problem? We will be using this

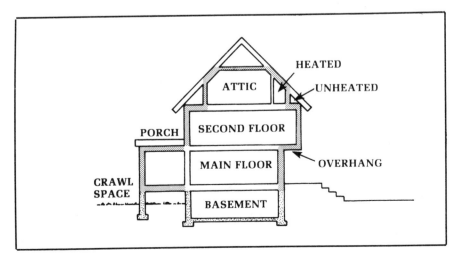

area for storage, now that it is accessible.

N.B., Levittown, Pa.

A.   Insulation itself does not create moisture problems. Moisture does. Insulation belongs between the areas you heat and the great outdoors. In the area you mention this could represent the floor if no heat will be used in the newly opened storage area. This could also mean the ceiling of the attic between the rafters, if you intend to heat the storage area. This does not necessarily mean that you have to run heat into that area. If you want to, you can heat the attic by the overflow from areas of your home that are already being heated. Otherwise, it is like leaving the doors and windows open and trying to heat the out-

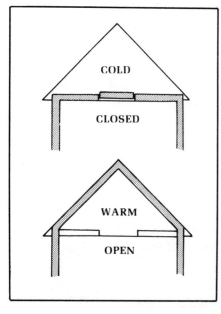

doors. So either close the opening that you recently made when winter comes or leave this section open and put the insulation in the roof and let it be warmed.

Wet rafters

Q.   I have a single-level, ranch-style home. The insulation in my attic is loose fill, 6″ thick. There is no paper or foil to serve as a vapor barrier. There is enough condensation in winter to make the rafters

and insulation wet. I would like to know if I should add some type of insulation under the present type and if so what kind and how to go about it.

G.M., Assonet, Mass.

A.   Your intention appears to be to add the vapor barrier and additional insulation at the same time. With loose-fill insulation already in place, this can be time-consuming, but still possible. Here's one way: First remove loose fill from the end between-the-joist space. Lay your new insulation, vapor barrier side down, toward the warm rooms below. Move the loose fill from the adjacent space over to top the just installed batt. That cleans out the second between-the-joist space, etc. It works if your attic is not more than partially floored. If it is floored, working in more loose fill is easier and you can add the necessary barrier with a good paint job on the ceilings of the rooms below. Either way, check ventilation in that attic. You should have 1 sq. ft. of free air opening for each 150 sq. ft. attic floor area.

Batts or loose?

Q.   I want to install insulation in my attic, which presently has none. Is it better to use batts or the loose insulation? Should I put down a vapor barrier first?

C.C., Warwick, N. Dak.

A.   Measure the distance between attic floor joists. Batt or blanket insulation can be bought to fit standard spacing, loose fill can be raked to fit any spacing. Batts or blankets are available with a vapor barrier; loose fill requires a separate vapor barrier. Either way, the barrier always goes on the warm side of the insulating material, towards the heated areas of your house. Make sure you do not obstruct eave vents when installing the insulation.

Fitting insulation

Q.   I have an insulation problem in my attic. I have already laid batts double thick across the floor except for the last 2′ on each side where the spaces between joists are 10″ instead of 14″. How does one go about squeezing 16″ batts into the narrower space?

B.W., Chicago, Ill.

A.   You can cut batt insulation to fit, thus reducing 16″ batts to any narrower width. Or you might buy a roll or two of blanket insulation to fit the 12″ joist spacing.

Fiber type insulation

Q.   I have a bungalow with an attic room finished in a soft pulp board. There is no other insulation. I want to put a more durable surface on the walls such as hardboard. Which is the better plan: remove parts of this board and go behind to apply batt insulation or add a reflector-type insulation between present wallboard and new planking?

L.L., Buffalo, N.Y.

A.   Since the wallboard is of insulating value, adding reflector type foil between it and the new wall surfacing material would give you better insulation without opening the walls. The drawback is in increasing the thickness which could mean resetting trim, electrical outlets, etc.

Partial insulation

Q.   I own a 2-1/2-story house. The attic is finished off already. Half of the eaves area is accessible but the other half is closed in completely by finished walls. Since my fuel bill is unusually high I wonder if it will do any good to insulate the side that can be reached.

W.A., Montclair, N.J.

A. As far as reducing the fuel bill is concerned, partial insulation will not be enough help. If the attic rooms are drywall it would not be much trouble to open the space between two studs to enter this area and insulate it. Also cover the floor area to save heat loss from rooms below. Even on a plastered wall such an opening would be worthwhile and could be replaced with a dry wall panel. In our opinion, insulation here would be worth the effort.

Insulation angle

Q. The upper part of the walls in our second floor rooms follow the roof slope. How do I get insulation down into this space between rafters 12" on centers? If I push batts down into this space, they pack up and don't go all the way down.

W.B., Cicero, Ill.

A. Insulation should not be packed tightly. You didn't say what thickness insulation you are trying to push down nor the size of the roof rafters. You would have trouble with full thick batts if the rafters are only 2x6s. With thinner insulation or larger joists you could probably make the job easier using a piece of hardboard as a slide for the insulation. I'm assuming it is rough lath and plaster that is causing the difficulty.

Attic floor insulation

Q. I've put a dormer in my attic. The builder put in 1/2" thick insulation between the floor beams. Should this be removed in the dormer room or not?

H.A., West Islip, N.Y.

A. You can leave the floor insulation provided you heat the attic rooms. Its purpose was to prevent heat loss from the rooms below and it should have been 2" thick. As it stands there will be little or

no effect from its presence. You should, of course, insulate the walls and ceiling of the new rooms.

Attic reinsulation

Q. I would like to reinsulate my attic. At present, the insulation is 2" fiberglass paper-covered batts. Should I get 4" fiberglass batts with aluminum on one side, or mica pellets?

P.L., Huntington Station, N.Y.

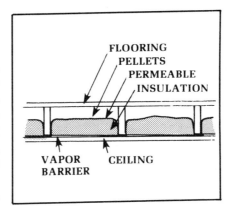
FLOORING
PELLETS
PERMEABLE
INSULATION
VAPOR BARRIER   CEILING

A. Assuming the current insulation has the vapor barrier down, and the paper cover facing up is vapor-permeable, you would get off easiest and probably cheapest using pellets on top of it to come up to the 6" total you desire. It may be that your current insulation has a vapor barrier on neither side, in which case check out your ceiling paint underneath. It should be sufficient.

Double barrier

Q. Our house had only 3-1/2" of asphaltic-paper-backed insulation laid with the backing down between the joists in the attic floor. Two years ago I laid more of the same insulation crosswise over the original insulation. I felt the new layer would bridge the old and not compress it since it was supported by the joists. I've since found out that you need a good vapor barrier on or under the original insulation: Was the original

asphaltic paper backing adequate or am I trapping moisture in that layer? Should I try to remove the backing from the added layer or sell it and replace it with unbacked insulation? Will turning over the added layer so the backing is up be helpful?

R.J., Fairport, N.Y.

A. Theoretically, you are trapping moisture between the layers. Actually if the vapor barrier on the first layer is doing the job, there is little moisture to trap. You may want to check this a couple of times a year by lifting the top layer in a few places.

You could lift the second layer and slash the backing to let any moisture through. Do NOT turn it over, unless you intend to slash the backing.

Roof insulation?

Q. Our two-story vacation home in the mountains is insulated everywhere but the roof. I suspect we are losing a great deal of heat through the present 1-3/8" x 6" tongue and groove decking. The roof is cathedral-type. Would 6" or 3" fiberglass insulation be best?

R.M., Massapequa, N.Y.

A. For the difference in cost between 3" and 6" insulation, I'd go for the thicker. It still takes about the same amount of labor to install either one. While you do not double the amount of heating dollars saved by doubling the insulation thickness, you do save more.

Wet insulation

Q. I have trouble up in my attic. There is a louver on each end of my two-year-old ranch house. I have 3" of insulation in the ceiling and it is moist and wet on top. How to stop this moisture is the problem.

P.M., Medford Point, Pa.

A. First step is to find out where the moisture comes from. If snow or rain can come through the louvers, block them temporarily till you can reconstruct them to stop such leakage. If there is a way, such as an open stairwell, for warm moist air to get into the attic above the insulation it should be closed. It might also be that condensation takes place between the roof rafters and drips down onto the insulation.

Attic conversion

Q. I would like to convert my attic into a bedroom. The roof has a steep pitch and beams 5-1/2" deep, 1-1/2" across. Under the floor boards of the attic there is loose-fill insulation.

What kind of insulation could I use between the beams that would have a pleasing appearance? I don't want to cover the beams, but prefer to keep a rustic look and as much headroom as possible.

C.M., Middletown, N.Y.

A. Don't rely on insulation for good-looking, decorative surfaces. Use blanket insulation,

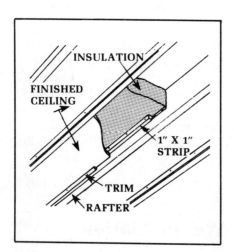

stapled against the sides of the rafters. Nail 1" x 1" wood strips against the sides of the rafters to support the insulation. The same strips will provide nailing surface for 3/8" plasterboard which can be

painted any desired color for an attractive finish. If you want, 3/4" quarter-rounds can be used to conceal the joists between plasterboard and rafters. The exposed edges of the rafters can be stained brown to provide the kind of decorative look you desire.

Dusty insulation

Q. I was thinking about putting foil insulation in my attic but I've been told that in time dust collecting on the foil makes it useless. Is that correct?

H.E., Oak Park, Ill.

A. We have been unable to locate any authority for the theory that dust will render foil or reflector-type insulation useless. It has been demonstrated that on a radiator, aluminum will deflect 15% of the radiant heat back into the coils, whether the radiator is dusty or not. Also foil between siding and sheathing of a house wall has a lot more than dust on it and it still performs its function as insulation. We feel you can discount this statement.

Peak insulation

Q. In my house, blanket insulation extends all the way to the peak. I am now making rooms in the attic and want to know if it is necessary to take down the insulation above the new room ceiling after placing new insulation across that ceiling. Would it be harmful to leave the insulation up to the roof peak?

W.P., Linden, N.J.

A. With insulation all the way to the peak you salvage heat in the entire attic. Presumably the space is adequately ventilated. The insulation is no longer necessary at the rafters and you might as well take it down and use it across the new ceiling.

Exposed rafters

Q. We plan a "pent-room" in our attic. We must insulate. We want to have the beams exposed. Instead of the bulky insulation that is generally used, is there some other type that could be placed directly on the ceiling so we could have the rafters visible?

E.D., Mattaplan, Mass.

A. We would hesitate to suggest any panel type insulation board against the sheathing since if condensation did take place it would quickly become saturated. With an exposed beam ceiling you usually do all the insulating on top

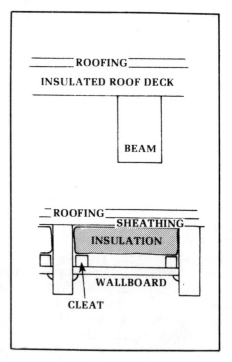

of the roof. Unless you want to reroof you can't very well do that. You could insulate in the regular fashion, apply 1/4" plywood to the ridge and install false beams over that. If you must have the rafters showing, you can do it with a great deal of trouble by using vapor barrier batt insulation against the underside of the sheathing. Fasten it on through nailing strips holding the flanges against the sides of the rafters. The strips also serve as cleats for inset wallboard or other ceiling surfacing panels.

Gambrel roof

Q. We have a house with a gambrel roof which was insulated with rockwool with a vapor proof backing stapled to rafters from eaves to ridge. Space from second floor ceiling to ridge is 26" and there is a louver at each end 9" x 20". Even in mild spring weather these upper rooms are hot and in summer as high as 115°. We wonder if it is possible to cool this area sufficiently to use it for living space?

J.M., Ridgewood, N.J.

A. Present insulation if 3" or 4" thick is fine. If only 1" or so thick, you have part of the cause of your trouble there. Your louvers do not seem adequate for ventilation. More than likely some form of exhaust fan would be necessary to discharge air from the rooms and draw cooler air up from the lower floors. Or you might install roof vents. Larger louvers would certainly help but you do not seem to have much more space available for them.

Blowing in insulation

Q. My single-story home seems to have been constructed without insulation in the outer walls. I would appreciate any information on availability for rental and any appropriate instructions for blowing granular insulation into the spaces between the studs to fill up the space between the outer sheathing and the interior plaster walls.

W.A., New Canaan, Conn.

A. Blowing insulation is pretty much of a professional job. There is a lot of detailed work involved besides just working the machinery.

Our advice is to hire a rock wool contractor to blow in rock wool insulation in your walls. It is a much better product for this purpose than granular insulation.

Insulate closet

Q. I'm building a cedar closet for clothing storage in my attic which is cold in winter and hot in summer. Should I insulate the walls?

S.G., Amsterdam, N.Y.

A. Unless the closet has some source of heat in winter, insulation would do no good since insulation can only keep in the heat that is present. With reflector type insulation you could probably reduce inside temperatures by as much as 15% in summer by deflecting some of the sun's radiant heat but your closet will still be hot unless ventilated with screened louvers.

Insulating brick

Q. The first floor of my home has brick walls. On the inside there is plaster directly on the bricks. The walls of the second floor are wood frame with aluminum siding, plasterboard inside. I feel I have considerable heat loss on the first floor. Next to the windows it is always cold. Is there an economical way to insulate these brick walls?

D.F., Cincinnatti, Ohio

A. Try to reduce heat losses through your windows and doors before worrying about insulating walls. Brick cavity walls can be insulated by pouring insulation into the void between the wythes, but getting at this space in a completed home is not easy.

Cheap insulation

Q. I am expecting to staple some corrugated board squares to the roof boards in-between the rafters in my hobby shop, to help keep it cooler in summer and warmer in winter. What I want is a liquid preparation that can be applied to the corrugated squares to fireproof them. I'm told that the cardboard

on the ceiling will be a fire hazard and likely not accomplish much of anything.

A.F., Lexington, Ky.

A. The cost of flameproofing liquid will reduce your savings to the point where you gain nothing. Besides, the placement you suggest will not accomplish much as you have only the dead air space in the thickness of the cardboard to act as insulation. You'll be far better off with commercial fireproof insulation properly applied over the bottom edge of the roof rafters.

Brick wall insulation

Q. How do I go about insulating my brick home? There is only 1" of space between the brick and the lath and plaster.

V.H., Chicago, Ill.

A. The easiest way to insulate masonry walls such as yours is to do it before you put on the interior surfacing material. At this point, you probably want to settle for adequate insulation in the attic—under the floor if you do not heat the attic, between the rafters if you do. You might also want to have your heating system checked to see if you are getting the best performance from the equipment you have.

Pattern of stains

Q. Across my ceilings, where the joists are, there are dark stain lines. A couple of the rooms were painted about a year ago with latex-type paint, and the kitchen with enamel. Now I see these stains on the newly painted rooms, and just lately in the kitchen. What's causing them?

C.M., Durham, N.C.

A. You evidently have insulation between but not on the joists. What's happening is that warm, wet air is picking up soil and depositing it on the coldest surfaces first—in your case the ceiling sections that are under the joists. You wouldn't notice the marks if the whole ceiling were uninsulated, because the soil would be evenly distributed.

These stripes should wash off easily. For a long-term solution, lay a little insulation over the joists and lower the house humidity.

Vapor barrier

Q. **The exterior walls of my home are solid brick with plaster applied directly to the block on the interior walls. I am planning to build another wall by placing 2x4s on the inside and insulating as you would a brick-veneered house. Should a vapor barrier of plastic be applied directly to the plastered brick wall before I place the studs?**
G.M., Red Boiling Springs, Tenn.

A. Condensation comes from the moisture in the inside air and the vapor barrier always goes on the warm side of the insulation. That means it does not go on the plaster, but the warm side of the insulation you expect to install in

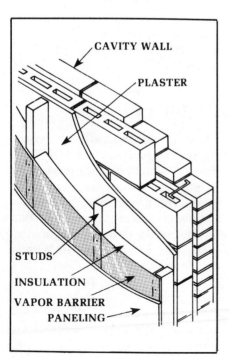

the stud space of the new wall, just under any paneling or wall surfacing material you apply. You can use batt insulation, stapled as shown, that has the vapor barrier on the warm side, just as you would in new construction.

Wall insulation

Q. **I am confused about wall insulation. Information I've seen recommends R-19 insulation for walls in my area (Spokane) which converts to 6″ of fiberglass or mineral wool. How do you get the recommended 6″ of insulation into 3-1/2″ of wall space available when using standard 2x4 studs?**

I am going to build a house next year and I want to insulate it to the maximum. Should I use 2x6s, two feet on center, for exterior wall studs?

J.T., Fairchild AFB, Wash.

A. You can stay with 2x4 framing, use fiberglass insulation 3-1/2″ thick, and use Styrofoam sheathing for a combined R-factor of 16.4 (fiberglass 11 R, Styrofoam 5.4 R). If you go to 2x6 framing, and 2′ center, be sure to use 5/8″ drywall on the walls for extra rigidity. As to cost, no matter which approach you take to increase the R-value of your walls, it will be expensive. But with rapidly rising heating/cooling expenses you're better off spending money on the wall, rather than in high utility bills.

Styrofoam & stucco

Q. **I recently saw an article on installing Styrofoam insulation on the outside of basement walls, then covering it with stucco. Where can I find more information on this method?**

R.A., Vestal, N.Y.

A. Your local Dow dealer or Dow sales office should have this information. If not, write Building Materials Department, Dow Chem-

ical Corp., 2020 Dow Center, Midland, Mich. 48640. Also, Dave Osborne, Conserv Products, 6701 Seybold Rd., Madison, Wis. 53719, can tell you more about the specific stucco mix noted in the article.

Windy boxes

Q. **I have a problem with cold air coming in around the electric wall boxes when the wind blows. I have a brick veneer home, all insulated.**

B.R., Vinetia, Okla.

A. Cold air is coming in around the electric wall boxes because there is room for it to get through. Sometimes the insulation is not properly installed behind the boxes. Fixing that properly requires temporary removal, not only of the plate and device, but of the box too—or else a lot of wall repairing. You will probably not go that far unless you are repaneling the room.

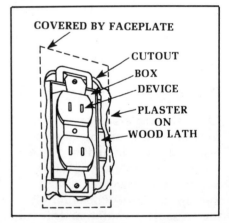

Short of that, remove the plate first and see what you find. Rough, oversize openings in the wall surfacing material can often be patched. At the very least, you can make sure the faceplate fits snugly against the wall. Use tape around the edges of the plate or go to an oversize plate. If a lot of cold air is still coming in, it would be a good idea to check the caulking around windows and doors in the general area. Should you find it necessary to remove or reset the box be sure to turn off the current.

Cold closet

Q. Two outside walls of my walk-in closet are always cold, though my house is adequately insulated. Should I cover the two walls with an additional layer of an insulating finish material?

B.N., Upper Saddle River, N.J.

A. Additional insulation probably won't help. Louvered doors can be installed to allow warm room temperatures to enter the closet.

Fluffy insulation

Q. A recent article on plugging heat leaks advises: "Fill gaps around windows and door framing with insulation. Do not pack insulation tight; leave it fluffed." Why?
M.B., Wilkes-Barre, Pa.

A. It's the trapped air that provides insulating qualities. When you pack such insulation tightly, the solid mass doesn't provide adequately thermal insulation. Also, you prevent any air movement between the back of the insulation batts and the inside of the sheathing which can lead to moisture problems within the wall. Cut the batts to fit snugly, keeping the vapor barrier on the warm side intact and in place.

Left-over foam

Q. We have several large rolls of foam. Can we use it as insulation in the walls of an older home we're fixing up? How many layers would we need?
R.J. Mueller, Isle, Minn.

A. First, you're not sure of the material's flammability, durability, or chemical make-up. Never stuff unknown material in an inaccessible place. Save it for seat cushion stuffing, nothing more.

Basement insulation

Q. I would like to make my basement into a playroom. Since it is an all-electric home, I will need a minimum of 3″ of insulation on the walls, according to my local electric company. Is there any way I can fur the walls with 1″ furring or must I use 2x4s? If I use 2x4s, how do I finish off the windows? They are wood frames in concrete block walls.

W.S., Nutley, N.J.

A. Use 2x4s and build a second wall inside your basement. Insulation is made in the right widths to fit 16″ center-to-center stud spacing, flanged for the 1-3/8″ face

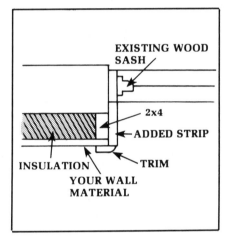

EXISTING WOOD SASH

2x4
ADDED STRIP

INSULATION
YOUR WALL MATERIAL
TRIM

width of the studs. Using 2x4 stock you will not have to fasten each piece to the basement wall as you would with thinner stuff; you'll be better off all around using 2x4s. On the window situation, essentially what you do is extend the jambs, head and sill the thickness of the paneling plus the furring, as the sketch shows.

Inside insulation

Q. After reading a story about styrene foam insulation, I would like to know if I could use this procedure in my house of wood construction with no insulation. I plan to panel several rooms. My thinking is to place furring strips over the plaster walls and put the insulation between them, on top of the plaster, then cover with wood wall paneling. Would this work?
R.M., Shadyside, Ohio

A. The styrene foam is a vapor barrier, and you should not apply a vapor barrier over an existing wall material such as plaster. Also, your furring strip/backer board/ paneling application will add 1-3/8″ thickness to your walls. You would then have to remove all trim around windows and doors, and baseboard. Strips of wood 1-3/8″ thick would have to be added over window/door frames to bring the frame flush to finished wall surface, so that trim would fit. This is a big job, because the old trim will split if you're not very careful in removing it.

Suggestion: If plaster/paint is sound, apply paneling directly over it, using a combination of nailing and panel adhesives to secure it to the wall. You may then fit small molding strips at base and other trim, thus not disturbing the trim. Insulation is another story. Is your home difficult to heat, or are your heat bills in line with other similar homes in your area? Your supplier (gas, oil, etc.) can tell you. Many older homes had no insulation in the sense of some form of batts between studs, but were "back-plastered" to trap dead air between the studs. These often are very easy to heat.

Insulation may be added into existing walls via blown cellulose- or rock wool. If you need to, have the applicator apply through holes inside the house, since you're going to cover with paneling anyway. Remember, too, that it will do little good to insulate only some of the walls in your house, as would be the case if you panel only a few rooms. Compare heating costs with similar houses, blow insulation in the walls if heating costs are high, and apply the paneling direct to plaster.

Ceiling insulation

Q. In my home I have an exposed wood ceiling, the underside of my 2x10 plank roof deck, which is supported on large wood beams. I seem to be losing a lot of heat; however, I don't want to close in the ceiling and loose the beamed effect. What can I put between the beams that would be a good insulating material?

F.M., Wallingford, Pa.

A. One way is to mount a finished ceiling material on cleats set on the sides of the beams with insulation above the new surface. You might also consider nailing Styrofoam TG to the underside of the roof deck and covering that with gypsum drywall, attached with mastic and nails. Finish the drywall joints according to manufacturer's instructions and cover the joint between beam and drywall with wood trim.

There's an alternative that will leave your ceiling looking the same. Remove the old roof shingles or work over them, if there's only one layer. Install Styrofoam TG

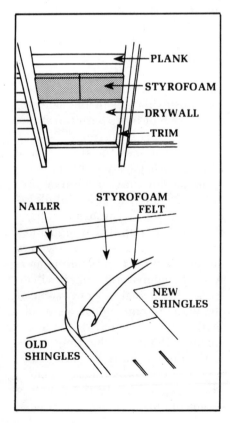

PLANK
STYROFOAM
DRYWALL
TRIM

NAILER
STYROFOAM FELT
NEW SHINGLES
OLD SHINGLES

and reshingle. For details, write Dow Chemical U.S.A., Dept. FH, Construction Materials, 2020 Dow Center, Midland, Mich. 48640.

Bedroom problem

Q. My carpeted bedroom is too cold in winter, and does not contain the coolness of my air conditioning unit in the summer, due to the fact that it lies directly above the garage. The ceiling of the garage is drywall and possibly already has insulation between it and the floor of the bedroom. Is this area simply insufficiently insulated, or must I add an extra ceiling?

F.Y., Wyckoff, N.Y.

A. You should check to see what insulation is currently between the roof of the garage and the floor of the bedroom. If there

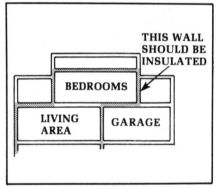

THIS WALL SHOULD BE INSULATED

BEDROOMS

LIVING AREA

GARAGE

isn't any in that area, definitely put some there. See a rock wool contractor and obtain an estimate on how much it would cost him to blow it in, that would give you the best insulation. If you wish to do the job yourself, first remove the drywall. Use 6" insulation if you want to do a thorough job. The second ceiling you name will help to an extent, but the most important insulation is between the floor of the bedroom and the garage ceiling. It would also be wise to check the insulation in the walls of the bedroom. If you plan to use the rock wool contractor, include this in your estimate if needed.

Dead air space

Q. I have a brick bungalow with furring, lath and plaster inside. There is considerable space in the unfinished basement between joist ends and the brick wall and air seems to blow up through here, behind the plaster. The attic floor is insulated with blankets between ceiling joists but the space in the walls is open here too. I could pour vermiculite into the spaces after plugging the basement end with blanket insulation or I could plug both ends with blanket insulation and let the dead air space serve as insulation. I would appreciate your advice.

D.J., Baltimore, Md.

A. If you can succeed in sealing both ends of these wall spaces you will have the least costly insulation. We would suggest you try this first as you can add the vermiculite later if you are not satisfied with the result. Use paint on your interior walls to provide a vapor barrier.

Existing walls

Q. My house has good metal siding. I don't want to remove the siding but would like to insulate the house and I don't want to have it blown in at the prices I've been quoted either. You have any suggestions?

J.N., Windham, N.Y.

A. You don't leave much choice but luckily there are pouring types that will do the job. This will take a small hole inside or outside between every pair of studs. If there are fire-stops between studs half way, the job gets complicated and under windows a new problem is made. You'll need two or three carefully applied coats of paint on these walls as pellet insulation has no vapor barrier. The only alternative is removal of all inside wall covering to work from inside the house.

Bay window

Q. Our all brick ranch house has projecting frame construction bay windows and they are cold. They're about 2' off the ground, clapboard exterior beneath the windows with hardboard 1/8" thick closing in the bottom. I don't know what if any insulation is used but wonder if this would help?

R.T., Mechanicsville, N.Y.

A. You may well find substandard insulation in wall areas as well as floor. Try removing the hardboard, installing batt insulation between the projecting joists and reclosing the bottom with thicker plywood. If that does not do enough, your next move would be pouring insulation in beneath the windows which can usually be done if you remove the apron and make a hole in the plaster or plasterboard through which you fill each area. If your complaint is really drafty construction, it may be flashing has been skimpy and dismantling the window area would be necessary to install it now. If the windows themselves leak cold air, the stop should be reset tighter and the putty checked.

Insulate basement

Q. I want to finish off the basement in my four-year-old ranch house. The basement is cement block with a poured concrete floor. The house is heated by oil-fired hot air. In making ceiling of gypsum board, is it of any value to insulate between the floor joists?

H.H., Poughkeepsie, N.Y.

A. Insulation between basement and the floor above would tend to keep all heat in the basement allowing none to warm the floor above. If the upper floor does not depend on this surplus heat for comfort, then you'd be wise to use some form of insulation to retain as much heat as possible in the basement.

Rigid foam

Q. My house is concrete blocks with no finishing on either side. I have purchased sufficient sheets of 1" thick Styrofoam® for insulating the house. Are commercial adhesives available for adequately gluing this material to concrete blocks? Is it practical to apply plaster to Styrofoam or can I glue wallboard to the Styrofoam?

D.L., Buford, Ga.

A. Yes, there are commercial adhesives available. All your questions are answered in much greater detail in a little folder "How to insulate masonry walls on the inside with Styrofoam TG brand insulation." Get a copy from Dow Chemical USA, Construction Materials, 2020 Dow Center, Midland, Mich. 48640, if your materials dealer cannot supply one.

Masonry wall

Q. I have a 25-year-old house with brick walls backed with hollow tile, plastered inside directly onto the masonry. I have trouble heating this house even though it is cool in the summer. I would like to know if there is any way to insulate these walls. The north end of the house is practically useless in winter.

J.A., McKeesport, Pa.

A. If there is a space between brick and tile or if the vents in the tile section run from top to bottom of the walls, you can have inorganic pellet type insulation poured into these wall spaces. If the walls are solid with no place for insulation, then furring, insulation and a new inner wall surfacing is the only solution.

Flooded insulation

Q. We have a house that was in a flood. The interior is all knotty pine with insulation in all walls. The entire inside has been washed with a detergent solution and a disinfectant but we still have a terrible odor. Can you tell me anything I can do to get rid of this odor?

C.E., Nutley, N.J.

A. No doubt the insulation inside the walls became saturated and has held dampness since the flood. This creates a situation where mold and dry rot and other smelly fungus can develop and grow. About the only way out would be to open the walls and remove the damp insulation or whatever else has been trapped behind the panels. At least you can salvage the wood and replace it. If air is allowed to circulate and dry out this area, new insulation may be substituted for that removed and the paneling replaced.

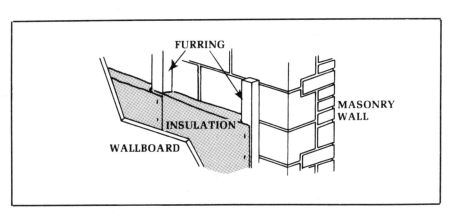

Block walls

Q. My house is of cinder block with gypsum wallboard on 2x3 studding. I plan using granular form of insulation in these walls between the studs. Is it necessary to put aluminum paint on the wallboard before applying finish paint to properly insulate these walls? Ceilings and floors already contain a pellet-type rock wool insulation.

F.P., Philadelphia, Pa.

A. It is unnecessary to use aluminum paint if you plan to use two coats of vinyl, alkyd, or latex base or oil enamel or semi-gloss paint as any of these provide a useful vapor barrier. None has any great insulating value.

Gas range question

Q. I want to place my gas range back against the wall flush with my base cabinets so it will have more of a built in look. Should I put insulating material between the wall and the range and if so what kind?

M.G., Detroit, Mich.

A. Most of the heat from a range goes up and concentrates above rather than behind or at the sides of a range. Usually the insulation built into a stove is sufficient to prevent any trouble. Some new models are designed specially to do just what you want done. With one not designed for this kind of an installation, you might add sheet asbestos on thin metal to the cabinet sides and to the wall immediately against the range.

Packed insulation

Q. I filled in the voids under a new triple window with tightly packed mineral wool insulation, packing it solid from the top before reinstalling the rough sill and placing the new window. Now I'm told I shouldn't have packed so tightly because the air doesn't circulate enough and consequently will breed silverfish. Is this true?

P.C., Cumberland, Md.

A. Packing loose fill insulation tightly cuts down the benefits of the enclosed air spaces and probably reduces the efficiency of the material as insulation. You'd have been better off to drop a section of batt insulation in the void, fastening it at the top. As for the silverfish, don't believe all you hear. They breed in damp places, not in cold and nothing breeds silverfish but other silverfish. Like any bug, two parents are necessary to start a crowd.

Vapor control

Q. I am insulating the ceiling of my bungalow using 3″ batts with a vapor barrier and do not know whether to lay the batts down onto the other side of the ceiling between joists or staple them up near the top of the joists so as to provide an air space between ceiling and batts.

R.G., Toronto, Ontario

A. Install the batts with the vapor barrier face down between the joists. It always goes toward the warmed side. Provide adequate ventilation in gable walls. Also, do not block eaves vents.

Paint vapor barrier

Q. I recently had my house insulated with the type of insulation that is blown into the spaces in the walls. This type of insulation does not include a vapor barrier but I've heard that a first coat of aluminum paint, prior to the final coat of interior paint, will act as a vapor barrier. Is there any truth to this?

D.H., Indian River, Mich.

A. Actually almost any interior paint with a vinyl, alkyd or latex base as well as washable enamels and semi-gloss paints can serve as vapor barriers. Make sure outer walls and ceilings are completely covered with two coats of one of these. Most fabric backed wall coverings also act as vapor barriers but old style flat interior paints do not.

Glidden's Insul-Aid® is a latex vapor barrier paint which more than meets FHA standards with a perm rating of .6. It goes on about as easily as any regular latex paint. Check your Yellow Pages for the Glidden dealer nearest you.

Sawdust insulation

Q. I am building a concrete block house. A friend told me to fill the core of the blocks with sawdust to make the house warmer. Will the sawdust have any insulation value?

A.M., St. Louis, Mo.

A. Sawdust does have some insulation value as long as it is dry, but the drawbacks to its use in the manner you suggest are many. If it gets wet it can rot or decay and it will compact leaving places without insulation. If you want a fill insulation, use an inorganic one that does not change when wet. A better solution is waterproof block walls plus furring plus a vapor barrier plus a panel material to finish the interior.

Balanced heating

Q. Considering the present concern with the "energy crisis" and conservation of fuel, the following question is posed. In a ranch house with an unheated, unneeded attic, which presently has full thickness (6″) fiberglass insulation in the flooring, is there any value in doubling the amount of insulation on the floor of this area? The question is raised in regard to the following points:

1. The conservation of fuel, i.e. an overall cost reduction in both the heating (hot air) during the winter and the central air conditioning during the summer.

2. The further evening out of temperatures in various rooms of the house.

J.K., Short Hills, N.J.

A. On the thermal insulation, check your utility company to find the R requirements for your area.

Regarding evening out the temperatures in the various rooms, balancing your heating system more closely might be a better way of achieving that.

Closed porch heat

Q. When we bought our 50-year old house we began several repairs on the closed porch. We replaced a single northern-exposure window with two storm windows facing east, we insulated, paneled with a dropped ceiling and carpeted. However, I would rather not keep the heat on in this room all winter long as it is seldom used. Instead, I thought we might open the door that connects the bedroom to the porch, using the bedroom's heat to also supply the heat for the porch. Could you tell me what I can do to keep this room warm without wasting fuel?

A.T., Brooklyn, N.Y.

A. For more economical heating of your porch, investigate the insulation under the floor. You could be losing considerable heat there. Other than this, there is not much you can do but keep the heat on in the porch if you expect it to stay warm enough to use during the winter. Leaving the door open to the bedroom and expecting that heat to be enough for both rooms just is asking more out of the bed-

room's supply than it is planned for. You may want to weatherstrip the exterior door on the porch more thoroughly since you don't use it much, but even this will not make heat.

Crawl space

Q. I have no basement but a complete foundation with a crawl space 24″ between ground and floor joists. There is a vapor barrier under the subfloor. The floors are cold and I wish to insulate them but have been advised against it because of their construction. Would appreciate your advice as the cold floors are bad for the children.

S.B., Crown Point, Ind.

A. Use insulation between the joists. Blanket types can be held in place between the joists with wire laced back and forth between staples driven into the framing or you can use rigid insulation boards fastened across the bottom of the joists. Chicken wire is another material which can be used. If your foundation is fitted with vents, provide covers for these which can be closed in winter, opened in spring.

Concrete slab

Q. I intend to put a heating system in my wood framed garage. I have already put 1/2″ insulating board on the ceiling and walls and now I would like to put down a concrete floor. I was told that the floor must be insulated but I'm not sure of the proper procedure. Is it necessary to put insulation underneath the entire area of the concrete floor?

W.S., Niagara Falls, N.Y.

A. There is no necessity for insulating underneath the entire area of a slab on grade. The usual practice in new construction is to

put a 2″ thick sheet of waterproof insulation at the edges of the slab, extending down vertically about 24″ or horizontally under the edge of the slab 24″. In your case it would be best to dig a trench inside the existing foundation wall and put in 2″ of an asphalt-enclosed insulation before you pour the slab.

Radiant heat loss

Q. I have 4-1/2 rooms on a concrete slab with radiant heating piping in it. The heat warms the foundation to such a degree that the ground outside is warm in a strip about 8″ wide; when fields are frozen, this area is wet. How can I stop this loss of heat?

D.V., Painesville, Ohio

A. The building contractor was definitely at fault here. This type floor is usually surrounded with some type of perimeter insulation to prevent this heat loss from the edges of the slab. We don't have sufficient detail on your problem to provide a good solution but the simplest thing to do is now provide perimeter insulation at the outside of the foundation by cementing on asphalt-impregnated insulating board, covering it for protection as required.

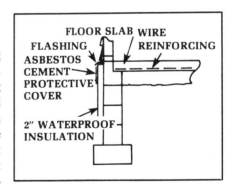

Damaged insulation

Q. Three years ago my husband and I built a family room addition onto our house. Under this addition is a crawl space only. We have tried to insulate this but the insulation has become saturated and pried loose from the floor joists. Is there some way to insulate this area permanently?

P.L., Westmoreland, N.H.

A.   Preventing the problem you describe would have been easier than remedying it now. In effect you've enclosed a damp area which became more and more damp. The insulation is acting like a sponge, absorbing the moisture as it rises from the earth. A layer of 4-mil polyethylene film over the earth in the crawl space is effective in keeping this moisture down in the earth where it belongs. You probably haven't provided sufficient ventilation for the area. Wet insulation does a poor job of insulating and holding dampness against floor joists will lead to wood rot.

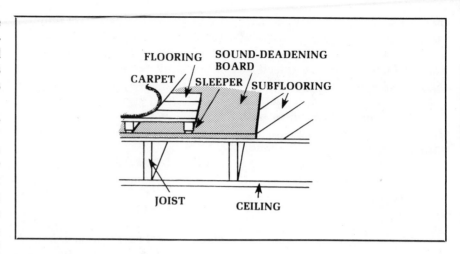

Soundproofing

Q.   I live in a two-story house and get a great deal of noise from the people living upstairs. Is there anything that can be done to soundproof floors and ceilings?

O.K., Atlanta, Ga.

A.   There have been tremendous advances in soundproofing new homes but, unfortunately, there is not much that can be done in existing dwellings without considerable alteration of the structure. If you can get your neighbor upstairs to put down carpeting over felt or sponge rubber padding, the noise will be greatly reduced. Acoustical tile on your own ceiling will also help but will not completely muffle noise from upstairs.

Noisy ceiling

Q.   I need information on soundproofing a ceiling to keep the noise from coming down from the upstairs apartment. There is enough room to drop the ceilings if necessary.

R.G., Port Lambton, Ontario

A.   You can cut the sound transmission somewhat between the apartment above and your own quarters by keeping your windows and storm windows closed. There is some bounce if you are near another house and both you and the people above have windows open on the same side of the house. Beyond that and stuffing any cracks around pipes and the like, your best bet is to go upstairs and fix from the top down. A good carpet for the floor upstairs is the first helpful hint. A second layer of flooring on sleepers, affixed with resilient clips, is the next thing to do. It will work even better if you put the clips on top of a layer of sound-deadening board or at least insulate between the floor and the new floor. There is very little you can do from down below. When the sound is that far, it has already come through the floor structure. Keep it above the floor as much as you can to lessen the problem.

Basement noise

Q.   I want to finish my basement to be as soundproof as possible. The floor above is 1/2" plywood with hardwood flooring and sound passes through it extremely easy. Cost is a big concern, but what do you suggest?

P.J., Coleman, Pa.

A.   Sound travels in different ways. You can keep some of the basement noise in the basement just by weatherstripping the basement-to-upstairs door so airborne sound doesn't go around the door. You can cut down noise at the source by resilient mountings on equipment that transmits vibrations. You can keep some of the noise in the basement with a solid, thick barrier. Cost-wise answer here is a gypsum wallboard ceiling, preferably mounted free of the floor structure. See your lumber or drywall dealer for a product made by U.S. Gypsum, called resilient channel. This is attached to the joists, then wallboard is screwed to it using an electric screwgun. The resilient construction reduces noise through ceilings. Perforated acoustical tile on the basement side of this will cut down the "bounced" noise within the basement area, absorbing it and making it quieter.

Noisy heating ducts

Q.   The expansion and contraction of the heating ducts from my gas, forced-air furnace, causes a lot of noise when the blower first begins and towards the end of the heating period. The ducts run between a plastered family room ceiling and upper bedroom floor. Is there any way to eliminate such noisy cracking and popping?

H.M., Saginaw, Mich.

A. The noise from the expansion and contraction of metal ducts is one of those phenomena that just cannot be eliminated. It can sometimes be lessened by having your furnace man adjust the furnace to go on and off more often, before the ducts get so cold, so that the temperature contrast is not as great. Sometimes the noise can partially be absorbed by insulating the ducts from the surrounding structure. With a plastered ceiling and a carpeted floor, though, this is not as easy to do as it sounds.

Lining a fan area

Q. The fan in our central air system was recently "boosted" to provide better distribution of cool air through the ducts. I am considering lining the area where the fan is located with some type of sound-absorbent material. Which material would be best: acoustical tile, rug samples, waffle type rug pads? I will probably try to put it on 1/4″ plywood and attach that to the wall of a closet-type area housing the air conditioner/furnace.

W.S., Datellite Beach, Fla.

A. Lining the fan area may help some. The rug samples would be as good as anything else. The answer might be a resilient type mounting of fan or fan and furnace/air conditioner unit. Ask your air conditioning man about this.

Bathroom noise

Q. Our upstairs bathroom is between the living room and master bedroom. As close as it is to the living room, I am frequently concerned about the normal sounds that can be heard if the user is not extremely careful. I had the floor carpeted but it helped very little. The door is a hollow core door. I read a long time ago about padding the inside of a door for decoration

as well as to deaden the sounds. Would this help?

T.T., Walla Walla, Wash.

A. Carpeting the floor would tend to quiet the bathroom. Padding the door would have much the same effect, absorbing some noise and interfering with its passage through the door. It would also help to weatherstrip the bathroom door to prevent sounds from simply traveling around the door. Any openings where pipes go into the common wall should also be gasketed or packed. Airborne sound travels wherever air can move. If there is a medicine cabinet set into the common wall, this is another easy path for noise to travel. Mechanically caused noises like water rushing through pipes are less easily subdued.

Duct noise

Q. I bought a 14′ × 68′ trailer house and the heating is not bad. The trouble is the heating pipe to the far end is very noisy when heating or cooling. Is there something I can do to quiet it?

E.H., Sedan, Minn.

A. The usual cause of noise in metal heating ducts is the contraction/expansion caused by a rapid change in temperature. Perhaps, if the duct that goes to the far end of your mobile home were better insulated, the noise might be reduced. You might use padded hanger straps to support the duct. It also is possible that the register and duct joint are loose and make a rattling noise. A couple of sheet metal screws will fix that, attaching the duct end more securely.

Condominium wall

Q. Is there any way I can soundproof one wall in my bedroom that joins my next door neighbor's bedroom wall? They are very noisy

and since this is a condominium, I would like to improve it.

B.R., Chicago, Ill.

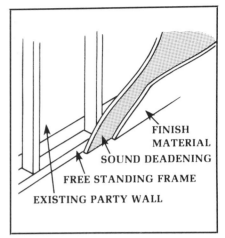

A. Although you didn't say what the construction of the party wall is, matters might be improved by building a second wall free from structural attachment to this existing wall. However, you would have to sacrifice the space required. There are various ways of building such a barrier (one shown in the sketch). Sound deadening board on studs with gypsum wallboard is helpful. You can write Homasote, Box 7240, West Trenton, N.J. 08628 and other makers of sound-conditioning materials. Find out whose line is carried locally and write that manufacturer for suggestions.

Terminology

Q. We have been looking at new houses lately and are constantly being told they are "sound-conditioned". Just what kind of malarkey is this? If they mean soundproof why don't the salesmen say so?

M.A., Glendale, N.Y.

A. It's not malarkey and it is not soundproofing. A totally soundproof room is the sort of test facility major manufacturers use to determine the noise rates of appliances, or sound transmission of various materials. You'd soon go out of your mind in a really sound-proof room. Sound conditioning is a term used rather loosely to indicate that some attention has been given to curtailing the transfer of objectionable noises and to reducing the reverberation of the normal noises of living to a generally quieter pitch. It may take the form of acoustical tile to absorb the clatter produced in a kitchen or the noise children make playing or it may mean planning practices which isolate the "quiet" areas of a house from the "noisy" ones have been employed. Sound conditioning would include insulated ducts, quiet-flush toilets, silent switches, medicine cabinets not back to back, double walling between bedrooms and living areas, etc.

New construction

Q. I wish to soundproof a bedroom and bathroom of a new cottage I am building. With drywall construction what would be the most effective method?

H.A., New York, N.Y.

A. If you use staggered 2 × 3 studs in your walls with rock wool blankets woven between them

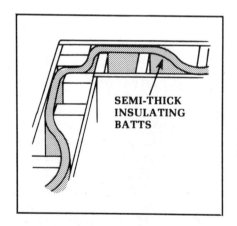

SEMI-THICK
INSULATING
BATTS

you'll find sound transmission cut considerably. Select the quietest fixtures you can afford and install them with all due regard for carefully supported, padded piping runs. Use a wall-mounted rather than a recessed medicine chest. Use acoustical tile on the ceilings

to lessen reverberation of sounds originating in the rooms and close off both areas with solid heavy doors, fully equipped with weather-stripping for a tight fit. If you use forced warm air or air conditioning ducts, have the layout made with quiet in mind and use lined ducts.

Exterior noises

Q. I have a room that faces a busy street at the foot of a hill and the sound of changing gears to climb that hill is twice as much noise as would be normal for this spot. I wonder if there is anything inside or out that I can do to soundproof this room?

N.E., Cincinnati, Ohio

A. A solid masonry wall without openings in the direction of the noise would be the ideal thing, particularly if the finish was gypsum lath and plaster on furring strips. You need to approach the solid heavy barrier idea to get any results at all. Sealing the window and setting in storm sash against felt or rubber cushions in the window frame will help some, particularly in taking up the vibration of low sounds. Planting and masonry walls between house and street are not usually thick nor high enough to have much effect, though in theory they would help.

Duplex noises

Q. We purchased a new duplex home this year. The problem is that we can hear conversation through the wall separating us from the owners of the other half. What can I do to make the wall soundproof?

F.F., Mays Landing, N.J.

A. You don't say what the wall between the two units is at present. Generally speaking, additional heavy-weight material independent of the present wall so as to enclose an air space would offer

the best chance of reducing sound transmission. This might be plaster on gypsum lath on 2x2 studs erected as a freestanding wall surface 1" to 2" away from the surface of the present wall.

Acoustical plaster

Q. I have a wall between two apartments which I desire to soundproof with acoustical plaster. Part of the wall will be bookcases but part will be hardboard plus wire plus this plaster. Question is will that be sufficient and will this wall be soundproof?

M.F., Chicago, Ill.

A. If you used acoustical plaster on lath on studding or metal furring channels on both sides of a good solid heavy concrete wall you might not be able to hear a thing between the two apartments. Plaster alone is not a good enough barrier and when you use bookcases as part of the wall you offer another path for sound to penetrate.

Lowered ceiling

Q. The first floor of my two family duplex resounds with most of the noise from the second floor. Is there any way to correct this? I thought that I would lower the kitchen ceiling about 6".

S.M., Syracuse, N.Y.

A. You should derive some help lowering the ceiling provided it does not act as a sounding box and multiply the noise that reaches it. If you will keep the new joists separated from the old ones, impact noise will not be directly transferred. Insulation in a double floor above would work better but you'll get some benefits using batts or blankets between the floor joists and the new ceiling's supports. Use gypsum wallboard as the barrier part of your new ceiling, covering it with acoustical tile if you wish to reduce the noises generated in your own kitchen.

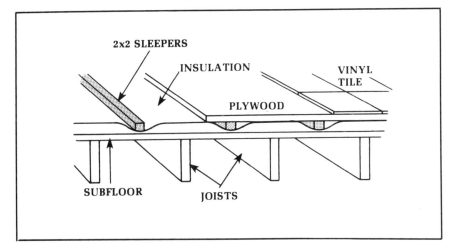

Labels: 2x2 SLEEPERS, INSULATION, VINYL TILE, PLYWOOD, SUBFLOOR, JOISTS

ability. Can they be washed and cleaned of kitchen grease, etc. satisfactorily?

R.B., Greenburg, Ind.

A. You say "they" as if all a-coustical tiles were identical in this feature. Far from it. There are some washing would just about ruin, some that can be washed gently once or twice and some, meant for kitchen applications, that can be washed as easily as a painted surface. Just make sure you look at the latter types when you make your selection.

Playroom floor

Q. What under vinyl tile in our attic would take care of footstep and "drop" noises? This will be a playroom for two little boys but we'd like to be able to hear our-selves think in the living room below it.

F.R., Saginaw, Mich.

A. Sound conditioning a floor is rather expensive. Double flooring is one good method you can use. Assume you have just a board subfloor now. Lay blanket insula-tion over this and using resilient clips attach 2x2 sleepers to the subfloor. On the sleepers put your 5/8" plywood subfloor on which you lay the vinyl tiles in the usual way.

Shop noises

Q. I would like to turn my base-ment area into a combination play-room and shop and to finish it in such a manner that no sounds will rise up to the apartment above. Can you tell me how I can sound-proof the basement completely and economically?

F.H., Brooklyn, N.Y.

A. Complete soundproofing cannot be achieved economically. Sound waves can be stopped by heavy rigid barriers that are not vibrated by the sounds and can be absorbed by loose materials by

which the sound waves are broken up and "lost". Keep all your noise-producing tools on the floor but mounted on vibration reducing mounts. A hung ceiling of acous-tical material will help greatly in absorbing sounds in the basement. A tight-fitting weather-stripped door at the head of the stairs is another possibility.

Footsteps overhead

Q. I have divided my home into two apartments and wish to tile the upstairs floor. How do I elimi-nate the noise of people walking which can be heard in the down-stairs apartment?

A.A., South Amboy, N.J.

A. Total elimination of walking sounds which are impact noises is difficult. You can quiet them some-what with cork or rubber tiles rather than harder types. Sub-stituting 90-pound felt for the usual layer under tiles has some advantage. Carpet and pad would be quieter than tile in any event. A double floor is your best bet.

Kitchen tile

Q. I'm sold on the idea that acoustical tiles in the kitchen and family room area would lessen noise and possibly save my nerves but wonder about their clean-

Attractive tile

Q. We have seen some of the very attractive patterned acous-tical tile for ceilings. Can these be put over not-too-badly-cracked plaster without furring strips?

E.S., Niagara Falls, Ontario

A. Plaster ceilings in good enough shape to support the tiles can be covered using adhesive. Pay careful attention to the instructions about amount of adhesive to use. It is usually 5 dabs on the 12" x 12" tiles. Also with some types you need to use a tongue and grooved tile.

French doors

Q. We have French doors, glazed, which separate our living room from a hall that leads to an apartment upstairs. We are anxious to make this arrangement more soundproof and incidentally make the room warmer. Can you tell me how to go about it?

M.R., Brooklawn, N.J.

A. You can improve matters on both scores by making flush doors. Either remove the glass entirely and fill the area with insulation board or cut bits of board to fill the pane recesses. Use 1/4" plywood or thinner hardboard to surface the doors, solid on your side, perforated on the hall side. Most important is to make a tight fit on the doors, you'll have to reset the stops for the thicker door anyhow. Set in a strip of rubber or felt for them to close against. This will save heat as well as bar sounds.

Soundproof shop

Q. I have a small room converted to a shop in an apartment where I have a power saw. While this is on a table with pneumatic wheels, it is important that the whole room be soundproofed. What material is available which will prevent the transmission of sound?

B.S., Bronx, N.Y.

A. Heavy mass lowers sound transmission while "fluff" absorbs noise. A combination of the two will help quiet your shop but it would cost far too much to make it absolutely sound proof. First of all, follow good maintenance practices to keep your table saw running as quietly as possible. Second absorb some of the sound created in the room with acoustical tile, probably on walls and ceilings both. Isolate or insulate any openings between your shop and surrounding rooms even to the extent of weatherstripping this interior door.

Tiles do not help

Q. I stripped the plaster and lath off two ceilings in our three-family house to replace the cracked and broken ceiling with what I hoped was something better. Put strapping to the joists and stapled 1/2″ × 12″ × 12″ block fiber insulation board ceilings up. I now find I can hear the family upstairs as if they were in the same flat with me. I put blocks on other ceilings in the house over the plaster and they don't let the sound through like these other two. Can I put 2″ of rock wool between the joists, fur and add another block ceiling below the new one?

J.P., Cambridge, Mass.

A. Putting insulation between the joists will not cut out impact noise which is transmitted through the joists themselves. Insulating tile is not acoustical tile. The plaster surface did the sound stopping before you removed it. You would probably be out less money if you remove the insulating tile, put two layers of 3/8″ thick gypsum wallboard over the furring, reinstalling the fiber tiles on that. Fiber tile does absorb some sound within the room though nowhere near as well as acoustical tile would.

Noisy closet

Q. My washer-dryer is in a centrally located closet in our ranch house and the whole place echos with the noise it makes. Is there anything that will help?

J.B., Cliffside, N.J.

A. First make sure the machine is operating as quietly as possible and is mounted on vibration reducing pads of some sort. Then you may absorb some of the noise it makes by lining the closet with insulation behind perforated hardboard or even acoustical tile on walls as well as ceiling.

Ceiling tile

Q. We are thinking about putting ceiling tile of the acoustical type in our bedroom but I do not like the looks of those little holes. I don't suppose it can be papered over but can acoustical tiles be painted?

R.G., Hickory, N.C.

A. Acoustical tiles can sometimes be painted without reducing their efficiency greatly but not wallpapered. If it is the appearance of the tile you do not like, we'd suggest you visit your building materials dealer again. There have been many attractive designs,

some even in color, developed in these products in recent years. You'll be pleasantly surprised.

Split level sound

Q. We have a lovely new home with a cathedral ceiling over kitchen, dining and living room area which is really all one big room with just the cabinet arrangement in the kitchen separating it from the other two areas. Trouble is I am not a quiet cook and the clatter from the kitchen is just too much in the living room. We wondered if something could be done.

L.D., Greenwich, Conn.

A. Something can be done but you'll no longer have a cathedral ceiling in the kitchen. Depending on how the cabinets are installed you can build or hang a ceiling surfaced with acoustical tile over that area, which will go a long ways toward absorbing kitchen-created noise. There are a number of suspended ceiling systems you might investigate, some of which incorporate lighting. You didn't mention countertop and floor surfacing—vinyl and vinyl tile would be quieter than, say, ceramic tile. Mounting small motored appliances on resilient pads will cut down noise there, using plastic shelf covering helps too. Studying kitchen storage habits to eliminate a lot of clatter-producing activities is another approach to the problem.

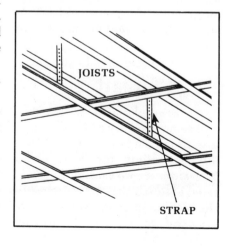

Attic ventilation

Q. We are planning to put a new roof on our one-and-a-half-story house and would like to know if you recommend putting ventilators on the sides of the roof to ventilate the crawl space in the attic? All of the aluminum ventilators that I have seen have stained the shingles on the roof after being in place for a while through rain and other harsh weather.

D.S., Wooster, Ohio

A. One of the good qualities about aluminum is that it will not stain through rust or corrosion. The ventilators that you have seen must have been made of galvanized (zinc-coated) sheet metal, or even ungalvanized sheet metal which

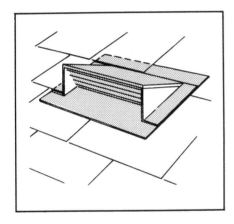

would be much less protected. The zinc has a tendency to wear off; so, unless the sheet metal is anodized, it will eventually rust and stain the roofing. One easy way to prevent this is to put a coat of lacquer on the sheet metal ventilators for protection. There should be no problems with aluminum, though.

Attic "breathing"

Q. Several years ago I insulated and remodeled my attic. Recently, a roofing company told me that I did not allow for "breathing." Therefore, condensation accumulated between the attic ceiling and the roof, causing the shingles and plywood to buckle. I've never heard of this "breathing" space. Is this a fact? If so, how can I remedy this problem without destroying my remodeling job?

T.S., Fairlawn, N.J.

A. The "breathing" space the roofers told you about is very true. by stuffing the area full of insulation, you did not allow for air circulation to carry off excessive humidity. That moisture condensed and deteriorated the shingles and plywood to the point where they buckled. That needs to be corrected. It may be that you installed the insulation properly except at the juncture of wall and roof where a lot of homeowners go wrong, running the insulation right over the undereave vents designed to let in air above the roof insulation. Open up these eave vents, and provide roof or ridge vents for the air to escape.

Trapped hot air

Q. I need some advice as to how I can get rid of trapped hot air in my now air conditioned cottage living room. The room is constructed with 2 x 8s, spaced 24" o.c., butting into a 2 x 8 ridge board covered with roof decking (1-3/8" thick planks). The roof is 1 in 12 pitch and the walls are all insulated, as are the drapes that cover all the Thermopane windows and sliding doors. There is an open-beamed ceiling without an attic. Can I use vents or a fan?

M.H. Conemaugh, Pa.

A. You can use either vents or a roof fan. Turbine roof vents would work for you, too, and you should examine and price fans and vents locally. Consider seriously some type of exhaust fan with louvers that could be closed when installed in each gable end, assuming your roof has a sufficiently deep overhang at the gables. Going through roof decking that is also the interior surface of the ceiling might be a bit sticky due to the weather staining possibilities, but it is easily controlled with good flashing. With a switch-controlled exhaust fan at each end you could take advantage of the wind and save electricity, running the fans only when necessary. For appearance, you might consider a matched pair of louvers, only one with a fan behind it, at both gables. Determine the cubic feet of air to be moved before you visit your local dealer so that he can show you fans and louvered vents in the right size range to control your problem.

Blistering paint

Q. My 60-year-old two-story wood frame house was painted five years ago but has blistered badly and needs repainting. I've been told that the problem is moisture escaping from inside and that I should "vent" the whole house. What's the best technique in "venting" a house?

J.H., Washington, D.C.

A. Moisture, like temperature, seeks its own level, which means that interior moisture will move through the wall to try to equalize with exterior moisture. This problem can be solved by (1) holding interior moisture levels at not more than 40 to 50%, (2) installing a vapor barrier so that moisture cannot pass through the walls and peel the paint when it reaches the siding and (3) through vents installed to provide the moisture an escape route. In your case, reduce interior moisture levels by using kitchen and bath exhaust vents. Apply two coats of oil paint, vinyl wallcovering, or Glidden's Insul-Aid to the interior side of outside walls to provide a vapor barrier so moisture cannot pass into the wall. Proper attic venting by use of soffit and ridge vents, gable vents or turbines will allow the moisture to pass out of the attic. There are also small round vents made to fit in siding. These must be installed between each pair of studs to vent each cavity. To find a source for siding vents write to Midget Louver Co., 800 Main, Norwalk, Conn. 06852.

Attic fan inadequate

Q. The attic fan in our home does not do nearly the job I feel it should. I have seen attic fans in similar size homes cause a strong breeze, whereas ours causes only a slight breeze in the hall where it is. There is no breeze from the windows, which are all casement. Someone has suggested that our problem is caused by the casement windows. What do you say?

K.D., Dallas, Tex.

A. The way the casement windows may be causing your trouble is that you may have too many of them open too wide. If you close all but one window, you could probably feel the breeze. The fans are rated to move so many feet of air per minute or hours. You should be using the fan to draw air from a window that allows greatest circulation in the house.

Another possibility is that the exit louvers in the attic are too small and a back pressure builds up. Then the fan would churn the air without exhausting it.

Noisy fan

Q. I have a very good portable fan with a reversing blade for intake and exhaust and a hi-lo speed for each direction. The fan is great except that it has a high velocity of air volume which is annoying to listen to in the background. How can I reduce the volume electric capacity to lower the speed and reduce the noise?

E.J., Orlando, Fla.

A. It may not be wise to try to alter the speed of the fan further.

Just run it on low and set the whole fan on a good rubber pad or other absorbent padding. Sound caused by vibration accounts for a good deal of the noise of a fan and this simple expedient will get rid of a lot of it.

Attic vents

Q. Recently we had insulation blown into our attic. Our house is a single story with a peaked roof. Dormers are at either end of the roof. Around the house were vents, under the eaves, about 4″ x 10″ in size. When the insulation was blown in, the small vents were covered over. The man doing the work said they should be covered. Is this true?

J.C., Orange, Calif.

A. Vents should *not* be covered. Ventilation prevents condensation. Vents in both sides of the attic permit cross ventilation. You

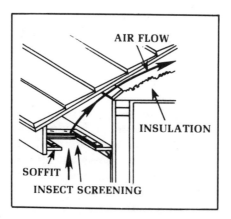

should clean out the vents, and may have to install baffle plates around them to keep insulation from plugging them again. You also need ridge vents or roof vents to let the upflowing air escape.

Wet attic

Q. Several years before I bought my present home, the previous owner installed aluminum siding

and a new roof over the old one. During my first winter, I discovered a bad condensation problem on one side of the roof. I removed part of the attic ceiling and found that the original louvers were almost completely blocked by the new siding. After I unblocked them, the condensation diminished slightly. How can I solve this problem?

N.D., New Hyde Park, N.Y.

A. Condensation is a frequent homeowner's problem. You partially solved it when you provided additional ventilation above the insulation in your attic. If you have not already done so, you should try ventilating the area behind the kneewall as well. Is there insulation in the floor area behind the kneewall? Properly vapor-sealed insulation in this area would also help alleviate your problem. Finally, check to be sure that air can circulate above the insulation in the slant-ceilinged portions of your attic.

Louvers in the roof

Q. I have just bought two aluminum ventilating louvers to install in my pitched roof. Can you tell me what to do first?

R.S., Ames, Iowa

A. Cut an opening in the roof sheathing to admit the louver so that the flange of the louver lies flat on the sheathing. If it is too large to fit between two rafters, you'll have to cut rafters to admit the louver. Place a header of the same size stock as the rafters across both cut ends. Metal flashing is then applied around the louver.

Too much ventilation

Q. I have a one-story 28′ x 40′ ranch type home with a wide roof overhang. In the underside of the overhang there is a 2″ wide slot running the full length of the house for ventilation, front and rear sides. My heating bill seems abnormally high. Is this much ventilation necessary? Would partial closure help in reduction of fuel use?

G.L., Livonia, Mich.

A. That much ventilation is good to keep condensation out of the house top. The problem is more likely to be insufficient insulation in the ceiling. You want to keep the heat in the house, and not let it escape to the attic.

Louvers and shingles

Q. I thought I'd be smart and reroof at the same time I installed venting louvers on our hip roofed house. I got the louvers on all right and with the help of your past issues think I have the shingling figured out all right. What I'm not sure about is exactly how the flashing is to go at the sides of the metal vent.

P.F., Baltimore, Md.

A. You're doing fine. Shingle your roof up to the vent. Extend the flashing for the down slope side over the top of the shingles, sealing it with asphalt and nailing it down. On the up-slope side and both lateral sides the flashing should extend under the shingles at least 6" and up to 12" if yours is a low pitched roof. Put this flashing in place and then shingle, cutting the shingles for a neat joint against the upturn of the flashing at the sides of the vent. Flashing extends up the sides of the louver and is sealed to it with asphalt. Bed the edges of the butting shingles in asphalt, too.

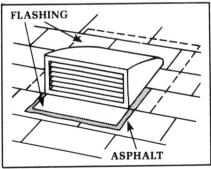

FLASHING

ASPHALT

Louvers for hip roof

Q. I have an unfinished attic under a hip roof. We think the house would be cooler if this were ventilated although the floor is insulated. How do you install gable end louvers when you have no gable ends?

S.F., Chicago, Ill.

A. You don't use gable end louvers. There are ventilating louvers designed for pitched roofs that you can use; if your overhang is large enough, soffit vents for intake and the others for outlet work very well. There is also on the market a ridge vent for homes which may present installation problems in some cases but is very effective and more attractive. Some builders use a triangular vent at the ends of the ridge, bringing out a peaked roof for protection over it but this would require considerably more construction in an existing house.

Leaking louvers

Q. I have a problem with my new home which has triangle louvers in the gable ends. Last winter we had a blizzard, dry snow, strong wind. Had about 2" of snow in the attic, moisture came through plaster. I was thinking of making a sheet metal hood that would stand away from the building 4" or 5" and open at the bottom or top and bottom. Do you think something like this is logical?

V.W., Sandusky, Ohio

A. The idea isn't too practical. Snow would probably work around the hood. If you have this sort of snow very much during the worst part of winter, it might be best to provide a cover for the louver on the more exposed side. If you want to go to the trouble and expense, you could substitute adjustable louvers for those you have, selecting a type that can be closed manually when desired.

Attic snowdrifts

Q. When there is a Northeastern, the snow sifts through the louver on the east side of my attic and lands on my insulation, building up to 2" or 3" sometimes. Here it melts and drips through to the ceiling below. We want to finish off the attic but must correct this problem first. Can you suggest a remedy?

R.B., Atkinson, N.H.

A. Why not close the louver in winter? Your other louvers will probably be adequate for the short time during the worst of the season. When you finish rooms in the attic, I would assume these same louvers will ventilate the remainder of the attic space. In that case, the present size will be more than ample and can probably be reduced by the 50% adding rustproof wire screening inside and out would cost in reduced efficiency. You could also substitute a louver with movable vanes that can be open or closed at will.

Choice of attic fan

Q. I have a house with a finished attic and air space about 5' high at the ridge. I plan to install an attic fan to cool these upper rooms. Some say the horizontal fan laid on rafters with gable end louvers is best. Others say the most efficient is a vertical fan placed at one end of the attic with a single automatic louver in front of it. What do you say?

R.G., Tuckahoe, N.Y.

A. Your choice would seem to be limited by possible louver area available. The horizontal type, mounted over a ceiling opening with automatically operating louvers in the ceiling would be best. Use of two gable end louvers with this type would not involve complete reconstruction of the area, just enlargement of existing louvers. Size of fan needed will decide the matter definitely but a vertical fan before a single gable end opening would probably have insufficient louver area.

Ranch house fan

Q. In a small, one story, no-basement ranch house, where is the best place for a large fan?
A.F., Riverhead, N.Y.

A. You probably have a center hall in the type of house you describe and it is the ideal location for an attic fan. Center it under the roof, directly above automatic shutters set in the ceiling. Make sure the exhaust vents in the gable ends are sufficient in size to permit the amount of air moved by the fan free passage to the outdoors.

Attic fan on flat roof

Q. I would like to install a large fan in my home similar to an attic fan but the house has a flat roof instead of an attic. Can you advise me where I can get information?
A.P., Brooklyn, N.Y.

A. It is quite possible to install an attic fan on a flat roof by building a sort of cupola on top of the roof to house the fan. Install a louver in the ceiling directly below the fan housing and mount the fan vertically to discharge in the direction from which you can expect the fewest heavy winds. Quite a few fan manufacturers include instruction on the erection of this type of housing in their installation details.

Ineffective attic fan

Q. I have an L shaped house with a truss roof. We recently installed an attic fan which has to move about 4976 cubic feet of air pulling air through two windows only as the house is not complete. But if you don't sit right in front of

a window you aren't cool at all. This is a 36″ fan with 1/5 HP motor, 600 rpm. Is the motor or fan too small or is there a certain way to box them in to get them to work?
C.N., St. Louis, Mo.

A. Your fan would probably work right if placed in the ceiling. Be sure you have adequate louver opening and equal amount of intake area, according to the manufacturer's recommendations. When placed in a confined area the fan develops a back-draft that makes it virtually useless.

Limited fan space

Q. My bungalow has two finished rooms upstairs with a total cubic content of 9,700 feet. There is a dead air space above 3′ high and the length of the house, with an 18″ square louver at each end. There is no way to get into this space so it would be impossible to install an attic fan in the ceiling. The only place I can figure to mount a fan would be over the stairwell that opens into one room upstairs. Is this method practical and efficient?
E.T., Baldwin, N.Y.

A. You could use a ceiling mounted fan into that dead air space. After the opening is cut you can get in although it would be cramped. For the cubic volume of air you would need a 36″ fan and a louver area of 13.4 sq. ft. You could get this area removing the gable ends entirely from the attic ceiling to ridge to make triangular louvers. To put the fan over a stairwell is good practice and so long as the attic rooms are open to the stairway the entire house should be cooled by this method.

Attic air currents

Q. I have a one story brick veneer house with an insulated

expandable attic. I plan putting an attic fan in one of the windows. I plan to intake air from my cellar rather than the first floor living quarters to take advantage of cooler air. There are four 30″ x 12″ screened basement windows. When figuring the fan capacity in cubic feet of air moved, do I include the cubic volume of my cellar as well as the living quarters?
R.R., West Springfield, Mass.

A. You should include the volume of the cellar in your calculations since you will be drawing air from this area as well as the rest. The important thing is that you have adequate louver area for the fan selected and that the fan should not move air more rapidly out through the louvers than it can be drawn in through those windows. Remember that screen wire over an opening reduces its actual capacity by 50%.

Installing fan

Q. Is it much of a job to install an attic fan in a single story house? There is only about 4′ to work in above the ceiling joists and only a trapdoor arrangement to get into it. Could you tell me enough so I know what to expect?
W.T., Hinton, W.Va.

A. Actual installation of modern packaged attic fans is not very involved. Most manufacturers include quite detailed installation instructions with the fan. What it amounts to is finding one joist for one side of the opening, marking and cutting the ceiling material to the dimensions required and then removing everything that is in the way—ceiling, insulation and intervening joists. You then need headers across the cut ends of the joists the same size stock as the joists. If necessary, threaded rods will carry the weight up to the roof rafters.

The framed opening is lined with 1x4s, usually, and the fan assembly set in place. Wiring is simple and the on-off switch set in a convenient wall as desired. The ceiling louver or shutter is installed in the ceiling opening, held in with screws. You probably won't even need your trapdoor as most of the work can be done from below and through the opening made.

Size of fan

Q. How do I find out how large an attic fan I need for a small Cape Cod with an expanded attic?
W.L., Hempstead, N.Y.

A. You can figure the size fan you need by first finding the number of cubic feet of air the fan must move. Multiply house length by house width by room height for the first floor, then in the case of your attic determine the additional cubic feet of air there. Deduct 10% from the total of the two for closets and other areas you needn't cool and you have the cubic feet of air to be moved. Fan blade size and speed determines the number of cubic feet of air a fan can move each minute. In your area, select a fan that can move about 2/3 your total air volume each minute.

Insect screening

Q. I am going to install a 36" attic exhaust fan. The manufacturer required 18 square feet of exhaust area with # 8 mesh wire. I have tried to find out what this is but have not had any luck. The soffit exhausts are going to be installed in a 30" wide overhang and I want to use a mesh screening that will keep out insects. How many soffit exhaust areas will I need to have 18 square feet of exhaust area using regular insect screening wire?
W.H., Far Rockaway, N.Y.

A. Insect screening reduces the available open air area of a screened square by 50%. # 8 wire is 1/2" mesh, number 8 wire weave, galvanized. With most makes this reduces the available open air space in an area covered with it by 25%. It does not insect proof the openings but it does keep out rats, mice, birds, etc. To calculate, multiply the total free air area by 2 if you use insect screening, by 1-1/2 if you use # 8 wire mesh to get the total opening area required. Divide this by the number of vents you'd like to use. For instance: you need 18 square feet open air space or 36 square feet of screened vents using insect screening. That's 18 vents if each is 2 square feet.

Louver area

Q. The gable end louvers in my one story house are only 18" across the bottom of the triangular grillework. There is insect screening behind this. We are getting an attic fan to put in the hall ceiling. Do I need bigger louvers?
I.O., Iron Mountain, Mich.

A. Chances are you do indeed need larger louvers at the gable ends but on the basis of the information you included I can't tell you how much larger. For instance, if your fan will move 7,200 cubic feet of air a minute and you plan metal louvers you need 12.2 square feet of louver area but if you use wood louvers, figure 16 square feet. Your fan dealer should be able to help you figure exactly what you need with the fan you are buying.

Clearance for fan

Q. My roof, over the place where it seems to me an attic fan should go, is only 3' high, measuring the clear height inside. Is this enough for a fan installed in the flat position on the ceiling?
E.T., Hays, Kans.

A. You need a minimum of only 2' so I'd say your clear height is OK. Check against the blade diameter if you like. It should be at least 1-1/2 times that. The important thing to be sure of is your vent area.

Excess moisture

Q. Our home has a bad case of mildew in the summer and in the winter we are bothered by sweating windows and glass doors. The house is well insulated (6" in ceiling, 4" in walls, 2" in floor) and we use storm windows throughout. Can you tell us how to beat this problem?
W.D., West Helena, Ark.

A. Mildew requires a condition of dampness which has to be corrected before it will disappear. With the amount of insulation you describe, the dampness in your home is likely caused by a lack of ventilation. And it's probable also that you are unknowingly adding to the moisture problem in some way. Seek out and cut down on the causes of your dampness: a lot of steam cooking, unrepaired leaks, hanging clothes indoors to dry. These few examples might not apply exactly in your case, but they may point you toward what is actually the problem. Open windows and doors once or twice a day in order to provide a complete change of air. Only after you have traced all possible sources of dampness, corrected them and observed the result should you begin to worry about making structural changes in your ventilation system.

Closet mildew

Q. What causes the clothing in my new storage closet to mildew and become musty smelling? Last year we built a cedar building and sealed with plywood. This should make the closet fairly airtight.

D.D., Whiefield, Houston, Tex.

A. From the construction you describe, we'd wonder first if the clothing was all put away in an absolutely bone-dry condition. If we read you right, this is a separate building and I wonder what damp-proofing was made beneath it. That could be a source of moisture contributing to the mildew growth. A musty smell is the usual result of stagnant air and your airtight closet may suffer from this. Hang the clothes outdoors for a couple of days to lose that smell.

Basement closet

Q. I built a cellar compartment 9′ x 3′ x 10′ for clothing storage. One side is made of beaverboard and rests against a cement wall. The closet is fairly airtight. Will the cellar air create mold? I think the air is reasonably dry.

C.O., Ansonia, Conn.

A. "Reasonably dry" isn't good enough. The chances of developing mold amidst damp clothing are very good. The fibrous material resting against a wall can absorb moisture and hold it. More moisture can rise through the floor. Provide louvers for the enclosure on opposite sides, one low and one high. For added safety, use a chemical dehumidifier.

Shower condensation

Q. I have a condensation problem in my bathroom. The room is in a dormer separate from the attic and there is no radiator. While it remains fairly warm throughout the seasons, when anyone takes a shower, condensation forms, leaving rust on the celing.

How can I prevent this condensation from forming?

M.D., New York, N.Y.

A. Warm the surface that the moisture condenses on and ventilate enough to remove the moisture-laden air. Insulation above the ceiling would keep it as warm as possible. An exhaust system to get the moist air out of your home would be best.

Range exhaust fan

Q. We are contemplating a range hood with fan and would like some advice. Do you recommend venting to the attic with crawl space available or to the outside of the house?

M.S., Maplewood, N.J.

A. Never vent to your attic from a kitchen range hood. You are trying to remove the grease and moisture from the house, not redeposit it in the attic. Run the duct the shortest direct path to the outdoors: straight up through the roof to the outdoors, over and out the wall or, in a pinch, up and over and out at the undereave.

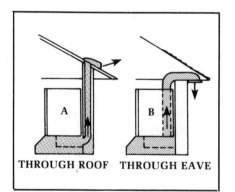

THROUGH ROOF THROUGH EAVE

Roof exhaust vent

Q. Is there any such thing as a grease trap I could install in my attic? What I need is a trap to replace the roof vent of my kitchen exhaust fan. This would also eliminate the

problem of snow blowing into the vent, melting and running under the roofing.

H.J., Columbus, Ohio

A. We know of no grease trap you could use as a substitute for a roof vent. What you can do is to install a flutter-type, louvered vent which opens only when the exhaust fan is running. With warm air blasting out, little snow will get in. Melted snow running under the roofing is more likely to be caused by faulty flashing than by snow in the vent and duct. Perhaps you should check the flashing first.

Dryer vent

Q. You showed a built-in laundry room in a recent issue where the exhaust pipe for the dryer was directed toward the ceiling. My question is: Can a dryer be vented through a ceiling?

B.E., Bryan, Tex.

A. The dryer in the story you mention not only vents up, it is ducted the full width of the room. Just try to keep the duct in as straight a run as possible and make sure you get it vented outdoors at the end. You've probably read some heat-salvage ideas about using dryer exhaust as a supplementary source. Never vent a gas dryer to an indoor space. If you want to use the humid heat from an electric dryer, slip a makeshift secondary lint trap over the open end, such as old nylon stockings. Be aware that you will be introducing increased moisture.

Vent kitchen odors

Q. My new home has a non-vented hood above the range which tends to blow the cooking odors through the rest of the house. I am thinking of venting to the outside in one of two ways: 1) Immediately behind the kitchen is a pantry. I could vent to the pantry, make a right angle turn, and penetrate the wall to the outside, or 2) Penetrate into the attic and blow the fumes into that space which is vented to the outside at each end of the house. I believe the second solution to be the best of the two. Could you offer an opinion and also give me a tentative list of materials?

J.S., Fredericksburg, Va.

A. Venting directly into the attic space from a stove hood isn't going to do anything except deposit in your attic the stuff that is now deposited on the filter in your vent hood, regardless of how fast the fan in the attic blows the "fumes" out the gable end vents. The fumes are not the major problem here. Warm, humid air is—and you want to vent that air outside. What you describe as the pantry route is alright, or you can go straight inside the cabinets with a duct and on out through the attic roof. You can also run ductwork through or above the cabinets to the outside wall if it is not going to be too tight up under the eaves. Go to your local dealer and ask him to explain to you ducting to an exhaust fan outlet or ask him whose exhaust fans he carries, and write that manufacturer for proper installation information.

Darkroom exhaust

Q. I want to build a dark room in my basement. It will have a labyrinth type of entrance and a door. I feel the need for an exhaust fan of some type. The door will only have a louvered opening for air. What type and where would it be best to install the fan?

E.S., Darien, Conn.

A. A ceiling fan, perhaps installed between the joists if they run at right angles to the wall, might be best. A mixed flow im-

peller or a blower wheel type fan on a switch would probably satisfy your needs.

Exhaust fan into attic

Q. I am remodeling a bathroom and wish to install an exhaust fan. Area is about 450 cu. ft. I have space available on one outside wall but it is the front of the house and I'd rather use the ceiling type. If I make a ceiling opening, can I vent directly to the unfinished attic above without using ducts?

G.I., Columbus, Ohio

A. The air you wish to exhaust will be warm and moisture laden. Chances are the attic area will be cold part of the year. Condensation on all cold surfaces will take place with attendant destruction. It would be better to run a duct through the attic area to an outside point, simpler still to go ahead and use a through-wall model.

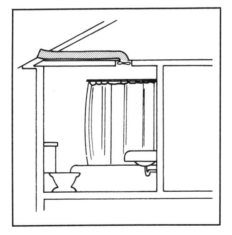

Vent dryer

Q. We have been told our basement would be drier if we'd vent the clothes dryer to the outdoors. How is this done?

E.T., Chicago, Ill.

A. The easiest way is with a venting kit. You need a hooded vent for the exterior wall and some means of conveying the damp air to it anyhow. The installation is

simple enough: prepare a hole in the exterior wall to accept the vent. You can use a piece of plastic with a vent in the center to replace one of the panes in a convenient window if you prefer. The flexible duct tubing attaches to inner end of vent and to dryer vent opening with screw-tightened ring clamps.

Exhaust vacuum

Q. We have a hot water tank with a side arm heater vented to the chimney. We cannot use the tank when the ventilating fan is on as it sucks the fire down through the bottom of the heater. We would like to install an automatic water heater but fear it might start up when the window fan is operating and ruin the contraption. What do other people do to prevent a downdraft?

E. N., Chicago, Ill.

A. The air removed by the fan must be replaced at once or a vacuum is created. There has to be a door or window or both open wide enough to admit air at the same rate of speed the fan expells it. Otherwise air is pulled down a chimney. If it happens to be a fireplace chimney you might get a house full of soot. In your case it blows out the flame of the heater. An electric heater would not be affected by the blast of air which may be why the difficulty isn't more widespread.

Flue as exhaust duct

Q. I wish to install a kitchen exhaust fan to get rid of odors. I can easily make a connection into a flue just over the range which is not being used for anything else. The size is 3-1/8" x 6-7/8". If this is satisfactory what size fan should be used or would the flue fill with grease and dust?

M.M., Fairmont, W.V.

A. You can place a hood over the opening designed to conduct hot air from the range toward the flue and let the natural rise of hot air take care of the discharge through the flue. A rotary fan at the top of the chimney would be about the only possible type fan that could be used. Do not worry about grease and dust deposits. It would be many years before the deposit could amount to much.

Vent condensation

Q. My house is so thoroughly insulated that condensation is becoming a problem. The answer seems to be ventilation. In view of the fact that the ceiling is 12″ square fiber tile with insulation immediately above it, would it be practical to remove one tile, install a fan and ventilate directly into the attic?

A.S., Utica, Mich.

A. Removing one tile is a convenient way to do it and sufficient for summer, at least it will vent the house to a degree while taking out some moist air. It won't do in winter when moist air expelled from the house will create a moisture problem in the attic. You'd get condensation on the colder undersurface of the roof. A better year-round solution is a duct from the removed tile to a louver venting outside with a grilled opening replacing the tile, or a regular exhaust fan.

Heater vent

Q. My 1-1/2-story house has an insulated attic, the rear half of which is mildewed. What's causing this? The flue for the hot water heater terminates in the attic. Could this gas burner be causing the trouble?

H.A., Charleston, W.Va.

A. The mildew originates from condensation of moisture on a cool or cold surface. Very likely the heater vent is responsible. It should be extended through the roof as a safety measure anyway. Once that's done, wash the mildewed area with a dilute chlorine solution to kill the fungus. Then provide louvers for ventilation of the attic space.

Fan vents to attic

Q. Two years ago we had a light/fan combination installed in our bathroom. The fan was vented into our unheated attic at the suggestion of the contractor. We have not yet had any problems. However, was venting the fan into the attic a wise decision?

P.M., Worcester, Mass.

A. With a fan vented into an unheated attic, warm, moist air is sent directly to a cold area where it can promptly condense. You are right to wonder if it was a good idea. It wasn't. Run the vent on through the attic to the outdoors. Insulate the duct where it passes through the cold attic so you won't get condensation in the pipe at that point. Make sure to flash well where the vent goes through the roof.

Inside bath

Q. I have a bathroom with all inside walls and wish to put in a ceiling exhaust. I can either run a pipe similar to a hot air duct through the roof or a similar pipe to an outside wall 12′ away. I would like to know which would give the most satisfactory results.

L.E., Pittsburgh, Pa.

A. You can run the pipe to the roof and put a rotary fan on the roof to draw up air from the bath. This is the wind driven type of exhaust that needs no motor. In a horizontal pipe exhaust you could use a motor-driven fan. The ver-

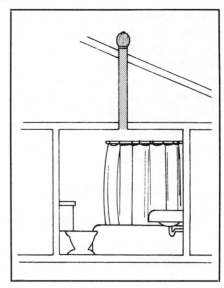

tical type would probably be more efficient, less costly and easier to install in your situation.

Fan in block wall

Q. Can a fan that just goes out through the wall be installed in the kitchen of a concrete house with brick veneer on the outside.?

T.G., Cicero, Ill.

A. Why not? If it is the thickness of the wall you are worried about, manufacturers make extension wall sleeves to increase the length of the air chamber to accommodate such walls easily.

Discolored walls

Q. A brownish film of dirt is forming on my painted walls, causing curtains and drapes to discolor. I have a gas furnace and a gas fired water tank. I also have a gas range which is not vented to the chimney but has a place for same in the rear of the stove. Is it the gas that's doing this?

G.B., Youngstown, Ohio

A. The average gas flame does not in itself leave a brownish deposit on anything. It does contribute to the excessive humidity within the house. This moisture picks up from the air any materials which might include residues from cooking, tobacco smoke, etc. the general tone of which is invariably a brown color. This is what is being deposited on your paint. A vent in the rear of the stove won't help as much as an exhaust fan to carry cooking smoke and vapor out of the house.

Kitchen ventilator

Q.   I recently installed a kitchen ventilator, venting it through the roof so that when I am ready to add an enclosed porch I won't have to move the vent. I used a 3-foot length of 6-1/2" pipe and I'd like to know how to break the vacuum the wind creates going down the pipe. It lifts the light baffle built into the fan and causes irritating flapping sounds as it rises and falls.

R.H., Louisville, Ky.

A.   You might install a roof vent pipe cap which revolves with the wind direction causing the wind to blow around rather than across the top of the pipe. This should stop any downdraft suction.

Deadly fan

Q.   I wonder if it would be practical to connect an exhaust fan in my kitchen to the chimney. I have a gas furnace connected to the chimney so would an exhaust fan have any bearing on the operation of the furnace?

C.D., Akron, Ohio

A.   DON'T DO IT. If you open the flue at this point, you may fill the house with odorless, colorless fumes that could kill you. Also any automatic drafts and dampers on the furnace might be upset. Furthermore the fan, directed against the back of the flue, could easily develop a back pressure that would overheat and burn out the fan motor.

Oven backfire

Q.   I have a built-in range with a hood and fan unit ducted outdoors. The oven vents via a 4" pipe into this same duct. When I put the fan on it backs up into the oven. If I block the oven flue the burners work well. How can I fix this?

P.S., Everett, Mass

A.   It is obvious that the fan forces air in both directions—out the vent and down the oven flue. Establish a second vent for the oven flue or conduct the oven flue into the hood so the same fan will vent the oven or the burners or both together.

Kitchen exhaust fan

Q.   Does it make any difference where in a kitchen a wall fan is installed? We can't use a vent hood as steel cabinets are already there and do not leave enough room below them.

E.J., West New York, N.J.

A.   Yes it does make a difference. Air should travel into the fan in such a way that it picks up odors, smoke and grease from the range. I would suggest the wall fan be located on the wall above the range if at all possible.

Fanless range hood

Q.   I do not understand how a range hood with no fan and no ducts works. Could you explain this please?

C.T., Westfield, N.J.

A.   This type of hood simply uses filters to clean the rising warm air somewhat and return it to the room. Without ducts, no heat and no moisture is removed from the kitchen. In an apartment or somewhere duct work could not be installed, it might be better than nothing but in a house a fan-and-duct type is preferable.

Chapter 15

Plumbing Problems

Attic baths...Basement baths...Cisterns...Drains, sewers...
Faucets...Fixtures...Pipes, tubing...Showers...Sinks...Septic tanks,
drainfields...Toilets...Tubs...Vents...Water heaters...Water softeners,
filters...Wells.

Attic bathroom

Q. I am finishing three small rooms in my attic. I have been advised to locate the bathroom directly over the one downstairs. Is this necessary?

B.M., Rochester, Mich.

A. The drainpipe of the attic bathroom toilet must slope 1/4" per foot from the toilet to the sewer pipe. This is the reason for the advice you received. The pipe is 4" in diameter, but the bell joints are about 6" in diameter. Assuming the joists to be 2x8s, you would be able to run the pipe only 6' from toilet to sewer pipe at the necessary slope. Therefore, your upstairs toilet must be located within 6' of the sewer pipe of the downstairs bathroom if you plan using that sewer line. The alternative is running a separate sewer from the upstairs bathroom directly to the basement and connect to the main line there—quite a costly operation.

Attic drain slope

Q. I am planning to install a sink and water closet in my attic. If I run the drain pipe at the usual slope to connect up to the main drain, I must break into the ceiling of the bathroom below which I do not want to do. Can I use an inverted Y fitting? Would it be satisfactory? I realize the water closet has a built-in trap, so I do not need another. However, does the fact the drain pipe has a reverse pitch affect the drainage? The level of water in the toilet would be above the top of the tap in the waste pipe.

W.H., Merrick, N.Y.

A. You cannot have an upward sloping drain. Aside from the fact no sanitary inspector would approve it, you'd shortly have a clogged drain. You need a slope of 1/4" per foot, so why not replace the section just below the upper floor with a Y which will cause little trouble on the floor below? Since you have 2x8 joists for clearance, you can raise the toilet on a 1" stone slab and your problem would be quickly solved.

Basement toilet

Q. My basement floor is about 4' below the first floor soil pipe. I would like to put a half-bathroom in the basement using a sump and pump to dispose of the waste. Do you recommend such an installation?

B.A., LaMesa, Calif.

A. We couldn't recommend that system of waste disposal—it would be a violation of sanitary codes. A sump is an open hole at best and raw sewage in it would be a health hazard. Also a sump pump won't remove solid wastes, only liquids. Only the waste from a sink, tub or shower might be disposed of in this way.

For this situation, you'll have to install a type of toilet that uses water pressure to carry wastes upwards. One such unit is made by MacPherson, Inc. P.O. Box 15133, Tampa, Fla. 33684.

Half bath

Q. I'd like to incorporate a half bath in our basement remodeling plans. The main drain line is about 10-1/2" from floor to center of end plug. Will it be practical to include a toilet?

J.H., Media, Pa.

A. If the drain pipe is only 10-1/2" off the floor, you can manage with one of the new wall-hung toilets which has a drain pipe that makes a U-turn and goes back into the wall leaving the whole fixture free of the floor. Your local plumbing supply house should be able to give you details.

Cistern soapstone

Q. Where can I find soapstone for a cistern?

D.M., Marshall, Minn.

A. Alberene Stone Co., P.O. Box 98, Schuyler, Va. 22969 quarries and sells soapstone. Also write Building Stone Institute, 420 Lexington Ave., New York, N.Y. 10017. They may be able to suggest another source near you. You should keep in mind that soapstone has a small iron content which affects water stored in a cistern. Perhaps you should consider using concrete.

Clogged drain

Q. The water in our bathtub drains out very slowly. I have checked the trap and it is clean. Can you tell me what could be wrong?

F.O., Hamburg, N.Y.

A. The cause of a sluggish drain may be far removed from the trap. The 2" drain line probably runs horizontally for some distance and this portion of the pipe can be clogged. We'd suggest you try one of the lye-base cleaners which is poured into the drain outlet. Another possible cause is a clogged vent pipe. This can be cleared from the roof by inserting a long flexible wire or plumber's snake into the top of the vent.

Noises in drains

Q. When we let dishwater run down our sink drain, a gurgling sound comes from the basement drain and usually water splashes out around that drain. As this is a new house, we can't understand it. The contractor pooh-poohs our concern, saying his own drain does the same thing. Can you tell us what causes this and how to correct it?

W.J., Gary, Ind.

A. The trouble is probably due to absence of a vent on the sink drain. Instead of air rising out the vent as it should, it is forced down the drain by water and the pressure forces out water standing in the basement floor drain—either in the trap if there is one (and there definitely should be) or the catch basin under the floor grill, which isn't draining properly. Quite often a sink vent pipe is installed but run up the wall and capped rather than continued through the roof. Sometimes it is omitted altogether. Check your roof above the sink for signs of a small vent outlet. If you have none, that's the main cause of trouble.

Sluggish drain

Q. In an effort to correct a sluggish floor drain, I have dug around considerably inside and outside of my basement and discovered a great many underground tile pipes. I was hoping to find either a point of connection between the floor drain pipe and the main sewer or a spot where the piping may have collapsed. Outside of the basement foundation, I found shorter sections of pipe that lead from the floor drain pipe, but these end abruptly. The drain is most sluggish during heavy rains and after the washing machine has been used.

P.S., Detroit, Mich.

A. As you suspect, the cause of your sluggish drain may be a collapsed pipe, a clogged connection, interference from tree roots or something similar that you have not dug far enough yet to discover. The other possibility is that your floor drain is tied into a dry well which has filled up over the years. This would also cause a sluggish draining situation, especially if the underground water table were high after a heavy rain. Depending upon the age of your house the drain may lead to a septic tank that is no longer in use. There are other possibilites that can only be guessed at.

If you determine the drain is clogged, you can clear it using a chemical cleaning agent or a drain auger. If you find the drain is collapsed at any point you can either replace the damaged section, which may mean more digging, or you can re-route the washing machine drain to your laundry sinks which will tie it directly into the sanitary sewer. This will lighten the amount of waste water entering the defective pipe. Finally, you may be able to control the heavy rain water back-up by installing a backwater valve at the proper location on the floor drain pipe leading to the storm sewer or dry well. Your plumbing supply dealer can tell you more about how, when and where to install a device of this kind.

Storm drain

Q. Every time the river rises, the flood tide rises back up from our floor drain. Is there some way to cap this so water will go down it and not come back up?

F.W., Des Moines, Iowa

A. There are some patented devices that will do the trick. One is a telescoping stand pipe affair that rises as the water level rises; another has a captive ball that floats up to close the opening when water rises beneath it and still another with a brass flap that works automatically to close the drain when water tries running the wrong way. We'd suggest you see what your local plumbing supply store has available.

Blocked drain

Q. The drain in my bathroom sink has me puzzled. When the plug is in the open position the water drains very slowly; let the water run and the water rises to the overflow drain level and doesn't flow out the basin drain at all. But remove the plug completely, and the basin drain takes the full flow of hot and cold water without difficulty. What's wrong?

P.B., Townshend, Vt.

A. You say that if the plug is out the full flow is easily drained. Did you examine the plug? Most plugs have a strainer that clogs easily, mostly with hair and lint. Clean it out and your problem should be solved. For the future, regular doses of a household drain cleaner should eliminate the problem.

Noisy drain

Q. When a quantity of water goes down the sink drain in our second floor kitchen, a loud gurgling noise occurs. The water drains rapidly so the trap is not clogged. The tenants below installed a new sink and connected it to the original sink drain in the wall as in my sketch. They agree to let me correct their drain if you think this is causing the trouble.

L.A., Chicago, Ill.

A. A partly clogged vent could create a partial vacuum in the vent

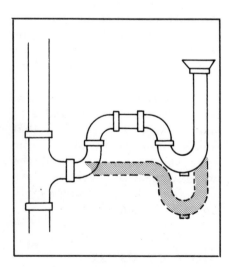

Clean out clogged vent if necessary. Trap should be lowered to eliminate upper loop.

pipe above the column of descending water. As your sink finishes draining, air would be sucked through the trap causing some strange noises in your sink drain. We suggest you inspect the vent and clean it if clogged. Your tenant's drain is installed incorrectly and should be corrected for greater efficiency but this probably has little to do with the noise in your drain. Suggest you lower it and reconnect as shown.

Root solution

Q. We have a problem with tree roots in our sewer. Every year the sewer must be rodded out which is expensive, as well as a nuisance. Is there any chemical we can put in the sewer to kill these roots?

E.J., London, Ontario

A. If you time it right, the problem can be treated economically with copper sulphate crystals. Measure two ounces of the crystals into the toilet and flush immediately using one gallon of water. Wait until sluggish draining indicates the sewer is nearly plugged up. That way the roots will stop the chemical and give it a chance to work. It burns off root ends without injury to the tree and slows their regrowth. One treatment a year should do the trick.

Caution: Do not use copper sulfate if you have a septic tank—only for sewer systems.

Frozen clean-out

Q. The cleanout plug seems to be frozen on and I can't open it to see if the main line is clogged. Is there another way?

A.L., Fairlawn, N.J.

A. Try soaking the cleanout plug threads with penetrating oil for several minutes, repeat the treatment, then open with a long handled pipe wrench.

Whistling faucets

Q. My bathroom and sink are awfully noisy, a loud whistling sound. I replaced all the washers and for a day or two the noise went away. Please let me know what causes it and how to stop it.

T.R., Atlanta, Ga.

A. Whistling noises are usually indicative of faulty packing. Air is moving in rapidly to the spindle of the faucet, either because the pack-

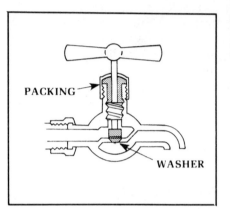

ing is not in place properly or because it is dry. When you have the faucet apart to make sure you got those washers on properly, rewind the stem with several turns of string packing.

Faucet leaks

Q. The faucet washers I buy from our hardware store don't solve my problem; when I put them in the faucet, it still leaks.

P.C., Endicott, N.Y.

A. If you have obtained the right style and proper size washer and you still have trouble, the problem may well be the faucet and not the new washer. After a time, the seat the washer fits against when it is closed becomes worn. This can sometimes be corrected by installing a new seat (if your faucet has a removable seat) or by dressing the seat if it isn't removable. Your dealer should be able to supply the tool that's needed for this job.

Noisy plumbing

Q. How can I stop the bang that occurs each time the hot water faucet is shut off?

F.S., North Valley Stream, N.Y.

A. A broken or damaged washer or a damaged washer seat can cause such a noise. A kit of washers and a reamer cure these two ills. There is the possibility the pipe is loose in its hangers on horizontal stretches and rattles against these as pressure is suddenly stopped when the faucet closes. Felt cushions in the hangers stop this.

Or this may be water hammer. The cause is lack of an air chamber in the system. Your system may have such a "cushion" that has become water filled. Drain the system and refill it to automatically replace the water with air. If you have no such device, install one on a T on the main water supply line.

Changing washers

Q. Is there any sort of trick in changing faucet washers? The hot water faucet of my bathroom makes a real racket when turned part way on. The noise stops when the water is on full. I assumed the washer was faulty and changed it but I still have the noise.

R.F., Newark, N.J.

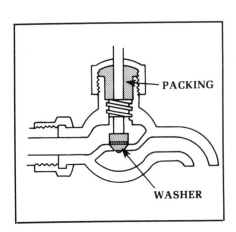

The packing around the faucet stem is as frequent an offender as a faulty washer.

A. The composition washers which will last for years are usually slightly larger than the recess at the bottom of the faucet stem into which they must fit and are held with a brass screw. It's easy to get them in place incorrectly. If the washer is improperly seated or the seat is damaged then there could be quite a lot of noise until pressure is stopped either by turning the faucet off or fully on. The other possibility is that packing around the faucet stem has deteriorated, permitting it to chatter. Rewind the stem with several turns of string packing when you check the washer.

Washer choice

Q. I just put neoprene washers in all my faucets. Now when I open up a faucet on the hot water side, the pressure drops to a trickle. I have to open it all the way in order for it to work correctly. What is causing this?

J.P., Garwood, N.J.

A. The temperature of the hot water swells neoprene washers quickly and causes them to reduce the flow of water. This reaction may be temporary and will pass as the washers wear down. One of the advantages of these washers is that they fit snugly and rarely leak. A fiber washer doesn't swell as much under heat.

Vintage fixtures

Q. My problem involves the maintenance of vintage plumbing fixtures. Our home, built in 1929, has a beautiful old American Standard bathroom that looks like it's right out of Hearst Castle. The problem is the old toilet. It is working still but some of the valve bodies are beginning to deteriorate. We've been told the parts are no longer made. Can you suggest a way out?

W.C., Long Beach, Calif.

A. Your problem requires a good deal of detective work and a lot of patience. First gather all the style, model number, year, manufacturer type information you can find. Then go to the manufacturer's representative, in your case American Standard, and try to get a copy of the catalog parts page that shows the pieces you need. Then, with plumbing parts, you'll usually have to work through a plumber. We'd pick the oldest plumber around on the off-chance that he might be more familiar with the fixture. His wholesaler may stock the part or something close enough to make a reasonable job possible. Or he may know that the Tapco Div. of Elias Industries, Epsilon Drive, RIDC Park, P.O. Box 2812, Pittsburgh, Pa. 15230 stocks parts for a number of outdated models. Even though most wholesale companies do not deal with the consumer, it sometimes becomes necessary for the consumer to do the research leg work simply because it doesn't pay the plumber to do it.

Pressure fade-away

Q. I moved into a new home which has copper tubing for water supply. Kitchen and bath are directly above the water heater, with no more than 15′ of tubing between heater and faucets, yet the hot water fades to a trickle. What causes this and what can I do about it?

D.F., Daly City, Calif.

A. Very likely there is some stoppage in the hot water supply line caused by mineral deposits. Water flows into the coil and slowly into the storage tank where it builds up enough pressure so the first flow is full volume. If it can no longer flow through the clogged coil as rapidly as it should, the pressure and volume diminish. If you find the heating coil is indeed fairly well plugged with mineral deposits, you need a new coil. Some of the tubing may also need replacement.

Pin holes in pipe

Q. Lime in our water supply leaves deposits that eat pin holes through our hot water pipes. We've replaced four or five sections already. Would a water softener stop this?

W.T., Lyons, Ill.

A. There's more than lime in your water. Lime could leave a crusty deposit in the pipes but wouldn't account for the pin holes. They're the result of an electrolytic process traceable to other minerals. A water softener is not designed to combat this. There are other filtering systems that remove unwanted elements, metal or mineral. It may be worth your while to have your water tested. Ask your local board of health how to do this.

Corroding copper

Q. One 3' length of copper tubing leading from the hot water boiler to a wash room develops a green "mold" and eventually springs a leak necessitating replacement. I have copper tubing throughout the house but this is the only section affected.

P.M., Lansford, Pa.

A. That section of tubing runs along a chimney and is exposed to sulfur bearing gases that escape from the chimney. These create a chemical action which ultimately will damage even copper. Suggest that you shield the tubing with a removable metal cover, such as aluminum foil wrapping and change this shield several times a year. Also, for the health of your family, be sure chimney gas leakage is stopped.

Chattering pipes

Q. I am having trouble with my hot water pipes. When the hot water faucet is turned on, they chatter badly. This condition only lasts for a few seconds, but they vibrate enough to make me worry that the soldered joints may be shaken loose with resultant leaks. The pipes are 3/4" copper tubing and are held down by metal saddles to the wooden joists. I was able to rectify a lot of this vibration by adding more anchoring saddles, but the section which I can't seem to correct is a 5" piece with two right-angle runs which are connected to the wash tubs in the cellar. This is the lowest point in the house for the hot water supply and the only place which is bothering me now. Any help you can give me will be appreciated.

R.T., Greenwood Lake, N.Y.

A. Is there an air chamber or "accumulator" in your water system? Is it working or is it full of water? If so, drain the system and refill to automatically replace water with air. If you don't have one, install one on a T on the main water supply line. Your plumbing supplier should be able to help you with this project. Your attempts with the additional saddle anchors is a good idea. However, you might have needed fewer of them if you had lined them all with a felt cushion. The pipes will still move some, but they won't make as much noise.

Lead water pipe

Q. Years ago I had central heating installed and hot and cold brass water pipes put in leading from the cellar where we still have the old main cold water line made of lead. In the past two years I have had three leaks in the lead pipes. Should I replace them?

P.F., Brooklyn, N.Y.

A. If you will consult the local water supply codes, you'll discover that lead pipe is now prohibited for water supply, because of the danger of lead poisoning. You would be wise to replace all lead pipe with iron, copper or plastic, depending on local codes.

Choice of pipe

Q. I plan to build my own home shortly and would like some information on the type plumbing to use. I want pipes that will last a long time and will require the least amount of time and tools to install. Then the cost must be right. What would you suggest?

P.W., Clermont, Ind.

A. Check your local building codes first. Where permitted, we would suggest plastic pipe for cold water lines, flexible copper tubing for hot water.

Tube vs. pipe

Q. I plan to install copper tubing in my house in place of the galvanized iron pipe. The house is a small four-room bungalow. Pipe from the main is 3/4" but I would like to replace with 1/2" tubing throughout, including the branch lines to faucets which are now 1/2" pipe. What size tubing do you think I should use?

W.M., New Hyde Park, N.Y.

A. Since copper tubing has a smaller inside diameter than iron pipe and since there is a definite volume loss as water is conducted through pipe, it's impractical to reduce the size of the tubing. Our advice would be to replace pipe with tubing of equal diameter.

Copper pipe leaks

Q. I have been living in my house for two years and during this time I've been plagued continually with leaks in the copper water pipes. I've called in a plumber a number of times to fix these leaks. However, so many new leaks popped up recently that I decided to save some money and do the repairs myself. I purchased a Bernz-O-Matic torch and some solder and tried my hand at a few of the leaks, with little success. I drained all the water out of the pipes, then sweated some solder into the leaking joints. These repairs seem to last only about two weeks, and then the pipes begin to leak again in the same places. Can you tell me how to sweat the copper tubing correctly so that the repairs will be permanent?

M.M., Syracuse, N.Y.

A. That old motto, "haste makes waste," really applies when making a sweat-solder joint connection. Fitting joints not cleaned correctly will be a problem to get apart and replace after the pipes are filled with water. The absolute rule when soldering copper pipe is clean it right the first time.

A professional plumber starts by cleaning the tubing that goes into the fitting at least an inch longer than the fitting requires. He also shines up the inside of a fitting whether it's a "T", elbow or anything else. Both fitting and tubing must be shiny bright.

After a professional has shined both fitting and tubing, he uses a good quality flux to further clean or etch the tubing for an even better solder joint. When selecting the solder, never purchase one with an acid or rosin core. Use only solder with a solid core. Use flux made for copper and a solid core solder. Be sure to buy fresh solder—it will work much better than stuff that's been laying around for years.

Your torch should have a soldering nozzle, which concentrates the flame instead of spreading it. The flame must be played all around the joint so that the entire fitting is heated evenly.

An experienced tradesman won't put his torch to the pipe to heat it up. This could cause contamination. Instead, he always heats the fitting and lets the solder flow in there before joining it to the pipe.

On horizontal work, solder is applied only at the top of the joint, and when it flows out at the bottom, you know the joint is filled. On vertical work, the ring of the joint must be filled all around. The torch should no longer be in use, for if

applied to the joint after the solder is applied, the solder will melt and flow out. If you find it necessary to reheat the joint, then the whole soldering job must be done over again. The heat of the metal, not the torch, should melt the solder.

Here's one other pitfall to watch out for when soldering. Just a few drops of water inside copper pipe will cool it off to a degree that you cannot get the pipe hot enough to sweat a fitting together or apart. Every trace of water must be out of the pipe.

Here is a clever way to dry out the pipe. Take a vacuum cleaner that can operate as a blower, and put the hose on the exhaust outlet. Tape or tie the other end of the hose to an upstairs faucet. Turn on the sweeper to blow air through the faucet, down the pipe and out the soldering opening. Or if you have an air compressor, that may work even better.

Accurate pipe cutting is also a must for a watertight solder. Copper pipe must be cut off square so that it goes snugly into the fitting. No matter how good your eye is or how talented you are with a hacksaw, never use one. You will always get a more accurate cut with a tube cutter. The modest price of a cutter will more than pay for itself in no-fuss connections.

Green pipes

Q. What can be done to copper water pipes to keep off green mold?
R.L., Cleveland Heights, Ohio

A. That green on the copper pipes is more apt to be corrosion than mold. You should make sure it has not eaten through the copper to create a leak. If the green appears near a joint, double check that the joint is tight. You probably can tell a lot by the pattern of the green. Take it as a warning sign and inspect the pipes carefully. Also, check for chimney leaks which may be emitting sulfur-bearing fumes into your home. Sulfur in the air, absorbed into

moisture condensing on pipes will combine with copper to form copper sulfate, and pipes will deteriorate.

Rust in pipes

Q. Can rust be removed from water pipes? I have a well in use for four years. We expect city water next year and wonder if filtered city water will clean out the rust from inside the pipes.
S.D., Clinton, Md.

A. Filtered city water will not remove rust. No water will remove rust. A water treatment system that coats the inside of the pipe with a rust resistant film can prevent further formation.

Pipes in cement

Q. I am going to put a new cement floor in the basement of my 65-year-old house. Why can't I install the water and gas pipes in the concrete floor?
M.F., Chicago, Ill.

A. Very likely you will discover regulations prohibiting the setting of gas pipe in the concrete floor. If you use copper tubing for the water lines and make no joints under the concrete, you would not be bothered with leaks from corrosion. This is all right for cold water but water heating bill would be high. The hot water line would become chilled in cold weather and you'd probably get only lukewarm water for quite a while after turning on a faucet.

Larger pipe

Q. I want to replace a 1/2" water pipe with a size large enough for about twice the water output. Would a 1" pipe be right?
L.T., Tampa, Fla.

A. One inch is a seemingly logical but wrong guess. The volume of flow through a pipe is determined by the cross section area of the pipe. The area of a round pipe is "pi" multiplied by the radius squared. Since we're using only round pipe, you can ignore the pi. Pipe cross section is in proportion to the square of its radius.

Square the radius of 1/2" pipe and you get .0625 (.25 x .25). Square the radius of a 1" pipe and you have 0.25, which is four times that of the 1/2" pipe. Just remember it you double the radius of a pipe, you quadruple the cross section area. Even a 3/4" pipe will more than double the flow of a 1/2" pipe with the 3/4" backing 2.25 times the cross section area of a 1/2" pipe.

Slow running hot

Q. Our cold water is running all right, but the hot water is down to a slow stream. Could you give a reason for this?

A.R., Chicago, Ill.

A. Chances are the outlet nipple of your hot water tank is partly plugged. Heating water breaks down chemicals in the water. They collect on the nipple plugging it and holding back the flow of hot water. Take the union apart above this nipple and clean both nipple and union thoroughly. Hot water flow should then be as good as cold water flow.

Replacing pipes

Q. We are renovating a 70-year-old house with galvanized plumbing. Is there any way we can replace the plumbing with plastic or copper piping without tearing things up too much?

S.R., Durham, N.C.

A. There are two solutions to this problem. First, get either flexible copper pipe or flexible plastic pipe. With an adapter, fasten the flexible pipe to the old galvanized pipe upstairs. Then one person

pulls the old galvanized pipe out in the basement while a second person shoves the flexible pipe down through the wall with the galvanized pipe. When the galvanized pipe hits the basement floor, cut a section out so that more pipe can be pulled down until all new copper pipe is downstairs.

The second way is to pull the galvanized pipe down as described above, but don't attach any flexible pipe to it. Then cut rigid pipe pieces that are about a foot shorter than your basement ceiling. Push one section up the hole left by the galvanized pipe. Take a coupling and fasten a second section to the first. With copper, sweat-solder these together. With plastic, cement them. Push more sections up the wall until your pipe is up to the bathroom.

With either method, you may have to cut out some of the bathroom floor to give adequate work room.

Pipe condensation?

Q. Condensation from the soil pipe from my upstairs bath falls on the ceiling below and is softening the plaster. It appears more often when the bathroom tub is in use and large amounts of water run through the outlet.

W.E., Portland, Me.

A. From your description, we'd say a leak is more likely. If the ceiling gets wet when warm water runs out of the tub, it is a leak. If you are draining cold water, it could be condensation. Repair a leak or wrap the pipe with insulation to prevent condensation.

Leaking pipe

Q. Two years ago I had a bathroom sink installed. Recently I discovered moisture around the threads of the pipe under the sink. I

looked for a leak but cannot find one. What's the trouble?

J.F., Bronx, N.Y.

A. There are two small, ring-like fittings on the sink drain pipe which join the pieces and each is fitted with a rubber gasket which eventually wears out. You can buy new rings, take the pipe apart, and put it back together with the new rings. There's a chance that the dampness could be a leak in the joint or it could be just condensation of moisture from warm air in contact with the cold pipe. A leak is steady. If you wipe the pipe dry and watch you can usually see where it comes from. A leak would call for replacement of the pipe length affected. If it is condensation, it will appear as long as the air is moist and the pipe cold. The solution is wrap the pipe in insulating tape.

Leaky pipes

Q. Are there any quick ways to repair leaks in pipes without replacing the entire pipe?

E.J., Princeton, Minn.

A. When plumbing leaks spring, you like to fix them as quickly and easily as possible. Here are a few fittings that can make life easier for the handyman.

One is Dresser fittings. They have been used by industrial plumbers for some time, but you don't often see or hear about them in home plumbing. A Dresser fitting looks something like the fittings on drain pipes under the sink. There's a rubber or neoprene O-ring that is sealed against the pipe when you tighten the nuts on the fitting.

If you have a leak in a pipe, no matter if it be steel, copper or plastic, you can cut the pipe in two and install a Dresser union over the leak. There's no need to drain all liquid out of the pipe as you would with a solder or cement joint.

Dresser fittings come in almost any size you want to name and some good hardware stores stock them. These fittings are UL listed and can be used for petroleum products.

Also on the market today are new fittings somewhat similar to Dresser fittings, only easier. These fittings just push together without threading, soldering or cementing.

You might wonder how they seal. Inside the fitting is a "V" washer or ring. Pressure of product in the pipe pushes against and out on this V making the seal. It's very important when using this type of push-together fittings that all burrs be removed first. Tubing or pipe must be extremely smooth.

Gas companies in some areas use push-together fittings on small gas lines going from the street up to the house, but not in homes. When company workmen use these fittings they have a special tool that takes all burrs off the ends of pipe or tubing.

There are a couple of disadvantages with this type of fittings. They're a one shot deal. They cannot be taken apart and reused as Dresser fittings can. Second, because they depend on the product in the pipe for the seal, you might run into problems with these fittings if you use them for outdoor water systems. Where water is drained out of pipes during winter, the V washer might dry out and fail to seal well next spring.

Like Dresser fittings, push-together fittings are a good thing for the handyman to know about. You can use them to repair a leak in a water line without having to drain all the water, which can sometimes be a problem.

Another place these fittings might come in handy is if you want to add a water line to your present system. Just cut the line and add a push-together tee or elbow to serve as a union for the new line. One company that makes these fittings is Larden Plastics, Davisburg, Mich. 48019. Their product is called "Grabber."

Softening copper

Q. I have cut some used copper tubing for a project, but the trouble is that, when I flare it, it often splits. Is there anything I can do?

L.Y., Lansing, Mich.

A. Most copper tubing, when it gets old, becomes stiff and hard to flare without splitting. Even new tubing may be hard to flare without a split. The answer is heat. With just a small amount of heat, the copper tubing can be made soft enough to flare without problems. (You should drain all the flammable or combustible liquids from the tubing before applying heat and avoid handling hot tubing with bare hands.)

Swinging iron pipe

Q. Is there anything galvanized iron pipe is good for that plastic or copper pipe can't do?

F.C., Glen Cove, N.Y.

A. When comparing copper, plastic and galvanized iron pipe, there's one case we can think of where galvanized is better. With plastic or copper, connections are rigid and cannot be moved. However, with galvanized the thread joint can be moved later without bothering the seal. Matter of fact, industrial plumbers use this to their advantage when making a swing-joint.

A swing-joint is a section of pipe that may be headed south. On to this a regular elbow is attached. Then into this elbow is screwed a street "L" and another section of pipe.

At first glance this seems like a lot of to-do over nothing. But almost all underground gasoline tanks at service stations are installed with swing-joints. When tanks are filled with gasoline they settle some due to the weight. If a swing-joint wasn't used, settling would break off the pipe. This versatile joint can swing down to absorb the strain and save the pipe.

Plastic plumbing

Q. I know how to handle galvanized iron pipe, but now I'm about to use plastic pipe in a renovation and would appreciate some pointers.

E.M., Sioux Falls, S.D.

A. Most older homes and all new homes have been upgraded or installed with plumbing techniques that weren't imaginable 50 years ago.

Today's plastic plumbing makes projects almost as simple as a mere cut and paste project. However easy it may look to a beginner, there are lots of tricks and knowledge to be learned from a professional plumber.

To start with, be aware that there are two major types of plastic—rigid and flexible. Any professional plumber knows not only his ABCs about these pipes, but his PVCs, CPVCs, FRPs and any other identification letters that plastic pipe manufacturers use to categorize types of plastic. These letters are the code to follow as you unravel the mystery of which pipe, fittings, solvent and cement to use.

For example, if you start with PVC plastic pipe, look for this code on all other materials you need for the project. This assures compatibility between all parts for a long-lasting job with no leakage. Here's a word of warning. Never trust color coding as it may not follow letter coding. When buying your joining supplies, remember that rigid plastic pipe is cemented together, not clamped. Never try to cement together two different types of plastic pipe unless the cement is coded to work on both. This is an important tip to remember when adding on to existing plumbing. You'll have less headaches in the long run if you identify the type of plastic already installed and purchase the same kind for the expansion project.

On the other hand, flexible pipe is clamped together, not cemented. Particular plumbers use a worm-gear type of clamp for clamping pipe to fittings. Stainless steel is the best material for clamps as it resists rust.

Be choosy about the type of worm-gear clamp you purchase. One acceptable clamp has a butter-fly-like nut that tightens with a pliers. A better type has a groove for tightening with a screwdriver. But the best type of worm-gear clamps are the ones with a hex head. You can really get these good and tight by using a small wrench or nut driver.

If a professional needs a connection that can later be taken apart with little trouble, he may use a flare. To do this, first put a flare nut on the plastic pipe, then dunk it into hot water to soften the pipe. While the plastic is still soft, put a flare on the pipe just like a flare on a soft copper pipe. You probably will need a flaring tool.

Increasing pressure

Q. **Would it be possible to increase water pressure for my lawn sprinkling system by installing 3/4″ pipe outside from the 1/2″ supply line I have inside the house?**

J.S., Pittsburgh, Pa.

A. Water pressure cannot be increased by running small pipe into larger. The flow is limited by the smallest diameter pipe on the system. To feed the sprinkler system, you'll have to cut into a 3/4″ main feed line.

Septic tank function

Q. **I recently purchased a house which has a septic tank. I would be very much obliged if you would kindly help me to understand the function of this installation.**

W.B., Bensonville, Ill.

A. Here's how the thing works: raw sewage enters the tank and meets a baffle which detours solids to the bottom for bacterial action

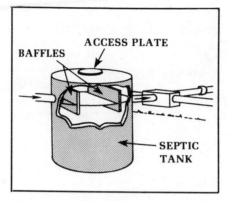

The septic tank proper is only part of this sewage system. Its purpose is to contain the sewage till bacterial action decomposes it into liquid form for further distribution via the drainfield.

and fluids continue on to the second section for ready disposal, being acted upon bacterially enroute. All fluids are then discharged into the drainfield system of field tiles in trenches. Disposal is by seepage (about 40%) and evaporation into the air (about 60%) with variations in these percentage figures in season.

Septic tank planning

Q. **We are contemplating moving to a place where there is no city sewage and septic tanks are used. I would appreciate information and specifications on a septic tank, what precautions to take, etc. We are a family of six with four small children.**

J.P., Bayside, N.Y.

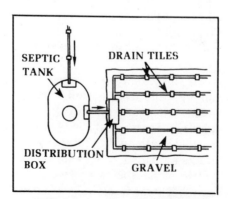

The purpose of the drainfield is to allow oxygen to work on the liquid effluent.

A. In a home, plan for the future and count children as adults. You will need a tank of 450-gallon capacity, 300′ of drainfield tiles. The tank is sealed, the sewer from the house to tank is also sealed with 4″ pipe. The intake is near the top of one end, the outlet about 2″ lower on the other side. The tank usually is fittled with baffles in front of intake and outlet to reduce turbulence. Top of the tank should be removed and at least 6″ below grade so it may be planted over with sod. Overflow is to a distribution box from which drain tiles conduct liquified sewage to the ground. These are 4″ tiles laid in gravel 18″ below the surface, spaced 1′ apart, the gravel brought within 6″ of the surface. A chemical stimulant is introduced into the tank to start bacterial action which under normal conditions continues indefinitely. Avoid laying drainfields near trees or large shrubs or roots will penetrate and foul the fields. Where property is poorly drained or subject to flooding the system will not function properly.

Septic sludge

Q. **I would like to know if coffee grounds and filter tips from cigarettes bother the action of a septic tank.**

F.S., Mishawaka, Ind.

A. Coffee grounds and those filter tips will not interrupt bacterial action in the septic tank but neither will they be reduced to liquid state. As a result they will pile up as sludge which will have to be removed eventually.

Drainage for washer

Q. **I have a 550-gallon septic tank and plan on installing an automatic dish washer and washing machine. I would like to know if everything should drain into septic tank, or if I should by-pass the septic tank and pipe these new**

additions directly to a drywell. I have been told to do it both ways and wish your recommendation.

D.E., Billerica, Mass.

A. It depends on local codes. By attaching these new water-using devices to the septic system you would flood the septic system unnecessarily. If codes allow, run them directly to a drywell but put a grease trap on the line to handle grease from the dishwasher. Since most of the grease will be dissolved by detergents, cleaning out the trap will be an infrequent chore.

Tank or cesspool

Q. I seem to have constant trouble with my septic tank or, rather, both of them. They are 4' deep and about 2' in diameter, joined by drain tiles, and flow into 200' of drainfield. There is no grease trap but most people around here don't have any. I recently replaced the drainfield which was set right in the ground and put it in gravel. Can I use a chemical to clean these tanks or do I need a larger tank? I have four in the family.

F.J., Frankfort, Ill.

A. From the description you haven't a septic tank at all. If open on the bottom and sides, they may be considered cesspools or leaching pools, with the drainfield carrying off liquids. No bacterial action would be possible to reduce solids to liquid for disposal. You need a larger, sealed tank with outlet to present drainfields. A septic tank, properly balanced and maintained, need never be cleaned. Your present system would have to be cleaned frequently.

Clogged drainfield

Q. Can a drainage field become clogged or saturated to the point where it no longer is effective? If so, what can be done about it?

W.G., Reading, Mass.

A. Drainfields can become clogged with use over a long period of time or when charged with more than capacity. Your trouble could well have its origin here. The ground loses its ability to absorb when the surface contacted by the flow of treated sludge and fluid can no longer absorb as may happen by solidifying during periods of inactivity or extreme cold, or when the porous soil is simply completely filled with such material. You can then "blow out" the drainfield system with a chemical cleaner. If space permits, extend the drainfield or add a new one, using the old as a sort of conduit between septic tank and new field if need be. At the same time, clean the old as mentioned and have not only extra space but workable old space.

Clean field

Q. Our hardware man tells me if I pour 20 gallons of muriatic acid into my septic tank it would then be like new—clean everything including the leaching field. Is he right?

J.O., Kankakee, Ill.

A. Don't do it. Muriatic acid is powerful stuff and could possibly cause worse problems than you seem to have now. This is one time to stick with commercially prepared cleaners such as Septic Aid (Vigilant Products Co., 27 Main, Ogdensburg, N.J. 07439). Follow the manufacturer's directions.

Copper sulphate

Q. I have heard of using copper sulphate crystals for tree root problems in the sewer. Will this work in a septic tank system?

T.B., Prescott, Ariz.

A. Although copper sulfate can be used in sewers, don't use it in your septic system or it will cease functioning. There are a

number of chemical products specifically for tree roots in drain lines, some safe for septic systems.

Greasetrap to drywell

Q. Years ago I lived in the suburbs where cesspools were needed and developed trouble with a gurgling and bubbling back into the kitchen sink. A visitor told me to take the sink off the main sewer line and make a separate disposal which turned out to be less work than I thought. I now have a lakeside camp where I need the same system but have forgotten some of the important details. There was a drum with one pipe in and one out but don't recall which was higher. I used an open T on one pipe but don't recall which. Can you help refresh my memory?

E.S., Johnstown, N.Y.

A. Your original advice was very good. The piping runs from the kitchen at a slope of at least 1/4" per foot, enters the drum as high as possible and this side has an open T. A short length of pipe should extend into the drum so that inflow will not be blocked by ac-

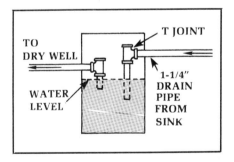

cumulating grease. The far side pipe should be 3" to 4" lower and fitted with a similar pipe extending downward below liquid level. The open T on the other side acts somewhat like a vent on a house drain line, permitting air to escape ahead of water flow. See if local codes allow this system.

Laundry drywell

Q. With the arrival of twins our septic tank has more than enough to do without the extra wash water. I've heard it is all right to run washing machine water to a drywell. Is this so?

F.T., Ottumwa, Iowa

A. Some local codes allow laundry waste water to be run to a drywell; a 4' x 4' x 4' hole filled with large rock or rubble to provide maximum spaces between pieces. Run the 2" drain into this. The drywell is covered over and may be planted over. Drainpipe should be kept below frost level, at a slope of 1/4" per foot. Locate the drywell at least 20" from house foundation. Check local codes.

Basement shower

Q. I am planning to build a shower in my basement but the floor where the drain is runs slightly downhill causing the water from the shower to run past the drain. Can I apply new cement over the old floor to divert the water toward the drain?

S.K., Willowick, Ohio

A. You can't just fill in with a thin film of cement on the low side and have it work correctly as water will gradually seep under it and crack it up. You can put new cement over old if you use a waterproof mixture of cement about 1-1/4" thick at its minimum thickness. The old surface must be free of any paint or grease. You can shape the cement base to provide the desired drainage to the existing floor drain.

Shower leaks

Q. Stained spots have appeared in the ceiling of the first floor under the front part of an upstairs shower. The shower was put in about 10 years ago. There apparently is a small leak in the front part of the shower or from a crack between the tile in the floor of the shower. How would you recommend that the leak be stopped?

T.R., Los Angeles, Calif.

A. It is quite possible that the leak occurs just in front of the shower where its sidewalls join the bathroom floor, a vulnerable point due to possible motion between the two areas. If the floor of the shower or a front tiled wall is suspect, re-grouting is the solution. If the joint between the tiled floor and the tiled walls seems to be open, a ribbon of caulking compound should be worked in deeply first, then enough removed to allow grouting that joint too. Stains on a ceiling don't always originate from a point directly above. You might examine the entire floor, points where pipes pass through walls and floors as well as all floor-wall joints.

No shower pan

Q. We were advised a bad pan was causing heavy leaking under our shower. We removed the floor tile and cement, discovered that there was no metal pan—only a segment of something like tarpaper under the cement. The subfloor has rotted away as well as wood framing around the shower. What is the best and easiest way to rebuild the shower?

M.B., Belmont, Calif.

A. Somebody settled for tarpaper which works for a time, then deteriorates. You have to start over with new flooring and possibly new joists, either a metal shower pan or a plastic one or a complete shower stall. Shower walls may also be damaged and had best be checked and probably replaced. Do it right this time, start from scratch.

Leaking shower

Q. The bottom of our shower is made of a plastic material and it developed several cracks. I crawled under the house and discovered a metal pan under the shower. The wood did not appear to have ever been wet.

I wonder if it is wise to continue to use the shower? Is there some-thing that could be poured over the floor part, such as cement, to seal the cracks and form a new surface? I have already tried filling the cracks with a special preparation a neighbor gave me, but the cracks opened again and lengthened.

M.B., Porterville, Calif.

A. Not knowing exactly what plastic material is involved, it is a bit risky to prescribe a remedy for your shower problem. However, anything that is cracking does need investigation to see if this indicates further disintegration in the near future due to continued movement. If so, then start over by securing the structure soundly first. Then install a new pan and a completely new shower base. The other alternative is to try to repair the existing one with a pour-and-toss seamless surfacing formula. This would mean cleaning the old base thoroughly, roughing it if the manufacturer so directs, painting on the base coat, tossing the flakes and working the transparent finishing coats over the flake layer.

Hole in porcelain sink

Q. I have a procelain-coated cast iron (or steel) kitchen sink. It has three holes in the top which accomodate a mixing faucet. I have purchased a new faucet set which includes a sprayer for dishes. I also purchased a water filter set that has a spigot for above-the-sink use. This is my problem: I need two extra holes in my sink to accommodate the two extra accessories. Can a porcelain-topped sink be drilled and how is it done?

L.O., Bayside, N.Y.

A. Some people report success in drilling jobs similar to yours by using a triangular file in a putty-walled puddle of kerosene to force a hole through the porcelain coating and on through the steel. Others use a glass cutting point, also lubricated, to cut through the porcelain and then they drill through the steel with a high-speed metal bit.

Dirty sink

Q. The sink in the kitchen of a house we just acquired is sound but there are lines in the bottom of the sink that look dirty. Can these be cleaned out with something or can they be painted over?

P.G., Torrington, Conn.

A. Before you go looking for paint for your sink, try letting a household bleach solution (like Clorox) set in it for a few minutes. Sometimes this is all that's needed to clean up a seemingly filthy sink. There are a few epoxy-type enamels designed for plumbing fixtures that your local paint store might be able to supply.

Cleaning a sink

Q. During a period when I was away from home, soap-and-hardwater curds formed such hard deposits on our bathroom sink that they are impossible to remove. Can you give me any information on how to remove these deposits?

D.P., Malone, Wis.

A. When the liquid bathroom cleaner won't do it, and the normal scouring abrasives (which shouldn't be used too much anyhow) don't touch it, and straight ammonia doesn't help, try a very gentle touch with a steel wool pad. Make sure you rinse well afterward.

Synthetic marble

Q. The vanity in our downstairs lavatory has a synthetic marble sink top. Not only is it scratched, but there are hair dye stains on it that won't come off. Can you help?

R.G., Encino, Calif.

A. Generally, these products are made of actual marble dust and polyester resin mix topped with a clear or lightly pigmented polyester resin gel, cast and cured as one piece. The high-quality products can usually be brought to an almost-new look with a good paste wax, well-buffed. Scratches can be removed with tooth paste or, sometimes, with wet/dry sandpaper—very fine, 400 or 600—used very gently; don't go through the top layer into the more porous mix. The original care and maintenance information should list substances that might stain the surface. Lacking this information, your best chance of removing or neutralizing stains is to write to the manufacturer, stating exactly what caused the stain.

Rust stains

Q. What is the best way to get water rust stains off bathtubs and sinks?

A.B., Miami, Ariz.

A. Boyle-Midway (South Ave. and Hale St., Cranford, N.J.07016) makes a product called "Zud" that will take the rust stains off most tubs and sinks. Your local housewares or hardware store should have it. It does contain an abrasive cleaner that you don't want to use on plumbing fixtures, so don't scour with it; gentle is the watchword. Wet the stain, sprinkle on the Zud and wait a minute before gently working over the area with a sponge. Rinse well.

Rising toilet tide

Q. Something is not right with our toilet. Water comes higher in the bowl each time it is flushed lately. It does go down eventually and has not actually overflowed yet but the way it's going, soon will. What can I do?

H.H., Bisbee, Ariz.

A. Chances are something that doesn't dissolve has caught, probably in the toilet trap, and you are building up to a complete stoppage. A flushed-down diaper would bring on just the symptoms you describe. Your first move is to try a plumber's friend. Press down sharply into the outlet of the bowl, forcing water and air down the pipe. Repeat rapidly several times. This will break up or push along an obstruction, can force it on down the drain or it may draw the offending object up into the bowl on the back stroke. A toilet auger (short "snake" fed through the curved pipe) would probably do the job if plunging doesn't.

Clogged toilet

Q. I would appreciate it if you would tell me how to bring a toilet back to normal operation. The bowl overflows. This is disconcerting on weekends when a plumber is not available. I've tried a plumber's friend and fed a couple of doses of chemical drain cleaner down with no results.

R.S., Tacoma, Wash.

A. It's a sure thing when a toilet bowl overflows there's a stoppage of some sort in the drain. We assume from your letter the water eventually flows out but you've not dislodged the stoppage. Arm yourself with a medium-size wrench and a 25′ snake. Remove a clean-out plug on the sewer line but stand by with a pail to catch a small flood of dirty water with dangerous chemicals in it when you do. If water runs out from both sides the stoppage is beyond the plug toward the sewer or septic tank. Probe that side first with the snake till you hook the obstacle to draw it back or push it beyond the next bend. Run a panful of water through the toilet bowl to determine if the stoppage is between toilet and clean-out. If so, probe that side to clear it. Replace clean-out plug.

Humming toilet

Q. Our toilet makes a humming noise which does not stop unless it is flushed or the water in the bathroom turned on. What can we do to stop this noise?

K.C., St. Louis, Mo.

A. The humming sound is due to a slight but constant flow of water. Flushing the toilet or turning on water elsewhere reduces the flow to the point where the noise cannot be heard but very likely does not halt the flow entirely. The ball valve that stops flow to the toilet bowl may be damaged permitting a slow trickle of water to

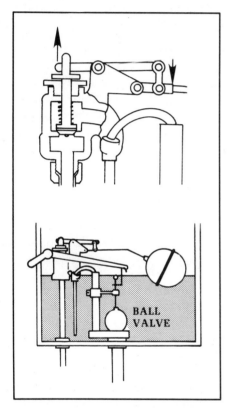

BALL VALVE

flow into the bowl and this keeps the intake valve open just enough to replace the amount flowing out. Or the intake valve—called a ballcock—may be damaged and permits water to flow into the tank which then flows out of the overflow pipe into the bowl. First check the ball valve. This is usually on a wire stem or chain and covers an opening in the center of the bottom of the tank about 2″ in diameter. If the rim of the opening is rough or the ball surface dented or roughened, replace the ball with a new soft rubber one. If this fails, replace the whole mechanism.

Inefficient flushing

Q. What can be done with a sluggish toilet? Sometimes it flushes efficiently, other times requires three or four flushings. The water level in the tank is as high as possible.

R.B., Lombard, Ill.

A. This could be caused by failure of the trip lever or handle to lift the ball valve to water level so it can float and settle into place as the water flows out. You can usually see what's needed by watching this lifting mechanism at work a few times. Could be the wire is bent, corroded so loop does not slide easily, etc. It could be a leaky ball valve which needs replacement. The outlets in the upper rim of the bowl can become clogged and require brush cleaning or it could be a partially blocked drain, the most common cause. The vent might be stopped up so air does not escape freely ahead of the water flow in which case a trip to the roof with the snake can clear the vent from the top. Less likely possibilities are a flooded municipal sewer system or an overloaded septic system but then you'd be apt to notice sluggish action in all drains.

Toilet tank crack

Q. Do you know of any way to seal a crack in a china toilet tank? It's only a hairline, but it does leak. The plumber cannot get a new tank to match the color of the sink and bowl, and doesn't know of any sealing compound that could be used.

O.R., Tulsa, Okla.

A. First thing to do is drain the tank and let it dry for a couple of days. Clean the crack and the surrounding area throughly; use coarse steel wool or even medium grit sandpaper to take off accumulated scum. You can try either of two materials for a repair. Both

may hold, but there's no guarantee of success. Lay a bead of silicone rubber along the crack on the inside of the bowl. Rub into the area with your fingers, then add a second bead on top the first. If you can get the interior clean enough, one of the epoxy adhesives would probably do the job best—if it bonds. Success will depend largely on how thoroughly you clean the surface.

Reducing water level

Q. Quite some time ago there was a mention in the local paper about a new device that would cut down on the amount of water used to flush a toilet. I have a vacation cabin and will soon be putting in a well. However, we don't want to waste water so if you can tell me the name of the device and the manufacturer I'd appreciate it.

C.S., Seattle, Wash.

A. One device we know of that is advertised as cutting down on the amount of water your toilet uses or loses, is the Fluidmaster ballcock. This eliminates the need for the floatball and works in a much more positive way. The water to refill the tank after flushing comes in at full flow, doesn't slow to a trickle as it does with a floatball. You'll notice if you hear water running very long, while you'll ignore the gradual diminishing that once in a while doesn't diminish all the way. This kind of signal happens when dirt or something clogs the valve. This doesn't happen as often with the Fluidmaster. It uses the movement of the water to shut off the flow positively. The ballcock now used shuts it off gradually. You can set it to use just as little water per flush as your toilet will work with, just as you could bend the floatball arm on the old style.

Write Fluidmaster Inc., 1800 Via Burton, Anaheim, Calif. 92805 and see if this isn't the device you recall reading about.

Bowl leaks

Q. My toilet leaks around the bowl (seal) at the floor. I have had to replace the floor three times because of water damage. I have used the circular seals with the extended tube, and I had a plumber install one at one time due to my own failures. The last time I thought it could be a hairline crack in the toilet bowl so I installed a new toilet. Now it is leaking again and the floor in front of the bowl is wet. The water also runs down into the basement. At one time I used a double seal to try to compensate for the flange possibly not being level. However, it still doesn't work. Any suggestions?

W.W., Dayton, Ohio

A. It seems as though you have tried every solution that is reasonable. Now you might check a couple of the unreasonable explanations. Are you absolutely certain that the difficulty is a leak and not condensation? Even though this problem is more likely to occur at the tank than at the bowl, it is a possibility. Another unreasonable explanation would be structural in nature. It is possible that the construction of the floor at that point is not rigid enough and movement continually loosens the joint. While not your most probable explanation, this is still a small possibility. You could also trace out the source, if the water was leaking from other plumbing fixtures, as sloppy washers at the bathroom sink can cause floor puddles. We suggest more detective work before you try another seal.

Composting toilets

Q. I saved a clipping about the Mullbank waterless toilet but can't find anyone here who sells it. It sounds like just the thing for my mountain cabin but I need more information.

R.S., New Ringgold, Pa.

A. The Mullbank was a Swedish import and may be difficult to find. Clivus Multrum USA, Inc., 14A Eliot St., Cambridge, Mass. 02138 currently offers the Bio Loo, which is also a composting toilet with added heat. We suggest sending them a self-addressed stamped envelope with a request for information. They're the same outfit, incidentally, that pioneered the Clivus Multrum Organic Waste Treatment System that also takes household kitchen waste.

Flushless toilet

Q. Recently I witnessed a demonstration of a flushless toilet. Details were sketchy, but I did perceive that the toilet works completely without water and the residue can be used as compost-fertilizer. Can you tell me where I can get more information?

W.W., Conneaut, Ohio

A. There are a number of composting toilets. In effect, it is an efficient compost pile contained within the unit. The odorless, earth-like final residue is removed at regular intervals (once a year on one model, assuming a five-person rate of use.)

Heat, oxygen and moisture are necessary to turn organic waste into humus. The natural compost pile creates its own inner heat. The composting toilet adds a heating element to speed up and even out the heat. Moisture is supplied by urine while the oxygen is forced through the pile by an electric fan drawing air from the intake and exhausting it up and out a vent. One relies on the design and continuous use of the unit to satisfactorily remove any unpleasant odor.

Peat moss is generally furnished to serve as the starter bed for the compost and it contains soil bacteria which interact with the bacteria in human waste. It should be safe and nonpolluting since it is an ecologically sound process; a natural solution where flush toilets or outhouses cannot be used because of soil conditions or zoning restrictions.

Big bathtubs

Q. My favorite place to relax is in the bathtub, but ours isn't built for comfort. Is there a company that makes a large, comfortable tub for a reasonable price? Or, is it more practical for me to build one myself?

J.J., Clanton, Ala.

A. Many of the plumbing fixture manufacturers make larger tubs (which cost more) but just don't advertise them. Your plumbing contractor should have the whole line catalog from his supplier and could show you what he can order. You could also build a tub of concrete and ceramic tile.

Cement bathtub

Q. My bathtub now has a cement floor and tile walls. Evidently the bathroom was too small to put a regular tub in it, and when we bought this house, it had tile on the floor. The grouting came loose and the water got underneath so we took out the tile and cemented the floor. Now I cannot keep any paint on it. I would like to know if there is a special paint I can use that will not peel in this situation?

I.M., Apple Creek, Ohio

A. We cannot conceive of a cement bathtub as being clean, comfortable or really paintable and suggest that you make every effort to get the abortive paint jobs off the cement. Then use a waterproofing cement coat and bed tiles for the bottom, if the wall tiles are still in good shape. If not, consider one of the vinyl chip, seamless flooring methods that will stand up to such use, such as the

Dur-a-flake system, which will go on over tile or cement, provided the proper preparatory steps are taken.

Unwanted non-slip

Q. Our bathtub has some of those non-skid cutouts. They've looked dirty since we bought the house, and I can't find any cleanser that will improve their appearance. I would prefer to remove them completely—how?

O.L., Coal City, Ill.

A. Alcohol will loosen some of the paste-on non-slip materials. Pour a bit on the high side so it will have a better chance to work under the offending cutout, hopefully loosening the adhesive.

Enclosing tub

Q. Could you please advise me how to enclose an old-fashioned bathtub?

J.R., Newark, Del.

A. First decide what surfacing material you'll use. Pre-decorated hardboard, laminated plastic, ceramic tile—these and more are all suitable. Make a rough basic framework of 2x2 or 2x3 stock to rest on a 1x2 nailed to the floor. Run it high enough so the covering material will be slightly higher and rest on the centerline of the tub rim. Space the verticals about 16" apart except a minimum of three is necessary at a free end. If the tub is recessed fairly close at ends, run the single side enclosure wall to wall. Cap the top with another 1x2, then exterior grade plywood on top of that extending from framework to tub rim, cut tub shape and beveled to fit radius of rim. Seat lower side of this in all-purpose adhesive to glue it to tub rim. At round end of tub, plywood may rest on cleat on wall. Run a similar piece, cleat sup-

ported, along the wall side of the tub. Cover the outer face of the enclosure with plywood too. A 1/2" thickness is suggested. With all plywood in place, cover with chosen surface material applied with necessary adhesive.

Bathtub crack

Q. I can't seem to get anything to stick in the opening between wall and top of bathtub. Plaster, grout, even tape either falls out or peels off. What's the answer?

B.S., Beverly Hills, Calif.

A. There is a special flexible mastic compound available in easy-to-use tubes for this trouble spot. Make sure you get all the loose stuff out first. Spread the mastic as you would toothpaste. It's sticky when applied but can be smoothed with a wet finger. Drys in a few hours, but stays flexible.

Resurfacing tub

Q. The former owner of my house evidently used the bathtub to soak something in lye. The bottom of the tub is rough and the porcelain has been eroded. Is there something I can use to fill the depressions and put a new surface over the whole thing?

A.F., Sheridan, Pa.

A. There is a spray enamel which can be used successfully on the interior of your bathtub. Available at most paint stores it is intended primarily for refinishing kitchen appliances but it does stick well to metal and porcelain and will withstand heat, water and cold. The surface must be absolutely clean and dry when the enamel is sprayed on. Apply several thin coats, allowing the first ones to fill in depressions and pockmarks. Successive coats will even out and create a smooth

surface. Allow each to dry before the following coat is applied.

Tub enamel repair

Q. I accidentally dropped a hammer into our new porcelain enameled bathtub, marring the enamel finish. Is there any way to repair this damage?

R.S., Hammond, Ind.

A. The damage can be fixed so you'll never know it happened. You can get a special spray paint in a pressurized can at most paint stores. The resulting finish is glossy and hard and won't be damaged by hot water or soaps. To apply, first scour the damaged area with wet steel wool to remove any rust and possible grease spots. Dry the area well and apply the spray carefully starting at the middle and feathering to outer edges. If the chipped spots are not filled to the surface, repeat the application as necessary after each coat dries. If after 24 hours the spot is not as smooth as the tub, rub down with a sheet of aluminum oxide sandpaper. Wet the sandpaper and rub in a tight circular motion. Wipe with a damp cloth and the job is done.

Removing lime

Q. What can be used to get accumulations of lime off basins and tubs? I have tried many chemicals, but to no avail.

D.D., Peoria, Ill.

A. If your fixtures are relatively new and unscoured, so that the surfaces are not already roughened, you can try a very light touch with steel wool to loosen lime deposits. Rinse well, though, or you could get rust stains from any remaining bits of steel wool. We wouldn't recommend this as an everyday treatment, but it will work in an all-out attack.

Clearing vents

Q. Can you suggest a way to clear the vents in a plumbing system? I live in a two-story house and the trouble seems to be on the second floor.

A.L., St. Louis, Mo.

A. What you need is a sewer rod or a sink cable. Either one of these, if long enough, should solve your problem. A sewer rod will enable you to push the obstruction further down the vent where it can be carried out through the drain line. With a hand crank sink cable you may be able to hook the obstruction up to the roof outlet. You may be able to rent one of these from a hardware store or a tool rental shop.

Water conditioners

Q. May I have your opinion of colloidal chemical water conditioners placed in the water line to prevent formation of scale and rust and also of magnesium rods and the bronze metal conditioner? How do the latter two compare?

J.S., Bergenfield, N.J.

A. Aside from the method of application, most of these devices are excellent for the purpose. They coat the interior of pipes and tanks with a smooth surface that defies rust and mineral scale formation. They are harmless. Many of the chemical types are in crystal form in a container which is attached to the feed line so the water flows over the crystals. The metal rod types are inserted into the storage tanks with a special coupling at the cold water intake. This coupling permits water to feed in around the rod which is held by the coupling itself.

Low pressure

Q. I have a hot water heating system in a hard water area. Re-cently the pressure for my hot water has become low. The pressure of the cold water is all right. Do I have to change the hot water pipes or just the hot water coil in the furnace?

J.F., Howard Beach, N.Y.

A. More than likely, the coil in your boiler is at fault. You can probably open either end of the heating coil for examination. If clogged, your answer is right there. The coil can be replaced. It cannot be cleaned out either quickly, cheaply or with any assurance that the cleaning job won't cause it to leak in a short while.

Heater troubles

Q. I recently installed an instantaneous hot water heater in my cottage. It works fine except that I cannot use the shower without getting lukewarm water, then steam. I have been advised by some dealers to discard it and use an automatic type but they come rather high. What is your advice?

P.W., Brisbane, Calif.

A. Your advice was good but it isn't necessary to go to the expense of an an automatic type. A very small oil or gas fired heater with a storage tank would cost considerably less. A storage tank of about 30 to 50-gallon capacity will provide a steady flow of properly heated water for shower use. You can fire the heater manually or add a thermostat control for "automatic" service.

Water shut-off

Q. When we shut off our main water valve to make repairs, is it necessary to do anything with the gas heater which supplies our hot water?

H.G., Woodhaven, N.Y.

A. When you shut off the water supply for repairs, the heating equipment that fires the hot water heater should also be shut off by turning off the valve in the gas line.

Quicker hot water

Q. My hot water heater is located at the far end of the cellar and hot water must travel as much as 50' to reach some of the faucets. The water must be run for some time before it is delivered hot. Is there any manner in which this system can be improved?

J.H., Freehold, N.J.

A. While wrapping the pipe with insulation will prevent some heat loss, it will not keep water in the pipe hot indefinitely. Best solution would be to set up circulation in the pipe. An adapter in a T on the pipe near the faucet receives a length of 3/8" or even 1/4" tubing. Conduct this back to and couple it into the heater at its base. A good location might be a T placed in the drain at the base or at any hole

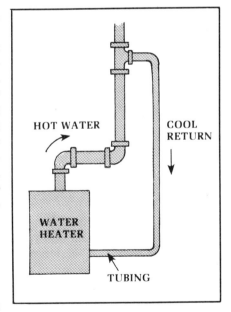

in the tank below the point where heated water enters. This way hot water rises to the faucet steadily but flows back to the tank for reheating when it cools. You will receive hot water from the upper T only a foot or so away instead of 50'. This will increase energy use for heating, but cut down on waste of water. If you insulate all pipes, energy waste will be reduced.

Clogged boiler heater

Q.   Three years ago I bought a house and installed a tankless water heater attached to the furnace. Recently, the flow has reduced in volume and the dealer states this is probably due to lime deposits in the copper pipes. He has tried reverse flushing and even acids to remove the deposits to no avail. A new unit is his only solution. Can you suggest a less expensive solution.

E.T., South Windsor, Conn.

A.   Your dealer is correct. The acid treatment is probably a failure in your area due to the presence of other mineral deposits in addition to lime. It may be possible to replace only the coils in the system but it may cost as much as a new unit. You can prevent this trouble in the future by installation of water-treatment devices on the main water supply line before it reaches the heater.

Leaky heater tank

Q.   My water heater tank has developed a leak. Water drips from the tank at the point where the nipple is inserted to lead to the drain valve at the bottom. I tried everything I know, including a new nipple and a special sealer but it still leaks. Would appreciate an inexpensive solution.

D.B., Philadelphia, Pa.

A.   It could well be that the threads of the tank opening are rusted and have been damaged in replacing the nipple. Have you tried winding the nipple threads with pipe joint thread and coating with compound? If that won't

work, try one of the compounds that harden into metal when dry, spreading this over the joint all around to a thickness of at least 1/4". The surface must be dry when applied. If that fails, there is only one solution—plug the present opening and have a new one made and threaded for the same size nipple now being used. The equipment for this job would probably cost more than having the work done by a properly equipped plumbing shop.

Instant hot water

Q.   My 40-gal. gas water heater is located 35' from my bathroom. I'm thinking of replacing it with a gas-fired instantaneous water heater. This requires a vent pipe through the roof. Is it possible to use either an "In-O-Vent" or a "Heat Saver" to capitalize on the heat that would be lost up this vent?

R.H., Gary, Ind.

A.   The whole point of the instantaneous water heater is to save fuel by not heating water you don't need. Burning gas only long enough to heat water saves fuel. Spending money to try and extract the last ounce of heat that might be wasted during those periods is probably not worth the investment. Doing it by allowing by-products of combustion to circulate in the house air is a very dangerous procedure.

Water softeners

Q.   I have a water softener, about 20 or 40-gallon capacity which does not function properly when salt is added. I think it requires renewal of the "permanent" chemical. I would like to know if you could give me the name of the chemical and the proportion used.

C.W., Chula Vista, Calif.

A.   The softener chemical is

usually one called zeolite. It's a form of silica, mostly of volcanic origin. It collects minerals from water which are then slowly rinsed out by salt application. This rinsing involves a period of as long as 24 hours—each softener device having its own peculiarities, which must be known to do a successful job. Your manufacturer is the proper one to consult. As a rule, a drain must be made and kept open and water introduced to bring the salt solution constantly through the zeolite to restore its function. In one type from 1-1/2 to 2 pounds of table or rock salt is required. Water must be used to slowly dissolve this salt and carry it through the "permanent" chemical and then to the drain. Since we don't know the make of your unit we can't be more specific.

Septic tank damage?

Q.   We have a cistern which provides hot and cold water for the laundry. When the cistern is dry we would like to fill it from the well but this water is hard. Could we install a water softener or make one ourselves? Would the chemicals be injurious to the water heater and the septic tank system?

G.A., Wellington, Kan.

A.   The chemical is known as zeolite and serves as a filter to remove minerals from the water. There are a number of such devices which need only be set into the water line, whether at the main intake point, or —for the hot water system only—near the water heating system. The chemicals need periodic renewal by the addition of salt. They cannot in any way injure the septic tank system.

Sinking a well

Q.   I would like to drive a well for my summer cabin. I need water for only a kitchen sink as there are no other fixtures. What is the procedure for sinking a well tip by hand?

R.S., Basking Ridge, N.J.

A. If water is locally available near the surface where you plan to drill the well, you will not have much trouble. A 2″ or 2-1/2″ well pipe is wide enough. Select the tips and point designed to fit the pipe. Simply drive the point straight into the ground. This is easy if the earth is sandy or clay, but you won't go far in hardpan or loose stone. The rig is fitted with a ring which fits over the top end of the top pipe to absorb the sledge hammer blows. An 8-lb. sledge is the usual tool, plus a large pipe wrench with which the pipe is rotated slightly after each blow. Special "well driver" tools are also available. The final operation calls for insertion of 1/2″ or 3/4″ pipe inside the driven pipe and attaching the pump to this pipe. For a kitchen sink, 1/2″ pipe is enough unless you want to conduct it more than 50′ from the well. In that case, use 3/4″ inside diameter pipe. You get a jet-like pulsating flow if you use just a pump; if you want steady pressure, use a small pressure tank between the pump and the house. Pump-tank combination units are available at reasonable prices.

Outdoor pump

Q. I have obtained an old-fashioned hand pump on a water well and need information on the best way to put the two together—thus, building a platform etc.

R.S., Madisonville, Ky.

A. There is a tiny little section drawing in *"Sanitation Manual for Isolated Regions"* by the Department of National Health and Welfare of Canada that might be of some help to you. Our own Department of Agriculture has probably also at some time or another published just the information you need. There are a number of ways one can find such information. Try your library first. Or contact your county extension agent. Or write the U.S. Government Printing Office, Washington, D.C. 20402. You might also contact the manufacturer of the pump for an installation detail.

Safe well casing

Q. I have bored a 3-1/2″ hole 30′ deep for a well giving me 5′ of water. I want to use a 3″ fiber pipe, impregnated with coal tar, for a casing. Will the water be safe for drinking with this kind of pipe?

J.K., Willimantic, Conn.

A. In your vicinity, you could be getting contaminated surface water in that well. Before worrying about the pipe, have the water tested for purity. As for the pipe, we'd suggest you use plastic approved for carrying potable water.

Electrical Problems

Aluminum wire...Attic fans...Bathroom wiring...Dimmer switches ...Door bells...Fire alarms...Light fixtures...Outdoor wiring...Outlets ...Overloads...Stereo wiring...Windchargers...Wiring methods.

Aluminum wiring

Q. **I've read stories that aluminum wiring in homes can cause problems. Should I be concerned with the aluminum wiring in my house?**

J.M., Philadelphia, Pa.

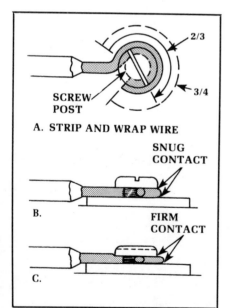

A. STRIP AND WRAP WIRE

A. Aluminum has been used for electrical wiring for over 70 years. Almost all large wiring used to transmit electricity across country and distribute it to individual homes is now aluminum.

Aluminum wiring now exists in a number of homes and some prob-lems of overheating at wall outlets have been reported. The problems have often been traced to loose connections at screw terminals.

A new type of aluminum wire and new switches and receptacles are now available that are designed to overcome these problems. The devices now listed by Under-writers' Laboratories for direct connection to aluminum wire have a "CU/ALR" marking on the mount-ing strap and they have been suc-cessfully tested under conditions far more stringent than those ex-pected in the home. Only these new devices should be directly con-nected with aluminum housewiring.

If aluminum wiring was used in your house, have a qualified per-son check the most heavily loaded circuits for loose connections or overheating. If you check the re-ceptacles yourself, make sure to first turn off the current at the breaker or fusebox.

If the inspection shows signs of overheating or loose screws, have the devices replaced with the new CU/ALR ones, available at your local electrical supply house. There is no need to replace the aluminum wire itself unless it is physically damaged.

The correct way to attach wire to a binding screw is to loop the stripped end 3/4 of the way around the screw in a clockwise direction. Tighten the screw until the wire is snugly in contact with the under-side of the screw head and the wiring device, then give the screw another 1/2 turn.

Aluminum wire and the CU/ALR marked devices are probably the most thoroughly tested combina-tion in the history of Underwriters' Laboratories (UL).

A report on the use of aluminum conductor with wiring devices prepared by a UL-sponsored com-mittee is available for 10¢ per copy from Public Information Office, Underwriters' Labora-tories, 333 Pfingsten Rd., North-brook, Ill. 60062.

Attic fan circuit

Q. **I plan to install an auto-matic attic fan this summer. Is it necessary that the fan be installed on a separate electrical circuit?**

G.R., Tuakahoe, N.Y.

A. Considering the line load needed for this type of fan, a sepa-rate circuit is probably better but it is possible to take current from an upper-floor junction box if a calculation of this line's load is made to ascertain that it will not be overloaded.

Non-stop refrigerator

Q. My refrigerator won't stop running, and I'm at a loss at what to do. Can you give me any suggestions?

K.K., Ortonville, Minn.

A. A common problem is a compressor that runs too long or won't shut off. As a result the temperature of the refrigerator may get too cold. The temperature inside the refrigerator should be above freezing, but below 45°F. The freezer compartment should be at 0°F. To test here, put a thermometer between two packages of frozen food and leave it there overnight. A defective thermostat is often the cause of a compressor that keeps running. The thermostat usually isn't difficult to replace. It is positioned under the temperature control dial. In many units the assembly is held in place with a single screw. When you replace the thermostat, carefully note the position of the sensing tube or bulb. Make sure the tube or bulb of a new unit does not touch any part of the compartment after you have installed it. Air must circulate freely around the tube or bulb if the sensing device is to do its work correctly.

Dead dryer drum

Q. The drum on our dryer won't turn, and my husband hasn't the slightest idea of what to do. Please help.

H.J., Fargo, N.D.

A. If the drum on your dryer quits turning, and the dryer motor is operating, the reasons can include a loose or broken drive belt, loose or defective pulley, broken tension spring or a heavy accumulation of lint. Check every belt to see if it has broken. Belts must be as tight as possible, with no more than 1/4″ of free play allowed when you press on the belt between pulleys. If the belts are okay, check the pulleys. Make sure each is tight by tightening its set screw.

See if pulleys have sustained damage by examining their grooves. If glaze has built up in the groove, it is probably allowing the belt to slip, which is hampering operations. Replace the pulley. Many dryers have a spring, or springs, between the motor pulley and drum and/or blower pulley that keep parts aligned with each other. See that a spring has not fallen loose or lost tension. Reconnect the spring tightly or replace it with a new one.

Blown fuses

Q. In our house, we have fuses that need replacing all the time, and we're tired of buying new ones. What is the cause of this and how can we correct it?

A.B., Story City, Iowa

A. When fuses blow or a circuit breaker trips, it indicates something is wrong within the circuit. Before replacing the fuse or resetting the circuit breaker, try to determine the cause. To replace a fuse, first locate the switch handle on the side of the fuse box. Pull this handle to the off position before you open the box or touch any fuses. If there's no handle, when you open the door you may find one or two cartridge-fuse holders at the top of the box. Pull both of them out, being careful not to touch the metal ends. If fuses are open to view, use a fuse puller. This turns the current off. When replacing a fuse, be sure to use one of the proper size, i.e., one that will blow before the current consumption becomes high enough to overheat the line. Do not substitute a larger fuse in place of one that keeps blowing. A circuit breaker works in much the same manner, except you merely have to flip a switch instead of replacing it.

Circuit failures

Q. Our problem is that we have one circuit that's always going out

on us. No other circuit is affected. Can you help us?

G.B., St. Louis, Mo.

A. Ignoring the cause of blown fuses or tripped circuit breakers can lead to fires, excessive power draw, or appliances running below optimum levels. Check the following reasons for circuit failures:

Loose connection in a fused panel. After turning off the power, remove the fuses. If the bottom of the fuse is blackened, discolored, or pitted, a loose connection is probably at fault.

Loose connection in a circuit breaker panel. After turning off power remove cover from panel. **WARNING:** The connections where the main wires enter the panel are **HOT** or **LIVE.** Inspect the panel for darkened or pitted marks on the box or circuit breakers. Also check the wires connected to the circuit breakers for signs of excessive heat.

Fuse poorly seated. Although the fuse window shows no indication of burnout and the bottom is not pitted or discolored, the fuse may not be making contact with the bottom of the fuse holder. Remove the fuse and replace with one of adequate length. If any of these conditions exist, look for an unused branch space in the panel. If there is an unused space, move the branch wire from the damaged fuse or circuit breaker to the unused space. Obtain a new fuse or circuit breaker and install it carefully. If there are no unused spaces, replace the entire panel. The damaged connection could cause a fire. If you replace the panel, consider installing larger service to meet future electrical service requirements.

Short circuits. If a fuse is blown, the fuse window appears discolored and the metal strip inside, visible through the window, is broken. This indicates a short circuit caused by either two bare wires touching or a hot lead grounding out to a metal object somewhere in the circuit. Cartridge fuses will give no visible indication that a short circuit has taken place. Circuits protected by circuit breakers can be identified by the handle of the tripped circuit breaker being in the "tripped" or "off" position. But the method for identifying the cause is the same for all types of circuit protection.

Overloaded circuits. If a fuse blows and the window remains clear, an overloaded circuit is the cause. Again, cartridge fuses give no visible indication of an overloaded circuit. Circuit breakers will be in the "tripped" or "off" position. Most circuit failures are caused by either temporary overloads or constant overloads. A circuit with a short should be repaired; constant overload means a new circuit should be added.

Temporary overload. Fused circuits can be corrected to handle temporary overloads by using a time delay fuse (also called a "slow-blow") of either 15 or 20 amps. This type of fuse will handle temporary power drains from start-up of appliance motors. Many electric motors require nearly three times the normal line current for initial starting. Circuit breakers are designed to automatically handle temporary overloads.

Constant overload. If one circuit repeatedly fails, there may be too many heavy appliances on that circuit. If removing some of the appliances from the circuit does not eliminate the overload, an individual circuit must be added for the appliance that requires the most current.

Bathroom electricity

Q. Is there any type of electrical outlet that can be safely mounted in a bathroom countertop, perhaps slightly raised above the surface?
H.L., Los Angeles, Calif.

A. There may well be a special outlet used, for example, in swimming pools, but why not put the outlet in the wall well away from the water and save yourself worry? Bathroom outlets must be pro-

tected by "Ground Fault Circuit Interrupters," in any case.

Dimmer power

Q. In one of your past issues, you featured dimmer switches. If a dimmer switch is left in the low position most of the time, would it use less electricity than a standard switch with a low-watt bulb?
B.J., Rockton, Ill.

A. Depends on the dimmer. A solid-state type would reduce the energy consumption. However, you need to include the cost of the dimmer switch in evaluating costs. A three-way bulb might provide you with an even less expensive option in the long run. Also consider the efficiency (more light per watt) of the larger wattage bulbs. One 150-watt bulb gives more light than two 75-watt bulbs.

Extra door bell

Q. How can I wire or rewire my door bell so that I can have another door bell in the back section of the house at the back door. I now have door chimes inside with a push button on the front door. Do I need another push button and another transformer?
E.S., Tampa, Fla.

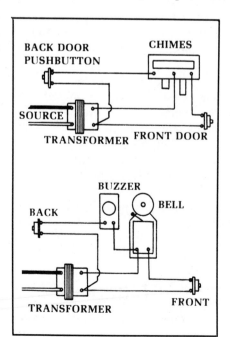

A. Some chimes are manufactured to produce two different kinds of sound, one for a front door and another for a back door. If yours is of this type, all you have to do is add an extra push button as per manufacturer's instructions. If not, you can connect another door bell and push button on the same transformer. Be sure that the new bell does not require a higher voltage than that of your transformer. Older chimes and bells required only 6 or 8 volts, newer ones require 12 to 18 or even as much as 24 volts. Connect a separate set of wires on the terminals of the transformer right where the first set that leads to the chimes are, so that there are two leads coming off of each terminal. Then connect the back door bell and push button to this second circuit, as seen in the sketch, and mount in place. It's a good idea to remove the fuse that controls the transformer while installing the door bell to avoid any possibility of a shock, although the voltage is very small. The one place where you can get hurt is if you attempt to touch the two heavy wires that connect the transformer to the house's electrical system.

Cord organizer

Q. I'm sick and tired of the mess I get with extension cords when I'm working around the house. Seen any slick tricks for keeping things organized?
M.R., Los Angeles, Calif.

A. If you need multiple electric outlets to run mixers, spray equipment and other tools simultaneously, or if you must work a long distance from a power supply, this idea may solve your problem. Long extension cords tend to become tangled, especially those which are flat, rather than round. Do this: Buy 100 feet of #12 round electric cord. Then bore a 1/2" hole in the side of a 5-gal. paint pail, at the bottom of the pail. Next poprivet a metal outlet box about 6" up the side of the pail, directly above the

1/2" hole. Next, run the extension cord into the bottom of the pail, out the hole, and up into the outlet box. You can also wire another outlet box in, and have four-outlet service.

A 100-ft. extension cord will coil into the 5-gal. pail. You can set the pail down at the work site, grab the plug end, and walk to your power supply. The extension cord will spin out freely as you walk, and you won't have any more cord strung out than is necessary; the unused portion stays coiled in the pail. When you're through with the job, it's a simple matter to re-coil the cord back into the pail.

The cord is always neatly coiled, with no tangles. The pail offers a handy carrying and storage device for the cord. Since you will experience "line-drop" or loss of power with lightweight extension cords, make sure you buy #12 or heavier cord if you're going to run power tools. Your extension cord will have three wires. One, colored green, you should attach to the ground on the plug end and the outlet. The black wire will attach to the lower screw on the outlet, with a jump wire to the second outlet. The white wire will attach on the opposite side of the outlet, with a jump to the second outlet.

Electrical fix

Q. The switch on my drill doesn't seem to make contact. Rather than replacement, is there an easy solution?

P.S., Raleigh, N.C.

A. Buy a can of electrical cleaner and keep it handy around the shop. The cleaner is sold in stores as TV tuner cleaner, and can be used to clean electrical contacts on small tools and appliances. A sticky switch or push-button control will often yield to a treatment with the cleaner.

Fire alarm system

Q. I want to install a fire detection system in my basement. I have five thermo-closing switches which will close at 300°F. What is the proper closing temperature for fire alarm switches and are there any specific places to install them?

A.J., Ozone Park, N.Y.

A. Proper setting of fire detection thermo-closing switches is 140° so that they will be activated before heat reaches such a point that it would be too late to do any good. Proper location for the switches is high up since heat rises. If the furnace is properly insulated, a switch may be located in its vicinity. You definitely need one near a stairwell going up and also above all of your windows and exterior door since heat seeks these exits. If you have enough units, any secluded storage areas would also be practical locations. The idea is to place them where a fire is most apt to break out.

Light fixture

Q. I'm fixing up the basement and have four recessed lighting fixtures to install in the ceiling which will be tile when I get done. The man I got the lights from told me how to wire them but I can't figure out how to hold the fixtures themselves in place. Do I put up tile and then cut holes for the fixtures or what?

E.T., Anadarko, Okla.

A. You could cut the holes as you suggest and install the fixtures last but we think this program will work better: after you have the furring up for the ceiling tile, nail a pair of wood blocks between the joists where the fixtures are to go. Run in your BX or cable and complete the wiring, fastening the boxes that are the hidden part of the fixture properly so that the tile thickness and furring allowance is made, bringing the face ring or finish flange on the surface of the tiles. Cut the tiles to fit closely around the box and then install the cover ring.

Green wire

Q. I have a new three pendent hanging ceiling fixture to install in place of an old fashioned one. The black and white wires are no problem but there is also a green wire on the new fixture. What for?

G.F., Albany, N.Y.

A. That green wire is a metallic ground. You should connect it directly to the metal box in which the black and white wires are connected. It grounds the metallic lamp parts to the house ground.

Remove old fixtures

Q. We have some old fashioned wall lights in our bedroom. Could you advise us how they may be removed?

R.J., Englewood, N.J.

A. Shut off all current. Remove the bulb. Remove knurled nut or screws that hold fixture to wall box. Detach fixture's wires from wires entering box from cable. Tape ends of heavy wires with electricians tape and replace solderless connectors if any. Fold wires back into box. Cover opening with standard box cover. Restore current.

Luminous ceilings

Q. How do people get that glowing ceiling effect where the whole area seems to be alight without showing any individual lights?

M.S., Meriden, Conn.

A. There are a number of package ceilings on the market which consist of a channel suspension system and diffuser panels. Fluorescent lights are mounted, usually on the existing ceiling, and the channels suspended so as to receive the diffusing panels and form a lowered ceiling through which the light is diffused. You can make up your own with aluminum sections and reinforced plastic sheet stock.

Lowered lights

Q. It is my intention to install a dropped ceiling of translucent plastic panels in opaque white in both kitchen and master bathroom. I intend to install fluorescent lighting to give the effect of a fully illuminated ceiling. Since the height of the ceiling is presently 8', the dropped ceiling will be set at 7'4" which does not allow much space below the light fixtures. Do you think there will be "hot" spots or will the light be evenly diffused?

S.Z., Plainview, N.Y.

A. With no more than 4" between light and dropped ceiling, you may have light in varying degrees of intensity. The panels will not overcome this effect entirely.

Dangerous tubes

Q. I am trying to figure a way to rig up used fluorescent tubes as a cover against frost for a vegetable garden at 3500' elevation. Do you have any suggestions?

B.C., Orville, Calif.

A. We have only one idea on using old fluorescent tubes: don't use them at all. Used tubes should be discarded, not reused, because the material inside the tube is a health hazard if the glass breaks. Discard old tubes with great care.

Buzzing light

Q. I have a fluorescent ceiling light that works but recently a buzzing noise occurs when the light is on. What do I have to do to stop the buzzing? The light is four years old.

J.M., Gary, Ind.

A. A buzzing sound here usually indicates a faulty starter which can easily be replaced. Another possibility is a defective transformer ballast but as a rule this would prevent the light from working at all. A general overhaul might also be of help. Check for signs of burn out. Loose parts in the fixture may be a source of buzz. Tightening up the parts of the fixture might help.

Outdoor lamp post

Q. I am planning to install an outdoor post light on our lawn and would appreciate any assistance you can give as to the correct procedure for bringing the current to such a light.

B.L., Boonton, N.J.

A. If the lamp post is not far from the house No. 14 wire is suitable but if the distance is beyond 50 feet you'll need No. 12 wire. The two basic items of importance in your project are a solid base for the lamp post and an underground electrical cable to supply the current. We'd suggest the use of nonmetallic sheathed cable, laid underground. At the house end connect the wires to a junction box or the fuse box, conduct them through a switch and then run the cable out of the house underground to the lamp post site. Where the wire passes through the house foundation, metal conduit is required by most building codes and should be used. Lead the cable up through base and post, on up to a junction box where you anchor the cable. From that a thinner set of wires goes to the light fixture proper. Check your local electrical codes before starting.

Glass for lamp

Q. For a lamp post light, what kind of glass is better for a glowing effect: plain glass in the fixture with a frosted chimney or frosted glass in the lantern and plain glass chimney? I want it more for a lawn decoration at night than a yard light.

P.N., Kirwan Heights, Pa.

A. Frosted glass for the sides of the lamp with a plain glass chimney will give you the soft glow you want.

Meter savers

Q. I use a costly VOM meter for trouble shooting electrical appliances, and it has very long test leads which tangle on tools and debris on top of my workbench. Then they get yanked to the floor and I've got a busted meter ready for an expensive repair job. What can I do?

R.T., New York, N.Y.

A. To help prevent such casualties, replace the original leads with the much-shorter coiled leads used on flash cameras. They pull out to use; retract out of the way when let go. Also, being short, they don't tangle. A fringe benefit is that these camera leads each contain two wires, so they last much longer.

Insufficient outlets

Q. Our big old house was a bargain but it does have a few flaws. Practically every outlet in the place is a maze of plugs in plugs in plugs and inconvenient as well as unsafe I'm sure. Is there a simple solution short of having the whole house rewired?

L.L., Riverside, Ill.

A. There is a system on the market that will partially solve your problem, at least where existing outlets supply sufficient power to handle the number of electrical gadgets you want to plug in. You substitute a connector unit for the outlet you have, mount the outlet strip to run where you need it, affix end caps, and twist in outlets anywhere along the inconspicious strip. You don't gain any additonal power but you can use it a lot more conveniently and much more safely.

Convenience outlets

Q. We are putting 1/2" gypsum wallboard on 1x3 furring over badly cracked rough plaster walls. What do I do about the boxes for the convenience outlets to get the cover plates out on the new wall surface?

G.B., New Market, N.J.

A. Some code requirements will force you to remove the boxes from their present locations and reset them properly in relation to the new wall surface. A second good method is the use of a box spacer or collar. This gadget is designed to solve the very problem you have encountered. Your electrical supplier should be able to show you these.

Light dimming

Q. Recently I purchased a heating and cooling air conditioner. When it goes on a light in the same circuit dims. This circuit is not over-loaded. The instructions recommend having a delayed action 15 amp fuse in the circuit. Our home has circuit breakers. Would installing the fuse in the circuit leading to the receptacle be of any help?

C.R., Dumont, N.J.

A. Apparently there is no serious overload or your circuit breakers would trip every time. If the light stays dim the line is under-supplied with current. If so, install a private circuit for the conditioner direct from the main fuse box, if you have an unused outlet there. Use heavier wire and install an outlet box with its own fuse or circuit breaker. Use the delayed action fuse and plug nothing else into the line. If the light returns to normal brightness as soon as the unit has reached operating speed you have nothing to worry about.

Floor lamp switch

Q. It's a nuisance to grope all the way across my dark living room to turn on the floor lamp. How can I control the baseboard outlet from a wall switch near the entrance?

F.M., New York, N.Y.

A. If you don't mind the looks you can buy surface mounted raceways at your hardware store and run the wiring in this along the top of the baseboard and up to the switch. If you want all the wiring hidden, run BX or Romex cable beneath the floor to connect the new switch. The switch should be mounted in a standard recessed box. The electrical hook-up is the same either way. Shut off the current, remove outlet plate. Take out the fixture and disconnect the black or "hot" wire from it. Connect one of the two wires from the new cable to the disconnected black wire and the other one to the screw from which the black wire was detached. Replace fixture in box and cover. Connect the new cable to the wall switch, turn current back on and grope no more.

Power at the switch

Q. I have two wires running from an overhead ceiling light fixture to a wall switch where I have a special fixture with a power outlet. Two wires are connected to the outlet from the switch but I get no power. How can I wire this to get power for a table lamp?

J.K., Forest Hills, N.Y.

A. Under the conditions you mentioned you cannot wire a socket to provide an additional outlet. The two wires that are now at the switch are really one continuous wire from the fixture into which the switch has been connected. The only way you could accomplish your purpose would be to bring a third wire from the fixture to the socket.

Wind power

Q. Just recently I saw a type of propeller that was set up on a house to harness the wind which in turn generated electricity to power electric circuits. I would appreciate any information you could give me on this system.

V.A., Merrick, N.Y.

A. "Wind-Catchers, American Windmills of Yesterday and Tomorrow" by Volta Torrey, published as a paperback by The Stephen Green Press of Brattleboro, Vt. 05301, is a great book to start with. It includes a historical survey, as well as practical aspects of wind energy. This is becoming a popular subject, and local libraries should have other sources.

Windcharger source

Q. Please tell me where I can buy the old-time Windcharger windmill that was popular during the 1930's?

A.S., San Antonio, Tex.

A. Though that same model may not be available today, try the Winco Division of Dyna Technology, 7850 Metro Pkwy., Minneapolis, Minn. 55420. If they can't help you, write to Wind Power Digest, 54468 Cr 31, Bristol, Ind. 46507. Ads for rebuilt windmills sometimes appear.

Electrical wiring

Q. I do not recall ever having read in your publication anything about wiring a house from scratch. Why this oversight?

E.D., Chicago, Ill.

A. We try to reflect the interests of the majority of our readers. While many have similar specific repair or improvement questions that have been covered, relatively few would undertake wiring an entire house. There is no way to give complete information in an article of reasonable length on this subject but there are a couple of good handbooks for individual study. In many communities it is difficult to secure the necessary building permit and inspection approval on any but professionally done jobs. Power companies will not furnish power until an inspection certificate is completed and many times insurance coverage is affected by non-licensed electrical work.

Wiring books

Q. Can you recommend a good book on electrical wiring in the home?

J.S., Rock Hill, S.C.

A. George Daniel's "*How to Be Your Own Home Electrician*" would be most helpful to you. This is a "Popular Science Skill Book" published by Harper and Row. Before you begin any large projects, check with your local building ordinances. Different areas have different laws concerning who can and who cannot legally do electrical work.

Hiding stereo wires

Q. My husband converted an old store cabinet into a stereo unit for all his equipment. He mounted the speakers above it on the wall. It really looks professional except for the wires visible on the wall from the two speakers and from a clock on a shelf. We just can't seem to think of any way to cover them up. Can you help?

N.T., Fort Lee, N.J.

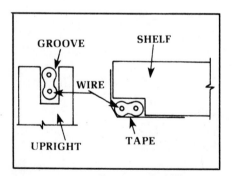

A. The answer may not be covering up the wires but simply running them where they won't show. Since your husband can mount speakers, see if he can't groove the back edges of the shelves and uprights as shown and move the outlet to a position behind the base cabinet. Even tape or staples to hold the wires against

the bottom of the shelves would help, simply painting the outlet and that part of the wire to match the wall.

Running wire

Q. I always have a problem fishing electrical wire through walls and ceilings. What's an easy way to do this?

R.L., Chicago, Ill.

A. To catch the end of a new electrical wire, use your steel measuring tape. Form your steel tape into a loop and push it through the outlet hole in the wall. The tape, pushed through the small opening, will take the shape of the space between the studs or floor joists. As the wire or snake runs through the loop, simply pull it to the opening.

Mixed wires

Q. Is it all right to use two different size wires on the same branch circuit? We used cable with No. 12 wire for new outlets tapped into an old circuit which probably is No. 14 wire.

R.R., San Francisco, Calif.

A. If the No. 12 wire is using its maximum current load it will cause the thinner, lighter No. 14 wire to get hot and this may result in a short. When the fuse blows you will have to remove many wires to find the burned-out insulation to repair it. Better use a 15 amp fuse in this line and do not put more than 1500 watts on the line at any one time.

Under concrete

Q. I would like to install a pole lantern 3' from the house on the street side of a concrete walk that is 4" thick and 3' wide. Is there some way of running a copper tube

under this walk without breaking up the concrete? The distance from the walk to the porch beams is 60". I had the idea of using an earth auger with a brace in a ratchet. Have you any suggestions that might help me?

L.W., Bloomfield, N.J.

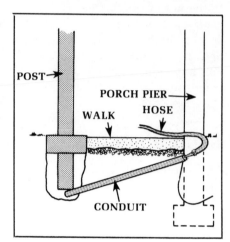

A. Using an earth auger is probably impractical. A regular auger is much too big and bulky for the job and the diameter of the cut for a 3' long hole would be too big for your purposes. There are also earth auger bits that fit electric drills that would not be too bulky for the job, but most of them drill about a 1-1/2 to 2' long hole. They are also very rare as most manufacturers seem to be discontinuing their lines. Finding one that would suit your purposes would be exceptional luck. A better idea—and a lot simpler one—might be the use of an ordinary garden hose with a high-powered stream as a digging tool. Use one with an old-fashioned type nozzle rather than a pistol grip handle. Success with this method depends upon what type of soil you have under the walk. You need to go deep enough to dig a tunnel rather than simply undermine the slab.

Another method, if the hose idea doesn't work, is to try and drive a 1" pipe through the soil beneath the walk, then wash out the pipe with a hose and run your wires through. Make sure that you hook them through with a stiffer wire to ensure that they don't get stuck.

About The FAMILY HANDYMAN Magazine . . .

The FAMILY HANDYMAN covers a wide range of home improvement, remodeling and repair subjects, along with woodworking projects and articles on other homeowner skills and interests. Published 10 times a year, the magazine serves an estimated total of more than 4,500,000 readers. For a subscription, send $9.95 with your name and address to: The FAMILY HANDYMAN, Subscriber Service Department, 52 Woodhaven Road, Marion, Ohio 43305. A limited number of back issues are available. Free list and prices available from The FAMILY HANDYMAN, Back Issues, 1999 Shepard Road, St. Paul, Minn. 55116.

Index